W9-BKI-884

*New Perspectives
on the House of
Representatives*

New Perspectives on the House of Representatives

FOURTH EDITION

Edited by ROBERT L. PEABODY

and NELSON W. POLSBY

The Johns Hopkins University Press

Baltimore and London

© 1963, 1969, 1977 Rand McNally & Company
© 1992 The Johns Hopkins University Press
All rights reserved
Printed in the United States of America on acid-free paper

The Johns Hopkins University Press
701 West 40th Street
Baltimore, Maryland 21211-2190
The Johns Hopkins Press, Ltd., London

'

Library of Congress Cataloging-in-Publication Data

New perspectives on the house of representatives / edited by Robert L. Peabody and
   Nelson W. Polsby. — 4th ed.
      p.   cm.
   Includes bibliographical references and index.
   ISBN 0-8018-4157-7 (alk. paper). — ISBN 0-8018-4158-5 (pbk. : alk. paper)
   1. United States.   Congress.   House.   I. Peabody, Robert L.   II. Polsby,
Nelson W.
JK1331.P4   1991
328.73'072—dc20   91-12346

Contents

Preface

This is the fourth edition of a book we brought out in 1963 in order to introduce to the classroom the results of a remarkable flowering of scholarly research on Congress. Nearly thirty years later, the study of the House has continued to expand, creating a bonanza for students of American national government, who face the perennial problems of decoding the events and understanding the processes that shape our lives. The House of Representatives is where a lot of the action—and inaction—in American politics takes place, and we have been fortunate that so much scholarly effort has gone into studying this complicated and interesting institution.

In this edition, we have chosen to group our selections in four clusters focusing on the working lives of members of the House so that the rest of us can form an appreciation of the way in which this particular institution shapes the behavior of its inhabitants. It is a fact that most of us have not the foggiest notion of how other people spend their working lives, and no harm done. Not knowing how our representatives in Congress go about their work is a different matter. After all, they are doing our business, not merely their own, and ultimately we, through our votes, are responsible for evaluating how well they do it. One of the purposes of this book is to help us discharge this responsibility more intelligently. Our lead-off section includes four different treatments of the conditions affecting the work lives of members.

Each member arrives at the House from a particular territory and relates in a unique way to the city, suburban, or rural district for which he or she sits. Within the constituency populations of each and every congressional district is the congressional archipelago, that set of groups and individuals to whom members are particularly connected and from whom they derive their sense of what the district wants, believes, and cares about. This construction of representative-district relations is in large part an achievement of modern scholars, some of whose work is represented here. They have observed that members of different parties are able over time to represent the same geographic territory and that representatives and senators who cover the same territory are able to do so successfully in different ways.

The fact that the organization of the House matters as much as it does constitutes a tribute to the uniqueness of the American Congress among the world's legislative bodies. Most legislatures provide arenas within which the programs of reigning governments and cabinets are debated but not altered. Whoever has a majority of votes in the parliament can count on success. Not so for Congress, which has the power through its committees to transform measures offered to it by the executive branch.* Committees are the main organizational features that give structure to the work lives of members. Our second section is mostly about committees.

The third section of the book pays attention to the fact that other subgroups in Congress matter, too. State delegations, for example, constitute primary groups for many legislators. They play a significant role in determining how members are recruited and distributed among committees. And because the inner structure of the House is so important, like-minded members who agree on public policy have formed organizations in order to coordinate their activity. Voting coalitions on the floor reflect these organizations.

Finally, there are the means by which the House is led and formally coordinated. The fourth section of this book presents essays describing the political leadership of the House and the powers and limitations of leaders. Much of what we know on this topic we have learned by watching how House leaders are chosen.

By focusing on members and their work lives we have made a book that is not too long or too expensive. We have sacrificed, among other things, articles about congressional elections and about the institutional history of Congress. Both of these topics have inspired so much work that they have grown into subspecialties that deserve their own books.

We are grateful to the authors of the articles printed here for the diligence and imagination they have brought to the study of the House

---

*For a fuller discussion of the distinction between arenas and transformative legislatures see Nelson W. Polsby, "Legislatures," in F. I. Greenstein and N. W. Polsby, eds., *The Handbook of Political Science* (Reading, Mass.: Addison-Wesley, 1975), 5:257–319.

of Representatives. In making their work available to a wide audience, we hope to stimulate curiosity about the workings of the larger half of the world's most interesting and complex legislative body, and to help American readers become better informed spectators and constituents of the most powerful representative institution on earth.

In addition to the debt we owe to our many professional colleagues, members of Congress, staff, journalists, and other congressional observers, we wish to acknowledge the sustained support of Terry Schutz, our copy editor, and the enduring efforts of the staff of the Johns Hopkins University Press, especially Heather Peterson, Lee Sioles, and Henry Tom.

RLP
NWP
Washington, D.C.
Berkeley, California

PART I   *Life in the House*

We begin this collection with a classic contribution, Lewis Anthony Dexter's "What Do Congressmen Hear?" This chapter provides a feel for the wide range of influences that impinge on members of the House of Representatives as they seek to perform their various legislative and representational roles. Dexter sets forth the menu, more or less, from which representatives must choose what they need to know in order to do their jobs. The broader study referred to is Raymond A. Bauer, Ithiel de Sola Pool, and Lewis A. Dexter, *American Business and Public Policy* (New York: Atherton, 1963), a book that won the American Political Science Association's Woodrow Wilson Award for the best book in American politics for 1963.

In a 1990 revision of the nearly last essay he wrote as a political scientist before he was elected a representative from the Fourth District of North Carolina to the One Hundredth Congress (1987–88), David E. Price explores the ethical ramifications of representational and governmental functions. He continues to ask not only, What do representatives do when they represent? but also, What ought they to do? How members confront these basic moral and ethical dilemmas has broad implications for legislative life and individual responsibility.

In the third contribution to this section, a representative communicates insightfully to his constituents. In the early 1960s, the late representative Clem Miller, Democrat of California, wrote a series of informal letters to friends and constituents. Three are reprinted here. Edited by John W. Baker, the letters were published as *Member of the House: Letters of a Congressman* (1962). Tragically, Congressman Miller was killed in an

1

airplane crash on 7 October 1962 while campaigning for a third term.

Building upon the findings of *Home Style* (1978), Richard F. Fenno, Jr.'s classic study of how House members cultivate their constituents, Glenn R. Parker and Suzanne L. Parker further explore the causes and consequences of attentiveness by members to their districts in the Ninety-second, Ninety-third, and Ninety-fourth Congresses. Changes in attentiveness—especially spending more time in the district—increasingly has had a positive influence on election margins and return of members over the past decades.

Chapter 1

What Do Congressmen Hear?

LEWIS ANTHONY DEXTER

This chapter derives from a book titled *Congressmen and the People They Listen To,* by the writer.[1] The report was done at the Center for International Studies, MIT, in connection with a transactional study of business communication about foreign economic policy. The reception on Capitol Hill of the communications from business was studied partly by interviews (more than fifty with congressmen and a similar number with congressional staff members, and about five hundred with businessmen, lobbyists and leading constituents) and partly by reading the incoming mail of a few members of each house. Except where otherwise indicated, the names of all congressmen in this report have been disguised; the words and illustrations are, however, reported exactly, except that where some interviewee used a phrase which would serve to identify him, this has been changed also.[2]

THE MAIL'S THE THING
(SUPERFICIALLY, AT LEAST)

Every congressman and senatorial assistant, when asked, "What do you hear . . . ?" or words to that effect, starts telling you about the mail. Most of the businessmen with whom we talked, when asked, "What have you done about such-and-such an issue?" tell you (if they have done

This chapter is reprinted by permission of the author. Part of it originally appeared as "What Do Congressmen Hear: The Mail," *Public Opinion Quarterly* 20 (Spring 1956): 16–27.

anything) that they've *written* to their congressmen or senators (or possibly telegraphed).

In the importance attached to it both by congressmen and by business constituents, mail outweighs every other form of communication. Strangely, many congressmen do not raise any explicit question as to whether the mail *represents* the views of the district. Some congressmen do, of course, question this. A senator, for instance, who received one hundred letters from a particular city urging that he support legislation for a higher minimum wage, checked on the senders and found out that at least seventy-five of them were eligible to vote but only thirty-three of these actually were registered.

Senator Service's assistant says, "If you put faith in that sort of thing [stimulated mail] you're lost. We can tell the day and hour when somebody or other starts those calls or doorbells ringing [to get people to write]; so what?" Another senatorial assistant says it is easy to identify stimulated letters by the fact that someone nearly always encloses a copy of the letter to the letter writer asking him to write his congressman. This assistant estimates that in any batch of a thousand letters, at least fifty will enclose the original request.

But these are the exceptions so far as formal statement goes. It is true that many congressmen and senators run counter to the mail in obedience to the dictates of conscience, party, or committee. But they frequently appear to think they are controverting something very significant. This may be merely a habitual genuflection toward the right of petition and the sovereignty of the citizen; in some cases it probably is. For whatever reason, older congressmen were much less inclined to quote the volume of mail as an authority than younger ones. This may simply mean that older ones had become sufficiently familiar with the point of view expressed by the mail (since it is similar on this issue over the years) that they do not pay as much attention to the current inflow on this subject. It may also be due in part to the fact that older congressmen are busier. It is also possible that older congressmen, by the very fact of being older, come from districts which seem safer and may therefore be less anxious to ascertain the views of the electorate. But even they on the whole appear to think that the mail is important and civically significant. There are several reasons that lead them to this attitude.

In the first place, members or their staffs spend an enormous amount of time on mail. And having invested that time on it, they like to feel that it means something.

Second, a great deal of the time congressmen operate in a pretty complete vacuum so far as the voters of their district go. Most people seem to prefer to know what they are supposed to do (in some cases, merely so that they can protest or revolt). The mail gives a sense that one is doing something that excites large numbers of people.

Third, as Paul Appleby and others have pointed out, many congressmen are irritated and annoyed because they come to Washington expecting to do and be something important; and because of the complexity of government and the seniority system they find they are hampered and shut off from effective action at every turn. Granted this rather general exasperation, handling mail is almost the only thing on which a congressman finds himself quite free; he can write any sort of letters he likes without let or hindrance from anybody. Thus letter writing becomes a disproportionately significant aspect of his job, for it represents the freedom and importance that he thought he would find when he got to Washington (but rarely does).

Fourth, most congressmen genuinely treasure the right of petition and the opportunity of the individual citizen to complain about mistreatment. This right has great importance on many issues where bureaucrats mistreat or overlook individual rights.

Fifth, whether realistically or not, some congressmen actually believe and many others like to feel that on any issue of national significance, rational communication between them and any constituent is possible. For this reason they spend a quite irrational amount of time on correspondence that is essentially academic in the sense that it is fairly clear that no political or legislative purpose is really served by the time they give it.

For these, and perhaps other, reasons congressmen come to believe that the mailbag is the secret of success. Senator Kefauver (D., Tenn.) reports that when first elected to Congress he asked Speaker Bankhead (D., Ala.) how to get reelected, and that Mr. Bankhead replied:

> Members get reelected term after term without substantial opposition (because they) give close and prompt attention to mail. Votes and speeches may make you well known and give you a reputation, but it's the way you handle your mail that determines your reelection.[3]

Nearly all the businessmen we talked with also regarded *writing* congressmen as the basic political-legislative act. In view of the supposed popularity of public relations in a wider sense, this was a little surprising. But nearly all of them said, "I wrote," "I telegraphed," or "No, I haven't written," when asked if they had done something about the issue.

In this article we shall review some of the characteristics of the mail that seem extraordinary in so highly valued a source of information.

Little or No Mail on Many Vital Issues

A substantial number of congressmen and probably all senators received a noticeable amount of mail about reciprocal trade legislation. This in itself differentiates reciprocal trade from many crucial issues. For example, a senator from a major industrial state heard *nothing* in the 1955 session of Congress on any of the following issues, all of which were considered by the Senate during that session, and several of which were decided so closely that he could have exercised a crucial vote: the Capehart amendment on policy responsibility of dollar-a-year men (WOCs), the Hickenlooper amendment on permitting construction of an atomic-powered merchant ship, home rule for the District of Columbia, the Statute of Forces Agreement (Jenner amendment), Marine Corps increase, mutual aid programs for Europe and Asia, the stockpiling of minerals, confirmation of SEC and ICC commissioners (both controversial in the extreme), a serviceman's voting proposal, the Congressional Amendment (actually passed by the Senate) permitting governors to appoint congressmen in event of emergency, the sale of rubber plants, the Housing Act of 1955, and the restriction of wheat and cotton acreage. Several of these are very important *in fact* to his state; some of them are considered by his committees. His experience is typical.

Most of the Mail Comes from Few Sources

In 1955, probably a majority of congressmen received a good deal of mail on the tariff. However, many rated it as tenth or fifteenth, relatively low in volume compared to mail received in connection with other issues. A few in 1954 heard nothing. Such figures mean relatively little, however, because a very large proportion of the mail on the tariff issue was organized and sent by a few sources. Westinghouse, Dow, Monsanto, and Pittsburgh Plate Glass may by themselves easily have stimulated 40 percent or more of all mail received by all congressmen in 1954 on reciprocal trade. In addition to them on the protectionist side, there were the coal, independent oil, and textile interests. One congressman is reported to have received well over five thousand letters on the topic from textile workers in early 1955.

On the reciprocal trade side, there is only one big producer of mail—the League of Women Voters. Very probably three-fourths of the mail received by all congressmen in favor of reciprocal trade was directly or indirectly stimulated by the league. Even in tobacco or automobile districts, league members produced a majority of the pro-reciprocal trade mail; and in districts where there was no strong protectionist group, the congressmen may have heard mostly from league members. In general, protectionist mail outweighed pro-reciprocal trade mail at least ten to one.

Inspired Mail Tends to Seem Unduly Uniform

Congressman Simpson (R., Pa.) received a number of letters and post-cards in 1953 urging him to vote against the Simpson Bill for the imposition of a fuel oil quota. To one of his colleagues this simply represented the ineptness and political uninformedness of the much-abused "women's groups."

By and large, most protectionist mail quantitatively speaking takes the line, "Save my job." Printed cards are distributed and often collected and mailed by firms in the woolen textile industry. A manufacturer in one big port city explained why his organization had gone to the trouble of collecting and mailing the cards.

> Oh, we found most of these people just didn't know who their congressman was, or they sent it to their state senator or something, so we asked them just to fill in their address and we did everything else.

One congressman from that city consequently got about 6 percent of the cards with an address but no name signed. A senatorial assistant comments, "That's doing better than par for the course."

Mail from almost any given industry tends to have its own special characteristics. The cherry industry, for example, seems to promote letters which are particularly "reasonable" sounding: "We know foreign trade is necessary but ours is a special case." It is almost impossible to organize a letter-writing campaign so skillfully that an experienced mail clerk does not spot it at once as stimulated and even identify its source.

The Mail Is Direct

We found that most of the mail to congressmen is quite direct; Mr. X writes to his congressman, and that's that. In the letter, Mr. X may identify himself but more often is simply satisfied to say he is a constituent. Mr. X does not go through channels to write his congressman. For example, I never saw a single letter from a county chairman or other *party* official on trade and tariff matters with one exception—an official Republican group in Midland, Michigan, had petitioned its senators against reciprocal trade. This is interesting because it differs from the prevailing political pattern on patronage where endorsements are often sought unless one is personally known to the congressman (and frequently when one is). It is unrealistic because in fact the attention a congressman pays to mail is *in part* a matter of how important the writer is; frequently the content and title make this obvious, but frequently they do not.

With letters to senators in the larger states, such endorsement or identification would seem still more appropriate since mail clerks for senators often know little about the state. I know one fairly skilled lobbyist who thinks that when he really wants something from a senator's office it is a good idea to write the senator a letter beginning "Dear so-and-so (first name)." Then the mail clerk, not to take a chance, will give the letter to one of the assistants instead of handling it himself. Ordinarily the assistant handles the subject, and the senator will never see the letter— so it will create no embarrassment.

Since we found that many senators and congressmen simply disregard out-of-state mail altogether, it is particularly odd that people who write them from out of state do not take some steps to identify themselves. Altogether, many thousands of dollars of postage must be spent in out-of-state mail which is unread except for the address or first sentence.[4]

Chaff in the Mail

I have hardly ever seen a letter which indicated any technical mastery of reciprocal trade legislation. I have never noted a letter which contained a new or unfamiliar thought about the issue; nor have I happened ever to read one (out of several thousands I have looked at) where one could say clearly as one sometimes can with letters: "Here is someone who writes with real conviction." (Letters I have seen on McCarthyism or on defense issues such as civil defense and stockpiling occasionally create such an impression). Put another way, a detailed study of the phrases and sentences in letters on reciprocal trade and the tariff would almost certainly show an enormously high proportion of clichés and stereotyped phrases. I do not recall seeing a coherent presentation of protectionist *theory*; the Careys and the other mercantile political economists and nationalist theorists might as well never have lived as far as the mail goes.

Handling and Effect of Senate versus House Mail

In several cases, I read mail to a senator and also mail to one or more congressmen from the same state. I noted little difference as far as the congressmen's districts were concerned.

A good many and perhaps most representatives read all their own mail, except that which is clearly routine. If they do not dictate answers themselves, they indicate who should be queried about the letter, etc. How they handle it—whether they pay attention to out-of-district mail, how much use they make of reference facilities in the Library of Congress or the executive departments, how far they try to use the letter as a basis for thinking of something *else* that will interest the constituent—depends enormously upon the representative, the subject, and how busy he or his staff are at a given time.

In the Senate, the situation is quite different. Senators from the larger states with whom we talked have mail clerks who handle the mail, attend to much of it themselves, and if in doubt consult one of the senator's assistants. But most senators rarely see their mail; some of them try to keep control by signing answers.

The inability to see mail results in odd situations. Senator Philip's legislative assistant assured me that no one in the state was concerned about reciprocal trade—the senator got practically no mail on it, for instance. However, the chief mail clerk told me that it was either first or second among the issues that the senator got mail about. One of the mail clerk's favorite ways of treating such mail was to reply, "I am turning your letter over to the chairman of the Senate Finance Committee which is now considering HR 1 and I am sure he will be interested in your comments." I looked at him quizzically. "No, I don't do it," he said, "but I don't think I'm being dishonest in saying that. I would if it said anything new." And this was probably true; every once in a while a letter that poses what is (at least to the senatorial or congressional office) a new question is sent to the staff of Ways and Means or Finance for comment or with the request that an answer be written for the appropriate signature.

No Great Difference in Mail to Committee Members

Mail to members of House Ways and Means or Senate Finance, the committees that consider reciprocal trade, did not seem to differ much in volume from mail to congressmen and senators not on these committees. This is surprising, since sometimes lobbying organizations list the members of the pertinent committees.

The Senate version of the Reciprocal Trade Extension Act of 1955 was quite different from the House version; so necessarily a conference committee (of five representatives and five senators) was appointed to decide on the final version. The measure was in conference for a number of weeks.

The conferees could have decided for a more "liberal" or a more "restrictive" measure. One would have thought, therefore, that they would have been bombarded with communications and attempts to influence them. There was a real question how far Messrs. Cooper and Mills, two Democratic conferees from the House, would go in opposing the Senate version; conceivably Senator George (D., Ga.), who had traditionally been a strong advocate of the old Hull position, and Senator Kerr (D., Okla.), who was then a potential Democratic candidate for president, might be open to some compromise on the numerous restrictive amendments written in by the Senate. Most observers felt Senator George sympathized with the House bill rather than the Senate version. So from the reciprocal trade standpoint, one might have expected a campaign directed at these four men at least. None took place.

On the other side, Senator Morse (D., Oreg.), one of the most vociferous advocates of local interests in the Senate on economic matters, had succeeded in getting into the Senate bill an amendment that was desired by Northwest fruit and nut producers and that would presumably have especially benefited them. The cherry producers in February and March had put on a fairly intensive campaign of letter writing; but as far as I heard, neither they nor the other Northwest, Michigan, and Georgia fruit-nut producers put on a campaign in May anywhere near resembling the March campaign. Yet, the fact was that in May they were in a special position where a campaign would have been more helpful. In any event the only loss "the" protectionists suffered in conference was the deletion of the Morse amendment.

Generally Constituents with Ideas Suggest Something That Is Procedurally Impossible

For our present purposes, it is sufficient to point out that because of the elaborate and technical nature of congressional procedure most letters to congressmen suggesting that they should do something, recommend things that they cannot, practically speaking, do. Procedural decisions or legislative custom may have allocated the responsibility to somebody else or have set the question up in such a way that what the constituent wants cannot be achieved. For instance, a large number of letters were sent to Senator Hennings (D., Mo.) asking that he support the Curtis amendment.[5] But the Curtis amendment never came to the floor of the Senate; it was not to the best of my knowledge seriously considered by the Senate Finance Committee; Senator Hennings belongs to more than a dozen subcommittees of his two major committees (Judiciary and Civil Service) and in addition serves on Rules.[6] This is quite enough to keep the senator and his staff busy. It would be difficult for them to take on new responsibilities of the magnitude involved in an effort for the Curtis amendment even if he should be convinced by the letters that this was important.

Of course, occasionally some senator or congressman is looking around for an issue or is impressed by particular ideas; so there is always an outside chance that letters of this sort may have direct influence. They may certainly have a long-run "educational" effect, so that if the matter does some day come to the floor it may be received with more friendliness.

"You Don't Know What They Mean"

Several congressmen pointed out—and a number of others implied—that much of the time, "When they write you, you don't know what they mean." For instance, a very large portion of the mail calls for protection for some one particular industry. Sometimes it says, "But we realize the necessity of foreign trade in general." What can the average House member do with this mail? For example, under the closed rule procedure under which tariff bills are usually considered, the House as a whole is very unlikely to have an opportunity to vote to protect the domestic cherry processors and producers. The members will have to vote for or against the Reciprocal Trade Extension Act as reported out of committee. They can, of course, urge the members of the Ways and Means Committee to do something to help the cherry growers and producers, but precisely what? Either there has to be somebody on Ways and Means who works out the method—or somebody in the cherry growers' association—or somebody in the cherry processors' association—or the congressman himself must do it.

On the cherry industry, three legislators at least have tried to make an effort to work out a tailor-made solution—Senator Morse (D., Oreg.), Senator McNamara (D., Mich.), and Congressman Holmes (R., Wash.). But most of the time on most of the mail they get, most congressmen and senators make no such effort. They simply receive the mail, and read and file it.

Or suppose a congressmen gets—as some do—letters saying, "Vote for free trade." There is no free trade measure on the calendar; there is not likely to be one. Probably in January this means support the Reciprocal Trade Extension Act, as reported from committee. The measure was so riddled by amendments in the Senate that some people felt it was no longer a free trade measure; a New Deal congressman who voted for the Cooper Bill voted against acceptance of the conference report for the reason that the revised bill was so restrictive and protectionist.

In January 1955, a letter from a League of Women Voters or a chamber of commerce in favor of "more liberal" trade presumably meant "Support the Cooper bill"; a petition from a cotton textile local to "protect our jobs," in January meant "Oppose HR 1"; but after the Senate had adopted the committee amendments, what then? How many of those who wrote letters on either side had any idea of the significance of the changes made by the Senate? Actually, the newspapers and newsmagazines and newsletters had given only a very general and frequently a misleading picture of the drift of these amendments.

"You Always Hear from Business Too Late"

Congressman Amiable says, commenting on his wide experience in a state legislature and in Congress, "You always hear from business too late." And this is true *in general* because businessmen and their representatives respond to the news; they write in to protest a bill that has been reported out of committee, for instance, because that is when they hear about it or when it really comes to seem a threat. But by the time it is reported out of committee, it is difficult to amend it; legislators have to say either yes or no. And by the time it is reported out of committee, the battle lines have formed, commitments and promises have been made, and it is harder for congressmen to change. For example, take Mr. L., a member of Ways and Means; he joins the committee in reporting out such-and-such a piece of tariff legislation. Then he hears that the manufacturers of some product in his district would very much like a particular change in the bill; however, several members of the committee majority are opposed to this change. If Mr. L. had advocated it before the measure was reported out, he might be free to continue his advocacy or look for supporters of the position. But he is under the obligation that most decent men feel—not to throw over an implied agreement without very strong reasons.

And this obligation is backed by a very real sanction or threat. If Mr. L. wants to keep on friendly terms with his colleagues, to preserve their respect, he cannot break many such agreements; if he does he will lose his influence with them. And if he wants to serve his district *not only at the moment but over the years, he must preserve his colleagues' respect.*

SOURCES OTHER THAN THE MAIL

It is apparent that the mail is but one of a number of important sources of information for congressmen. Hattery and Hofheimer, in a study of legislators' sources of expert information, listed ten.[7] These were ranked by the congressmen as follows: (1) committee hearings, (2) personal reading and consultation, (3) office staff, (4) committee staffs, (5) arguments on the floor, (6) Legislative Reference Service, (7) executive departments, (8) interest groups, (9) political party, (10) legislative counsel.

No congressman mentioned to me his office staff, committee staff, the Legislative Reference Service, or legislative counsel as sources of communications which had shaped his thinking about the tariff issue. All four of the sources, of course, are not supposed to try to influence members but merely to aid them as requested, so the omission is perfectly natural. It will be helpful to comment more specifically on the role of a number of the others with respect to the tariff issue itself and to mention still other sources of influence that are absent from this list.

1. Committee Hearings. I asked a distinguished member of the Ways and Means Committee early in 1954 whether there would be hearings on the Reciprocal Trade Extension Act in that year. "O my God," he said, "I hope not. I get so bored with those repetitious hearings. We've been listening to the same witnesses saying the same things the same way for ten years."

Statements by witnesses from different industries are extremely repetitious not only from year to year but from witness to witness. Almost all of the statements were criminally dull. I spent portions of several days listening to the Senate hearings, and I wish I may never go through the same boredom again. Even some major government witnesses, such as Assistant Secretary Butz (Agriculture), who led off for HR 1 before the Senate committee, sounded as though they were reading statements which they only half understood and found thoroughly boring themselves.

After the first few days of House and Senate hearings, a good many of the members found it necessary to be absent. Since they walk in and out of a good deal, no figures are available on how many hearings the "average member" attended.

Some of the questioning, particularly by Mills (D., Ark.) and Eberharter (D., Pa.) in the House, and by Millikin (R., Colo.) in the Senate, was adroitly contrived to embarrass witnesses opposed to the questioner's position. Very few witnesses seemed prepared for fairly obvious questions; yet a reading of hearings several years back or consultation with informed sources would have shown that Millikin, for example, has certain "traps" he has successfully baited his opponents with. Secretary Butz, the government lead-off witness, fell into several of these—apparently he had not been briefed on what to expect.

There was practically no evidence of any effort *systematically* to check facts or to follow through a line of argument except by Senator Malone (R., Nev.), an extreme protectionist who asked probably more than half the questions in Senate Finance. His questions were designed to get all witnesses to admit the unconstitutionality of the reciprocal trade program.

The reciprocal trade issue is, of course, an old one—and many of the members have heard it all before. But the factual basis of the subject has to some extent altered since the matter was last considered by Congress, and many of the members had probably had no occasion to consider the economics of the matter or the political theory, systematically, for years.

No member outside the committee in talking with me referred to the hearings in any way.[8] Probably with them, as with the public, it is the indirect effect of the hearings that counts rather than the direct ones. Newspapermen take the press release of witnesses and write stories on them, and these stories are often published. So members of Congress read the stories. Since newspapermen are far more apt to get the releases than they are to sit through a session and listen to the questions, even quite inane testimony has a better chance of receiving publicity than quite pertinent questions have. Limitations of time affect the press as well as members of Congress.

2. The Floor Debates and the Record. Some debate takes place in the House and often a good deal in the Senate on issues such as reciprocal trade. Some Senate speeches cover a subject widely—for example Senator Gore's four-hour speech on reciprocal trade in 1954, and speeches by Senators Douglas, Langer, and Malone in 1955 on that topic.

It is unusual for many senators or House members actually to listen to a speech; during most of Senator Gore's speech six other members on the average were in attendance, and those who paid closest attention were close sympathizers and supporters on the reciprocal trade issue.

On this basis, it might seem that the fairly common impression that the floor debate makes no difference and is chiefly for the benefit of the galleries is correct. However, there seems to be general agreement among those in a position to know that Senator Gore's speech in favor of the Randall program in 1954 was four hours long for this reason: The senator and his associates, in offering the amendment which would have provided for a three-year extension (instead of the one-year extension voted by the House), feared the general attitude of his colleagues would be (1) "Gore's trying to put the Republicans in a spot," or (2) "Gore's just trying to show that he fills Hull's shoes."

But his associates felt that if the senator made a four-hour speech developing the issue in terms of the relationship of reciprocal trade to the discouragement of East-West trade then it would make clear the fact that he really was serious in pushing his amendment.

Hattery and Hofheimer, commenting on the importance of floor debate, assert:

> [Our] findings present a challenge to some assumptions which may have been too readily accepted. . . . One of these relates to floor debate. . . . Although it is true that members of the committee which studies the bill obtain little additional information through floor debate, the majority of legislators have not had the benefit of the committee deliberations. . . . Floor debate in cases of controversy often represents the results of careful research and marshaling of facts and consideration.

Several congressmen cited floor debate as the best source of information on minor matters, . . . [and] on amendments (to the bill) it may be the only source of information available to the member before a vote is called for.

Unfortunately, neither their report nor this study enable us to distinguish between the importance of floor debate *as such* and floor debate and speeches as preserved in the *Record,* which members may study at leisure. I suspect it is the latter which is important.

However, no member referred directly to the debate as influencing him; although several members stated that when they went on to the floor 17 February 1955, before the key votes on the closed rule, they did not yet know how they were going to vote.

3. How Much Do Congressmen Hear from Congressmen? It is likely that congressmen hear more from other congressmen about most legislation than from anybody else. Our study unfortunately was not conducted in such a way as to make it possible to be as certain on this point as we might wish.

Relatively few congressmen in answering our questions referred to other congressmen as sources of information or ideas.

Evidently, the communication of ideas and information between congressmen takes place in such a matter-of-fact way that the congressmen who had heard something from a colleague did not often think of it as "hearing" something from an external source, but as an exchange of views within a work or friendship situation. Nevertheless, party leaders in the Congress, as well as individual congressmen with a specific interest in given issues, are clearly in a strategic position to influence congressional thought, and we have some evidence that they do so.

4. "Pressure" from Other Congressmen: The Leadership. A number of references were made to the "pressure" exerted by the Democratic leadership on the 1955 vote. This pressure is indicated by Speaker Rayburn's often-quoted remark at the breakfast of the freshman congressmen just before the vote: "If you want to get along, go along." Those who had read or heard the 1954 debate might also remember that the speaker (then minority leader) had made an impressive speech stating his view that the Reciprocal Trade Act ought to be extended for twenty-five years. Similarly, one of the Boston newspapers reported that Majority Leader McCormack (D., Mass.) made a remark to Representative Macdonald (D., Mass.) which indirectly and euphemistically, but quite clearly, implied that Macdonald, by voting against the leadership, had let his district down—in front of a newspaper reporter! Since Macdonald was serving his first term, and since Medford, the key city in the district, was the scene of unusually public factional struggles, and since the district is traditionally very close, McCormack's remark, under the circumstances, was, in design or not, a threat.

Far more important than such hints are direct efforts to get members to change. On some measures, this is effective. One bill which was extremely vital to the leadership in 1955, actually appeared to squeeze through by five votes or so, but the leadership had in its pocket about twenty-five sure changes if the bill were in danger.

"Changes" takes place in this fashion. A member answers to his name and votes yea or nay as the case may be, but while the vote is being checked changes it. A member may also announce an intention to vote yea or nay but fail to answer at the appropriate point in the roll call and switch if the vote is close. On the closed rule votes on 17 February, the leadership in fact won by one vote according to the *Record*. But at one time, members report, it had lost by seven votes.

5. *"Pressure" from Other Congressmen: Cleveland Bailey.* The only other member reported as exercising "pressure" was Representative Cleveland Bailey (D., W.Va.). Representative Bailey is unusual among members—probably unique—in that protection is the most important issue to him and that he creates the sense of having a deep-felt conviction on the subject. In 1953–54 he went around and pleaded individually with a number of members to vote against reciprocal trade and for the West Virginia miners. As one member put it, "He was rough, real rough. . . . I had to be rough with him." Another said, "In the 1954 vote, Cleve Bailey was worth fifteen votes to his side easily." In 1955, Mr. Bailey was generally admitted to be the leader of the protectionist fight.

Members who propose something *new* are likely to send statements about it to their colleagues. For example, Congressman Thomas Curtis (R., Mo.), who introduced the Curtis amendment which would materially change the basis on which reciprocal trade is administered, made an effort to publicize it and even testified before the Senate Finance Committee on its behalf. Similarly, Congressman Bolling (D., Mo.) circulated amongst his colleagues explanations of his measure for facilitating industrial dispersion.

6. *Informal Contacts with Other Congressmen.* As has been noted, the influence of other congressmen is very important, but frequently this is exerted in a casual, unplanned way, so it is not recognized or remembered except in the clear-cut cases. The study of legislative bodies as work groups is one of the crying needs of political science at present.

A couple of cases where friendship seems to have been the dominant factor in the vote in 1955 may be cited. A newspaper correspondent told me:

> Oh, yes, you know those two boys [congressmen]. . . . Well you know why Jack voted against the leadership? Just to oblige Joe to whom he's very close. Joe was afraid he'd be the only fellow from the state to vote against the leadership and he'd get into trouble with the leadership and party organization so Jack went along with him to prevent his sticking his neck out all alone. Then of course on the final vote Jack switched back, so he's OK if anybody in his district asks him.

Similarly, the whip for the area told me:

> Oh, Don went along against the leadership on this, but I don't think he cares at all or heard much about it from his district. It was just that Dave to whom he's very close is pretty strong against foreign imports and Don was more concerned to help him out than to help the leadership. And Tom rather wanted to go along with the leadership, but he found Dave and Don and four other guys from surrounding districts were against the leadership, and he decided he'd better go along with them, because after all he's hearing a lot from his district against it, and how could he explain his being for it and Dave and Don and the rest being against it?

7. Personal Contacts. No congressman in any way indicated that his wife or secretaries influenced his views, but I suspect that this was the fault of our method of interviewing plus the fact that in many cases congressmen are quite unaware of views picked up through daily contacts.

8. Visitors. Visitors do come in and see congressmen. Congressmen also talk with people back home about issues. On some matters, congressmen get as much and hear as much from visitors as they do from the mail, but it seems to be quite generally agreed that the tariff and reciprocal trade are mail issues, not visitor issues. To my knowledge, no congressman except a representative from Detroit received a visitor *from his district* simply to talk in favor of reciprocal trade. Most of the protectionist people from a district come in to talk about the sad state of their sales. Now, in regard to any given commodity, there are a number of ways government can help, of which tariff legislation is only one.

Mr. Serious Consideration, for example, and Mr. Fourth, who were certainly open to persuasion, had, according to their statements, no visitors come to see them particularly in behalf of protection.

The few cases I know of where someone came to see a congressman *specifically* against reciprocal trade extension and nothing else fall into two types:

1. People who, it sounded, were glad of a trip to Washington; and if the congressman helped them on gallery tickets, hotel accommodations, etc., that more than offset any disappointment on his views as to trade.

2. People who buttonholed congressmen in the lobbies the day of the vote 17–18 February; I'm not sure how many (if any) of these were actually from congressmen's districts, but some of them may have been. However, the opportunity for influencing congressmen by a hurried word just before they went on the floor was not great.

One reason why delegations and informal conversations back home count for little in what a congressman does on reciprocal trade is that many congressmen are much more expert in diverting visitors than visitors are in influencing congressmen.

9. Reading. Few of the congressmen interviewed quoted specific published sources as the basis of their opinions. With one probable exception (Mills, D., Ark.), there was little indication of familiarity with the economic literature on international trade, convertibility, and so forth. This may depress economists, but it should be remembered that many congressmen feel that economists are generally biased in favor of free trade. The history of economic thought tends to support this feeling. Thus, those congressmen who are much worried about unemployment or threatened unemployment among their constituents will find little credible in the published material on international trade. Journalists and newspapermen, on the other hand, may be encouraged by the fact that several congressmen evidently had obtained ideas from columns. Perhaps a dozen referred to some item in the press (e.g., an article by George Sokolsky, the most active protectionist columnist). The local and business press was not referred to by any of the interviewees.

In addition, few congressmen referred to the various reports recently issued by government agencies or distributed by interests groups; in most cases they had probably skimmed rather than read them.

On these points, congressmen appear to differ in degree at least from the executive department officials with whom I talked. Very likely, however, some executive department officials make a greater effort to impress a scholar than congressmen do. On the other hand, it must be remembered that there was little or nothing available in 1956 which was of any real use to congressmen on the topic of foreign economic policy. For essentially what they need is material which *reconciles* the claims and desires of their individual constituents with the overall general economic problems. What they find for the most part is (a) theoretical (e.g., abstract, high-level) discussion of the virtues of international trade, and (b) occasionally a theoretical response to that argument.

Congressmen—and everybody else in this area—also badly need *simple* or at least *simpler* explanations of what the whole apparatus of quotas and tariffs achieves and how they hang together legislatively. But there was nothing clear, usable, and readable on the topic, thus blocking this significant material as a source of information for legislators.

Epilogue

VOLUME OF COMMUNICATIONS AND ITS EFFECT ON CONGRESSMEN IN THE 1980s AND 1990s

The preceding chapter is an account of what congressmen heard in 1953–55 and how they used and evaluated some of what they heard. Since then, some things have changed on and off Capitol Hill, but, as far as I can tell, many things have remained more or less constant. The way in which parliamentarians are related to their constituents, as these words are written, appears to be shifting rapidly, almost day by day, for example, in Czechoslovakia or East Germany. And the growth of a committee system has altered the opportunity for and the style of communication between Canadian MPs and their constituents and interests in the last decade, so that MPs are *somewhat* freer of caucus and leadership than was the case thirty years ago.

What has changed on Capitol Hill? Above all, the *volume* of communications. There has been a tremendous increase in the number of communications congressmen receive. The congressmen who read most of their own mail in the 1950s are now, probably, completely outdated because there is so much more of it and because they have learned—partly from the studies by professional congressional specialists, more from their own experience[9]—that most mail expresses an opinion without presenting worthwhile new information or workable ideas. Visits and personal meetings, in general, also duplicate each other and a lot of the mail.

Volume of communications in two other ways makes a considerable difference in what congressmen hear and how they hear it. The individual congressman in the 1990s is, in fact, the administrator of an (unusual type of) small business; funds for assistants have been multiplied and so have funds for subcommittee and committee staffs. In the nature of the case, staff people know more about many of the issues and problems that congressmen hear about than do the congressmen themselves: many of the staff people become reasonably well-informed specialists, while most congressmen perforce are generalists. But staff members' views, concerns, professional connections, chagrin at appearing ignorant or unprofessional, interaction with staff in other offices and on committees, are in many instances communicated to and translated by the representative — often probably without his being aware of where they come from. I am not saying such relationships never happened in 1953; of course they did; but the *volume* of professionally influenced communications about any subject with which Congress deals is greater now than it used to be. This in turn means that the average, middle-of-the-road congressman is somewhat less able to check and balance, to offset the prevailing doctrines of the bureaucracy (and the intelligensia on which the bureaucracy largely relies), than was the case in 1953.[10] The "inner-directed," intellectually autonomous congressman, for instance, who can now, for good or ill, assume an offsetting, balancing role will be of an unusual temperament or ability, not the most likely type to survive contests in party primaries.

Volume of communications affects the congressman in still a third way. There are, obviously, a greater number of issues and concerns that the House and Senate and, therefore, congressmen are expected to know about and, often, to act on. Vice versa, in 1953, congressmen could respectably claim ignorance of much more than they can now. Among subjects that were not then prescribed reading for anyone on Capitol Hill but are today are the politics of El Salvador, Vietnam (and Vietnamese refugees), Chile, Brazil, Lebanon, Colombia, and Burma (because of drugs). Congressmen may also be asked to state their position on many social welfare matters that once were left mostly to the states or to private agencies. For example, they may be asked where they stand on natural catastrophe insurance.

No one, of course, can master even a small proportion of these issues. In addition there are taxation, the environment, highway construction, and many more. But on all these issues and many others there are organizations that try to influence representatives through visits, correspondence, articles, invitations to meetings, campaign contributions, and so on. Fortunately for congressmen, it is still true that many and probably most of these communications are presented in a way that makes it relatively easy to acknowledge them courteously and then refer them on somewhere. The average communication is *processed* and perhaps counted but has no particular effect on the legislator to whom it is addressed; he may never see it at all. Yet, it is a perfectly plausible hypothesis that every once in a while a particular communication or set of communications has considerable impact upon some given representatives. So far as I know, we have little more knowledge as to when and how such uncommon but potentially significant happenings occur than we did thirty years ago. Despite considerable increase in knowledge about Congress and the legislative and representative processes since 1953, many such areas still demand reflection, analysis, and further study. Such study ought to be placed, as it too frequently is *not,* within a *general* social science framework, rather than in an almost *technical* or *journalistic* study of Capitol Hill.

The general issue that this chapter raises thirty years after it originally appeared is that of a world, a society, and a role in which too much information is available so that the attention and capacity for analysis of the processors (in this case congressmen and their staffs) are unduly strained. Herbert Simon and others point out in an article,[11] the significance of which was not sufficiently appreciated, as far as I know, that what is needed in such tasks as that of congressmen is to *buffer* them (in some systemic way, presumably, rather than through intuition and interest) against the richness of information likely to be communicated to them. Although Simon does not make the point, it can be argued that the frontier lawyer Abraham Lincoln, because he was restricted from information pressure by knowing only a few books, learned *better* how to reflect and evaluate than today's political scientists or law school teachers, who are victims of scarcity of attention, which is the obverse of richness of information. Scarcity of attention means, for instance, less opportunity or prospect of weighing relevance[12] and of determining what needs to be evaluated critically and how this should be done. "We need to know," says Simon, "the costs of consuming attention (by getting drowned in information or fearing we must try to be). Progress lies in the direction of figuring out more manageable ways of storing information, rather than insisting that all of us must personally store it."

NOTES

1. Lewis Anthony Dexter, *Congressmen and the People They Listen To* (Cambridge: Center for International Studies, MIT, 1956, Mimeographed). The copyright of this material belongs to MIT, and permission for reproduction should be obtained through the author, School of Public Administration, Dalhousie University, Halifax, N.S. B3H 3J5.

Copies of the duplicated report, now out of print, are available in part at the Library of Congress and some university libraries; and it may also be obtained through University Microfilms, Ann Arbor, Mich. (Ph.D. diss. in sociology, Columbia, 1960).

2. Since 1955, a good deal of my experience has been in political activities and I have also been engaged in a study bearing on the way congressmen are approached by businessmen on defense *contracts.* I want to emphasize that this is a report of what I saw as to mail and contacts on reciprocal trade. Contacts in the statehouse in Massachusetts are very, very different; some contacts on defense contracts are probably different in Washington; and, in quite another way, mail and contacts on defense *policy* are different—there being practically no mail on issues of defense policy. (See my "Congress and Military Policy" in the 2d ed. of this work (Chicago: Rand McNally,

1969). The picture derived from our report of a soft, nonpressure relationship does not apply to patronage in the governor's office on Beacon Hill, although my experience and observations suggest that even there the "pressure" on the Furcolo office was much tougher than on the Volpe office, because of sociological and social-psychological differences between the two administrations.

3. Estes Kefauver and Jack Levin, *A Twentieth Century Congress* (New York: Duell, Sloan, and Pearce, 1947), 171. It may be an interesting comment on public preconceptions and expectations that a columnist in a popular magazine, who frequently summarizes academic articles, summarized the present piece from the *Public Opinion Quarterly* by giving the Bankhead quote *as though it were the point of my article* and stated, when I protested, that that was what I had in fact said.

4. In other words, where the mail seems routine, repetitious, or uninspired, or where the mail clerk of the congressional office is busy, much such out-of-state mail gets little attention. But a serious, original letter from a person who obviously knows what he is talking about or has some known claim to attention may and often does receive careful consideration.

5. No doubt this occurred because both he and Mr. Curtis are from St. Louis and Mr. Curtis had stimulated local attention on the matter.

6. A minor committee in the Senate, although a very major one in the House.

7. Lowell H. Hattery and Susan Hofheimer, "The Legislators' Source of Expert Information," *Public Opinion Quarterly* 18 (Fall 1954): 300–303.

8. There can be little doubt that committee executive meetings, where the text of the bills is discussed and amendments considered, often involve a lot of give-and-take and also result in members on both sides changing their minds.

9. See L. A. Dexter, "The Representative and His District," in the 1st ed. of this book (Chicago: Rand McNally, 1963), 3–29.

10. See Dexter, "Checks and Balances," in A. de Grazia, ed., *Congress: The First Branch of Government* (Washington, D.C.: American Enterprise Institute, 1966), 83–113.

11. "Designing Organizations for an Information-Rich World," in Martin Greenberger, ed., *Computers, Communications, and the Public Interest* (Baltimore: Johns Hopkins Press, 1971), 37–72.

12. See F.C.S. Schiller, "Doctrine of Relevance," in *Logic for Use* (Orlando, Fla.: Harcourt, Brace, 1930), chap. 5.

Chapter 2

Ethics and the Work of the Legislator

DAVID E. PRICE

As a member who came to the Congress in 1987 from a teaching career that included a good deal of work in ethics and public policy, I have found it strange to hear talk of an "ethics craze" in government and indeed to witness a continuing preoccupation with ethical matters, centered around the fall of House Speaker Jim Wright but by no means limited to that episode.

My first assignment upon joining the Duke University faculty in 1973 was to devise an ethics course to be a required component of the graduate public policy curriculum. Over the ensuing decade I worked with a growing group of academics and practitioners across the country, holding workshops, writing papers, attending conferences—promoting the study and the teaching of ethics while developing the intellectual content and broadening the applications of my ethics course. But while I thus stepped into the swirling waters of "ethical" agitation and debate in the House with considerable background in that subject, that background often seemed to have precious little relevance to what passed for ethical discussion there.

I say that not in criticism of the fields of political ethics and public policy as they have developed. Indeed, I am more inclined to be critical

This article is adapted from the Sorensen Lecture given at the Yale University Divinity School on 13 February 1990 and is reprinted by permission of the author. The author is grateful to Andrew Sorensen for his sponsorship of this annual lecture, and to Dennis Thompson for his helpful suggestions. David E. Price, a Democrat, represents the Fourth District of North Carolina.

23

of prevailing public and congressional conceptions of ethics, what I will somewhat disparagingly term "Ethics Committee" ethics. My point, however, is not that the ethics committees and the congressional code of conduct should appreciably broaden their domain. Rather, it is that the implications of ethical reflection and analysis for the Congress—for the policies it makes and how its members function—go far beyond what can or should be contained in a code or enforced by a watchdog committee. It is that broader conception of ethics and its relevance to legislative life that I want to explore in this chapter.

Numerous colleagues and I examined the ethical content of the legislator's role and the inherent limitations of "Ethics Committee" ethics as part of a major Hastings Center project in the early 1980s.[1] What I encountered in 1987 was an intensifying ethical concern in Congress itself, culminating on the House side in the appointment of the Bipartisan Task Force on Ethics and the passage of the Government Ethics Reform Act of 1989, but with hardly any broadening of the terms of discussion and debate.

A readiness to believe the worst about the motives and the integrity of public officials has characterized American political culture from the beginning. Historians like Bernard Bailyn and James Sterling Young have documented the prevalence of a strong antipower ideology in the revolutionary and subsequent generations, a conviction that those with political power would invariably abuse it, that corruption and self-aggrandizement were endemic to government.[2] Young, in fact, attributes the disabilities and demoralization of the early congresses in large measure to the tendency of the members to internalize the dominant public view of "power-holding as essentially a degrading experience. . . . The power-holders did not, in their own outlook, escape a culturally ingrained predisposition to view political power and politics as essentially evil."[3] Such cynicism and mistrust of officeholders and public institutions have been heightened in recent years by highly publicized scandals and by the capacity and the tendency of modern mass media to publicize the foibles and failings of politicians.

For most of their first two centuries, the House and Senate had no written codes of behavior but dealt sporadically and often inconsistently with discrete acts of wrongdoing.[4] I came across one such instance in researching a brief bicentennial piece on those who preceded me in representing my district in North Carolina. I discovered that one of my predecessors, a Reconstruction congressman named John Deweese, had resigned his seat in 1870 one day before he and two other members were censured for selling appointments to the military academies. Progressive-era reform sentiments and various election scandals led to a series of federal campaign practices statutes beginning in 1907. But it was not until after World War II that Congress moved to adopt more general codes of conduct for its members. The first was a governmentwide aspirational code, adopted in 1958 in the wake of the Sherman Adams-Bernard Goldfine scandal in the Eisenhower administration. Widely publicized congressional scandals a decade later—involving Senator Thomas Dodd, Senate Majority Secretary Bobby Baker, and Representative Adam Clayton Powell—led both chambers to adopt their first formal codes of conduct. These were toughened considerably in 1977 and again in 1989.

The most recent changes, passed after the resignation under fire of Speaker Jim Wright, tightened limits on outside employment and eliminated speaking fees, or "honoraria"; strengthened financial disclosure requirements; prohibited members from converting campaign funds to personal use upon retirement; and prohibited lobbying by members and staff for one year after leaving their positions. Most of these provisions were contained in the report of the Bipartisan Task Force on Ethics, accurately described by its co-chairman as "the most sweeping reform of congressional ethics in the last decade."[5] But the proposals did not break new ground conceptually and were "comprehensive" only in relation to the already defined domain of congressional ethics.

Dennis Thompson tells of one instance in which a breakthrough did indeed occur. In Tennessee in 1977, in the wake of a political scandal, the leaders of the state senate decided they needed a tough code of ethics:

> Senators who did not want the code were reluctant to vote against it in the prevailing climate of reform, but when the code came to the floor, they thought they had found a way out. One senator proposed, as a substitute amendment, the Ten Commandments and the Golden Rule. The leaders knew that in Tennessee no legislator could vote against the Ten Commandments or the Golden Rule, and they scrambled to find a parliamentary compromise that would save the code. The substitute amendment became a regular amendment, and Tennessee became the only state to have a code of ethics that included, along with strong conflict-of-interest provisions, all ten of the Commandments. From Article IV with its detailed procedural rules, the document jumped immediately to Article V, which read in its entirety: "Thou shalt have no other gods before me."[6]

But even Tennessee has now fallen into line; when the code was revised in 1985, Thompson reports, the Ten Commandments quietly disappeared!

The 1985 Hastings report, while acknowledging that a code of official conduct should only be "one element in a well-rounded effort to inspire the conduct of legislators as well as to engender trust on the part of the public in those legislators," still is critical of the limits of existing codes: "They are generally narrow in scope, short on aspirational statements, and fail to deal with the full range of representative or legislative functions.[7] The report proposes three touchstones for legislative ethics: *autonomy* (the "obligation to deliberate and decide, free from improper influence"), *accountability* (the "obligation to provide constituents with the information and understanding they require in order to exercise responsible democratic citizenship"), and *responsibility* (the "obligation to contribute to the effective institutional functioning of the democratic legislative process").[8] Existing codes address the first two principles in their conflict-of-interest and public disclosure provisions, but they still construe "autonomy" and "accountability" quite narrowly and deal with "responsibility" hardly at all.

The Hastings authors suggest that a more adequate code of legislative ethics might, like the former code of professional conduct of the American Bar Association, contain aspirational elements and espoused ideals as well as precisely defined rules of conduct.[9] They probably underestimate the difficulty of reaching consensus on aspirational maxims and do not suggest what kind of enforcement mechanisms, if any, might be appropriate in this realm. But they are correct in pointing up the severe limitations of "Ethics Committee" ethics. Using that as my point of departure I want to proceed, not precisely to delineate what might or might not be codified, but to look beyond personal and official probity and to ask what further ethical dilemmas and challenges confront the legislator as he defines and carries out his job.

ETHICS AND POLICY

Members of Congress and other legislative bodies continually make policy choices, not just in hundreds of roll-call votes each year but in crafting legislation for introduction, refining bills in committee, and engaging in debate at each stage of the process. These policy choices are, among other things, choices of value. Legislators, like most citizens, value human liberty, feel that policies should be just and fair, argue for taking the public interest or the common good into account, and may speak of furthering human solidarity and community. They are aware to varying degrees, of course, of the historical, philosophical, and theological grounding of such concepts, of how they might complement or contradict one another, and of the implications they might hold for specific questions of policy. But such concepts do describe valued social states and help shape, however loosely, the process of deliberation and debate.[10] For years I taught a course called Ethics and Public Policy that was based on the assumption that policymakers and the policy process would benefit from more careful and critical reflection on our inherited notions of human well-being and the public good, and more explicit efforts to discern the implications of these ideas for particular policies and institutions. Much of what I have experienced during more than two terms in the U.S. House has strengthened that conviction.

This is not to say, of course, that the ethical assessment of policy among practicing legislators generally takes the same form that it does in the academy—or indeed that it should. Dennis Thompson argues persuasively that the demands of the role of the legislator, in particular the *ethical* demands, may conflict with the "generic requirements of ethics." "Ethics demands a general perspective, but legislators are also obligated to look after their own particular constituents. Ethics requires autonomous judgment, but legislators are also expected to defer to electoral decision." Legislators, moreover, if they are to give effect to their values and intentions, must collaborate with and defer to colleagues whose values and goals they only partially share. Nor do legislators normally operate from a universalistic perspective. On the contrary, they occupy *particular* positions within the legislative system, and their roles may be partial or "one-sided," depending on the opportunities they have and their expectations about what others will do. "The duties of any single representative depend on what other representatives do or fail to do, and thus the proper role of a representative cannot be determined without reference to the state of the legislative system."[11]

Still, as members develop, articulate, and justify their own positions, their notions of social value come into play. And one element in the viability of a legislative proposal, or in the credibility of a critique of executive or administrative policy, is its resonance with widely held notions of justice or the public good.

One of the few books that has attempted to describe and characterize the process of valuation as it takes place among policymakers is *A Strategy of Decision* by David Braybrooke and C. E. Lindblom. It is a book that has held up remarkably well in its account of how public officials cope with their environment, and my service in the House has led me to appreciate it anew. Braybrooke and Lindblom show that the process of social evaluation does not normally conform to the conventional (or, one might say, stereotypical) "rational-deductive" or "synoptic" ideal. Various features of legislative and other policy-making settings—the multiplicity of values and interests, and conflicts among them; shortages of time, information, and analytic capabilities; the multiplicity of decision points; the dominance of margin-dependent choices and of remedial orientations—render synoptic decision-making impractical.[12] But this is not to say that normal practice—what Braybrooke and Lindblom describe as the strategy of "disjointed incrementalism"—is value free. On the contrary, they suggest that existing practice comports remarkably well with utilitarianism, that "family of theories" that "allow meliorative and distributive considerations a decisive role in confirming all moral judgments that are open to dispute, and . . . suppose that, among these meliorative and distributive considerations, social welfare and group happiness justify supporting an action or policy, while their opposites do not."[13]

It is no secret that distributive considerations loom large in congressional policy-making and that distribution is often conceived in terms of the benefits or breaks sought by organized, active interest groups. But aggregative notions of utility—the sort of value we are getting at when we speak of "the public interest"[14]—are also frequently considered and may serve as a standard against which narrower professions of interest are measured.

Life on the Banking Committee could be considered the supreme test of this, I suppose, for the committee's environment is replete with organized interests, and policy deliberations sometimes seem to reduce to pulling and hauling among them. But even the legislative battle that best exemplified this in the One Hundredth Congress—the attempt to repeal the Glass-Steagall Act, to expand bank powers, and to rationalize banking regulation—also demonstrated something more. On one level, the episode displayed familiar group conflicts: banks *versus* securities firms, money-center banks *versus* independent banks, and so forth. In the end, unfortunately, these conflicts (plus a major turf battle between two House committees) killed the bill. But one reason the proposal got farther along than similar proposals had previously—and may yet be enacted—is that public interest arguments were developed and used and were, in many cases, persuasive.[15] Proponents of Glass-Steagall reform were thus not simply responding to the interests of major American banks but were also attempting to increase the availability and lower the cost of capital in many regions of the country, bolster American banks' slipping competitive position internationally, move toward a rationalized system of functional regulation, and so forth.

In the Banking Committee's second major area of jurisdiction, housing, competing concepts of social value often arise with unusual clarity. How, for example, should community development block grants be targeted? I used this as a "textbook case" in my class on ethics and public policy, and it is still debated from time to time on the Banking Committee. One's sense of justice, reinforced in the case of my class with a reading of John Rawls's *A Theory of Justice*,[16] might lead one to give priority to the poorest neighborhoods, to those most in need. But the sort of utilitarian calculations described by Braybrooke and Lindblom might lead one to a different—and, in my view, more defensible—conclusion, at least as long as community development (CD) funding does not go far beyond its present level. CD funding, which mainly is used to rehabilitate dilapidated housing and to provide local infrastructure improvements, is quite modest. Yet it can be quite effective in halting deterioration and in turning a *marginal* neighborhood around, providing benefits that extend far beyond persons who are directly assisted. In the poorest neighborhoods, by contrast, such funds might sink without a trace. Other types of housing programs are needed in the poorest areas, of course, but it would be a mistake to target CD funds too narrowly; the money should be used where it can be effective and can do the most good for the most people.

A related dilemma in the area of public housing was explored at a Raleigh field hearing of the Banking Committee's Subcommittee on Housing and Community Development as we prepared to write the 1990 housing bill. Ever-tightening "federal preference" rules in public housing have required that priority be given to those who pay more than 50 percent of their income in rent, who are involuntarily displaced, or who are living in substandard housing. "At face value," the director of the Greensboro Housing Authority testified, "these rules suggest fairness, providing that scarce housing resources go to the most needy."[17] But she went on to describe how the rule was requiring the authority to replace working families who left public housing with multiproblem families and people who could not function independently, who placed a great strain on the inadequate network of community services (budget counseling, job training, tutoring, etc.), who aggravated community drug and security problems, and so forth. What was being lost was the socioeconomic *mix* that had given public housing projects some stability and had provided indigenous role models and leadership. The obligation to assist the most destitute obviously stood in some tension with the need to promote the well-being of those already in the project, to ensure the viability of the project as a whole, and to enable it to function as a community.

These are difficult dilemmas, but it is often possible to devise solutions that address the competing values effectively. In the 1990 housing bill, for example, I successfully pushed an amendment to allow up to 30 percent of the slots in public and assisted housing to go to persons who met the income eligibility requirements but fell outside the federal preference criteria. Another type of solution—more difficult to come by, unfortunately, in these tight budget times—is to "expand the pie" or otherwise alter the policy so that the tradeoffs are less painful. In this case that would mean increasing federal support for public and assisted housing so that the waiting lists are not as long and the unmet needs not as desperate. My point here is simply to stress that policy choices are value choices, and that to initiate or to support a policy is to affirm a certain notion of social value. Legislators will make such choices one way or another, but I believe they will be better choices—more ethically responsible choices—if they are made in explicit awareness of the goods one is pursuing and with a conscientious and thoughtful effort to relate those values to the problem at hand.

REPRESENTATION AND RESPONSIBILITY

I now want to look at the legislator's responsibility from a different perspective, moving beyond the ethics of policy choice to the *role* the legislator assumes as a member of an ongoing institution. Legislators must define themselves in relation to forces impinging on them from outside and from within the legislature, and in terms of their responsibility for the institution's collective performance. Dilemmas of role definition and institutional responsibility depend, for the specific form they take, on the character of the legislative system and the possibilities it offers its members. I will thus highlight some critical features of the U.S. Congress as it currently operates and then focus on specific dilemmas of role and responsibility that arise in this setting.[18]

The New Congress

An examination of the picture painted by leading students of Congress of members in their institutional environment reveals a significant shift over the past three decades: from an emphasis on members' *adaptation* to well-defined norms and procedures to a portrayal of them as purposive *agents* in a fluid organizational setting. In the former category, one thinks of Richard Fenno's landmark studies of the appropriation committees and Donald Matthews's 1960 study of the Senate centering on the "folkways" of the institution, "its unwritten rules of the game, its norms of conduct, its approved manner of behavior"—just like, as one senator put it, "living in a small town."[19] Consider, by contrast, the premise of David Mayhew's influential 1974 essay, *Congress: The Electoral Connection.* "I have become convinced," Mayhew wrote, "that scrutiny of purposive behavior [of individuals] offers the best route to an understanding of legislatures—or at least of the United States Congress."[20] Mayhew thus posited the assumption that members of Congress were "single-minded seekers of reelection" and found a close fit between the behavior such an assumption led one to predict and actual congressional performance.

While this shift reflects changing fashions in social-service research,[21] it also owes much to changes in the institution being studied: a number of developments have made an individualistic portrayal of Congress an increasingly plausible one. Many observers have chronicled changes in House and Senate folkways and a decline in their influence on member behavior. Particularly significant has been the fading of the expectation that one would serve an extended apprenticeship before taking an active role in committee or on the floor. While members still value subject-matter specialization and expertise, they have become less hesitant to get involved in areas beyond their committee assignments. The introduction of bills and issuing of pronouncements on a wide variety of subjects, formerly the hallmark of a few "mavericks," had become widely engaged in and tolerated, and members are less concerned to maintain a facade of committee or party unity as they take their causes or their amendments to the floor.

These changes are rooted to a considerable extent in the altered context in which members are elected and seek reelection. Of primary importance is the decline of the political parties, both as shapers of electoral choice and as organizations controlling critical campaign resources. Members are increasingly on their own electorally and less dependent on the parties. They face electorates less inclined to vote for them on partisan grounds alone and a public largely unaware of and unconcerned about their party regularity once they are in office. They are generally nominated not by party caucuses or conventions but by direct primaries, and the number of districts with party organizations strong enough to control the nomination process has declined substantially. Candidates must raise their own funds and build their own organizations at the primary stage and often for the general election as well. National partisan swings have become less and less determinative of election outcomes in most congressional districts, and ticket splitting has become endemic. Understandably, members are inclined to see the services they render to their districts and the visibility they maintain there as more crucial to their electoral fortunes than their ties to the organized party, either at home or in Congress.

The electoral environment has changed in other ways as well. Both senators and representatives face larger, more heterogeneous districts; better educated and more demanding constituencies, with expanded expectations of the role and obligations of government; and electorates less easily reached through traditional friends-and-neighbors or clubhouse politics. Television has become the dominant campaign medium, with far-reaching consequences for candidate and congressional behavior. It places a premium on highly visible posturing in Washington—"showhorse" behavior of the sort the folkways proscribed. By promising to reach voters directly and persuasively, it further reduces member dependence on party organizations. It requires huge outlays of money, thereby increasing candidate dependence on groups with money to give and on direct-mail technology.

Members have responded to this complex of environmental forces in a variety of ways. Mayhew stresses the prevalence of three strategies: *position taking* (making speeches, introducing bills and amendments, assuming postures designed for maximum electoral appeal), *advertising* (building name familiarity and a favorable image through newsletters, media reports to the district, and targeted mail), and *credit claiming* (performing favors for constituents and helping secure projects for the district).[22] What these strategies have in common is their *entrepreneurial* character; they are more readily understandable in terms of the profit-and-loss calculations of individual political agents than in terms of the established norms of the legislative institution.

Anxious to gain visibility and leverage earlier in their congressional careers, members have also pressed for "reforms" that dispersed authority and resources more widely within the institution. The most visible result of this has been a proliferation of subcommittees—senators are currently spread among 96 subcommittees and House members among 135–and a series of rules changes, mainly in the House Democratic Caucus, mandating a high degree of subcommittee autonomy. At the same time there has been some democratization and expansion of the functions of the party caucuses and whip organizations, making them more promising as vehicles of participation.

Many members have found this reduction in the power of full committee chairs and the spreading around of legislative resources quite serviceable in terms of their desire for a piece of policy "turf" and enhanced visibility. But organizational fragmentation has posed certain problems for Congress as an institution. It has heightened the tendency toward "particularism," the servicing of narrowly based interests with limited regard for broader considerations, as members have gravitated toward subcommittees in whose jurisdictions they and their districts have a particular stake. It has complicated congressional policy-making by making mobilization of the chamber more difficult and by providing numerous checkpoints for those who wish to oppose new departures in policy. It has, in fact, helped prompt a sort of congressional reform—the centralized budget process, for example, and the increased powers over committee assignments, scheduling, and other processes granted to the party leadership—that represents a partial corrective to those changes that have dispersed power. But the net effect of congressional reform has been to put more resources in the hands of individual members while making Congress as a whole more difficult to manage and to mobilize.

What Sort of Member Shall I Be?

Thus does a survey of members in their legislative and electoral settings reveal an organizationally fragmented, almost atomistic Congress with many of the norms and structures that formerly ordered behavior in a weakened state; particularistic pulls from constituency and other interest groups, increasingly unmediated by party; increased opportunities for electoral and policy entrepreneurship, but in a volatile environment that requires constant attention and offers few reliable mechanisms of support; and weakened inducements to committee or party solidarity or to institutional patriotism. Now we return to the question: what sorts of ethical dilemmas—decisions as to role and responsibility—does the legislator in this setting face?

In posing these questions I assume that members cannot eschew the profit-and-loss calculations related to the maintenance of their electoral viability and to the preservation of their power base within the institution. I also assume, however, that a broad range of legislative strategies and involvements are compatible with, and indeed can be supportive of, self-interest in these senses. Most members of Congress, most of the time, have a great deal of latitude as to how they define their roles and what kind of job they wish to do. If they do not have the latitude, they can often create it, for they have a great deal of control over how their actions are perceived and interpreted. I thus conceive of these ethical dilemmas as choices a politician makes within the bounds of political "necessity."

1. *To what range of values and interests should I be responsive?* It is tempting to believe that one is being properly representative and responsive by giving a respectful hearing to groups that present themselves on a given issue and then reaching a reasonable accommodation among them. Such an assumption finds support within the pluralist school of political science. Braybrooke and Lindblom, for example, expect those most intensely interested and directly affected to make their voices heard on a given policy question: "Normally, people are not slow to protest when a policy looks like worsening their condition."[23] Public officials, such analysts conclude, will generally feel constrained to be attentive to such groups and to strike some sort of balance among them. Perhaps that is an acceptable operationalization of representative government under contemporary conditions.

But perhaps not. A number of analysts have argued persuasively that the politically active organizations or constituencies prepared to press their views on a given question are likely to be a highly selective sample of those whose interests and values are affected.[24] One cannot assume that all affected interests will find ready access to the political arena. Some lack the organizational or other resources to make their voices heard. Others may be frozen out by virtue of the ties that exist between dominant groups and clientele-oriented committees and agencies. And broader and more diffuse interests will generally have more difficulty mobilizing their constituencies and developing effective organizational structures than will those more narrowly based interests whose stakes are more immediate and tangible.

A responsible legislator will take the initiative in looking to those poorly organized or deviant interests that the system might exclude, and to broad, shared public interests and values that are inadequately mirrored in the "pressure system." Many of the developments we have surveyed promote an uncritical particularism: the fragmentation and clientele orientations of subcommittees, the increased campaign role of organized interests, the decline of parties as institutions mediating between those interests and public officeholders. But taking a broader view of one's representative role need not be seen as self-sacrificial behavior, at least not most of the time. Legislators often find it politically profitable to cultivate new constituencies, or to appeal over the heads of contending groups to a broader public concerned with one issue or another. Such strategies do not succeed automatically: legislators must *work* at increasing the salience and attractiveness of their policy stances. To transcend the "brokering" role and to make such moves politically viable and attractive to their colleagues, members must shore up supportive groups, cultivate the media, and otherwise attempt to "broaden the *scope* of conflict."[25]

Responsible representation does not require a dark view of any and all collaboration with "the interests." But neither does it permit a sanguine view of representation as a mere balancing of pressures, or an expectation that competition among the interests organized and active in a given area will ensure an equitable outcome. It is important to take account of the biases and exclusions of the group system and to take independent account of the full range of values and interests a policy question entails.

2. *To what extent and in what fashion will I contribute to the work of the legislature?* It is often said—and as members we often say it—that we are very thinly spread. But such complaints may miss the mark in accounting for institutional performance; the real problem is the erosion of the inducements to engage seriously in the *work* of Congress. Pulling one's weight in committee and developing a substantial area of expertise are still serviceable strategies for members who would gain the esteem of colleagues. But the weakening of the norms of apprenticeship and specialization, together with the pressures for self-promotion created by the

new electoral environment, have made showhorse behavior more profitable and less costly than it was in the past.[26] Members have stronger incentives to latch onto a piece of policy turf, to gain control of a subcommittee, and to cultivate an image of policy leadership. But their incentives to engage in the painstaking work of legislative craftsmanship, coalition building, and mobilization may actually be weaker. Such activities are more difficult under conditions of organizational fragmentation, and the pressures to do one's homework are less compelling. Moreover, as Mayhew stresses, the electoral payoffs for merely taking a position or introducing a bill may be just as great as those that reward more extensive or conscientious efforts: "Would Senators Hatfield and McGovern," he asks, "have been any the more esteemed by their followers if their [anti-Vietnam War] amendment had won rather than lost?"[27]

In stressing the importance of serious legislative work, I do not mean to denigrate the nonlegislative aspects of the job. I believe that constituent communication and services are worthwhile in their own right and, moreover, can support the member's legislative efforts in important ways— enhancing the two-way "representative" relationship and giving the member the kind of leeway he needs for flexible and cooperative legislative involvement.[28] But alterations in both the electoral environment and the congressional ethos have made it thinkable, perhaps even profitable, for a number of members to engage almost exclusively in constituency-cultivating activities to the detriment of Congress's legislative and oversight tasks. And even when members do turn their attention to policy, their involvement is too often superficial and fleeting.

This sort of "position taking" can be just as deceptive and manipulative as other forms of self-promotion. "Appearing to do something about policy without a serious intention of, or demonstrable capacity for, doing so," as Richard Fenno stresses, "is a corruption of the representative relationship."[29] And of course such behavior robs the legislative institution of the energy and persistence needed to make it work, at precisely the time when the tasks of coalition building and mobilization have become appreciably more difficult. Congress still contains many skilled and persistent legislators—more, I think, than Mayhew's model would lead one to predict—and some have managed to make of their legislative power and productivity a substantial electoral asset. The institution still depends on members' assuming such roles and adopting such priorities, but this behavior is more dependent on the choices and proclivities of the members themselves and less on institutional pressures and constraints than was formerly the case.

3. *What responsibilities do I bear for the functioning of the committee and party systems?* "Public duty," wrote Edmund Burke, "demands and requires

that what is right should not only be made known, but made prevalent; that what is evil should not only be detected, but defeated": "When a public man omits to put himself in a situation of doing his duty *with effect,* it is an omission that frustrates the purposes of his trust almost as much as if he had formally betrayed it." Such a demand for seriousness of purpose speaks directly, of course, to the superficial and symbolic gestures that too often pass for policy-making in the contemporary Congress. But what Burke specifically had in mind was the need for members of Parliament to associate, to cooperate under the standard of a party:

> No man, who is not inflamed by vain-glory into enthusiasm, can flatter himself that his single, unsupported, desultory, unsystematic endeavors, are of power to defeat the subtle designs and united cabals of ambitious citizens. When bad men combine, the good must associate; else they will fall, one by one, an unpitied sacrifice in a contemptible struggle.[30]

Public duty, Burke argued, gives powerful ethical support to party fidelity. He was profoundly skeptical of the tendency of politicians to tout their own independence or to portray themselves as motivated by conscience; too often, he suspected, this was a cover for the pursuit of private advantage. Party operations, Burke believed, could and should leave room for occasional dissent, but the desire for concord and for effectiveness would properly nudge fellow partisans toward agreement:

> When the question is in its nature doubtful, or not very material, the modesty which becomes an individual and that partiality which becomes a well-chosen friendship, will frequently bring on an acquiescence in the general sentiment. Thus the disagreement will naturally be rare; it will be only enough to indulge freedom, without violating concord, or disturbing arrangement.[31]

Such a view, of course, squares imperfectly with the individualistic notions of moral autonomy to which Americans typically repair. Former Senator Jacob Javits no doubt anticipated his readers' applause as he declared: "In this clash of loyalties—loyalty to constituents, loyalty to party, and loyalty to myself—my constituents and I had to prevail."[32] But we should beware of imputing ethical superiority to the "loner." If the committees and the parties play a legitimate and necessary role in developing and refining measures, in aggregating interests, in mobilizing the chamber, should not the burden of proof be on the member who would violate the comity and the discipline necessary to their successful functioning? This is neither to endorse mindless party regularity nor to deny that members should sometimes resolve conflicts with their party or committee in favor of personal convictions regarding constituency interests or the public good. But such choices should be difficult and not arrived at lightly.

Party voting has displayed a long-term decline in both houses over the course of this century, although in recent years the decline has leveled off and the average member's party-support score has slightly increased.[33] For this, the renewed role of the parties, especially the Republican party, in recruiting and supporting candidates may bear some responsibility, as may various measures that have enhanced the role of the House leadership. But neither constituency nor chamber pressures constrain most members to support or work within the party; how closely they do so is largely a matter of individual choice. The same is increasingly true of work on committees, most of which have seen their ability to maintain a united front on the floor and to command the deference of the parent chamber decline. Although many members may welcome the reduced hold of these systems on them, they also have reason to reflect on the price the *institution* has paid in its reduced capacity to act in an orderly and concerted fashion. It will not do simply to revel in one's status as a free agent; an adequate ethic will give substantial weight to the need to maintain mechanisms of *collective* action and responsibility.

4. *How should I present myself in relation to the legislature's practices and performance?* Every member of Congress, former Congressman Bob Eckhardt (D., Tex.) suggests, functions in three roles: lawmaker, ombudsman, and educator.[34] The third role, as we have seen, may be closely related to the first: any lawmaker who wishes to do more than simply defer to the strongest and best-organized interests on a given matter must give some attention to explaining his actions and educating his constituents, helping them place the issue in broader perspective or perhaps activating alternative bases of support. The extent to which a member is willing and able to undertake such explanations, I have suggested, is ethically as well as politically significant.[35]

Here I turn to another facet of the legislator's educative role: his portrayal of Congress itself. Richard Fenno describes as his greatest surprise, upon traveling with House members around their districts, the extent to which each one "polished his or her individual reputation at the expense of the institutional reputation of Congress":

> In explaining what he was doing in Washington, every one of the eighteen House members took the opportunity to picture himself as different from, and better than, most of his fellow members in Congress. None availed himself of the opportunity to educate his constituents about Congress as

an institution—not in any way that would "hurt a little." To the contrary, the members' process of differentiating themselves from the Congress as a whole only served, directly or indirectly, to downgrade the Congress.

"We have to differentiate me from the rest of those bandits down there in Congress," Fenno heard a member say to a campaign strategy group. "'They are awful, but our guy is wonderful'—that's the message we have to get across."[36]

So much for the traditional norm of institutional patriotism! Opinion polls regularly reveal public officials in general and Congress in particular to rank low in public esteem, an evaluation reinforced by the recent spate of ethics charges in both houses but rooted much more deeply in our country's history and political culture. Every indication is that members reinforce such an assessment by distancing themselves from any responsibility for the institution's functioning. And we are phenomenally successful at it, matching a 30 percent approval rate for Congress with a 90+ percent reelection rate for ourselves.

My point is not that a member should defend the legislature right or wrong. I understand very well the disadvantages of being put on the defensive about Congress's ethical problems—pointing out that only a small number of members are involved, that Ethics Committee proceedings are generally bipartisan and fair, etc.—although I believe many of these defenses have merit. I am speaking of a more general tendency to trash the institution. It is often tempting—but, I believe, also deceptive and irresponsible—to pose as the quintessential outsider, carping at accommodations reached as though problems could simply be ignored, costless solutions devised, or the painful necessities of compromise avoided. The responsible legislator will communicate to his constituency not only the assembly's failings, but also what it is fair and reasonable to expect, what accommodations they would be well advised to accept, and so forth. In the past, institutional patriotism has too often taken an uncritical form, assuming that whatever the process produces must be acceptable. But self-righteous, anti-institutional posturing is no better. The moral quixotism to which reelection-minded legislators are increasingly prone too often serves to rationalize nonproductive legislative roles and to perpetuate public misperceptions of the criteria it is reasonable to apply to legislative performance.

Thus, although it may be politically profitable to "run *for* Congress by running *against* Congress," the implications for the institution's effectiveness and legitimacy are ominous. As Fenno concludes, "The strategy is ubiquitous, addictive, cost-free, and foolproof. . . . In the short run, everybody plays and nearly everybody wins. Yet the institution bleeds from 435 separate cuts. In the long run, therefore, somebody may lose. . . . Congress may lack public support at the very time when the public needs Congress the most."[37]

Legislative Structures and Legislative Ethics

Although the American founders regarded public virtue, a willingness to forego private advantage for the sake of the commonweal, as essential to the health of the new republic, they were unwilling to trust human nature to its own devices. On the contrary: government must be *structured* in such a way, not only to anticipate self-serving behavior but to turn it to good account. "Ambition must be made to counteract ambition," wrote James Madison in *The Federalist* (no. 51).

> This policy of supplying, by opposite and rival interests, the defect of better motives . . . [is] particularly displayed in all the subordinate distributions of power, where the constant aim is to divide and arrange the several offices in such a manner as that each may be a check on the other— that the private interest of every individual may be a sentinel over the public rights.

It can be argued, analogously, that certain of Congress's organizational features have structured the pursuit of political advantage and turned it to the institution's account. The committee system, for example, accommodates the aspirations of disparate members but also represents a corrective of sorts to congressional individualism—a means of bringing expertise and attention to bear on the legislature's tasks in a more concerted fashion than the free enterprise of individual members could accomplish. The committee system channels members' desires for leverage and status into activity that serves the institution's needs and builds its policy-making capacities.

Such an institutional maintenance function is even more obvious in the case of Congress's powerful "control committees"—Appropriations, Ways and Means, and, now, Budget—and the party leadership. Mayhew argues that the willingness of members to defer to these control mechanisms and to reward those who operate them with power and prestige can be understood as the "purchase" of a collective good—the preservation of the institution against the consequences to which unchecked individualism and particularism could otherwise lead.[38] But members do not make these calculations in a vacuum; they come into an institution where these structures and the norms, patterns of authority, and powers to reward and punish that support them are already in place. If members are to function effectively they must, to a significant degree, honor these norms and direct their own initiatives through approved channels.

It is important to subject such institutional structures and norms to ethical scrutiny. Despite Madison's expectation that the checking and balancing of power would protect the public interest, we know that in fact the constitutional system has historically given advantages to certain types of interests at the expense of others. Similarly, the norms and structures that gave inordinate power to Congress's committee chairmen in the 1950s had a distinctive policy impact, inhibiting overdue changes in civil rights and other areas. As Roger Davidson argues, that period's folkways were promulgated by, and served the interests of, the conservative coalition that ran both chambers during the 1950s.[39] There were powerful ethical arguments for modifying this particular pattern of institutional maintenance. I do not mean to suggest that the directions in which Congress has moved and the policies it has adopted in the ensuing years represent some sort of ethical decline. Indeed, the contrary case could convincingly be made.

What I do mean to suggest, however, is that congressional behavior has become less structurally and normatively constrained in the past thirty years and that this loosening, rooted mainly in the electoral incentives facing individual members, poses serious problems for the functioning of Congress as an institution. Both Congress's capacity to produce coherent policy and the quality of its policy product are at stake.

These dilemmas demand renewed attention to congressional organization and structure. Of particular importance are efforts to strengthen party organs—to strengthen the caucuses as forums for policy discussion and to increase the leadership's capacity to overcome committee fragmentation and parochialism in bringing proposals to the floor. And while our budget difficulties are more political than structural, it is still important to strengthen and streamline that process.

Strengthening the structures and norms by which the Congress "supplies the defect of better motives" and protects its institutional capacities, however, will not dispense with the need for a heightened sense of individual responsibility. In today's Congress, members are often essentially on their own—in dealing with the entreaties of interested groups, in deciding what kind of contribution they will make to the work of the legislature, in making the party and committee systems work, and in shaping citizen perceptions and evaluations of the institution. Such dilemmas will continue to be central to legislative life, questions of value that members cannot help addressing in one way or another. How we deal with them will decisively shape the capacity of Congress for leadership and the quality of its performance.

NOTES

1. Bruce Jennings and Daniel Callahan, eds., *Representation and Responsibility: Exploring Legislative Ethics* (New York: Plenum, 1985); Callahan and Jennings, *The Ethics of Legislative Life* (Hastings-on-Hudson, N.Y.: Hastings Center, 1980).

2. Bernard Bailyn, *The Ideological Origins of the American Revolution* (Cambridge: Belknap, 1967), chap. 3; James Sterling Young, *The Washington Community, 1800–1828* (New York: Harcourt, Brace, and World, 1966), chap. 3.

3. Young, *Washington Community*, 56, 59.

4. A useful overview is provided in Richard Allan Baker, "The History of Congressional Ethics," in Jennings and Callahan, *Representation and Responsibility*, chap. 1.

5. Rep. Vic Fazio, in 16 November 1989 *Congressional Record* (daily ed.), H-8745.

6. Dennis F. Thompson, *Political Ethics and Public Office* (Cambridge: Harvard University Press, 1987), 10.

7. Callahan and Jennings, *Ethics of Legislative Life*, 53, 55.

8. Ibid., 34–42. This framework was first developed by Amy Gutmann and Dennis Thompson in "The Theory of Legislative Ethics," in Jennings and Callahan, *Representation and Responsibility*, chap. 9.

9. Callahan and Jennings, *Ethics of Legislative Life*, 55. Note the aspirational character of most of their suggested "next steps," 60–62. For a more cautious view see John D. Saxon, "The Scope of Legislative Ethics," in Jennings and Callahan, *Representation and Responsibility*, chap. 10.

10. See David E. Price, "Assessing Policy," in Joel L. Fleishman et al., eds., *Public Duties: The Moral Obligations of Public Officials* (Cambridge: Harvard University Press, 1981), chap. 6.

11. Thompson, *Political Ethics*, 96, 101.

12. David Braybrooke and Charles E. Lindblom, *A Strategy of Decision* (New York: Free Press, 1963), chaps. 3, 5 and *passim*.

13. Ibid., 206. The authors also claim that the strategy conveniently compensates for some of the defects commonly attributed to utilitarianism (212–23).

14. See Brian Barry, *Political Argument* (London: Routledge and Kegan Paul, 1965), chaps. 10–11.

15. See, for example, Gerald Corrigan, *Financial Market Structure: A Longer View* (New York: Federal Reserve Bank of New York, 1987); *Mandate for Change* (Washington, D.C.: Federal Deposit Insurance Corporation, 1987); House Committee on Government Operations, *Modernization of the Financial Service Industry* (1988).

16. Rawls's theory of justice places a burden of proof on social and economic arrangements: do they maximize the well-being of the "least advantaged" members of society? This might not always require giving first priority to those most in need, but assistance to other groups would depend on whether it improved the lot of the worst off in the long run. John Rawls, *A Theory of Justice* (Cambridge: Harvard University Press, 1971), chap. 13 and *passim*.

17. Testimony of Elaine T. Ostrowski, "Affordable Housing," field hearing before the Subcommittee on Housing and Community Development, House Committee on Banking, Housing, and Urban Affairs, 101st Cong. 26 January 1990 (serial no. 101–75), 97.

18. An earlier but more detailed version of what follows may be found in David

E. Price, "Legislative Ethics in the New Congress," in Jennings and Callahan, *Representation and Responsibility*, chap. 7.

19. Donald R. Matthews, *U.S. Senators and Their World* (New York: Vintage Books, 1960), 92. Fenno likewise drew heavily on concepts from functionalist social science—role, function, integration, and adaptation—terms suggesting that members conformed to the institutional environment more than they shaped it. See Richard F. Fenno, Jr., "The House Appropriations Committee as a Political System: The Problem of Integration," *American Political Science Review* 56 (June 1962), 310–24; and *The Power of the Purse: Appropriations Politics in Congress* (Boston: Little, Brown, 1966).

20. David R. Mayhew, *Congress: The Electoral Connection* (New Haven, Conn.: Yale University Press, 1974), 5.

21. See Brian Barry's exposition of "sociological" and "economic" modes of social analysis: *Sociologists, Economists, and Democracy* (London: Collier-MacMillan, 1970).

22. Mayhew, *Electoral Connection*, 49–77.

23. Braybrooke and Lindblom, *Strategy of Decision*, 185–86. These analysts proceed to treat "disjointed incrementalism" as a tolerable substitute for—and in some ways an improvement on—utilitarianism's felicific calculus (chap. 10).

24. See, for example, E. E. Schattschneider, *The Semi-Sovereign People* (New York: Holt, Rinehart and Winston, 1960), chap. 2; Theodore J. Lowi, *The End of Liberalism*, 2d ed. (New York: W. W. Norton, 1979), chap. 3; Robert Paul Wolff, *The Poverty of Liberalism* (Boston: Beacon Press, 1968), chap. 4; and Mancur Olson, Jr., *The Logic of Collective Action* (New York: Schocken Books, 1968), chap. 5.

25. The phrase is Schattschneider's; see *Semi-Sovereign People*, chaps. 1–2.

26. For an attempt to operationalize the showhorse-workhorse typologies and to discuss the conditions of their occurrence, see James L. Payne, "Show Horses and Work Horses in the United States House of Representatives," *Polity* 12 (Spring 1980): 428–56. Payne finds that the orientations are indeed distinctive, with few members ranking high on both "legislative work" and "publicity" indices. He also finds evidence that "being a show horse pays off electorally," and is far less costly than it once was in terms of advancement within the House.

27. Mayhew, *Electoral Connection*, 117.

28. On this latter point, see Richard F. Fenno, Jr., *Home Style: House Members in Their Districts* (Boston: Little, Brown, 1978), 240–44.

29. Ibid., 243.

30. Edmund Burke, "Thoughts on the Cause of the Present Discontent," in *Works* (London: George Bell and Sons, 1893), 1:273–75. Emphasis added.

31. Ibid, 378.

32. Jacob K. Javits, *Javits: The Autobiography of a Public Man* (Boston: Houghton Mifflin, 1981), 134.

33. See David E. Price, *Bringing Back the Parties* (Washington, D.C.: Congressional Quarterly Press, 1984), 51–57.

34. Norman J. Ornstein, ed., *The Role of the Legislature in Western Democracies* (Washington, D.C.: American Enterprise Institute, 1981), 96–97.

35. For discussions of various techniques—and difficulties—of "explanation," see John W. Kingdon, *Congressmen's Voting Decisions*, 2d ed. (New York: Harper and Row, 1981), 47–54; and Fenno, *Home Style*, chap. 5.

36. Fenno, *Home Style*, 164, 166.

37. Ibid., 168, 246.

38. Mayhew, *Electoral Connection*, 141–58; see also David E. Price, "Congressional Committees in the Policy Process," in L. Dodd and B. Oppenheimer, eds., *Congress Reconsidered*, 3d ed. (Washington, D.C.: Congressional Quarterly Press, 1985), 168–75.

39. "Socialization and Ethics in Congress," in Jennings and Callahan, *Representation and Responsibility*, 110–16.

Chapter 3

Member of the House:
Letters of a Congressman

CLEM MILLER

Dear Friend:

Here follows, in answer to numerous (at least three) requests, an account of the way I spend a typical day. I arise at 6:45, eat breakfast, and spend ten minutes with the *Washington Post,* skimming the news and reading the editorials and columns. Leave for the office at 7:55 A.M., arriving at congressional parking lot at 8:20 A.M. (Alternatively, I may breakfast at 8:00 A.M. with a veterans group, Boy Scouts or some other group—Thursday last, with the British Ambassador. I enjoyed good conversation with a British member of Parliament and three other congressmen and had a chance to do a little indirect complaining about the legislative program, under the guise of social discussion. Breakfast seems to be the best time of day to talk to someone seriously.)

Back at the office, your congressman is at the desk from 8:30 to 10:00 A.M. at least, or possibly till 12:30 P.M. First off, I look at the mail, perhaps a carryover from the preceding day, dictating replies and stashing aside the reports, memos, mimeographs, speeches, publicity blurbs, brochures, for later study. The average daily onslaught of mail, excluding newspapers, makes a stack about fourteen inches high.

Generally, at 9:00 comes the first office appointment: A trade asso-

Reprinted with permission of Charles Scribner's sons, an imprint of Macmillan Publishing Company, from *Member of the House: Letters of a Congressman,* by Clem Miller, edited by John W. Baker, 66–68, 74–77, 80–83. Copyright © 1962 by Charles Scribner's Sons.

ciation to discuss an industrial problem, or a lobbyist to explain his position on a bill. I invite them to come in. Right now, I am wrestling mightily with the problem of what to do about fair trade laws. I invite interested parties to meet with me and discuss their point of view. I have just recently concluded a similar study on the administration's proposals for taxing cooperatives. At 10:00, there may well be a hearing of the committee to which I am assigned, or of the subcommittee currently holding extensive hearings on the depressed areas bill. One of our major problems consists of getting to our committee hearings on time. Frequently it seems almost impossible to arrive on time for these hearings, what with the press of office work. However, the committee work is vital to the work of Congress, and I think it well-nigh a national disgrace to observe witnesses who have traveled many miles speaking to a committee of one member. So, I make it a point to be there on time.

The House meets at 12:00 noon. Usually, it is in session four or five days a week. Members are rather erratic in their attendance. If there is a debate on a bill, I will generally be there.

Fitting lunch into this schedule often becomes difficult. Frequently I have luncheon engagements. Frankly, I do not have time for them. I usually eat at my office, and relax with a newspaper from the state capital or my district.

Then, during afternoon hours, I am busy cramming committee meetings between duties on the floor or in the office. Yesterday, for instance, several of us had a 2:00 P.M. meeting with John K. Galbraith on tight money and economic policy. The debate over Hawaiian statehood was also on and I listened to that for a while. Then, a meeting with a member of the Appropriations Committee on our district public works.

About 5:00 P.M. I return to the office to work over the mail, sign letters, and see people. Getting away from the office is more and more difficult. In the beginning, I left at 5:45 P.M. Now I am leaving at 6:15 or 6:30 P.M.

Evenings I spend at home as much as possible. A congressman can eat out five and six nights a week if he wishes to. After having attended several functions, I have now cut them down to a minimum. I have been invited to dinner with the assurance that it is "strictly social." However, the socializing is somewhat difficult and quite flat. The feeling will not down that behind the tenderloin steak is the cold and indifferent practicality of the Washington lobby. So, I tell the inviters "no." Instead, I invite them to my office to speak frankly about their problems. I learn more faster, and feel better.

At night, after supper, I read another district paper as well as the reports, speeches, and magazines that have accumulated during the day. I throw some out, keep others for filing, and separate others for condensing on five-by-eight cards.

About 11:00 or 12:00 P.M. the day is at an end. I like to top it off with a chapter from a book. This is a busy day, six days a week. I present it to you neither for commiseration nor vainglory. I like it. It is very lively, and may some day be rewarding. (I hope the account may prove instructive and helpful without being sickly. Each of us has his own tolerance in this department.)

Very sincerely,
CLEM MILLER

Dear Friend:

The congressional recess is that period in the fall, after adjournment, which offers respite from the steady press of legislation. Congressmen, extremely weary of themselves and their fellows, are eager to be home—to see how things are.

Congress remains in session for longer and longer periods as the complexity of government mounts. In the early days of the republic, sessions lasted from one to three months. Today, a nine-or-ten-month session is routine.

Recess at home is traditionally a time for checking grass-roots reaction; it is also a time for public viewing of the congressman. Citizens have a right to see their representative, to talk to him and observe him.

In a city district, a central office with daily office hours is sufficient. In a district covering as much territory as the First California (if transplanted to the East Coast it would reach from Boston to Baltimore), this is impossible.

As soon as I know about when Congress will adjourn, my field representative and I frame in certain dates from the requests for appearances which come in to us. We spot invitations on the calendar, providing a schedule that will move us from one community to another, in a sequential manner. A great deal of time must be spent actually on the road. Our station wagon is loaded with files of research material, congressional reports to distribute to constituents, and all the personal paraphernalia we need for a two-month safari—including cookstove and stenographic recording equipment.

My home and office for two or three months is a series of motels. The pressure of the schedule and the distances involved make use of my real home in Corte Madera impossible.

We usually begin with three or four days in Marin County with headquarters in a San Rafael motel, ready for engagements in nearby towns.

From Marin, we move to my district office in Santa Rosa in reach of various Sonoma County towns. Then, a swing north along Highway 101, from Ukiah to Cresent City. Returning, we tour through Lake County, into the Napa Valley, and back to Marin to prepare for a renewal of the cycle. Such a swing around the 300-mile-long district takes at least ten days and preferably, fifteen to eighteen days. Two such complete swings are made during a recess, with side forays into smaller communities. Time is set aside to talk to a dozen federal and state agencies in San Francisco and Sacramento.

We lay out the schedule with reasonable attention to population densities, and allot time for the ordinary continuing duties of a congressman. This time out for routine duties is important. The continuing duties of a member of Congress—answering the mail from constituents, seeing individuals on special problems, and keeping up with events—do not come to a halt simply because you are on the road. The press of the routine is insistent, and must somehow be sandwiched in between service club speeches, church socials, local group barbeques, and visits to defense installations.

When we first begin a tour, the commitments are well spaced out. But as time goes on, the schedule becomes choked with a succession of extra events that make each day tighter and tighter. Telephone calls begin to follow us around from place to place. Can I spare a few minutes on this? Can I see that person for five minutes? Can I talk to the annual meeting of the Soil Conservation District directors? It may mean skimping on lunch, shaving travel time, and postponing bedtime, but we generally work them in.

A recent typical day went like this: At 7:00 or 8:00, breakfast with a small group to talk over a legislative program on dairy products for school lunches. The next engagement was set for 10:00 in a nearby town to talk to the high school civics class. The ample time allotted to get there was cut to ribbons by the fact that a constituent had driven up from San Rafael to see me about a harbor project. The worked-in appointment for twenty minutes took forty, so the daily rush was on—behind schedule already.

The civics class ended at 10:50; we had planned time for the drive to another town and time to collect my thoughts and make a few notes for a Rotary luncheon speech. However, the schedule did not provide for the senior problems class, which blocked my exit from school with some very serious questions demanding answers. The principal also wanted a word about science equipment available through the National Defense Education Act. According to the schedule I should have left at 11:30, but the final breakaway came fifteen minutes later.

Service club luncheons you can count on. They must be over by 1:30. This gave from 1:45 to 2:45 to work on the backlog of accumulated telephones calls. (They come from everywhere. Invariably, the caller begins, "Well, you *are* a hard man to track down. . . .") While I was telephoning, a delegation of Indians arrived to talk to me about their reservation hospital. At 3:00 I accompanied the board of supervisors to inspect the site of a much needed river levee to keep back floods; this took longer than anticipated. So it was a strain to arrive clean and ready for a veterans' dinner at 6:30. I had been asked to speak for twenty minutes on veterans' legislation and national defense. A part of the meal was given over to reviewing that portion of my portable file pertaining to these subjects and to formulating notes on my remarks. This was accompanied by frequent interruptions to shake hands and to be introduced to new friends. I had to finish the dinner, the speech, and move on for an 8:30 meeting at the local farm center to discuss the farm bill. We arrived at 9:00 after a hectic nighttime drive over a strange road. The meeting lengthened with lively and forceful questions until 11:00; the room was hot and crowded. The tone of the meeting at the start had been quite hostile. At the end, as understanding grew closer, the extra cake and twentieth cup of coffee (for the day) were hard to refuse. The relief of the group as tensions relaxed was obvious, and their friendly attention was hard to break away from. They followed us to the car and talked while the engine ran. Finally, we were off and down the road, with the necessity of driving to a neighboring town to position myself for the next day. Bedded down at-last, the last half hour of the day was spent reading mail, a newspaper or two, and a memo from Washington in order to keep up with what was going on in my own office there and in the world, and then lights out.

This is the schedule for more than two months, seven days a week. It is a life of constant movement and relentless physical activity. It imposes a constant vigilance, unrelieved, hour upon hour. An inappropriate off-hand remark, misplaced flippancy, or a flash of irritation are not readily forgiven. People ask meaningful, serious questions on all conceivable subjects, and they demand and are entitled to informed, thoughtful answers. This means an ever-active brain. Even a social evening is turned into a mental exercise. The time for solitude, for refueling of the machine, is nonexistent. As representative, I am constantly exposed to the represented—to our mutual education and benefit.

What the recess trip home also means is that my capacity, like any congressman's, is taxed to the limit. We are called on in this field of legislation one moment, in another the next moment, and a third shortly afterward. This is in the approved tradition of the United States. It is a kind of testing which Americans insist on. We use it as a yardstick for off years as well as election years. It's an exhilarating experience but an exhausting one. The long hours of work in Washington, keeping oneself up to the mark on district and national and world affairs, pay off. When I return to Washington I know that I have been through the mill. I have sheaves of notes for action on new proposals: a mental health bill, an upgrading in priority of a proposed harbor project, a new outlook on the civil defense and shelter programs, the need for a new post office, and on and on. . . . A rest of several weeks is in order, then a new session of Congress, and I'm off again.

Very sincerely,
CLEM MILLER

Dear Friend:

The opening day of Congress is a time of great excitement and ferment. During the off season, Capitol Hill simmers along, hardly a ripple breaking the empty silences of the long halls and passageways. Opening day is moving day. A vast game of musical chairs takes place as some congressmen move out of their offices and newcomers move in. Restless senior congressmen with priority move from one floor to another. Furniture heaps up in the hall while squads of painters renovate whole rooms in a matter of minutes among secretaries stolidly sorting through mounds of mail.

The matter of room assignment is the jealously guarded privilege of seniority. The matter of furniture is a vital symbol of status. The exact desk. The proper chairs. The perquisites of public office are relatively few in number so that the capture of a special desk seems quite important.

When the buzzers sound for the opening call of the House, the corridors begin to seethe; people emerge from everywhere—pageboys, clerks, and attendants of all sorts bustle here and there. Everyone moves a bit faster. You feel good. You feel friendly toward everyone. It's like the first day of school; it seems brand new and hopeful. When you shake hands, you mean it. You may not know the man very well. But he, too, is back from "the district."

Congressmen flood into the tunnel that connects the offices with the Capitol. The hubbub is fierce. A booming jollity. Everywhere hands are grabbed. They set off smartly in platoons of four and six, waves of men and women proceeding along the gentle incline. Deep smiles of greeting, halloos, and backslapping.

This may appear to outsiders as part of the ordinary political spectacle, the general overfriendliness of the trade; but it is much more than that. The emotions are real. The affection is a heartfelt display. It is the camaraderie of the shared experience. These people, these congressmen, have all been through the mill. They have returned from the indifferent cruelties of the political wars. They may have been saddened by the failure of friends to understand, as much as they were outraged by the indignities suffered from their opponents. Elections are unrelenting and painful. The public image of the thick-skinned politico is an inaccurate stereotype which conceals private feelings. So, the freshly painted office, the familiar furniture, the trusted staff, their fellow ambulants, constitute a refuge, warm, friendly, understanding.

They are really glad to see one another. As the Members come piling into the chamber through the glass door, the reading clerk must pause time and again for the clamor to subside. He smiles indulgently and quite happily as he nods to familiar faces. There is no great effort to keep order amid the surging throng. People squirm in their seats to greet friends. There is zip and crackle to the "hellos" ringing about the room.

The greetings on the floor extend across the aisle to the Republican side, perhaps a trifle less effervescent, but the warmth is there. The camaraderie of the return is bipartisan. The harsh words which divide the two parties are for the moment put aside and rendered impersonal. He was not *my* opponent. He did not call *me* that. The bitterness is shelved in the joy of reunion.

The members crowd in on the floor, piling up along the side aisles, packing together, overflowing in front of the Speaker's dais, chattering and gesticulating, gradually finding seats. The southerners take their accustomed places in the center, the northerners along the edges. Everything is customary, familiar. The clerk of the House calls the House to order under the rules. As the names of the members are called by states, the cliché goes round and round—"Well, boy, it's official, you're on the payroll now!" Somberly, patiently, the teller records the vote for Speaker: each Democrat for Rayburn, every Republican for Halleck, 258–170. Mr. Speaker, Mr. Sam Rayburn, marches firmly and stolidly to the seat he has held so long, and Halleck, accompanying him to the dais, delivers the accustomed sententious amenities.

It is Speaker Rayburn's birthday. Curious how angular and grim in profile, so broad and rather complex in full face. He remains stolid and dignified throughout, stirring to smile-traces when the chairman of an important committee, his implacable legislative foe, rises to speak his words of congratulations.

You search the Speaker's face for some sign as former Speaker Joe

Martin rises. Martin leans heavily on his cane, his words are slow and full, deep affection showing through their formality. The chamber is silent, each of us pondering what is between these two, while Martin talks throatily of long, long ago. He speaks from the center of the chamber, next to the Democratic side, away from Minority Leader Halleck, who has succeeded to his place. Martin, the silent, is speaking to his friend, Sam Rayburn:

> Mr. Speaker, and my colleagues, it is a great privilege to have the opportunity, even for a few moments, to pay my respects to a dear friend, an old friend and a member whose friendship has lasted over thirty-five years without a jarring note. It has been my privilege to know Sam Rayburn all these years, and I can testify, as few men can testify, to his rugged Americanism, his loyalty to country, and his intense desire above everything else to maintain the high honor and integrity of the House of Representatives.

Rayburn's face never flinches, but he shifts his weight heavily from one side to the other, cups his jaw in one and then the other hand, as he looks unblinkingly at his friend Joe Martin.

The Speaker's acceptance is restrained, stripped of all histrionics, with the simple resonance of his voice carrying his feeling. When he says, "The House of Representatives has been my life, and it is today and always has been my love," it brims with emotion. One perceives from these words why he has been Speaker for twenty years. When he says

> I feel a deep sense, of humility, because my talents are not beyond those of the average member of the House or the average American citizen. They are all good folks; and I know that when they are geared to having faith and confidence in you, you are the only one who can destroy that faith and confidence.

—when he says these words you understand why he gets the allegiance of that disparate mixture called the Democratic members of the House of Representatives. He does have faith in people. His roots are deep in the humanitarian populist tradition of the West. It is this faith which enables him to bridge the gap between the Texas of 1913 and the national prospect of 1961. And then he says:

> I make no promise except to say that every man and woman in this House will be treated like every other member of the House and have all the rights of every other member of the House, because you are chosen by the people, you are a selected group. There is not a district in this country

where many men and women would not like to sit where you sit today and would run against you any time they thought they could defeat you either in the primary or in the general election.

When he says this he lines up with every member of the House personally. He is not an institution. He is not Speaker. He is one of us.

Very sincerely,
CLEM MILLER

Chapter 4

Correlates and Effects of Attention to District by U.S. House Members

GLENN R. PARKER
and SUZANNE L. PARKER

Most of our knowledge of district attentiveness comes from three sources. In *Home Style,* Fenno (1978) undertakes an extensive individual-level analysis of incumbent behaviors in the district. He is able to isolate three kinds of district behavior: allocation of resources, presentation of self, and explanations of Washington activities. The incumbent's ultimate goal is to generate trust among constituents; such trust helps to maintain the electoral support necessary to win reelection. Further, the diffuse support that a member is able to generate in the district may afford him greater freedom in his legislative decisions in Congress.

Glenn Parker's (1980a, 1980b) aggregate analyses of the amount of time members spend in their districts indicate that in the House some members have been converted to more attentive home styles and others have replaced less attentive members.

It appears that the replacement of less attentive incumbents elected prior to 1965 by more attentive cohorts (elected since 1964) has helped to increase the overall levels of district attentiveness exhibited by House members. These data indicate that the process of replacement, as well as conversion, has operated to increase attentiveness. [1980b, 121]

All three of these analyses seek to answer a basic question posed by Fenno: "Which members go home most often and which less so—and why?"

This chapter was originally published in *Legislative Studies Quarterly* 10 (May 1985): 223–42. Copyright © 1985 by the Legislative Research Center. It is reprinted by permission.

(1978, 35). Parker's aggregate analysis indicates which members go home more; in the aggregate, members elected since 1964 spend more time in their districts than members elected prior to 1964. In addition, while older members have increased their time in the district, newer members entering the House place even more emphasis on such travel; this finding suggests that newer members have brought a new style of representation to the House—a style that emphasizes personal attention to constituents.

This chapter seeks to further our knowledge of the causes and consequences of district attentiveness. It focuses first on the influences which motivate some members to spend more time in their districts than other members. Where previous analyses examined the effects of cohort, period, and seniority on district attentiveness (Parker 1980a, 1980b), this one explores several other factors that may influence attentiveness, such as demographic characteristics of the district and partisan characteristics of the member. Further, it expands Fenno's analysis, examining district attentiveness over a longer time period and using a different data base.

The second part of the analysis provides empirical evidence to explain why members find district attentiveness so attractive; it explores the link between time spent in the district and the electoral margins of incumbent representatives—the consequences of district attentiveness. We suspect that district attentiveness among newer cohorts accounts for their increased electoral safety. Increased attentiveness on the part of Democrats elected between 1965 and 1970 can account for the changes in their reelection margins, and the increased attentiveness of newer members elected in the 1970s can explain the continued generational change in election margins that Born (1979) has documented.

The data for this analysis—time spent in the congressional district—are coded from the travel vouchers filed by members to obtain reimbursement and reported by the clerk of the United States House of Representatives (*Report of the Clerk of the House, 1971–76*). A member is coded 1 for every week in which he or she spent two or more days in the congressional district. Members who chose to take a lump sum cash allowance rather than filing individual travel vouchers for each trip are excluded from the analysis. This presents only minor problems for this analysis, since most members file vouchers. The members most likely to choose the lump sum allowance are those who live close to Washington, D.C., since they can then take more trips than those allocated under the voucher system. The data cover a six-year period from 1971 through 1976 (Ninety-second, Ninety-third, and Ninety-fourth Congresses).[1]

Additional data described district and member characteristics for the six-year period. These data include 1972 census data on district characteristics: the percentage of central-city residents, the percentage of suburban residents, the median family income, the percentage of families with an income below $3,000, the median years of education, the percentage of white-collar workers, the percentage of blue-collar workers, the percentage black, and the percentage of foreign-born residents. Electoral information for each member includes the district congressional vote for the years 1968 through 1976, the district presidential vote for 1968, 1972, and 1976, the year of the member's entry into Congress, the year of the member's retirement, the year in which the member made a bid for higher office, and the number of years the member had served in office. Finally, data on the personal characteristics of each member include year of birth, region, party, presidential support scores, Conservative Coalition scores (CCS), and party unity scores.

THE CAUSES OF DISTRICT ATTENTIVENESS

Variables

Underlying all of the hypotheses presented in this part of the analysis is the assumption that members behave as they do in order to win reelection. Factors that might threaten that goal, therefore, can provide an impetus to district attentiveness. The dependent variable in this section is the number of weeks in which a member spends two or more days in the district. In an attempt to explain the variation in the amount of time members spend in the district, we use several types of independent variables: electoral circumstances, district characteristics, and divergence from the party, the president, and/or the district. To identify the most important influences on district attention, we use regression equations to delineate the most important explanatory variables.

The most obvious threat to a member's reelection would seem to be an electoral threat. Yet discovering a link between electoral margins and district attention has proved to be problematic: Fenno (1978) finds no relationship between vote margin and his measure of district attention (trips to the district). Safety (and its obverse, marginality) has no truly objective measure; member's perceptions of electoral safety may not correspond to the actual vote percentages that separate them from their opponents. It has been hypothesized that a measure of the homogeneity of the district might serve as a surrogate measure for perceptions of marginality or safety (Fiorina 1974; Fenno, 1978, 29). We examined electoral margins and several measures of the degree of homogeneity within the district in this analysis; there were no significant relationships between these measures and the time members spend in the district.[2]

However, we have explored several other influences that could have a significant impact on district attention. There are two explanations of how the socioeconomic status of the district might affect district attention. One postulates that members from higher-status districts would spend more time in their districts than those from lower-status districts. The literature on political participation and constituency influence on leaders suggests that higher-status citizens are not only more politically active but also more likely to interact with political leaders (Schattschneider 1975; Verba and Nie 1972). It would be expected, therefore, that members who represent districts high in socioeconomic status spend more time cultivating their districts because citizens with higher income and education have both the leisure time and skills necessary to understand and to be attentive to politics (Converse 1975). As a result, these districts would place greater demands on the representative than lower-status districts. The second explanation emphasizes the special needs and demands of lower-status districts. In contrast to higher-status districts, lower-status districts have a greater need for the ombudsman activities provided by the representative. The representative from a lower-status district would spend more time in the district because of the greater need for his services and the greater opportunities to serve the constituents. We introduce three variables to capture the effects of constituents' socioeconomic status: median years of education, median family income, and the percentage of white-collar workers in the district.[3]

In his analysis, Fenno (1978, 38–39) uses region to measure proximity to Washington, on the assumption that members with districts farther from Washington will have time for fewer trips to the district. The analysis in this article uses distance to measure proximity. States located within five hundred miles of Washington, D.C., are coded 1; distances are then coded in five-hundred-mile intervals, with states over two thousand miles from Washington receiving a code of 5. It is expected that distance has a negative relationship to time spent in the district.

In *Home Style*, Fenno (1978) suggests that district attentiveness may be one way in which the representative secures policy leeway in Congress: the member cultivates the district and by doing so increases citizen trust. Thus, members whose legislative actions diverge from the desires of the district would need to cultivate their districts more than members whose actions are more in line with their constituents' positions. Divergence from constituents' positions, however, has been difficult to measure (Fiorina 1974, 1–28). Here we examine divergence from the constituents' interests: we hypothesize that conservative members who represent lower-status districts would be in conflict with their districts, particularly in the area of economic policy. Similarly, liberal members who represent higher-status areas would also diverge from their constituencies. These members are expected to spend more time in their districts than members who are not similarly divergent.[4]

Finally, the analysis includes several member characteristics in order to measure their impact on district attention. Parker (1981) has shown that Republicans place more emphasis on personal contact than Democratic members. Therefore, party has been included to measure the influence of this difference; it is hypothesized that Republicans spend more time in their districts than Democrats. It is also expected that members who decide to run for higher office and members who decide to retire from Congress will behave differently from members who do not make these decisions. Members running for higher office may use their reimbursed travel to cultivate a wider constituency in preparation for their campaign. Thus, they would be expected to spend more time in their districts than other members. Members retiring from Congress could be expected to spend less time in their constituencies than other members because they no longer have a pressing need to cultivate their districts. Dummy variables are introduced to capture the effects of retirement and bids for higher office.

Since prior analyses (Parker 1980a, 1980b) have shown that the member's cohort, indicated by the year he or she entered Congress, is an important variable in explaining aggregate patterns in district attention, it is included in this analysis. Members elected before 1965 are coded 0, and members elected after 1965 are coded 1. It is expected that members elected after 1965 spend more time in their districts than the cohort elected before 1965.

Findings

Two variables are significant across all three congresses (Ninety-second, Ninety-third, Ninety-fourth) — cohort and the divergence of conservatives from their lower-status districts. The unstandardized regression coefficients for the cohort variable show a monotonic increase over time (see table 4-1). Further, the betas indicate that cohort effects increase in importance relative to the other variables. In the Ninety-second Congress, cohort is the least important of the four variables; by the Ninety-fourth Congress, cohort is the most important explanatory variable. Members elected after 1965 spend more time in their districts than members elected before 1965. These findings coincide with those of Fenno (1978) and Parker (1980b), and indicate that members elected since 1965 display a different home style than earlier cohorts, a style which places heavy emphasis on spending time in the district.

Divergence from the district also appears to serve as an impetus for

Table 4-1. Correlates of District Attentiveness (Regression Coefficients)

Variables	92d Congress			93d Congress			94th Congress		
	b	Signifi-cance	Beta	b	Signifi-cance	Beta	b	Signifi-cance	Beta
Variables significant in all three congresses									
Cohort	2.0	.009		3.3	.002	.17	9.1	.000	.32
District divergence (conservatives from lower-status districts)	3.3	.001	.22	3.1	.009	.14	3.5	.03	.11
Variables significant in two congresses									
Bids for higher office				5.4	.045	.10	7.4	.02	.12
Distance	.85	.003	.18				−1.8	.001	−.17
Variables significant in only one congress									
Party				−3.4	.002	.18			
Income	−.0005	.011	−.16						
Retirement							−8.2	.009	−.14
Multiple *R*	.38			.35			.46		
N	266			336			321		

district attention. Conservative members elected from lower-status districts spend more time in the district than other members. This variable, however, decreases in relative importance over the three congresses. This is the only divergence measure that has a significant relationship with district travel. (See notes 2, 3, and 4 for descriptions of other variables tested.)

The decision to run for higher office appears to encourage members to spend more time in the district. This variable first attains significance in the Ninety-third Congress and remains significant in the Ninety-fourth Congress. As the allocation of reimbursed travel increased over the six-year period,[5] members running for higher office increased the amount of time they spent in the district compared to other members (fig. 4-1). The differences in the means for retiring members and members running for higher office, and the mean for all members of the Ninety-fourth Congress are substantially larger than in the previous two congresses. Further, the gap between retiring members and those running for higher office had increased significantly by the Ninety-fourth Congress (see fig. 4-1). It appears that members running for higher office found that the increase in the travel allocation provided increased opportunities to use the perquisites of their present office to campaign for a new one.

The relationship between the proximity variable and time spent in the district is more puzzling. This variable is significant in the Ninety-second and Ninety-fourth Congresses (table 4-1); the direction of the relationship changes, however, between the two Congresses. In the Ninety-second the relationship is positive, indicating that members with districts closer to Washington, D.C., spent less time in their constituencies than members with districts farther from Washington. By the Ninety-fourth Congress, members with districts closer to Washington spent more time in their districts than members from more distant districts. It may be that representatives from districts within five hundred miles of Washington frequently opted for lump sum allocations rather than a fixed number of trips in the earlier Congress. Thus, the only members who filed vouchers in the "within five hundred mile" category were those who traveled less. As the number of reimbursed trips increased, more members from districts closer to Washington, or their replacements, opted for the fixed allocation rather than the lump sum.

In the Ninety-second Congress, members from lower-income districts traveled more than members from districts with a high median family income, as table 4-1 shows. This finding suggests that lower-income districts demand greater attention from the representative than higher-income districts. This may be caused by a variety of factors; it may be that there are more opportunities for a member to provide services to lower-income districts. It may also be that the tendency for lower-income people to vote less frequently than higher-status citizens makes it necessary for the representative to appear in the district frequently to remind his constituents that he is looking after their interests and deserves their support. Members in lower-status districts may feel constant pressures to enhance their reelection constituency because they cannot be sure their supporters will turn out to vote.

Party attains significance only in the Ninety-third Congress. The negative relationship indicates that in 1973 and 1974 Republicans spent more time in their districts than Democrats. This finding is not surprising in light of the events of 1973 and 1974. President Richard Nixon's problems with Watergate increased his unpopularity as well as that of the Republican party. The rise in Republican travel in the Ninety-third Congress probably reflects the efforts of these House members to try to disassociate themselves from Watergate and Richard Nixon.

The only other significant variable is retirement (table 4-1). By the Ninety-fourth Congress, retiring members were spending significantly less time in their districts than other members of Congress. In the Ninety-second, Congress, the mean number of weeks spent in the district by retiring members was twenty-one weeks—five fewer than the average of

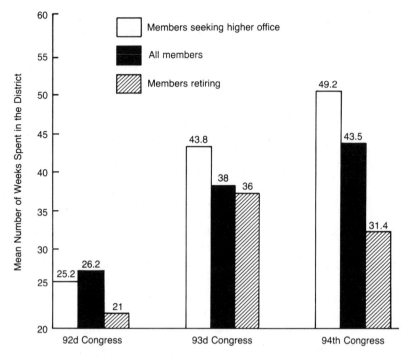

Figure 4-1. Weeks Spent in the District, by Members Seeking Higher Office, Members Retiring, and for All Members for Each Congress

all members included in the analysis (fig. 4-1). In the Ninety-fourth Congress this gap had increased to 17.8 fewer weeks. It appears that members who decide to retire are less motivated to be attentive to the district than other members.

Clearly, the analysis indicates that a large amount of variation is left to be explained and that few of the variables hypothesized to have an effect seem to have one. Perhaps expanding the number of hypotheses and variables would help to uncover other factors that affect district travel; then again, perhaps the causes of attentiveness are less systematic and more unique to the individual members.

DISTRICT ATTENTIVENESS AND ELECTORAL SAFETY

The aggregate changes in the attentiveness of House incumbents have a pattern: they indicate that congressmen are placing a greater emphasis on constituency affairs. Generational changes have occurred also in the allocation and duties of congressional staff (Schiff and Smith 1983), the increased travel to congressional districts (Fenno 1978), the growth in district offices (Fiorina 1977), and the expansion of congressional case-work (Johannes 1980). In short, there is ample evidence to suggest that stylistic changes have occurred in House incumbents and that the cornerstone of these changes is their attention to constituency affairs.

These aggregate stylistic changes appear to have occurred in senators as well as congressmen (Parker 1984) and appear to coincide with periods during which House and Senate incumbents were experiencing increases in electoral safety. These corresponding developments lead to the proposition that stylistic changes in the constituency orientations of members of Congress (i.e., greater displays of attention to constituency affairs) have helped to promote the electoral safety of House and Senate incumbents. Since there is evidence that these stylistic changes have continued through the 1970s (Parker 1980b), the question arises whether they have been accompanied by electoral change and how the stylistic changes could translate into some measure of aggregate electoral change and safety in the 1970s. In this section, we confine our attention to the impact of stylistic changes in the constituency orientations of representatives on their electoral safety.

There are two mechanisms through which stylistic changes in the district attentiveness of House incumbents could translate into the types of aggregate patterns of electoral safety that have been observed in House elections (Mayhew 1974; Fiorina 1977): the conversion of older members to greater attentiveness, and the replacement of less attentive (older) members by more attentive (newer) members. If older members were to adopt more attentive home styles, the systematic conversion of these members to greater district attention could help to enhance their reelection margins. There is reason, however, to doubt that the conversion of older congressmen to greater attentiveness would have a profound impact on the electoral safety of House incumbents. First, it may be more difficult for older members to adopt a more attentive home style. As Richard Fenno (1978) has observed, once a home style has been established, very little alteration in that style is likely to occur. Therefore, older cohorts of congressmen (i.e., those elected before 1965) may have difficulty in adapting to a newer, more attentive style because they have already adopted styles that place less emphasis on attentiveness than those of newer members elected in later cohorts. The difficulty in changing home styles explains why those elected before 1965 are less attentive than more recent cohorts (Parker 1980a): their home styles were largely established before district attentiveness had become recognized as an electoral resource, and before congressional perquisites had improved enough to facilitate such attention. Since their styles were formed without exploiting their attentiveness to the district, most do not avail themselves of the electoral benefits that can derive from a more attentive style. Further, even if such stylistic changes occur in older members, the electoral benefits may be negligible, since electoral safety appears to increase only among members elected to the House since the mid-1960s. "House cohorts elected since 1966 have achieved more electoral value from their incumbencies than those they replaced, while members of the pre-1966 generation have not benefited from any general pro-incumbent swing" (Born 1979, 811). In sum, the available evidence points to the conclusion that the conversion of older cohorts of congressmen to greater levels of district attentiveness in the 1970s would have a minimal impact on the electoral safety of House incumbents during this same period.

A more compelling argument can be made that the aggregate stylistic changes during the 1970s, produced by the replacement of less attentive congressmen by more attentive ones, have promoted the electoral safety of House incumbents during the 1970s. As we have already noted, recent congressional cohorts (i.e., those elected since 1965) have been more successful in boosting their election margins and have displayed higher levels of district attention than older House members. In fact, Fiorina (1977) views the process of replacement as instrumental in promoting the electoral safety of House incumbents, especially Democrats:

> The new representatives placed relatively greater emphasis on constituency service than did those who they replaced. The average freshman in 1965 replaced a congressman elected in 1952 or 1954. The latter had formed their homestyles in a different era. Moreover, particularly in 1964 many of the freshmen were Democrats who had won election in heretofore Republican districts. They can hardly be blamed for assuming that they could not win reelection on policy grounds. They had every incentive to adopt homestyles that emphasized nonprogrammatic constituency service. [54–55]

Fiorina's argument suggests that the electoral safety displayed by some House incumbents during the 1970s can be traced to the adoption of attentive home styles on the part of Democrats elected during the 1960s: "Paradoxically, then, the electoral upheavals of the 1960s may have produced the electoral stability of the early 1970s. New congressmen chose homestyles best adapted to the changed congressional environment" (Fiorina 1977, 55).

There are three reasons why we might expect that Democrats elected in the mid-1960s (1965–1970) would continue to be a source of electoral change during the 1970s. First, stylistic changes on the part of members of this cohort continued into the 1970s (Parker 1980a). Second, these members formed their home styles during periods when perquisites were increasing and incumbents had greater opportunities to cultivate their constituents through lavish displays of district attention. Hence, these incumbents should have had little difficulty in adjusting to the higher levels of attentiveness that were made possible by further increases in House allowances (e.g., travel, staff) during the 1970s. In addition, the home styles of these members would not have solidified to hinder their adaptation to further changes. Finally, given that many of the Democrats from this cohort replaced Republican incumbents during the 1960s, they may not have felt so electorally secure that they could afford to eschew the increased opportunities to expand their attentiveness during the 1970s.

We suggest a corollary to Fiorina's hypothesis about the impact of replacement on the electoral margins of House incumbents. Since stylistic changes in constituency attention are also exhibited by congressmen elected in the 1970s (Parker 1980a, 1980b), we expect that such changes in attentiveness would also be accompanied by increased electoral safety. That is, the electoral safety of House incumbents in the 1970s could be attributed to the adoption of a more attentive home style by Democrats elected in the 1960s and the adoption of attentive styles by congressmen elected in the 1970s. In sum, the stylistic changes in district attentiveness could translate into aggregate levels of electoral security during the 1970s.

The purpose of this section of the analysis is to examine the hypotheses of how changes in constituency attentiveness may have affected the electoral margins of House incumbents in the 1970s. We will attempt to determine which process—conversion or replacement—can best account for the changes in the electoral safety of incumbents during the 1970s. Four hypotheses are tested; one deals with conversion and three with replacement. If conversion is a significant factor in increased safety, members elected before 1965 who increase in attentiveness should also increase in electoral safety. The absence of such a relationship mitigates against the conversion hypothesis.

The test of replacement is a little more complex since it contains three separate components. First, if the replacement of less attentive members by more attentive members (no matter which party) is responsible for increased safety, there should be a positive relationship between changes in attentiveness and changes in electoral margins for all members elected between 1965 and 1970. Second, if Fiorina is correct and Democrats elected between 1965 and 1970 were the primary beneficiaries of increased attentiveness, we would expect to find Democrats from this cohort displaying a positive relationship between attentiveness and electoral safety. Further, if the second replacement hypothesis holds, we would also expect increases in the attentiveness of all members elected during this period to have no significant effect on their reelection margins. That, is, the relationship between increases in attentiveness and increases in safety would be insignificant for all members elected between 1965 and 1970, but significant and positive for Democrats elected in that period. The final replacement hypothesis examines members elected since 1970. Here, the same positive relationship between increases in attentiveness and increases in election margins is posited.

Our measure of stylistic change is the change in the amount of time spent in the congressional district during successive terms of office. This relationship must be further qualified, however, in order to distinguish between members who have actually altered their constituency styles and those who spend more time in their districts because of an immediate electoral threat. Members who have already established an electorally successful home style but who nevertheless increase their attention to their districts can be viewed as exhibiting a stylistic change in district attentiveness. The measure of stylistic change represents the interaction, for members free from electoral threat, between an existing successful home style and increased attentiveness. This variable is computed by multiplying the change in time spent in the district by a dummy variable that indicates whether the member won the last two elections by more than 65 percent:

$$
\begin{pmatrix} \text{Stylistic} \\ \text{change} \\ \text{between} \\ \text{the 92d} \\ \text{and 93d} \\ \text{Congresses} \end{pmatrix} = \begin{bmatrix} \text{Time} \\ \text{spent} \\ \text{in the} \\ \text{district} \\ \text{during} \\ \text{the 93d} \\ \text{Congress} \end{bmatrix} \text{minus} \begin{bmatrix} \text{Time} \\ \text{spent} \\ \text{in the} \\ \text{district} \\ \text{during} \\ \text{the 92d} \\ \text{Congress} \end{bmatrix} \text{times} \begin{bmatrix} \text{Prior} \\ \text{success} \\ \text{(last two} \\ \text{elections} \\ \text{65 percent} \\ \text{of vote)} \end{bmatrix}
$$

$$
\begin{pmatrix} \text{Stylistic} \\ \text{change} \\ \text{between} \\ \text{the 93d} \\ \text{and 94th} \\ \text{Congresses} \end{pmatrix} = \begin{bmatrix} \text{Time} \\ \text{spent} \\ \text{in the} \\ \text{district} \\ \text{during} \\ \text{the 94th} \\ \text{Congress} \end{bmatrix} \text{minus} \begin{bmatrix} \text{Time} \\ \text{spent} \\ \text{in the} \\ \text{district} \\ \text{during} \\ \text{the 93d} \\ \text{Congress} \end{bmatrix} \text{times} \begin{bmatrix} \text{Prior} \\ \text{success} \\ \text{(last two} \\ \text{elections} \\ \text{65 percent} \\ \text{of vote)} \end{bmatrix}
$$

This formulation allows us to differentiate between those incumbents who exhibit a stylistic change in their constituency attentiveness and those who temporarily alter their existing patterns of district attention in response to electoral threat. It is well known, for instance, that incumbents who are defeated for reelection have spent inordinate amounts of time in their congressional districts in efforts to stave off electoral defeat. Such changes in attentiveness may not indicate any systematic and enduring change in constituency attentiveness. Members who are electorally safe, on the other hand, have little electoral incentive to alter their levels of attentiveness; hence, electorally safe members who increase their attentiveness can be viewed as exhibiting a stylistic change in their constituency attention. While this formulation is admittedly imprecise, it is the only manner in which we can distinguish between those increases in time spent in the district which result from stylistic change and those which are a by-product of electoral threat.

If stylistic changes among our earliest cohort of House incumbents (those elected before 1965) increased the election margins of these members, this relationship will be interpreted as evidence that the conversion of incumbents to greater levels of district attention enhanced their electoral safety during the 1970s. If stylistic changes among those elected since 1965 enhanced their electoral safety, we will interpret this finding as evidence that replacing less attentive incumbents by more attentive ones can have lingering effects on electoral safety in the 1970s. If this relationship occurs only among Democrats elected between 1965 and 1970, we will interpret the effects as supporting the importance of replacement processes in enhancing electoral safety, but only among Democrats.

When this variable is analyzed among our most recent cohort (those elected in 1972), the relationship reflects how their adoption of an attentive home style affects their reelection margins—further evidence of the impact of replacing less attentive members by more attentive ones. For cohorts elected during the 1970s with experience in only one or two elections, these members' home styles have not solidified to the point that we can speak of conversion effects. That is, these members are still developing their home styles. If attentiveness is incorporated into home styles early in a congressional career and members are electorally successful, that attentiveness is apt to become an established feature of their home styles.

> Whereas, in the beginning, prospective House members are uncertain as to what kinds of home activities will work, once they have one or two testing elections behind them, they become more confident. They probably have no clear idea, as we noted earlier, of what element of home activity was responsible for how much of their support. But they do know that the sum of the elements contributed to victory. So the temptation is to keep the support they had "last time." [Fenno 1978, 189]

As this cohort of members increase their attention to district affairs, we expect their election margins to increase.

In order to measure the effect of stylistic changes on the part of attentive Democrats elected between 1965 and 1970 we also created an interaction term, which the change in the amount of time spent in the district between time$_1$ and time$_2$ is multiplied by a dummy variable indicating party (coded 1 if the incumbent is a Democrat and 0 otherwise):

$$
\begin{bmatrix} \text{Stylistic} \\ \text{changes} \\ \text{by Democrats} \\ \text{between} \\ \text{the 92d} \\ \text{and 93d} \\ \text{Congresses} \end{bmatrix}
=
\begin{bmatrix} \text{Time} \\ \text{spent} \\ \text{in the} \\ \text{district} \\ \text{during} \\ \text{the 93d} \\ \text{Congress} \end{bmatrix}
\text{ minus }
\begin{bmatrix} \text{Time} \\ \text{spent} \\ \text{in the} \\ \text{district} \\ \text{during} \\ \text{the 92d} \\ \text{Congress} \end{bmatrix}
\text{ times }
\begin{bmatrix} \text{Party} \\ \text{(coded} \\ \text{1 if} \\ \text{Democrat)} \end{bmatrix}
$$

$$
\begin{bmatrix} \text{Stylistic} \\ \text{changes} \\ \text{by Democrats,} \\ \text{between} \\ \text{the 93d} \\ \text{and 94th} \\ \text{Congresses} \end{bmatrix}
=
\begin{bmatrix} \text{Time} \\ \text{spent} \\ \text{in the} \\ \text{district} \\ \text{during} \\ \text{the 94th} \\ \text{Congress} \end{bmatrix}
\text{ minus }
\begin{bmatrix} \text{Time} \\ \text{spent} \\ \text{in the} \\ \text{district} \\ \text{during} \\ \text{the 93d} \\ \text{Congress} \end{bmatrix}
\text{ times }
\begin{bmatrix} \text{Party} \\ \text{(coded} \\ \text{1 if} \\ \text{Democrat)} \end{bmatrix}
$$

If Fiorina is correct about the impact of stylistic change on electoral safety among Democrats elected during the 1960s, we can expect to see a similar phenomenon during the 1970s. That is, as these Democrats expand their attentiveness to district affairs, their election margins should respond in the same manner as Fiorina suggested they did during the 1960s. In sum, we expect increased attentiveness on the part of Democrats elected between 1965 and 1970 to increase their election margins during the 1970s.[6]

Before we can evaluate the effects of conversion and replacement on changes in election margins we need to control for the effects of two confounding forces: partisan trends and electoral slippage. Shifts in the strength and direction of partisan forces can produce fluctuations in election margins; our measure of the level and direction of partisan forces is a dummy variable that is coded 1 if the incumbent is a Democrat and 0 otherwise. Electoral slippage—a natural erosion in high election margins but continued electoral safety—can also produce shifts in election margins, if only temporarily; this variable is also a dummy variable that takes on the value of 1 if the incumbent has maintained an electoral vote greater than 65 percent in the past two elections.

Our data for this stage of the analysis are restricted to a panel of members who remained in office and filed vouchers between 1971 and 1976; incumbents who lost or retired during this period are excluded in order to create the panel of continuous members. Repeated measurements of the electoral vote and the attentiveness (time spent in the district) of these members provide an opportunity to examine the effects of behavioral change on electoral support. We use the stylistic change of members toward greater attentiveness, the stylistic change among Democrats elected between 1965 and 1970, the natural erosion in safe margins, and the vagaries of partisan forces to explain the change in election margins between 1972 and 1974, and between 1974 and 1976 (dependent variables). The explanatory equations are examined within three cohort groups (members elected before 1965, between 1965 and 1970, and in 1972) to determine the relative importance of idiosyncratic forces, such as electoral slippage and partisan trends, and changes in attentiveness in explaining the changes in electoral safety among House incumbents elected before and after 1965. Such intercohort comparisons can provide evidence of whether stylistic changes in district attentiveness influence electoral safety in the 1970s.[7]

Analysis and Findings

All of our analyses were first performed with the main effects as well as the interaction effects of these variables included. Since none of the main effects proved to be statistically significant, these variables have been removed from the final equations. It is clear from table 4-2 that any changes in the election margins of House incumbents elected before 1965 are largely due to idiosyncratic forces—shifts in partisan trends and declines in previously high electoral percentages (greater than 65 percent of the vote). For instance, between 1972 and 1974, members elected before 1965 increased their margins by about 13 percentage points (column 1), and members of this cohort who had compiled healthy election margins in 1972 and 1974 experienced a 9 percent decline in their vote support between 1974 and 1976 (column 2). Changes in attentiveness appear to have little noticeable influence on the election margins of the cohort elected prior to 1965.

The effects of attentiveness are far more evident when we examine later cohorts. For example, increased attentiveness on the part of House Democrats elected between 1965 and 1970 explains changes in their electoral safety in the 1970s (column 3). Partisan trends also affect House incumbents elected since 1965. An increase of about five weekends each year spent in the district by Democrats elected between 1965 and 1970 could increase their election margins by about 5 percent. This interaction

Table 4-2. Changes in District Attentiveness and Electoral Changes between 1972 and 1976 (Unstandardized Regression Coefficients)

Variable	Cohort 1: Elected before 1965		Cohort 2: Elected between 1965 and 1970		Cohort 3:[a] Elected in 1972
	Electoral change from 1972 to 1974	Electoral change from 1974 to 1976	Electoral change from 1972 to 1974	Electoral change from 1974 to 1976	Electoral change from 1974 to 1976
Electoral slippage	−4.50	−9.22[b]	1.72	−2.22	−7.09
Partisan trends (toward Democrats)	13.02[c]	−5.98	8.55[d]	−11.13[b]	−9.31[c]
Change to increased attentiveness	−0.14	0.29	−0.41	−0.67[c]	1.07[c]
Increased attentiveness of Democrats	−0.26	−0.22	0.54[d]	0.45[c]	0.05
Constant	−19.70	11.57	−16.42	18.82	15.16
Multiple *R*	0.49	0.44	0.55	0.52	0.50
R²	0.24	0.20	0.30	0.27	0.25
(N)	(79)	(79)	(78)	(78)	(50)

The equation tested in each cohort is: $Y = a + b_1S + b_2P + b_{3(XM)} + b_{4(XD)}$, where S = electoral slippage, P = partisan trends, XM = increased attentiveness for cohorts 1 and 2 or establishment of an attentive style for cohort 3, and XD = increased attentiveness on the part of Democrats.
[a] In this cohort, the variable (change to increased attentiveness) represents the adoption of an attentive style. Hence, for this cohort the effects of the variable reflect replacement and not conversion processes.
[b] $p < .01$
[c] $p < .05$
[d] $p < .07$

variable distinguishes between stylistic changes on the part of "replacement" Democrats and changes on the part of all members of the cohort. Clearly, stylistic changes on the part of the members of this cohort did not increase electoral safety uniformly; only Democratic members of this cohort appear to gain an electoral advantage from their stylistic changes. In sum, increased attentiveness on the part of Democrats elected between 1965 and 1970 accounts for the increased electoral safety of this cohort during the 1970s.

Members elected after 1970 appear to be best able to capitalize on attentiveness to improve their election margins. We have only a single cohort, and only one pair of elections in which to observe the impact of changing attentiveness, but the results are consistent with our hypothesis. House incumbents who were elected in 1972 and who have increased their attention to the district gain considerable value from their attentive styles: an additional five weekends spent in the district during each session of Congress could raise election margins by about 10 percent between 1974 and 1976 (column 5).

These findings suggest that the mechanism for translating stylistic changes into electoral safety is the replacement of less attentive members by more attentive ones. There is no evidence from this analysis that the conversion of older members to greater levels of district attentiveness has had a noticeable effect on their reelection margins during the 1970s. Newer members, particularly Democrats elected between 1965 and 1970 and members elected during the 1970s, appear to have increased their reelection margins by increasing their attentiveness to district affairs during the 1970s. Thus, stylistic changes can affect electoral safety in the 1970s, but the process is apt to involve the replacement of less attentive incumbents by more attentive legislators, rather than the conversion of older members to higher levels of attention.

CONCLUSIONS

Several hypotheses about district travel are examined in this analysis. We find several indications that certain district characteristics affect the amount of time that members spend in the district. We find that two district characteristics, proximity to Washington, D.C., and socioeconomic status as measured by median family income, have a significant effect on the time members spent in the district. In the Ninety-second Congress members from lower-income districts spent more time in the district than did members from higher-income districts. In addition, proximity to Washington, D.C., seems to influence the amount of time spent in the district, although the exact nature of this relationship is unclear.

The analysis failed to uncover any effects of electoral marginality or insecurity. Year of entry (cohort) into Congress did have a significant effect on the amount of time spent in the district. In fact, a substantial proportion of the explained variation in each of the equations is due to cohort effects. The monotonic increase in the importance of cohort effects over the three congresses suggests that newer members have adopted different home styles than earlier cohorts. This finding confirms both Fenno's and Parker's assertions that replacement is an important variable in explaining changes in district attentiveness over time. Members seeking higher office appear to use the perquisites of their present office to increase their chances of winning a new position. In both the Ninety-third and Ninety-fourth Congresses, these members spent more time in their districts than other members. In the Ninety-fourth Congress, retiring members showed little motivation to devote their time to district travel.

Two of our measures of partisanship and ideological divergence have a significant impact on the time members spend in their congressional districts. Conservative members from lower-status districts consistently spend more time in their districts. We suggest that the ideological divergence of these members from their constituency serves as the motivating force for their increased travel. These members may use their time in the district to build constituency trust, which Fenno notes also buys them policy leeway. Further, members who are ideologically divergent from their districts may also need to spend more time explaining their Washington activities and votes to their constituents. Party has a significant influence on travel in the Ninety-third Congress, with Republicans spending more time in their districts than Democrats. This suggests that national events can act as an impetus for increased travel.

While our analysis of the causes of district attentiveness explains only a modest amount of the variation in the amount of time members spend in their districts, this is not unexpected. Fenno has pointed out that allocations of personal and staff resources "are the product of both personal and constituency factors" (1978, 50). Personal factors may be the reason why our measures explain only a portion of the differences in the time spent in the district.

The benefit provided by increased district attention is illustrated in the second part of our analysis. Members are able to exploit their district attentiveness to increase their election margins. The ability to capitalize on the benefits of district attention, however, is not the same for all members. Members elected after 1965 seem better able to increase their election margins in the 1970s. This finding seems to reflect Fenno's contention that once members establish a successful home style, they are reluctant to change that style. We have interpreted these findings as suggesting that stylistic changes brought about by the replacement of less attentive members by more attentive ones can serve to increase the electoral safety of incumbents; there is no evidence that the conversion of older members to a more attentive home style has had a positive influence on their reelection margins during the 1970s.

NOTES

1. For a fuller explanation of the coding scheme used to record the data, see Parker 1980b, 118–20.

2. The homogeneity variable was formulated as Fenno suggested. Homogeneous districts were defined as those in which at least 75 percent of the population fell into one of three categories—rural, suburban, or urban. This characteristic was introduced into the analysis as a dummy variable, coded 1 if the district was heterogeneous and 0 if the district was homogeneous. It was hypothesized that heterogeneous districts, because they are more competitive and correspond to members' perceptions of marginality, require more district travel than homogeneous districts. In addition to the above measure of homogeneity, other potentially divisive cleavages were examined: racial splits, ethnic antagonisms, and white collar/blue collar splits. Lagged electoral margins were also included in the analysis in the following manner:

Election margin 1970–District travel Ninety-second Congress
Election margin 1972–District travel Ninety-third Congress
Election margin 1974–District travel Ninety-fourth Congress

None of these variables are significant, however, and they have been excluded from the final regression equations.

3. The degree of urbanization (percentage of central-city residents) in the district was included as a variable in the analysis. We hypothesized that community size and degree of boundedness affects the degree of political participation (Verba and Nie 1972, 247) and that this affects the amount of time a member spends in the district. We find, however, that this variable has no significant impact on the amount of time members spend in the district. The variable is, therefore, excluded from the final regression equations. We also included region as a dummy variable to account for differences in styles; this variable is also insignificant.

4. Interaction terms are used to capture the effects of this type of divergence. Two variables are used: conservatives (CCS ≥ 70 percent) from districts that are lower status (percentage of white-collar workers < 50); liberals (CCS < 50 percent) from suburban (percentage suburban > 50) districts. An additional ideological divergence variable, formulated to capture (*a*) the difference between the congressman's electoral margin and the vote for the president in the district, and (*b*) conservatism of the member (conservative coalition score) was included in the analysis. The logic of this measure rests on the findings of Waldman (1967). In trying to explain member voting records in the House, Waldman finds that members who lagged behind Lyndon Johnson tended to vote more liberally in Congress (85). In this analysis, the 1972 election and Richard Nixon's vote in the district are used to determine leaders and laggers. From Waldman's findings, we would expect that laggers would tend to vote more conservatively. Of particular interest here are laggers who vote more liberally, because they could be expected to spend more time in their districts in order to compensate for their divergence from the district. This, however, does not seem to be the case, since the variable fails to attain significance. It is not included in the final regression equations.

Party unity has also been used as a measure of divergence in studies of legislative voting behavior. It was included in the analysis under the expectation that members with lower party-unity scores would spend more time in their congressional districts, since members might buy leeway from party control with constituency support. Members who display little party loyalty are conceived as deviating not only from the majority of their party in Congress, but also from the majority party preference of their district. Thus, these members would need to cultivate their constituency more than members who are more loyal to the party. Party unity (support for the Democrats and Republican opposition) scores were also used to determine party divergence.

Finally, we measured divergence from the president, using the presidential support score of each member. Members who are less supportive of the president should spend more time in their districts than members who are more supportive. None of the measures of ideology, party unity, or presidential support are statistically significant. Hence, they have also been excluded from the final analysis, which concentrates on the significant variables.

5. The allocation of reimbursed trips increased over the six-year period: 1971–72, twelve trips per year; 1973–74, eighteen trips per year; 1975–76, twenty-six trips per year.

6. Members elected in 1970 are combined with those elected between 1965 and 1968 because of the small number of cases in the 1970 cohort (N = 21). This cohort (1970) was not added to the members elected during the 1970s because cohort changes in district attentiveness did not begin to appear until after 1972 (Parker 1980a).

7. Other variables were included in earlier analyses to insure the reliability of the relationships. Many of the variables included in the first half of the analysis, as well as different formulations of the effects of district attentiveness, were also tested in the analysis. Because none of these variables attained significance, they are excluded from the final equations.

REFERENCES

Born, Richard. 1979. "Generational Replacement and the Growth of Incumbent Reelection Margins in the U.S. House." *American Political Science Review* 73:811–17.

Converse, Philip. 1975. "Public Opinion and Voting Behavior." *Handbook of Political Science,* vol. 4, edited by Fred Greenstein and Nelson Polsby. Boston: Addison-Wesley, 75–169.

Fenno, Richard F., Jr. 1978. *Home Style: House Members in Their Districts.* Boston: Little, Brown.

Fiorina, Morris P. 1974. *Representatives, Roll Calls, and Constituencies.* Lexington, Mass.: Lexington Books.

———. 1977. "The Case of the Vanishing Marginals: The Bureaucracy Did It." *American Political Science Review* 71:177–81.

Johannes, John R. 1980. "The Distribution of Casework in the U.S. Congress: An Uneven Burden." *Legislative Studies Quarterly* 5:517–44.

Mayhew, David. 1974. *Congress: The Electoral Connection.* New Haven: Yale University Press.

Parker, Glenn R. 1980a. "Cycles in Congressional District Attention." *Journal of Politics* 42:540–48.

———. 1980b. "Sources of Change in Congressional District Attentiveness." *American Journal of Political Science* 24:115–24.

———. 1981. "Incumbent Popularity and Electoral Success." In *Congressional Elections,* edited by Joseph Cooper and Sandy Maisel. Sage Electoral Studies Yearbook. Beverly Hills, Calif.: Sage Publications.

———. 1984. "Stylistic Changes in the Constituency Orientations of U.S. Senators: 1959–1980." Paper delivered at the Annual Meeting of the Midwest Political Science Association, Chicago.

Schattschneider, E. E. 1975. *The Semisovereign People.* Hinsdale, Ill.: Dryden Press.

Schiff, Steven H., and Steven S. Smith. 1983. "Generational Changes and the Allocation of Staff in the U.S. Congress." *Legislative Studies Quarterly* 8:457–67.

Verba, Sidney, and Norman H. Nie. 1972. *Participation in America: Political Democracy and Social Equality.* New York: Harper and Row.

Waldman, Loren K. 1967. "Liberalism of Congressmen and the Presidential Vote in Their Districts." *Midwest Journal of Political Science* 11:73–85.

PART II   *Committees*

Organization is what makes the United States Congress the most extraordinary legislative body known to political science. Not merely is the Congress genuinely bicameral, with two separate and powerful halves—an unusual feature in and of itself—but the assembly with the most members, the House of Representatives, is intricately wired. An understanding of the organization of the House is absolutely essential to those who wish to follow the forces at work there. It is not enough to know which party has the most members in Congress to predict legislative outcomes. Because the population of the American nation is diverse and spread out across the land, belonging to a particular political party means quite different things in different parts of the country. When representatives from all these different places come together under the same party banner in the House, all manner of compromises and trades must be struck and all sorts of responses can be found to the common stimulus of outside issues and events.

All this would be true even if members of Congress moved in a great herd and did their business only by voting on the floor of the House. But, of course, they do not: each and every member plays a part, large or small, in forming the agenda for the whole by virtue of bills introduced and work done in committees. All House business flows first to committees, and committees in turn shape the substance of legislation and prepare it for consideration by the whole House. Committees maintain subject matter jurisdictions, staff, and, consequently, expertise. The House sustains itself as a major actor in the national policy-making process by virtue of its division of labor into committees.

This section is primarily about committees: how they operate to sustain the interest and loyalty of their members; how they divide labor and power among themselves; how they recruit, reward, and educate new members; how they select their leaders; how they watch over the activities of the executive branch; and how they connect members to the interests of their constituents.

Important as they are, committees and subcommittees are not the only significant organizational features of Congress. But they are the principal reason for the importance of the House seniority system, the system by which committee positions are parceled out. By no means as venerable as observers of Congress once believed, the system is not as perfectly automated as it once was. And influential as committees are, they are less influential today as determinants of floor action than they were only a few years ago.

Nevertheless, the twenty-two standing committees of the House of Representatives and their Senate counterparts are the basic building blocks of the institution. Without committees and subcommittees and the specialization they provide, it would be impossible to process the thousands of bills introduced, a national budget of more than a trillion dollars, and the countless controversial issues that come before the Congress.

Since committees are central to the life of Congress and the careers of members, how places on these committees are allocated is clearly a subject of the highest importance. In "Committee. Assignments," David W. Rohde and Kenneth A. Shepsle analyze how these key choices are made. From 1911 until 1975, the Democrats vested these powers in the hands of Democratic members of the House Ways and Means Committee, who, in turn, were selected by the entire Democratic Caucus. Just after this article was published, control shifted to the House Democratic Steering and Policy Committee, chaired by the Speaker. The new arrangement is more like the way in which House Republicans make their assignments. Although the Democratic party leadership now plays an even more central role, the process of committee assignments remains substantially the same for both parties.

When, during the 1970s, power in the House shifted from committee chairs downward to subcommittee chairs, an organizational revolution took place in which new and complex relationships were created across the board. Charles M. Tidmarch, with the assistance of Paul D. Ginsberg, explores variations on these relationships by asking: What new powers did the subcommittees capture? What powers remained in the hands of the full committees and their chairmen? How do these complex relationships vary from committee to committee?

The third article in this section is a reprinted chapter on "Committees" from a major source of information on Congress, *Vital Statistics in Congress, 1989–1990,* compiled by three leading students of the institution, Norman J. Ornstein, Thomas E. Mann, and Michael J. Malbin. It provides statistics on a number of important trends, from the 84th (1955–56) to the 101st (1989–90) Congresses. Students are encouraged to note some of the major parallels, but especially the differences, between House and Senate committee systems.

The final selection, one of the few extensive studies of committee leadership in Congress as distinct from formal party leadership, is contributed by Joseph K. Unekis and Leroy N. Rieselbach. They develop a threefold typology of leadership among chairmen as: (1) partisan-extremist, (2) partisan-middleman, and (3) bipartisan-consensual, showing how these patterns of leadership are often related to committee integration and success on the House floor.

Chapter 5

Committee Assignments

DAVID W. ROHDE
and KENNETH A. SHEPSLE

Since Woodrow Wilson wrote *Congressional Government,* the dominance of the standing committees in the House of Representatives in determining legislative outcomes has been accepted by students of Congress. In light of recent studies of groups of House committees[1] and in-depth studies of individual committees,[2] the generalization about the central role of committees in the legislative process remains intact. These studies, however, indicate that there are major differences among these "little legislatures" in regard to their organization and behavior, and that these differences are in part a function of differences in their memberships. Furthermore, as Charles Clapp has said,

> Not only is the fate of most legislative proposals determined in committee: to an important degree the fate of individual congressmen may be decided

This chapter is reprinted by permission of the authors and publisher, from David W. Rohde and Kenneth A. Shepsie, "Democratic Committee Assignments in the House of Representatives: Strategic Aspects of a Social Choice Process," *American Political Science Review* 67, 3 (1973): 889–905. Copyright © 1973 by the American Political Science Association. We would like to express our gratitude to Richard Fenno of the University of Rochester and John Manley of Stanford University for making available to us the request data for the Eighty-seventh, Eighty-eighth, and Ninetieth Congresses, and to Robert Salisbury of Washington University, St. Louis, for the request data from the Eighty-sixth Congress. We also wish to acknowledge the research assistance of Robert Delgrosso of Michigan State University. We finally want to thank Richard Fenno, Morris Fiorina of the California Institute of Technology, and the two anonymous referees for their helpful comments on previous versions of this study. An earlier draft of this paper was presented at the Sixty-seventh Annual Meeting of the American Political Science Association, Chicago, 8–11 Sept. 1971.

there too. A person's congressional career may rest largely on the kind of committee post be is given.[3]

Therefore, given the importance of committee membership, both in policy-making and in determining the success of individual congressmen's careers, the process by which members are assigned to committees is of the greatest importance.

A good deal of research has been devoted to the committee assignment process in the House.[4] Most of this research, however, has been based on the *results* of the process, i.e., the committee assignments that were actually made. For example, the desirability of committees has been measured in terms of the proportion of freshmen on each committee, or the number of transfers from a committee versus the number of transfers to it. The variable missing from such treatments has been the desires of the members. Also, success in achieving committee assignments has been treated in only the most general terms, again because of the absence of data on what committee members requested.

The purpose of this paper is to analyze committee assignments by focusing on this "missing link." Our subject will be the committee assignments of Democratic members of the House of Representatives. Committee assignments, as Clapp's observation above suggests, are valued, are in limited supply, and are allocated by rather well-defined mechanisms and procedures. By viewing committee assignments as the culmination of a special sort of allocation process, we shall be in a position to *explain* the results of this process, the *descriptions* of which have constituted the bulk of research on this topic to date. It is explanations we seek, and we find more general theories of social choice particularly well suited for this purpose. More specifically, we examine the data of committee assignments in terms of actors in pursuit of personal goals, constrained only by scarcity and institutional procedures. We will consider the process from the point of view of the members requesting assignment and the members who make the assignments: who wants what committees, and whose requests are satisfied. The basic data which will be employed are the requests for committee assignments, by all House Democrats, made to the Democratic Committee on Committees in the Eighty-sixth to Eighty-eighth and Ninetieth Congresses.[5]

DEMOCRATIC COMMITTEE ASSIGNMENTS

In the House, the Democratic Committee on Committees is made up of the Democratic members of the Ways and Means Committee.[6] At the beginning of each Congress they are faced with the task of filling vacancies on the other standing committees on the House. Each member of the committee is assigned a geographic zone, containing his own state and perhaps others, and he is responsible for handling requests for assignments from members in his zone.[7]

Sometimes after the November election, new Democratic congressmen submit to the Committee on Committees their requests, in order of preference, for committee assignments. At the same time, returning congressmen may submit requests for second assignments or for transfers from committees they held in the previous Congress.

After members submit requests, lobbying for assignments begins. Many representatives seeking assignments write letters to some or all members of the Committee on Committees, setting forth arguments on their own behalf. Many also pay personal visits to the members of the committee (especially their zone representative), to the Democratic leaders, and to the chairmen of the committees they are requesting. Often letters are written to members of the Committee on Committees to support the cause of some requesters. Typically these letters came from the deans of state delegations (either from the deans alone or from them on behalf of the whole delegation), from party leaders or officeholders outside the House, from committee chairmen, and from leaders of interest groups relevant to the work of the committees requested.

At the beginning of the Congress, the size of committees as well as party ratios are set by negotiation between the leaders of both parties.[8] Thus the members of the Committee on Committees are faced with the task of filling the vacancies on the standing committees which have resulted either from the failure of some Democratic members to return or from the creation of new positions. The committee meets in executive session, and the committees are called up (usually alphabetically). For each committee the members proceed in order of seniority to nominate candidates from their zone.[9] The names of nominees are written on a blackboard, and they are discussed by the members. After nominations are completed, the members vote by secret ballot.

Finally, after the Committee on Committees has filled all the vacancies, their decisions are placed before the Democratic Caucus for ratification. This is, however, almost always a pro forma action.

For our purposes, then, the time sequence of the committee assignment process, which culminates in the creation of a committee structure, for a new Congress, may be characterized by the following stages:

1. the committee configuration in the previous Congress
2. an election
3. requests for assignments by newly elected members and by return-

ing members who held assignments in the committee configuration of the previous Congress

4. the establishment of size and party ratios for committees in the new Congress

5. committee assignments by the Democratic Committee on Committees for the new Congress.

Stage 1 provides initial conditions, which are "disturbed" by an election (stage 2). The election disturbs the initial committee structure in several obvious ways. First, aggregate party proportions in the chamber are altered, requiring the renegotiation of the committee structure by party leaders: committee sizes and party ratios are fixed at this stage (stage 4). Second, individual and aggregate election results effect a change in the opportunity structure in the chamber. Individual defeats of party members in the election create party committee vacancies, which may or may not be lost to the party depending on the aggregate election results and its effect on stage 4. At the outset of the new Congress, then, there are unfilled committee vacancies and demand for those slots by newly elected and returning members (as expressed at stage 3).

Our concern in this chapter is with the process of committee assignments for the Democrats. We take the first, second, and fourth stages of the process as exogenous to our concerns (though, as we suggested earlier, stage 4 may well be conceived of as endogenous, since it is probable that deviations from the aggregate party ratio on any given committee are partly a result of the configuration of requests at stage 3). Before getting into the details of our analysis, we should first outline the general theoretical context within which we view the requests of the members and the decisions of the Committee on Committees.

MEMBER GOALS AND COMMITTEE ASSIGNMENTS

We view the committee assignment process as an instance of "social choice" (or "collective decision-making"). That is, a group (the Committee on Committees) is charged with allocating the valuable resources (places on committees) of the collectivity (the Democratic members of the House). We view the participants in the process as rational actors, that is, actors who have goals that they want to achieve, and who, when confronted with a decision-making situation, examine the available alternatives and choose the alternative which seems most likely to lead to the achievement of those goals.

On the question of goals, Richard Fenno has argued that "of all the goals espoused by members of the House, three are most basic. They are reelection, influence within the House, and good public policy. There are others, but research on the House acknowledges these to be the most consequential."[10] If this view is accepted, we may now consider the participants in the assignment process and show how the outcomes of that process affect their goals.

1. Requesters. The impact of committee assignments on the members requesting those assignments is so obvious that it hardly needs to be discussed. If a congressman holds any or all of the goals mentioned above, his committee assignment will have a substantial impact on the probability of achieving them.

> A "good" assignment may greatly enhance his value to his constituents and provide unusual opportunities to publicize his activities in Congress; here he can develop the expertise and the reputation as a "specialist" that will enable him to influence his colleagues and important national policies.[11]

2. The Committee on Committees. The interest of members of the Committee on Committees in what assignments are made is less direct than that of the requesters, but important nonetheless. If a member has a general interest in the policy area of a particular committee, he may support the assignments of congressmen whose views are most congruent with his own. Furthermore, when a piece of legislation important to a member of the Committee on Committees comes before the House, he may call in debts owed to him by congressmen he has sponsored for committee assignments in order to influence such legislation.[12]

3. The Leadership. The filling of committee vacancies is also important to the Democratic leadership, for much the same reasons as it is to the members of the Committee on Committees.

> Committee assignments are vital to the leadership in two ways. First, to the degree that the leadership affects assignment it has an important resource for doing favors for members, for rewarding members for past favors, and for establishing bonds with members that may provide some leverage in future legislative situations. Second, committee assignments are vital to the policy for which the leadership is responsible.[13]

4. State Delegations. Members of a state delegation serving on committees which affect the interests of their state serve as a source of information about the committee's business and a resource for influencing the course of legislation on that committee.[14]

This discussion could be extended to include the committee chairmen and persons outside the House (e.g., interest groups), but the essence of our point is established. How committee slots are assigned is of vital interest to many individuals and groups, because those assignments will have an impact on the achievement of their goals within the House.

DATA AND ANALYSIS

The empirical analysis, which constitutes the bulk of this current study, employs *request* data from four Congresses. In all, we have data on the committee requests, in order of preference, of 106 freshman and 89 nonfreshman Democratic representatives. It is important to reiterate the distinctiveness of these data. Ordinarily, analyses of committee assignments are based on the *results* of the process, from which inferences about the process are drawn.[15] By using request data, however, we are in a position to assess the extent to which the process links requests, on the one hand, with final assignments, on the other. Moreover, we may now determine who benefits and who is harmed by the assignment process, not in terms of so-called objective standards of "good" and "bad" assignments, but rather in terms of the subjective preferences of the actors affected. All these possibilities permit somewhat keener insights into the characteristics of this important internal process.

The first aspect of the assignment process we will consider is the requests themselves: what committees are requested most often, and how many requests are made. For this part of the analysis we will consider only the requests of freshman congressmen. Nonfreshmen already hold committee assignments and, because of service restrictions,[16] are prevented from applying for certain committees (unless they are trying to transfer from the assignment they hold).[17]

Table 5-1 presents these data on freshman requests. The first column gives the total number of requests for each of the standing committees. The second column gives the percentage of all requesters who applied for a slot on each of the committees. The last column indicates the percentage (and number) of all requests that were the requesters' first choices. Thus, fifteen congressmen (nearly 14 percent of all freshmen) requested Agriculture Committee slots. It may be further noted, however, that of these fifteen requests, seven were first-preference requests.[18]

Although this table does indicate the distribution of preferences for the various standing committees, consideration of aggregate demand to determine committee desirability is potentially misleading. First, the distribution of preferences reflects the *opportunity structure* as well as the preference structure, so that observations about committee popularity on this basis are necessarily ambiguous.[19] Second, even if we discount the effects of opportunity, the aggregate demand for a committee vacancy

Table 5-1. House Committee Requests and First-Choice Preferences of Freshmen

Committee	Total Requests	Percentage Requesting [a]	Percentage of Request's First Choice (N) [b]
Agriculture	15	14	47 (7)
Appropriations	12	11	42 (5)
Armed Services	26	24	26 (12)
Banking and Currency	34	32	41 (14)
District of Columbia	3	3	0 (0)
Education and Labor	17	16	29 (5)
Foreign Affairs	23	21	61 (14)
Government Operations	8	7	13 (1)
House Administration	1	1	0 (0)
Interior and Insular Affairs	20	19	50 (10)
Interstate and Foreign Commerce	34	32	38 (13)
Judiciary	25	23	36 (9)
Merchant Marine and Fisheries	5	5	20 (1)
Post Office and Civil Service	13	12	23 (3)
Public Works	29	27	31 (9)
Science and Astronautics	15	14	33 (5)
Un-American Activities	2	2	0 (0)
Veterans Affairs	8	7	13 (1)

Note: Number making requests = 108.
[a] Since requesters submitted multiple requests, this column sums to more than 100 percent.
[b] The number totals to 109 because one requester asked for "Foreign Affairs or Agriculture," and so both requests were considered first choices.

may not accurately reflect the intensity of preference for that vacancy. To take one example, although aggregate demand for Agriculture and Post Office–Civil Service is approximately the same (14 percent and 12 percent respectively), there is a great difference in the proportion of those requests that are first choices (47 percent and 23 percent, respectively).

More important than the two previous points, however, is that attempts to provide an aggregate measure of committee desirability are inconsistent with the conception of the legislator's behavior as goal directed. All congressmen are not the same. Their goals differ, and the kinds of constituencies they represent vary. Thus, we would expect committees to have *differential* appeal to different types of congressmen.

The next two tables lend credence to this expectation. While it is difficult to measure the personal goals of legislators, it is probably safe to assume that most freshmen are initially concerned with firming up relationships with their constituencies. This is probably a minimal requirement for the pursuit of policy goals and internal House influence,

Table 5-2. *House Committees Most Requested by Freshmen,*
Controlling for Region and Population Density

Region	Density [a]	Committee	Percentage Requesting
South	Sparse	Interstate Commerce	45
(N = 18)		Banking and Currency	39
		Public Works	33
Midwest	Sparse	Interior	57
(7)		Interstate Commerce	57
		Public Works	43
West	Sparse	Interior	75
(16)		Public Works	38
East	Medium	Armed Services	50
(8)			
South	Medium	Interstate Commerce	44
(9)		Foreign Affairs	33
Midwest	Medium	Judiciary	44
(9)		Public Works	44
		Education and Labor	33
		Interstate Commerce	33
East	Concentrated	Banking and Currency	40
(15)		Interstate Commerce	40
		Judiciary	33
West	Concentrated	Banking and Currency	71
(7)		Interstate Commerce	71
		Education and Labor	57
		Foreign Affairs	43

[a] See note 20 for definitions.

and is, of course, directly relevant to the goal of reelection. Thus, we can classify members according to the kinds of districts they represent in order to demonstrate the extent to which "committee popularity" varies with constituency types.

In table 5-2 we have classified districts according to region and population per square mile. Although the classification is crude and the choice of variables somewhat arbitrary,[20] this scheme suffices to exhibit the very real differences in committee appeal. We have listed those committees requested (at any preference level) by 30 percent or more of the members in each category containing at least seven requesters.[21] Immediately one notes that committees differ greatly in their relative attractiveness to the various groups of representatives. Interior is one striking example. That committee was the most requested for both midwestern and western congressmen from sparsely populated districts. These members, moreover, accounted for 80 percent of the total requests for that committee (sixteen of twenty). The reason is clear. Congressmen from these constituencies can probably serve the interests of their districts better on that committee than on any other. In the words of one western representative on the committee:

> I was attracted to it, very frankly, because it's a bread-and-butter committee for my state. I guess about the only thing about it that is not of great interest to my state is insular affairs. I was able to get two or three bills of great importance to my state through last year, I had vested interests I wanted to protect, to be frank.[22]

Other specific examples may be cited. Public Works is requested by seventeen of the forty-one representatives from sparsely populated districts in the South, Midwest, and West, and they account for 59 percent of the requests for that committee. Banking and Currency, part of whose jurisdiction includes housing legislation, was the most requested committee by members from districts with concentrated populations in both the East and the West.

Thus, as these data demonstrate, there is indeed a difference in the attractiveness of committees to various groups of representatives, and in most instances there is a clear relationship between the type of district represented and the committees most requested.

Table 5-3 provides even more direct evidence on this score. For five selected committees, we partitioned members into two groups—interesteds and indifferents—depending on constituency characteristics.[23] Although the relationship between ascribed interest and request behavior varies from committee to committee, it is always in the predicted direction and quite strong. The ratio of the proportion of interesteds applying for a committee to the proportion of indifferents applying varies from a low of nearly two to one (Armed Services) to a high of more than sixteen to one (Agriculture). Moreover, a high proportion of requests for each committee is accounted for by interested requesters.[24]

These findings lead us to the following conclusions: Since the attractiveness of a committee does vary from member to member, a broad-gauged, systematic property like "committee desirability" may not be appropriate for an understanding of congressional behavior. A few committees (e.g., Appropriations, Ways and Means) may be almost universally desired, but beyond these few, the attractiveness of a committee, and the value of an assignment to it, may depend solely on the interests and preferences of the member under consideration. While to an urban congressman an assignment to Agriculture might be viewed as disastrous, a farm belt member might prefer it second only to an appointment to Appropriations.

Table 5-3. Requests by Freshmen for Selected House Committees,
Controlling for Interesteds and Indifferents

	Requested		Not Requested		Total		Percentage of Requests by Interesteds
	N	%	N	%	N	%	
Banking and Currency							
Interesteds	17	47	19	53	36	100	
Indifferents	9	20	36	80	45	100	
Total	26	32	55	68	81	100	65
Education and Labor							
Interesteds	11	30	25	70	36	100	
Indifferents	3	7	42	93	45	100	
Total	14	17	67	83	81	100	79
Interior and Insular Affairs							
Interesteds	11	65	6	35	17	100	
Indifferents	5	8	59	92	64	100	
Total	16	20	65	80	81	100	69
Armed Services							
Interesteds	9	30	21	70	30	100	
Indifferents	9	18	42	82	51	100	
Total	18	22	63	78	81	100	50
Agriculture							
Interesteds	11	33	22	67	33	100	
Indifferents	1	2	47	98	48	100	
Total	12	15	69	85	81	100	92

Note: See note 23 for definitions of "interested" and "indifferent."

To this point we have been characterizing the empirical request configuration. Before we turn to the data on assignments proper, we should report several additional features of this configuration as it relates to the opportunity structure of the House.

Clearly the decision about *which* committees to request is a complex strategic one for a member to resolve. Additionally, however, he must decide the strategic question of *how many* committees to include in his preference ordering. In many instances (at least with regard to freshmen) the final preference ordering submitted comprises the entire "information environment" of the Committee on Committees. In any event, it does provide one of the few pieces of hard data on members' desires. The

Table 5-4. Number of Requests by Freshmen and Nonfreshmen

Number of Requests	Freshmen		Nonfreshmen	
	N	%	N	%
1	24	22	71	82
2	15	14	9	10
3	49	45	3	3
4 or more	20	19	4	5
Total	108	100	87	100

Note: Here also the two unassigned nonfreshmen are included with the freshmen (see note 17).

extent to which a goal-directed member chooses to vary that information environment, then, becomes an important strategic consideration. (Shortly, we examine the relationships among length of preference ordering, assignment success, and other features of the opportunity structure.)

Initially, we consider this decision as faced by freshmen and nonfreshmen. The strategic problems facing these two groups are very different. The freshman has no committee assignment at all. He desires a good committee, but he knows for certain that he will be assigned to *some* committee. That is, any committee assignment is possible, the range of alternatives open to the Committee on Committees is maximal, and the member is entirely at the committee's mercy. The nonfreshman, on the other hand, already has a committee, one which he may keep as long as he wishes. Thus, he need not worry about being given a committee less desirable than the one he holds.

Therefore, if the member assumes that, circumstances permitting, the Committee on Committees will attempt to satisfy his request (obviously he must assume this, or else it would be irrational to bother making any requests at all), the two groups are likely to follow different strategies regarding the number of requests they make. Freshmen are likely to offer the Committee on Committees a wider range of alternatives (i.e., make more requests), while nonfreshmen will probably be much more specific in their requests. As table 5-4 shows, the data are in accord with these expectations. Only 22 percent of the freshmen make only one request, while 82 percent of the nonfreshmen do so.

Within the freshman category in table 5-4, there is considerable variation in the number of requests.[25] Some of this variation in request behavior reflects variations in opportunities confronting members.[26] The data of table 5-5 are wholly consistent with this hypothesis. In this table we look at two features of the opportunity structure (unfortunately, our

Table 5-5. Number of House Committee Requests by Freshmen, Controlling for State Vacancy and State Competition on First-Choice Committee

| Number of Requests | State Vacancy | | | | No State Vacancy | | | |
| | State Competition | | No State Competition | | State Competition | | No State Competition | |
	N	%	N	%	N	%	N	%
1	0	0	5	42	1	9	18	26
2	0	0	4	33	3	27	7	10
3	8	67	1	8	4	36	32	47
4 or more	4	33	2	17	3	27	11	16
Total	12	100	12	100	11	99[a]	68	99[a]

Note: Five members whose most preferred committee had no vacancies are omitted here.
[a] Error is due to rounding.

total N is too small to permit the meaningful introduction of other relevant features). The first is whether a member is confronted by competition for his first-choice committee by another member of his state delegation. Since the only way a member can get assigned to a committee is to be nominated by his zone representative, a member's probability of getting a particular assignment is substantially reduced if the zone representative or the Committee on Committees must choose among two or more members from the same state. Therefore, we would expect a member to "hedge his bets"—that is, make a greater number of requests—if another member from his state is requesting his most preferred committee.

The second feature of the opportunity structure that may influence the decision concerning the number of requests a congressman makes is the source of vacancies. It is apparent that at least the large states regard themselves as entitled to one or more seats on important committees, and that members, when requesting assignments, feel that a claim made on "their state's" vacancy is a persuasive argument in their favor.[27] Thus a member whose most preferred committee (as revealed by him in his preference ordering) contains a state vacancy may be more likely to list few options, *ceteris paribus,* than other members.

As table 5-5 reveals, when a state vacancy exists, the presence of state competition makes a great deal of difference in the number of committees requested. With state competition, no member makes fewer than three requests, but without state competition, 75 percent do so. When no state vacancy exists, state competition has no effect; 36 percent make fewer than three requests with state competition, and 36 percent make fewer than three requests without it. (There is a large difference, in the predicted direction, in the number that make a *single* request.) Furthermore, in the

Table 5-6. Number of House Committee Requests and Assignment Success, Freshmen and Nonfreshmen

| Number of Requests | Member Received: | | | | | | | |
| | First Choice | | Other Choice | | No Choice | | Total | |
	N	%	N	%	N	%	N	%
A. Freshmen								
1	18	75	—	—	6	25	24	100
2	6	40	5	33	4	27	15	100
3	16	34	15	32	16	34	47	100
4 or more	9	45	8	40	3	15	20	100
Total	49	46	28	26	29	27	106	99[a]
B. Nonfreshmen								
1	32	45	—	—	39	55	71	100
2	1	11	5	56	3	33	9	100
3 or more	2	22	5	56	2	22	9	100
Total	35	39	10	11	44	49	89	99[a]

[a] Error is due to rounding.

absence of state competition, a member is much more likely to submit fewer than three requests if there is a state vacancy than if there is not (75 percent versus 36 percent). Thus, as we expected, both the existence of state competition and the presence of a state vacancy exert an independent impact on the number of committees requested by freshmen.

So far, we have examined the committee assignment process from the point of view of the requester. We now consider who is successful in getting the assignments he requests, viewing the process in terms of the goals of the members of the Committee on Committees and the leadership.

Above we stated that the member must assume that, if circumstances permit, the Committee on Committees will try to satisfy his request. We also argued that the number of requests a member makes depends on certain strategic considerations, and thus we implicitly argued that a member would think that his probability of getting *some* requested committee depends (at least in part) on the number of requests made. In table 5-6 we present data relating to these points. Freshmen and nonfreshmen are treated separately to prevent seniority from contaminating the results.

When the data are examined we find that in regard to freshmen our first statement is more correct than our second. That is, almost three-fourths of the freshmen do get *some* committee that they requested, and the probability of getting *no* choice is affected little by the number of

Table 5-7. Seniority and Success in Assignment to House Committees

Number of Previous Requests	Member Received:							
	First Choice		Other Choice		No Choice		Total	
	N	%	N	%	N	%	N	%
0	49	46	28	26	29	27	106	99[a]
1	19	41	8	17	19	41	46	99[a]
2	9	43	1	5	11	52	21	100
3 or more	7	32	1	5	14	64	22	100[a]
Total	84	43	38	20	73	37	195	100

[a] Error is due to rounding.

requests. For nonfreshmen, on the other hand, more requests do increase chances of some success.

The most striking finding in table 5-6, however, results from our treating freshmen and nonfreshmen separately. Contrary to what one might expect in a body in which seniority is often important, freshmen are much more successful in getting requested assignments than are non-freshmen. This finding is reinforced by the data in table 5-7, which shows assignment success by amount of seniority. We find that the probability of receiving *no* request monotonically *increases* as seniority increases.

This result should not be entirely unexpected, for many references in the literature on committee assignments claim that seniority is often ignored when circumstances dictate. For example, Clapp claims that

> given a contest for an important committee assignment, in which returning members of Congress may wish to transfer from another committee and find themselves competing with each other and with freshmen congress-men, seniority is not infrequently brushed aside, if it will not bring about the outcome desired by those making the decisions.[28]

Another observer of the process stated:

> Seniority may control if all other things are equal. But other things usually are not equal. Sometimes you begin to think seniority is little more than a device to fall back on when it is convenient to do so.[29]

To assess the accuracy of this last statement, we examined a situation where it is more likely for "other things" to be "equal": the case when two members from the same state are competing for the same committee. We looked at all committees that had vacancies and determined for each requester whether another member from the same state was applying for that committee and if so, whether the other member was more senior.

Table 5-8. State Competition, Seniority, and Success in House Committee Assignments, in All Committees with Vacancies

	Member Assigned		Member Not Assigned		Total	
	N	%	N	%	N	%
No same state competition	103	36	187	64	290	140
Same state competition; competitor not more senior	20	26	56	74	76	100
Same state competition; competitor more senior	1	7	13	93	14	100
Total	124	33	256	67	380	100

The relevant data are presented in table 5-8. It is clear that a request for which there is no same state competition has a likelihood of about one chance in three of being granted. When there is competition, however, a member has about one chance in four of success if his competitor is not more senior, while he has only one chance in fourteen if the competitor is more senior. Thus in this instance, where "other things" are more likely to be "equal," seniority may become very advantageous, although it is generally not.

What, then, are the things that in other situations are not "equal"? That is, in terms of the goals of members who determine committee assignments, what factors cause them to ignore seniority? Clearly, many kinds of interacting and even conflicting motivations may influence the members of the Committee on Committees. Thus it is dangerous to posit either a single motive for all members of the Committee on Committees or even for any one member. Still, it is not unreasonable to assess the extent to which the data support any of these motives.

The first motive or goal for Committee on Committees members we have posited might be termed the *management goal*. The Committee on Committees, in this view, is concerned solely with satisfying requester demands. Thus, it acts as an "impersonal" preference aggregation device in an effort to keep requesters happy. In reporting on this motive, we find it useful to contrast it with another, the *constituency interest goal*. According to this goal, committee makers ignore request data, concerning themselves instead with matching individual members to committee vacancies on the basis of constituency characteristics and interests.

The data relevant to this comparison are presented in table 5-9. For the committees investigated in table 5-3 we partitioned freshman[30] members according to two criteria: whether they qualify as interested and whether they requested the committee. The results suggest that the man-

Table 5-9. Interesteds, Requests, and Success in House Committee Assignments, Freshmen

Interested[a]	Yes	Yes	No	No	
Committee Requested:	Yes	No	Yes	No	Total
Banking and Currency	47	0	33	3	15
	(17)	(19)	(9)	(36)	(81)
Education and Labor	64	4	67	2	14
	(11)	(25)	(3)	(42)	(81)
Interior and Insular Affairs	64	17	20	3	14
	(11)	(6)	(5)	(59)	(81)
Armed Services	33	0	11	2	6
	(9)	(21)	(9)	(42)	(81)
Agriculture	27	14	100	4	11
	(11)	(22)	(1)	(47)	(81)

Note: Each cell gives percentage of N assigned to that committee (N in parentheses).
[a] See note 23 for definition of interesteds.

agement goal dominates the constituency interest goal. In most instances (the small *N*'s make firm conclusions difficult), interested requesters get the nod. Moreover, for *every* committee, requesting indifferents are more successful than nonrequesting interesteds. Minimally, we conclude that committee makers do not take member requests lightly—that in requesting a committee a member is not waltzing before a blind audience.

A third obvious candidate as a motivational hypothesis for members of the Committee on Committees, is *party maintenance.* Whether a member is interested in influencing policy outcomes or in influence for its own sake, one thing that in part determines the amount of such influence is the majority or minority status of his party. A member has more influence if he is Speaker than if he is minority leader, more influence if he is chairman of a committee than if he is ranking minority member, and probably more influence if he is on the majority side of the committee than if he is in the minority. Therefore it is in the interest of most Committee on Committees members to help insure the reelection of party colleagues. Thus the question arises, Who needs the most help? Clearly, the members most in need of help are those who were elected by the smallest margin. *Ceteris paribus,* a member elected with 51 percent of the vote is more likely to be defeated than one elected with 61 percent. Thus, we would expect members from marginal districts to be more successful than members from safe districts. (We have termed a district marginal if the member was elected with less than 55 percent of the vote.)

As the data in table 5-10 show, our expectations are correct. Marginal freshmen are slightly less likely to fail to receive a requested committee

Table 5-10. Margin of Election and Success in House Committee Assignments, Freshmen and Nonfreshmen

	First Choice		Other Choice		Member Received: No Choice		Total	
District Is	N	%	N	%	N	%	N	%
A. Freshmen								
Marginal	31	56	10	18	14	25	55	99[a]
Safe	18	35	18	35	15	29	51	99[a]
Total	49	46	28	26	29	27	106	99[a]
B. Nonfreshmen								
Marginal	7	39	5	28	6	33	18	100
Safe	28	39	5	7	38	54	71	100
Total	35	39	10	11	44	49	89	99[a]

[a] Error is due to rounding.

and are much more likely to receive their first choice than are safe freshmen.

Marginal nonfreshmen are *much* less likely to receive no choice than are safe nonfreshmen, but they are about equally likely to receive their first choice as are safe nonfreshmen. We also find that some of the difference in success between freshmen and nonfreshmen disappears here—that is, safe freshmen are treated about the same as marginal nonfreshmen. When one recalls that these nonfreshmen, even though they are marginal, have demonstrated (at least once) their ability to get reelected, it does not seem surprising that these two groups are about equally successful.

The perceived stand of the individual member on specific issues is yet another basis on which committee makers may determine assignment.[31] Their prime concern here is the degree to which members will support the party position on issues which come before the standing committees (*party support goal*). While detailed considerations of individual committees are beyond the scope of an initial study such as ours, two pieces of evidence may shed some light on this question. Generally speaking, southern Democrats are less likely to support their party's position than are northern Democrats. Therefore, whether we consider the granting of a specific request a reward for past behavior or an attempt to gain influence over future behavior, the leadership should be less likely to intervene with the Committee on Committees on behalf of a southerner than a northerner. Moreover, since the Democratic members of the Ways and Means Committee are more liberal and more supportive of their party than is the average House Democrat,[32] those members, even when acting on their own, are likely to be more favorably disposed toward the requests

Table 5-11. Region and Success in House Committee Assignments, Freshmen and Nonfreshmen

| | | | | | Member Received: | | | |
| | First Choice | | Other Choice | | No Choice | | Total | |
Region[a]	N	%	N	%	N	%	N	%
Freshmen								
South	8	31	7	27	11	42	26	100
Non-South	41	51	21	26	18	23	80	100
Total	49	46	28	26	29	27	106	99[a]
Nonfreshmen								
South	7	27	2	8	17	65	26	100
Non-South	28	44	8	13	27	43	63	100
Total	35	39	10	11	44	49	89	99[a]

[a] The South includes the eleven states of the Confederacy.
[b] Error is due to rounding.

of northern Democrats than toward those of southerners. Therefore, we would expect southerners to be less successful than northerners in obtaining requested committees.

As table 5-11 shows, the data support this hypothesis. For both freshmen and nonfreshmen, southerners are more likely than nonsoutherners to receive *no* request. They are less successful than their colleagues from other regions in getting their first choices as well. One might wonder, however, whether this finding of lesser success among southerners does not simply repeat our finding concerning marginal versus safe districts. That is, since southerners are more likely to come from safe districts,[33] they may be less successful than nonsoutherners simply because they are elected by larger margins. To examine the possibility we present in tables 5-12 and 5-13 data on regions, margin of election, and assignment success for freshmen and nonfreshmen, respectively.

Since there are few marginal freshman southerners and no marginal nonfreshman southerners, we will focus our discussion on members from safe districts. As the data demonstrate, even when marginal members are removed, southerners are less successful than are nonsoutherners. Among both freshmen and nonfreshmen, safe southerners are more likely to receive no request than are safe nonsoutherners and are less likely to receive a first request. The evidence is unequivocal: Region has a strong, independent impact on committee assignment success, even when election margin is controlled.[34]

The second piece of evidence bearing on the party support goal is

Table 5-12. Region, Margin of Election, and Success in House Committee Assignments, Freshmen

Region[a]	First Choice		Member Received: Other Choice		No Choice		Total	
	N	%	N	%	N	%	N	%
Marginal districts								
South	1	25	0	0	3	75	4	100
Non-South	30	59	10	20	11	22	51	101[b]
Total	31	56	10	18	14	26	55	100
Safe districts								
South	7	32	7	32	8	36	22	100
Non-South	11	38	11	38	7	24	29	100
Total	18	35	18	35	15	29	51	99[b]

[a] The South includes the eleven states of the Confederacy.
[b] Error is due to rounding.

presented in table 5-14. To construct this table we examined the party support scores of nonfreshman requesters[35] for each of the Congresses in the sample, and compared the assignment success of those whose support surpasses the mean for the party in the previous Congress with those who gave the party less than the mean support. In each of the four Congresses, high party supporters were more successful in securing assignments (i.e., being granted any one of their requests) than low party supporters. Part E of this table gives the aggregate totals: 58 percent of the high party supporters, as opposed to 37 percent of the low party supporters, secured a requested committee.

SUMMARY AND CONCLUSIONS

In this chapter we have viewed the Democratic assignment process as an instance of social choice. We have examined the process from the point of view of the members requesting assignments and of the members making assignments. We have assumed that both groups are goal directed and that an understanding of their behavior derives from an analysis of alternative goals and alternative means (behaviors) of achieving them.

In regard to those members requesting assignments, we have shown that their choice of committees is related to the type of district they represent. Also, the data indicate that the decision concerning the number of requests to make appears to be affected by certain strategic considerations, such as whether the requester is a freshmen, whether there is a

Table 5-13. *Region, Margin of Election, and Assignment Success in House Committee Assignments, Nonfreshmen*

Region[a]	First Choice		Other Choice		Member Received: No Choice		Total	
	N	%	N	%	N	%	N	%
Marginal districts								
South	0	—	0	—	0	—	0	—
Non-South	7	39	5	28	6	33	18	100
Total	7	39	5	28	6	33	18	100
Safe districts								
South	7	27	2	8	17	65	26	100
Non-South	21	47	3	7	21	47	45	100[b]
Total	28	39	5	7	38	54	71	100

[a] The South includes the eleven states of the Confederacy.
[b] Error is due to rounding.

vacancy from his state on his most preferred committee, and whether another member from his state is competing with him for his most preferred committee.

We next considered the making of assignments. Here we found that about three-fourths of the freshmen are granted some committee they requested. The data showed, however, that nonfreshmen are much less successful. Indeed, the probability of success decreased as seniority increased; therefore other factors were sought in order to explain assignment success. We considered several alternative goals for committee makers—the management goal, the constituency interest goal, the party maintenance goal, and the party support goal—and found strong support in the data for most of them. However, the interaction (and collinearity) among goals precludes any unqualified conclusions.

The assignment process in the House of Representatives is obviously complex, and it is affected by a host of factors, some of them detailed in the body of this paper. Our purposes here have been severalfold. First, we believe it is useful to view the assignment process as an institutionalized allocation process involving goal-seeking actors, scarce but valued commodities, and behavioral constraints. Second, given this view, we have sought to supply a "missing link" in the literature on committee assignments, namely the preferences of committee requests. Not only does this link provide some interesting insights about one group of actors in the process (requesters); additionally, it provides empirical knowledge about the constraints and information confronting the other significant group in the process—the committee makers. Third, the heuristic use of a social

Table 5-14. Party Support and Success in House Committee Assignments, Nonfreshmen

	Assigned	Not Assigned	Total
A. 86th Congress			
Supporter[a]	62	38	100
	(8)	(5)	(13)
Nonsupporter	40	60	100
	(2)	(3)	(5)
Total	56	44	100
	(10)	(8)	(18)
B. 87th Congress			
Supporter	50	50	100
	(8)	(8)	(16)
Nonsupporter	45	55	100
	(5)	(6)	(11)
Total	48	52	100
	(13)	(14)	(27)
C. 88th Congress			
Supporter	62	38	100
	(8)	(5)	(13)
Nonsupporter	40	60	100
	(4)	(6)	(10)
Total	52	48	100
	(12)	(11)	(23)
D. 90th Congress			
Supporter	60	40	100
	(9)	(6)	(15)
Nonsupporter	0	100	100
	(0)	(4)	(4)
Total	47	53	100
	(9)	(10)	(19)
E. All Congresses			
Supporter	58	42	100
	(33)	(24)	(57)
Nonsupporter	37	63	100
	(11)	(19)	(30)
Total	51	49	100
	(44)	(43)	(87)

[a] Supporters are members whose party support scores were above or equal to the mean for the party for the previous Congress. Cell entries are percentages; Ns are in parentheses.

choice construct and the new data on the preferences of committee requesters have brought into focus and provided some order to the complex
of strategic factors involved in this process.

The questions for future empirical analysis appear to be almost limitless.
For example, future research should consider, instead of surrogate variables like region, the position of members on specific issues before and
after the assignment decision. Another aspect to be examined is the
behavior of individual members of the Committee on Committees. What
requesters from which zones are most successful? Do zone representatives
appear to nominate members whose views are like their own? A third
aspect of the process which deserves further consideration is the opportunity structure: Are members who are granted their first choice more
likely to make further requests in the future, and if so are they very
successful? Are members who receive no request initially granted a good
assignment at some later time, or are they perpetually unsuccessful?

The research reported here is not distinctive in one respect: It raises
as many questions as it answers. Nevertheless, we feel this study has
provided some initial direction for a more comprehensive, formal understanding of the committee assignment process, and thus of internal
relationships in the House as a whole. In this fashion, we believe, students
of the public sector will begin to ascertain some of the operating characteristics of its institutions and thus be in a better position to make
sound evaluations and prescriptions.

Epilogue
DEMOCRATIC ASSIGNMENTS AFTER REFORM, 1990

Our original research reported above analyzed Democratic committee
assignments during the 1960s. In the early 1970s, the House was swept
by a wave of reform that changed many of the procedures under which
it operated.[36] Among the changes was a shift in the responsibility for
committee assignments among Democrats. Initially, the change was small:
in 1973, the Democratic Caucus added the three elected party leaders—
the Speaker, majority leader, and chairman of the caucus—to the Committee on Committees. Two years later, however, a much more substantial
alteration of procedure was made: the responsibility for making assignments was taken away from Ways and Means Democrats and was given
to the Steering and Policy Committee.

The Steering and Policy Committee had been created by House Democrats in 1973 as a forum for shaping legislative strategy. It had twenty-
four members, twelve of whom were elected by the membership from

geographic zones, and a requirement that there be a mix of senior and junior representatives. The other twelve members included the three elected leaders plus nine others appointed by the Speaker. Among them were the majority whip, the four deputy whips, and representatives from specific groups within the caucus (the Black Caucus, the Women's Caucus, and the freshman class). This gave the Steering and Policy Committee an approximately even mix of leadership and rank-and-file members. Thus when committee assignment responsibilities were shifted to it, the party leadership had a much larger voice in the process than it had had on the old Committee on Committees. The reformers wanted to strengthen the leadership. One of them said at the time that committee assignments "ought to be a function of the leadership, and if the leadership doesn't want it, I want them to have it anyway. I want members to owe their assignments to the leadership, not to the Ways and Means Committee."[37]

The early research on the effects of this reform was similar in character to what was described above—dealing with Democratic requests and the assignments made from them—and thus it provides a useful comparison.[38] Kenneth Shepsle's analysis dealt only with freshman assignments in the Ninety-fourth Congress. He concluded that the change in assignment responsibility had only a small impact on each of the variables that had been found to be important influences on freshman assignments, but that these impacts collectively added up to a statistically significant difference between the two systems. "*Conclusion.* Things have not remained the same in the Ninety-fourth Congress, but the changes are hardly revolutionary."[39]

Shepsle's conclusion was reinforced by the more extensive analysis of Smith and Ray, which also included consideration of nonfreshmen transfer requests. They concluded that "the process has become even more a routine effort to accommodate the requests of as many members as possible."[40] They also concluded, however, that the new system had given party leaders a more regularized say in assignments, and they found that nonfreshmen who were more loyal to the party were advantaged in getting assignments.

Unfortunately no data on member requests has become available for Congresses after the Ninety-seventh. There is substantial evidence, however, that party leaders have had a growing impact on assignments, especially to the major committees, such as Appropriations, Budget, and Ways and Means,[41] and that party loyalty on important issues has a significant impact on these decisions. For example, in 1983 a set of southerners who were loyal to the party were given choice assignments in preference to more conservative Southerners who had supported major proposals of President Reagan in the previous Congress.[42] Thus, it is fair to conclude from these analyses that changing the rules under which social choice decisions are made can have—and in this case, did have—a significant impact on the outcomes of those decisions.

NOTES

1. Richard F. Fenno, Jr., "Congressional Committees: A Comparative View" (Paper presented at the Sixty-sixth Annual Meeting of the American Political Science Association, Los Angeles, 8–11 Sept. 1970); George Goodwin, Jr., *The Little Legislatures* (Amherst: University of Massachusetts Press, 1970).

2. Richard F. Fenno, Jr., *The Power of the Purse: Appropriations Politics in Congress* (Boston: Little, Brown, 1966); John Manley, *The Politics of Finance: The House Committee on Ways and Means* (Boston: Little, Brown, 1970).

3. Charles Clapp, *The Congressman: His Work As He Sees It* (New York: Doubleday, 1963), 207.

4. The classic treatment of the process is Nicholas A. Masters, "Committee Assignments in the House of Representatives," *American Political Science Review* 55 (June 1961): 345–57. Assignments are discussed at length in Clapp, *The Congressman*, 207–40, and Goodwin, *Little Legislatures*, 64–79. Some recent studies include Louis C. Gawthrop, "Changing Membership Patterns in House Committees," *American Political Science Review* 60 (June 1966): 366–73; Charles Bullock and John Sprague, "A Research Note on the Committee Reassignments of Southern Democratic Congressmen," *Journal of Politics* 31 (May 1969): 493–512; Charles Bullock "Correlates of Committee Transfers in the United States House of Representatives" a (Paper delivered at the Annual Meeting of the Midwest Political Science Association, Chicago, 29 April to 1 May 1971); Charles Bullock, "The Influence of State Party Delegations on House Committee Assignments," *Midwest Journal of Political Science* 15 (Aug. 1971): 525–46; and Charles Bullock, "Freshman Committee Assignments and Reelection in the United States House of Representatives," *American Political Science Review* 66 (Sept. 1972): 996–1007.

5. In addition to our own data, this description relies heavily on Masters, "Committee Assignments," and on Clapp, *The Congressman*, chap. 5.

6. The Democratic delegation on Ways and Means is made up almost entirely of members drawn from the southern and border states and from the large industrial states. They are elected to membership by a vote of the full Democratic Caucus. During the period covered by this study the committee was dominated by the southern and border state group, who were greatly overrepresented compared to their proportion of the Democratic delegation in the House. In the Eighty-sixth to Eighty-eighth Congresses, they had eight members out of the total of fifteen, and in the Ninetieth Congress they had seven of fifteen. For a discussion of assignments to Ways and Means, see Manley, *Politics of Finance*, 22–38.

7. Zone assignments in the Eighty-sixth Congress are listed in Masters, "Committee Assignments," 347. The number of states represented varies greatly, with Keogh of New York, for example, representing only his own state, while Metcalf of Montana represents seven small western and midwestern states.

8. While party ratios usually reflect the partisan division in the House, it is not unlikely that decisions on both these questions are influenced by the leadership's knowledge of the requests of the members of their party.

9. It is important to note that the only way a requester can be nominated for a committee post is to be nominated by his zone representative.

10. Fenno, "Congressional Committees," 3.

11. Clapp, *The Congressman,* 207.

12. It is clear that such debts are recognized, and that they are called in. One member, commenting on the influence another member had within the House, said, "Much of his power rests with the fact he is on Ways and Means. Since that committee determines committee assignments, he is in a very important and strategic spot. He makes his deals with various groups as to which people he will support for certain spots. Naturally when the time comes that he wants something, he can make a request and people reciprocate." Quoted in Clapp, *The Congressman,* 29–30.

13. Manley, *Politics Of Finance,* 24.

14. See Bullock, "Influence of State Party Delegations."

15. Most of the individual committee studies (e.g., Fenno, Manley) also draw on interviews with committee members to generalize about what led them to seek assignment to the committee and why they were successful.

16. The standing committees of the House are divided into three classes: exclusive, semiexclusive, and nonexclusive, and there are rules which govern assignments to each class. Members of exclusive committees may serve on no other committee. Members of semiexclusive committees may be given a second assignment only on a nonexclusive committee; and members of nonexclusive committees may be given second assignments on any semi- or nonexclusive committee. During the period covered by this study the committees in these classes were: *exclusive:* Appropriations, Rules, and Ways and Means; *semiexclusive:* Agriculture, Armed Services, Banking and Currency, Education and Labor, Foreign Affairs, Interstate and Foreign Commerce, Judiciary, Public Works, and Science and Astronautics; *nonexclusive:* District of Columbia, Government Operations, House Administration, Interior and Insular Affairs, Merchant Marine and Fisheries, Un-American Activities, and Veterans Affairs. In addition, Post Office and Civil Service was changed from semiexclusive to nonexclusive status at the beginning of the Eighty-eighth Congress. Finally, the twenty-first standing committee, Standards of Official Conduct (established in 1967), seems to occupy a special status since it is a third assignment for a number of members.

17. We do, however, include the requests of two nonfreshmen who were first elected in special elections near the end of a Congress. They were not assigned to any committees then, and thus they are in the same position as freshmen.

18. The reader will note that only eighteen committees are listed in table 5-1. Ways and Means is excluded here and throughout the rest of the analysis, because its vacancies are filled by the caucus. Rules and Standards of Official Conduct are excluded because they were never requested by either freshmen or nonfreshmen. In regard to Rules, this absence of requests probably reflects the special importance this committee has to the leadership, since almost never is a vacancy on Rules filled by a member not first sponsored by the leadership. See Clapp, *The Congressman,* 218, and Manley, *Politics of Finance,* 77.

19. Thus a problem with using requests or appointments as a measure of committee desirability results from anticipated reactions. A freshman will probably refrain from requesting the committee he most wants if he believes there is no chance of getting it. Table 5-1 seems to support this view in regard to requests for Appropriations, which (along with the other two exclusive committees) is generally recognized to be the most sought-after committee. It is, however, also recognized that freshmen have little chance to be appointed. (Indeed, in the four Congresses analyzed here, no

freshman was appointed.) There does not, however, seem to be any evidence of anticipated reaction in regard to requests for other committees.

20. Differences among districts on a regional basis are well known, hence the selection of that variable. Regions are defined as follows: *Northeast:* Conn., Del., Maine, Mass., N.H., N.J., N.Y., Pa., R.I., Vt.; *Border:* Ky., Md., Mo., Okla., W.Va.: *South:* Ala., Ark., Fla., Ga., La., Miss., N.C., S.C., Tenn., Tex., Va.; *Midwest:* Ill., Ind., Iowa, Kans., Mich., Minn., Nebr., N.Dak., Ohio, S.Dak., Wis.; *West:* Alaska, Ariz., Calif., Colo., Hawaii, Idaho, Mont., Nev., N.Mex., Oreg., Utah, Wash., Wyo.

Population per square mile was selected to tap the relatively urban or rural nature of districts. While percentage urban would have been a preferable measure in this regard, such data were available on a district basis only for the Eighty-eighth and Ninetieth Congresses. To operationalize this variable the districts were divided into three categories: sparse (fewer than 100 persons per sq. mi.), medium (100 to 999 persons per sq. mi.), and concentrated (1,000 or more persons per sq. mi.). Population data were obtained from *Congressional District Data Book: Districts of the Eighty-seventh Congress* (for the Eighty-sixth and Eighty-seventh Congresses) and from *Congressional District Data Book: Districts of the Eighty-eighth Congress* and its supplements (for the Eighty-eighth and Ninetieth Congresses). Both books and the supplements are published by the Bureau of the Census, Washington, D.C.

21. The excluded categories and the number of members in each were: East, sparse (3); Border, sparse (4); Border, medium (5); West, medium (3); Border, concentrated (0); South, concentrated (0); Midwest, concentrated (4).

22. Quoted in Fenno, "Congressional Committees," 6.

23. These committees were selected because of the availability of constituency data which seemed reasonably related to representatives' probable interest in the committee. We borrowed the terms "interested" and "indifferent," and the basic ideas on measuring interest, from Charles Bullock (see "Correlates of Committee Transfers," 22–23), although our specific measures are somewhat different. Bullock, in turn, adopted the terms from David R. Mayhew, *Party Loyalty among Congressmen* (Cambridge: Harvard University Press, 1966).

Data on constituency characteristics were obtained from the *Congressional District Data Book: Districts of the Eighty-eighth Congress* and its supplements. In this source data were available on freshman representatives in the Eighty-sixth and Eighty-seventh Congresses only if they came from states which were not redistricted after the 1960 census. Therefore the number of members considered in table 5-3 is 81 instead of 108.

For each committee a constituency measure was selected, and each representative's district was ranked as either above or below the national average on that measure. If the district was above the national average, the congressman was classed as an interested; if the district was below the national average, the congressman was classed as an indifferent. The measures of the committees are as follows (national averages are in parentheses): Banking and Currency and Education and Labor, percentage of population residing in urban areas (69.9 percent); Interior and Insular Affairs, land area of district (8,159 sq. mi.); Armed Services, percentage of the total labor force who are members of the armed forces (2.5 percent); and Agriculture, percentage of the employed civilian labor force employed in agriculture (6.6 percent).

24. The proportion of Armed Services requests made by interesteds is by far the lowest. This is probably because interest in this committee is determined by other things besides a relatively large number of servicemen in a district (e.g., large defense plants or a hope of attracting defense bases or plants to a district in the future).

25. We restrict the following discussion to freshmen because the argument about a nonfreshman's ability to be more specific in his requests applies as well here as it did above.

26. Here we consider opportunities to depend upon certain objective conditions, such as number of vacancies for a given committee (supply), number of requests (demand), and service restrictions regarding dual requests (formal rules) and upon informal norms which may guide the allocation of committee vacancies, such as "same state" norms for appointment.

27. See Bullock, "Influence of State Party Delegations," and Clapp, *The Congressman,* 220, 238.

28. Clapp, *The Congressman,* 26–27.

29. Quoted in Clapp, *The Congressman,* 226. We should note here that the data in tables 5-6 and 5-7 indicate only overall success and not success in those instances where the requests of freshmen and nonfreshmen are in direct competition. Masters states that "when two or more members stake a claim to the same assignment, on the ground that it is essential to their electoral success both party committees usually, if not invariably, will give preference to the member with longer service" (Masters, "Committee Assignments," 354). We do not know what arguments were made about electoral success, but in our data fifty nonfreshmen were in competition with one or more freshmen for assignments to semi- or nonexclusive committees which had insufficient vacancies to satisfy all requests. Of these fifty members, twenty-three were passed over in favor of freshmen. This does not include instances where the passed-over members received another, more preferred, assignment.

30. We restrict our attention here to freshmen, not only because of the effects of seniority on both request behavior and success, but also because the situation is much more complex in regard to nonfreshmen. Minimally we would have control for whether a representative is already a member of a committee for which he would be classified as an interested. Further, we would probably want to control for whether the requests made are for transfers or dual service assignments. Also we would want to exclude prestige committee requests. These controls would make the *N*'s so small and would break them into so many categories that a meaningful test would be impossible.

31. In addition to our discussion of member goals above, see Masters, "Committee Assignments," 354–55, and Clapp, *The Congressman,* 228–30.

32. See Fenno, "Congressional Committees," 33–34, and Manley, *Politics of Finance,* 29–32.

33. Using a different definition of safe seat, Wolfinger and Hollinger found that while southerners held only 38 percent of the Democratic seats in the Eighty-eighth Congress, they held 63 percent of the safe seats. See Raymond E. Wolfinger and Joan H. Hollinger, "Safe Seats, Seniority, and Power in Congress," in the 2d ed. of this work (Chicago: Rand McNally, 1969), pp. 60–61.

34. This finding is all the more striking in light of the southern Democrats' dominance of the Committee on Committees during this period (see note 6). It is, admittedly, dangerous to treat a variable like region as a surrogate for, in this case, expected policy behavior. Support for party policies clearly varies within regions. Moreover, other informal, nonpolicy, behavioral norms are likely to cloud the relationship between region and appointment success. A clear indication of this intraregional variation is the rather startling differential in success between members from the South and those from outside the South when we control for the state of their zone representative. As the data in table 5A show, the southern member who is from the same state as his zone representative is much more likely to secure a requested

Table 5-A. Assignment Success, Region, and Zone Representative's State Delegation

	First Choice		Other Choice		Member Received: No Choice		Total	
	N	%	N	%	N	%	N	%
Freshmen, non-south								
Same state[a]	16	52	8	26	7	23	31	100[b]
Not	25	51	13	27	11	22	49	100
Total	41	51	21	26	18	23	80	100
Freshmen, South								
Same state	5	46	4	36	2	18	11	100
Not	3	20	3	20	9	60	15	100
Total	8	31	7	27	11	42	26	100
Freshmen, non-south								
Same state	13	46	3	11	12	43	28	100
Not	15	43	5	14	15	43	35	100
Total	28	44	8	13	27	43	63	100
Nonfreshmen, South								
Same state	3	30	2	20	5	50	10	100
Not	4	25	0	0	12	75	16	100
Total	7	27	2	8	17	65	23	100

[a] Same state means that the member making the request and his zone representative are from the same state.
[b] Error due to rounding.

assignment than are his southern colleagues who are not from the same state as their zone representatives. Whereas 60 percent of the freshmen who are *not* from the same state as their zone representative fail to receive any committee request, only 18 percent of those from the zone representative's state delegation are in the same unenviable position. The differential is somewhat smaller for nonfreshmen (75 percent versus 50 percent receive no request), but the pattern is the same. For members from outside the South, however, this differential does not appear. There is virtually no difference between the success of members who are from the same state as their zone representative and that of members who are not.

35. We exclude the two nonfreshmen elected in special elections near the close of the preceding Congress for whom there was no party support score data. For each Congress, a member's party support score is tabulated from his voting behavior in the previous Congress. Party support data are found in the appropriate volumes of the *Congressional Quarterly Almanac* 14 (1985): 124–25; 16 (1960): 140–41; 18 (1962): 764–65; 22 (1966): 1030–31.

36. The literature on reform is quite large. Some general treatments may be found in Leroy N. Reiselbach, *Congressional Reform* (Washington, D.C.: Congressional Quarterly, 1986); Burton D. Sheppard, *Rethinking Congressional Reform* (Cambridge: Schenkman, 1985); Norman J. Ornstein and David W. Rohde, "Political Parties and Congressional Reform," in Jeff Fishel, ed., *Parties and Elections in an Anti-Party Age*

(Bloomington: Indiana University Press, 1978), 280–94; and Kenneth A. Shepsle, "The Changing Textbook Congress," in John Chubb and Paul Peterson, eds., *Can the Government Govern?* (Washington, D.C.: Brookings Institution, 1989), 238–67.

37. David Obey (D., Wis.), quoted in *Congressional Quarterly Weekly Report* (16 Nov. 1974): 3119. For more general discussion of the efforts of Democratic reformers to strengthen the leadership and the party structure, see Ornstein and Rohde, "Political Parties"; Rieselbach, *Congressional Reform*, 63–66; and David W. Rohde, *Parties and Leaders in the Postreform House* (Chicago: University of Chicago Press, 1991), chap. 2–4.

38. See Kenneth A. Shepsle, *The Giant Jigsaw Puzzle: Democratic Committee Assignments in the House* (Chicago: University of Chicago Press, 1978), epilogue; and Stephen S. Smith and Bruce R. Ray, "The Impact of Congressional Reform: House Democratic Committee Assignments," *Congress and the Presidency* 10 (Autumn 1983): 219–40. Shepsle's analysis deals with the Ninety-fourth Congress, while Smith and Ray's covers the Ninety-fourth to Ninety-seventh (1977–83). Most of Shepsle's book is a much more extensive analysis of assignments in the Ways and Means era. Unfortunately space will not permit us to discuss those findings here.

39. Shepsle, *Giant Jigsaw Puzzle*, 281.

40. Smith and Ray, "Impact of Congressional Reform," 238.

41. In addition, as part of the reforms in 1975, the Speaker was given the power to appoint (with caucus approval) the Democratic members and the chairman of the Rules Committee.

Beginning in 1981, the membership of Steering and Policy was expanded further. By 1989, it had reached thirty-one members, twelve of whom were still regionally elected. The others included the elected leaders, who now number six (Speaker, majority leader, majority whip, chairman of the congressional Campaign Committee, and the chairman and vice chairman of the caucus), the chief deputy whip, the chairmen of the four most important committees (Appropriations, Budget, Rules, and Ways and Means), and eight members appointed by the Speaker. Thus, the influence of the leadership was even greater.

42. See David W. Rohde, "Something's Happening Here; What It Is Ain't Exactly Clear: Southern Democrats in the House of Representatives," in Morris P. Fiorina and David W. Rohde, eds., *Home Style and Washington Work: Studies in Congressional Politics* (Ann Arbor: University of Michigan Press, 1989), 137–63. For a more extensive account of the party's and the leadership's roles in assignments after reform, see Rohde, *Parties and Leaders*, chaps. 3, 4; and Gary W. Cox and Mathew D. McCubbins, "Parties and Committees in the U.S. House of Representatives" (Manuscript, 1989).

Chapter 6

Politics, Power, and Leadership in Congressional Subcommittees

CHARLES M. TIDMARCH
with the assistance of PAUL D. GINSBERG

If what we do not know about a given subject is the chief source of research motivation and intellectual excitement, then students of Congress should be in a veritable frenzy about subcommittee politics. The congressional scholarship fellowship has within the last decade seemingly arrived at a consensus about the importance of subcommittees in the affairs of the Congress, especially the House (Davidson 1981; Dodd and Oppenheimer 1981, 40–49; Smith and Deering 1984, 125–65 and passim). But the scope and depth of research on the varieties of subcommittee behavior and impact are still surprisingly limited. As Sinclair (1983, 122) has observed, "We lack systematic comparative studies of subcommittees or of their presumably variable relations to their parent committees. Before any firm conclusions about the impact of subcommittee government upon policy can be reached, we need to know more about the actual focus of decision-making and how this varies across committees." The 1984 publication of Smith and Deering's volume on committees has taken us some distance toward meeting the concern expressed by Sinclair, but there is a vast amount yet to be done.

What ought to be done is, in a certain sense, quite clear. We might well undertake a replication and expansion of Fenno's masterful work (1973) on committees, with a special eye on the consequences of "sub-

This chapter was originally prepared for delivery at the annual meeting of the American Political Science Association, Washington, D.C., 30 August–2 September 1984. Copyright © 1984 by the American Political Science Association. It is reprinted by permission.

108

committee government" as it has evolved since the reforms of the 1970s. Further, the vast body of public documents and available data on sub-committee and committee activity constitutes a rich empirical crop for harvest. Whether all of this would lead us to a level of theoretical achieve-ment proportionate to the empirical largesse is open to serious question. As Dodd (1983) has persuasively argued, legislative study has no mature, broad-gauged theory to call its own. Yet one suspects that the committee-subcommittee nexus may be central to the development of such a theory.

This study has goals more modest than its title may imply. We do not seek, for obvious reasons, to treat all subcommittees of both houses of Congress. Nor do we strive to articulate an encompassing theoretical framework. Our major objective is to compare the roles and activities of the subcommittees of five House committees in order to determine: (1) whether and how subcommittee "systems" differ among committees, and (2) whether and how subcommittees within the committee context differ among themselves. The five committees are Appropriations, Energy and Commerce, Government Operations, Public Works and Transportation, and Veterans' Affairs. Our goal is to generate some hypotheses pertinent to an enhanced understanding of the particulars of subcommittee gov-ernment. Frankly, our presupposition is that subcommittees differ in important (and not-so-important) ways. The greatest challenge lies in determining which similarities and differences are the consequential ones with regard to quality of performance and influence upon the organi-zational and legislative processes of the House.

Our data sources include thirty semistructured personal interviews with members (fourteen) and committee or subcommittee staffers (sixteen) of the five committees. These interviews were conducted during the period from August 1983 to June 1984. The interviews lasted an average of about forty-five minutes, none were shorter than twenty minutes, and several were longer than an hour. Interviewees were assured anonymity in order to encourage greater candor in the discussion of what sometimes became the politics of personal rivalry among members and among sub-committees. We are well aware that the number of interviews is insufficient to permit full and detailed characterization of each subcommittee. There are, after all, thirty-seven subcommittees among the five committees. Accounting for majority and minority viewpoints, as well as full com-mittee and subcommittee staff perspectives, we might need closer to 100 interviews in order to approach a genuine cross section of respondents. (One resists the temptation to call it a sample.) Yet we strongly believe that our interviews are sufficient in number and quality to permit the generation of hypotheses and the identification of interpretive insights. Perhaps even more important, we were encouraged by our interview experiences to believe that the great majority of respondents resonated with the objectives of the research and genuinely sought to shed light on an admittedly amorphous subject.

The interviews represented but one portion of the research effort. In addition, we have consulted journalistic sources and public documents, including committee rules, reports, and calendars. One of the more important components of the research is a study of subcommittee membership patterns, especially patterns of mobility between subcommittees and what we have chosen to call "integration" of subcommittees by means of overlapping membership.

THE COMMITTEES

The committees chosen represent a good variety of types. At one extreme is the selective and prestigious Appropriations Committee. If not the formidable force (Schick 1980, 415–40) that it was when Fenno (1966) first studied it, it remains one of the most attractive committees to members (Granat 1983; Ray 1982). At the other extreme is the Veterans' Affairs Committee, low in general prestige, visibility, and member attractiveness. Between the two extremes we have Energy and Commerce, Public Works and Transportation, and Government Operations.

Energy and Commerce (called Interstate and Foreign Commerce until 1981) is one of the premiere policy committees, possessing broad jurisdiction in various key sectors of the American economy. Membership on this committee has become increasingly desirable in recent years.

Public Works and Transportation provides a substantial menu of policy and constituency-benefit opportunities to its members. Environmentalists and "pork-barrelers" alike can find challenges and rewards from service here. It is, however, not nearly as attractive to members as Appropriations and Energy and Commerce (Ray 1982, 610–11).

Government Operations is primarily an investigation and oversight committee, but it also exercises a modicum of legislative responsibilities. It provides few opportunities to deliver tangible benefits to constituents. For members interested in improving the quality of governance, the committee does provide nearly boundless opportunities to examine and critique federal agencies and programs. Hence its attractiveness has traditionally been moderately high.

Such thumbnail sketches of the committees are tendered with reservations, of course, for there are a host of reasons why a given member of the House might value or depreciate service on a particular committee. We know from the work of Shepsle (1978) that the matching of requesting members and committees is often an intricate exercise in the accom-

Table 6-1. A Portrait of Five House Committees, Ninety-eighth Congress

		Subcommittees		Committee Staff	
	Size	No.	Mean Size	No.	Assigned to Subcommittees
Appropriations	57	13	10.5	139[a]	40.3
Energy and Commerce	42	6	13.1	147	65.3
Government Operations	39	7	9.6	79	57.0
Public Works and Transportation	48	6	21.1	75	32.0
Veterans' Affairs	33	5	12.6	30	20.0

Sources: *Congressional Quarterly Special Report: Committees and Subcommittees of the 98th Congress*, 2 Apr. 1983; U.S. House of Representatives *Telephone Directory*, Spring 1983.
[a] Includes associate staff attached to members' office.

modation of perceived political needs that are not always amenable to rational explanation. Hence, a freshman might take a seat on Judiciary not because he really wants the seat but because the leadership needs a willing warm body to fill the committee roster. The good will that is thus earned might be converted at a later date into the Speaker's support for an assignment switch to, say, Ways and Means.

In any event, we would argue that our choice of committees is a defensible one on the grounds of variety. On the other hand, because we have in common with Fenno (1973) only the Appropriations Committee, we are unable to update his analysis (assuming that we wished to adopt his analytical framework, which we do not).

Table 6-1 provides a concise overview of the five committees as of the Ninety-eighth Congress.

A few cautions are in order before moving beyond table 6-1. To begin with, the counting and classification of staff is notoriously tricky business. Full committee staffers may be detailed to subcommittees without a change of title. The General Accounting office may detail people to work with a committee or subcommittee who are not listed as staff members. Minority staff arrangements may be highly flexible; in the case of Energy and Commerce, for example, Republican staff members must be generalists prepared to shift attention to subcommittees where they are needed. Finally, all staff—from file clerks to chief counsels—are counted equally in the table.

Nonetheless, certain aspects of table 6-1 are worth comment. First, one should note that Appropriations has relatively small subcommittees with carefully delineated jurisdictions. The ratio of staff to members is about 2½ to 1. Yet the share of staff assigned explicitly to the subcommittees is rather modest. Indeed, one minority staffer is listed as having sole responsibility for three subcommittees. If associate staffers are set aside, the proportion of subcommittees to subcommittee staffers changes from 40 percent to 63 percent, a very major adjustment. Even so, the differences in subcommittee staff resources are marked: the Defense Subcommittee lists fourteen majority and one minority staffers; the Legislative Subcommittee lists but one majority and one minority staffer.

There is comparatively little ambiguity about the role of staff on the Energy and Commerce Committee. Majority staff are clearly identified as either full committee or subcommittee employees, with no evidence of multiple subcommittee duties for any subcommittee staffer. Our interviews with persons associated with this committee conveyed a clear sense of "them and us" mentality among staff, which is not to say there was hostility so much as autonomy and identity. The various subcommittees have substantial staffs of their own, ranging in size from fourteen to nineteen. A good sense of how several of these subcommittee staffs got "built" in the mid to late 1970s can be found in Malbin (1980, 97–165), who shows us that aggressive and shrewd subcommittee chairs such as John Dingell and John Moss left a profound imprint upon the nature of the subcommittees.

Government operations is a committee with a high ratio of staff to members (21 to 1) and a healthy subcommittee staff infrastructure—one that is rather equitably apportioned among the units. The largest minority staff is seven and the smallest is four. No separate minority subcommittee staff is identified.

Public Works and Transportation represents a departure from the pattern of small subcommittees with substantial staffs. Instead, the configuration is unusually large subcommittees (among the largest in the House) and rather small subcommittee staff details (one or two majority staffers is the standard, along with a like number of minority staff). This suggests a degree of centralization in staff that is reminiscent of the prereform House. We will say more on this point later.

The Veterans' Affairs Committee is the smallest in size and has the fewest subcommittees and one of the smallest staffs of any standing committee. The proportion of subcommittee staffers here is by far the smallest of our five committees. Majority subcommittee staffers usually work out of their chairmen's personal offices rather than out of full committee offices. One additional curiosity about Veterans' Affairs subcommittees is that the Hospitals and Health Care Subcommittee is markedly larger (twenty-two) than the other four. The reason for this, we were told by two members, is the need to put onto the subcommittee as many people as possible who have veterans' hospitals in their districts. As one Republican member put it, "Everybody would like to be on that subcommittee." Yet even this relatively attractive subcommittee has only one majority staffer.

All in all, we suspect that simple numbers such as those in table 6-1 have real, though limited, value in helping to understand the structural aspects of subcommittee politics. Clearly, "understaffed" (however defined) subcommittees are at a disadvantage in dealing with "adequately" staffed full committees. At the same time, larger subcommittees may be more cumbersome to manage and lead than smaller subcommittees (*ceteris paribus*).

In any case, such figures represent a starting point and a potential source of speculation and hypothesis about influences upon subcommittee performance. Let us now turn from structures to evidence about the behavior of committee and subcommittee members.

IDEOLOGY AND PARTISANSHIP OF COMMITTEE MEMBERS

There is less than a professional consensus about how important partisanship and ideology are in influencing the behavior of legislators, but there is no real disagreement about the need to study these two central facts of congressional life (Clausen 1973; Kingdon 1981; Schneider 1979). A thorough consideration of party and ideology in committee and subcommittee deliberations would necessitate, *inter alia*, the analysis of voting patterns at both the subcommittee and the committee levels. What data we have at this point in our inquiry are too fragmentary to permit discussion here. Instead, we will present data on the floor roll-call voting behavior of the members of the committees and subcommittees of interest. We do not believe that in the era of open meetings and recorded votes it is likely that very many members would risk "schizophrenic" voting behavior—i.e., voting like a liberal in subcommittee and like a conservative on the floor. At the same time, we are well aware that issues are framed differently early in the legislative process, and iterations and adjustments may cause members to modify their views and votes along the way from subcommittee markup to final passage.

Table 6-2 presents evidence about the ideological proclivities of committees and subcommittees in the aggregate during the first session of the Ninety-eighth Congress. While there are obviously more sophisticated ways to measure ideology in House roll-call voting, Americans for Democratic Action (ADA) scores have the virtues that scholars traditionally use them and that they correlate demonstrably strongly with several other "ideological" group ratings.

Table 6-2 makes clear that although full committees differ relatively

*Table 6-2. Ideological Differences among Subcommittees,
Controlling for Party: Mean 1983 ADA Scores*

Committees and Subcommittees	Democrats	Republicans
Veterans' Affairs	*65*	*13*
Oversight and Investigation	61	16
Hospitals and Health Care	75	17
Compensation, Pension, Insurance	46	7
Education, Training, Employment	73	5
Housing and Memorial Affairs	66	17
Range of subcommittee means	29	12
Government Operations	*73*	*17*
Commerce, Consumer, Monetary Affairs	64	10
Environment, Energy, National Resources	86	22
Government Activities and Transportation	85	10
Government Information, Justice, Agriculture	71	7
Intergovernment Relations and Human Resources	83	13
Legislation and National Security	67	18
Manpower and Housing	78	14
Subcommittee range	22	15
Public Works and Transportation	*73*	*11*
Aviation	73	8
Economic Development	80	19
Investigations and Oversight	65	15
Public Buildings and Grounds	65	5
Surface Transportation	73	9
Water Resources	77	6
Subcommittee range	15	14
Energy and Commerce	*79*	*13*
Commerce, Transportation, Tourism	76	10
Energy Conservation and Power	77	7
Fossil and Synthetic Fuels	68	10
Health and Environment	85	8
Oversight and Investigations	83	13
Telecommunications, Consumer Protection, Finance	86	25
Subcommittee range	18	18
Appropriations	*75*	*16*
Agriculture	69	6
Commerce, Justice, State, Judiciary	79	20
Defense	52	11
District of Columbia	78	32
Energy and Water Development	57	7
Foreign Operations	85	8
HUD, Independent Agencies	78	32
Interior	78	18
Labor, HHS, Education	83	24
Legislative	71	24

Continued on next page

Table 6-2—Continued

Committees and Subcommittees	Democrats	Republicans
Military Construction	65	10
Transportation	89	30
Treasury-Postage-General Government	88	7
Subcommittee range	37	26

ADA scores are from *Congressional Quarterly Weekly Report*, 14 July 1984: 1696–97.

little from each other in what we might call their central ideological tendencies, the subcommittees of the parent committees present some surprisingly large differences. Thus, while the least liberal committee Democrats (those of Veterans' Affairs) are only 14 points lower on the ADA scale than the most liberal committee Democrats (those of Energy and Commerce), some intracommittee disparities are of great magnitude. The ranges reported in the table are eye-catching, especially those for Veterans's Affairs and Appropriations. The Defense Subcommittee of Appropriations (ADA = 52) is unarguably representative of a different segment of the Democratic party than is the exceptionally liberal Transportation Subcommittee (ADA = 89). Both subcommittees are chaired by northern liberals, but their supporting casts are rather different. The most homogeneous set of Democratic subcommittees is to be found on Public Works.

The Republican subcommittee means are, on the whole, less variable within committees, but the Appropriations set closely parallels the Democratic array (Spearman rank-order correlation is .57). What this suggests to us is that Democrats and Republicans have developed a somewhat complementary relationship in the subcommittees of Appropriations. A very low or a negative correlation would suggest a more conflictual pattern in which, perhaps, the most liberal Democrats and the most conservative Republicans gravitated to the same subcommittee, and so forth.

The extent of such complementarity between the subcommittee delegations of the other four committees is variable. The ideological rank order correlation for Public Works is a high .71, while the coefficient for Energy and Commerce is .35, for Veterans' Affairs .22, and for Government Operations .17. We do not propose to make much of such numbers, except to argue that they may say something about the notion of complementarity. What they most assuredly do not tell us is that liberals of both parties flock to the same subcommittees and that conservatives of both parties seek their own kind as well. Obviously table 6-2 reveals a profound degree of ideological difference on every last one of the subcommittees.

Table 6-3 offers us a glimpse of the partisanship of the subcommittee and committee members. We have chosen to use the familiar *Congressional Quarterly* party unity scores, specifically for 1983. Party Unity score is the percentage of recorded votes on which the representative voted yea or nay in agreement with the majority of his party, when majorities of Democrats and Republicans voted differently.

Again we find that full committees differ relatively little with each other in the mean levels of party unity voting, but that subcommittees differ substantially. The ranges for each committee are somewhat narrower than were the ADA score ranges, but they are still noteworthy. The differences among the Appropriations subcommittees for both parties are once more the greatest. This should come as no great surprise, given the fact that majority party positions tend to be correlated with ideological voting as we have opted to measure it.

Quite clearly some subcommittees have a good many more ardent partisans on them than other subcommittees do. Appropriations has eight Democratic subcommittee contingents with 80 percent or higher unity scores (but only one Republican subcommittee group with a score as high as 80 percent). Veterans' Affairs has no Democratic subcommittee bloc with a mean unity score as high as 80 percent, but it does have two Republican subcommittee contingents with scores over 80. By one means of reckoning, the most partisan subcommittee of the lot is Government Activities and Transportation (of Government Operations), where both party delegations have 86 percent unity means. The combined means provide a fairly good guide to the strength of party loyalties of the memberships. Hence, the least partisan subcommittee on our list is perhaps Appropriations Defense (combined total 135).

It would be worthwhile to follow this analysis with an examination of how much partisanship there is *within* the subcommittees as they go about their legislative and investigatory business.. We know from prior research on committees (Fenno, 1974 83–94) that internal committee norms may discourage overt partisanship in doing essential business of the committee. Thus, a fire-breather on most issues might become an accommodationist once the markup begins. In future work we hope to explore the consequences of ideology and partisan membership "mixes" on selected subcommittees.

THE WORLD OF THE SUBCOMMITTEES

Without question the Subcommittee Bill of Rights (Ornstein 1975) and other Democratic Caucus reforms of the 1970s solidified the position of the subcommittee as a legislative subunit. These measures guaranteed the

Table 6-3. *Partisanship Differences among Subcommittees:*
Mean 1983 Party Unity Scores

Committees and Subcommittees	Democrats	Republicans
Veterans' Affairs	70	76
Oversight and Investigation	69	76
Hospitals and Health Care	78	72
Compensation, Pension, Insurance	54	81
Education, Training, Employment	74	83
Housing and Memorial Affairs	72	72
Range of subcommittee means	20	11
Government Operations	78	71
Commerce, Consumer, Monetary Affairs	69	74
Environment, Energy, National Resources	86	59
Government Activities and Transportation	86	86
Government Information, Justice, Agriculture	71	82
Intergovernment Relations and Human Resources	78	83
Legislation and National Security	75	65
Manpower and Housing	77	77
Subcommittee range	17	17
Public Works and Transportation	76	76
Aviation	77	81
Economic Development	82	72
Investigations and Oversight	72	69
Public Buildings and Grounds	71	73
Surface Transportation	75	79
Water Resources	80	78
Subcommittee range	11	12
Energy and Commerce	78	79
Commerce, Transportation, Tourism	74	73
Energy Conservation and Power	80	87
Fossil and Synthetic Fuels	68	81
Health and Environment	78	85
Oversight and Investigations	82	85
Telecommunications, Consumer Protection, Finance	86	70
Subcommittee range	18	17
Appropriations	80	67
Agriculture	75	79
Commerce, Justice, State, Judiciary	82	67
Defense	67	68
District of Columbia	80	56
Energy and Water Development	69	76
Foreign Operations	84	71
HUD, Independent Agencies	81	54
Interior	84	69
Labor, HHS, Education	88	57
Legislative	77	61

Continued on next page

Table 6-3—Continued

Committees and Subcommittees	Democrats	Republicans
Military Construction	74	75
Transportation	90	51
Treasury-Postage-General Government	87	81
Subcommittee range	23	30

Source: *Congressional Quarterly Weekly Report*, 31 December 1983: 2792–93.

demarcation of subcommittee jurisdictions, the prompt referral of germane legislation to the appropriate subcommittee, and the procurement and funding of subcommittee staff. Finally, after decades of relative incarceration, the subcommittee began to emerge from the hegemony of the full committee. Increasingly, members have begun to view subcommittee chairmanship as a vehicle for accruing prestige, power, and further positions of leadership in the House. To be sure, not all have relished the emasculation of the full committee chair and the diminishment of the chair's imperium. One senior Veterans's Affairs staffer, in disdain for what he termed the "reconstructionist" Democratic Caucus, and in longing for the more "traditionalist" member and Congress, lamented: "Congressional reform in 1968 and 1972 and through that period, in my opinion, changed the Congress dramatically. The proliferation of subcommittees I think has been one of the most damaging forces in the ability of Congress to pass legislation, in the ability of chairmen to control the direction that committees will go."

No matter what the normative judgment, there is little doubt that the contemporary House of Representatives is an institution vastly different from its predecessors of as few as fifteen years ago. The difference is in large measure attributable to the changing nature and role of the subcommittee.

The question arises, What specifically about the House of Representatives has the rise of subcommittee government affected? The most observable difference between the contemporary and previous Congresses is understood in terms of congressional power and influence—who has it, how did they get it, and how is it utilized? During the years when subcommittee members and subcommittee chairmen were commonly designated by the full committee chairman, that chairman was able to bridle effectively the power of the subcommittee. Except for the degree of control derived from "ex officio" membership on subcommittees, the full committee chair has lost several formal channels of influence. The chair can no longer capriciously establish or disband subcommittees, determine their composition, size, and party ratio, or control totally the referral of bills. The Democratic Caucus ensured that the provisions for subcommittee operation would be codified within the House rules or within the written rules of each standing committee. Logically, the anticipated results would be an increase in the independence of House subcommittees and in the power of subcommittee chairmen vis-à-vis the full committee chair.

Most congressional staffers, when asked degree of influence they believed the subcommittee chair now has over setting the agenda for the subcommittee, noted that the subcommittee chair almost always "calls the shots." A staff member for one of the Government operations subcommittees, in recording the prevailing sentiment concerning the expanding dominion of subcommittee chairmen, stated:

> Now the control ultimately resides with the subcommittee chairman. In terms of our investigations, what we decide to look into, he has total control. So far everything that we have had has been a hearing that he wanted to hold. There is no influence coming down from the full committee chair. I think that one of the really good things about this committee is that the subcommittee chairmen are autonomous individuals. I mean there are things the full committee wants us to do, there are hearings and reports we do for the House administration and that kind of thing, which are in the interests of the full committee. But when it comes to subject matter it's pretty much hands off.

A staffer for the Veterans Affairs full committee concurs:

> If one considers that at the maximum there can be 240 subcommittees depending on how you count them, statistically every sophomore Democrat can chair a subcommittee. You can do it with virtual autonomy as opposed to the old days when the chairman had significant control over what his subcommittee chairmen did, how [the chairmanships] were handed out, and under what conditions they would be held. A young man today can use the subcommittee position as a really brilliant soapbox limelight in order to bring a bill to national prominence. A subcommittee chair can now significantly gather support for a co-sponsored bill on the floor of the House, whereas before the full committee chairman decided whether it goes to the floor or doesn't.

We need not be content with participants' perceptions only in considering this matter, for the role of subcommittees in the legislative process can be measured in various ways. Smith and Deering (1984, 132) report that the percentage of legislation referred to House subcommittees more than doubled between the Ninety-first Congress (prereform) and the

Ninety-sixth Congress (1979–80). Similarly, the percentage of all committee meetings and hearings held by subcommittees increased markedly during the same period. However, the differences among committees in the degree of change undergone is striking. Considering our committees only, we learn from Smith and Deering that Public Works increased from 18 percent to 99 percent of reported legislation with subcommittee action. Veterans' Affairs increased from 62 percent to 91 percent. Government Operations started at 100 percent and ended at the same level. Energy and Commerce increased from 67 percent to 92 percent (Smith and Deering 1982, 136).

LEVERAGE FROM THE CHAIR

One should resist the temptation to infer that subcommittees enjoy legislative autonomy merely because they have come to play an integral role in the process. As Davidson (1981, 117) points out, the scope and autonomy of the subcommittee depends on various intra- and extracommittee variables. Subcommittees need funds to operate, and the disposition of committee budgets is still largely a constrained prerogative of the full committee chairperson. Virtually all of our interviewees made reference to the enduring power of the purse held by the committee chair. One senior Democratic full committee staff member commented, "They (the subcommittee chairs) know that we can make life easier or harder for them in the way that the budget is carved up." A petty budget struggle between John Dingell and his Energy and Commerce subcommittee chairs became the subject of a 1983 *Washington Post* article by David Maraniss, much to the chagrin of some Democratic members of the committee. Matters such as whether or not a subcommittee chair will be given travel money to conduct field hearings can be important tests of the full committee chair's influence. One subcommittee chair spoke with obvious residual unhappiness about having been denied without satisfactory explanation a field hearing opportunity a year prior. And one Public works subcommittee staffer commented, "If a set of hearings is going to be embarrassing to the full committee chairman, he has a set of devices he can use to discourage us from holding hearings. He controls the administrative budget, the travel budget. If we have to travel in the field and he doesn't like the whole investigation, he can scrub the travel. We have to schedule our hearing rooms through him. If he doesn't like a particular issue we're into, he can just refuse to give us a hearing room."

An intriguing variation on the theme of dislike for the proposed hearing emerged from one of our interviews with a Democratic member of the Veterans' Affairs Committee, who indicated that Chairman Sonny

Montgomery occasionally likes the proposed subcommittee hearing subject so much that he tries to adopt it for his own subcommittee on oversight and investigations. This has led to a game of subcommittee "cat and mouse" in which the initiating subcommittee "schedules around" Montgomery or moves more rapidly than originally planned. We suspect that a more vindictive chairman would not often tolerate such tactics.

Another budgetary tool available to the full committee chair is staff hiring. It became clear to us from our interviews and reading of committee rules that there is a variety of practices in the realm of hiring. Although full committee chairs are all accorded de jure power in the matter of hiring, some do not exercise the power with regularity and gusto. Others exercise it idiosyncratically or only when they distrust a subcommittee chair's judgment.

An Appropriations subcommittee chair told us that Chairman Whitten is very conscious of his prerogative to hire and fire. "That isn't to say that I would not go to him with a recommendation for the subcommittee," said our respondent, "but I certainly couldn't go to him and tell him that I want to move somebody off my personal staff onto the subcommittee or committee staff."

Two subcommittee chairmen from the same committee told us that they saw themselves as having nearly free rein to hire whomever they wanted as subcommittee staffers. Yet the chief counsel of the same committee described the hiring process in different terms: "We try to give the subcommittee chairs their way if they have somebody they really want for an opening, but the [full committee] chairman is absolutely not going to sign off on too many $50,000-a-year counsels for a given subcommittee. He insists on staggering or balancing these things by subcommittee." While these member and staff perceptions are not totally incompatible, the disparity suggests subcommittee staff recruiting is constrained by the committee chairman's budget powers.

The model staff hiring arrangement for the subcommittees that we have specific knowledge of appears to be one of consultation between the full committee chair and the subcommittee chair, with the chief committee counsel or the staff director playing an advisory role. To read the rules of, say, the Energy and Commerce Committee is to gain the impression that the subcommittee chairmen have carte blanche in the choice of subcommittee top staff. To talk with the subcommittees, chief counsels and staff directors is to strengthen the impression that these are, indeed, the hand-picked choices of the subcommittee chairs. But a discussion of the subject with a top full committee staffer leaves one with the impression that, subcommittee bill of rights notwithstanding, Chairman Dingell is interested in the quality of certain subcommittee staffs.

If we must generalize on the matter, we would say that on three of the committees (Energy and Commerce, Government Operations, and Public Works) subcommittee chairs have substantial freedom in personnel matters. In Appropriations and Veterans' Affairs, the committee chair and the chief committee counsel exercise tighter control over subcommittee hiring. Our omnipresent caveat is that there is no accounting for deviations from the norm as a result of unusually good or poor relationships between the committee chair and a subcommittee chair.

A more subtle leadership tool of the full chair is control over the outflow of paper and the exercise of editorial control over documents. This power was mentioned explicitly by senior staffers of Government Operations and Energy and Commerce. The Energy staff member emphasized (with obvious relish) that in the editing of subcommittee documents, he deletes inappropriate and unnecessary references to the subcommittee. The purpose in this is to establish that all of the documents are in the last analysis *committee* publications. The task of curbing subcommittee self-promotion has been made easier by the advent of word processing and computerized document files.

On Government Operations, the chairman insists that all press releases must be cleared through him and the chief counsel, lest an impetuous subcommittee head get the full committee "out on a limb." The chairman also bars full committee and subcommittee staff alike from speaking with the media or giving public speeches without prior approval by the chair of the contact and content. We cannot say whether Energy Chairman Dingell would like to exercise the same types of control in press affairs, but it was obvious to us that the media-wise subcommittee chairs and counsels would quickly find ways of circumventing the rules. Two key subcommittee staffers mentioned their congenial relationships with reporters who were more than happy to catch leaks and leads.

While it is true that a component of full committee chairs' leverage over subcommittees is the capacity to deny valued resources and opportunities, this is not the only form of leverage. Refusal to move a bill after the subcommittee has acted is a weapon a chairman must use with discretion. Repeated denials of requests to hire, refusals of hearing rooms at convenient times, tightfistedness in matters of travel—all such confrontational tactics can only lead ultimately to subcommittee rebellion. Our interviews turned up very few specific complaints from members about hostile and obstructionist committee chairs. Indeed, quite the opposite was found. Consider these exemplary quotes:

I get along great with Brooks. . . . No problems.

I make him [Whitten] nervous, but he's willing to let me play a role on the right issues.

I make him [Montgomery] nervous, but he lets me do my thing.

Dingell doesn't feel any overpowering need to try and interfere in the ——subcommittee. He's satisfied to wait until the legislation moves to the full committee. Besides, Oversight and Investigation provides him plenty of opportunity to use a subcommittee. He can also be a help to the subcommittee chairmen on issues where they have a similar outlook.

No small part of a chairman's influence may be grounded in his facility for creating and sustaining a mood of mutual trust and (at least in the early stages of the legislative process) deference. Of Dingell, one sub-committee staffer said, "He doesn't like all of the subcommittee chairmen, but he respects them . . . and they respect him." Another subcommittee staffer, reflecting partly upon Dingell and partly upon the ideal type, stated, "The full committee chairman can be a facilitator, an expediter. He can use the subcommittee chairs as his good right arms. He can use the committee budget as an incentive. He can let them set agendas, but he can help them develop the policy agenda cooperatively."

An Energy and Commerce minority staffer, in characterizing the working relationship between Dingell and ranking minority member James Broyhill, underscored the point that both men were effective because they understood the necessity for give-and-take.

A similar dynamic seems to be at work in the relationship between Jack Brooks and Frank Horton in Government Operations. Brooks, although reputed to have some flair for old-fashioned arm twisting, was described as being sensitive to matters of procedural fairness most of the time. For example, the committee requires that any subpoena must be issued through Brooks, who normally consults with Horton. Both majority and minority staffers interviewed strongly emphasized the need to maintain credibility in the use of the subpoenas that are so integral to the work of an investigative body like Government Operations. This example in some sense stands as an exception to the rule that committee chairs let subcommittees set their own agendas. Surely, if Brooks were to oppose the issuance of a key subpoena on behalf of a subcommittee, it could have direct impact on the subcommittee agenda. We were given no example of a subpoena denial.

The Public Works and Transportation Committee serves as an excellent example of how the relationships between full committee chair and sub-committee chairs can vary from one subcommittee to the next. A moderately senior Democrat who does not hold a Public Works subcommittee chair told us that several of the subcommittees had become quite formidable during the Howard regime (1981–88), especially Aviation under Norman Mineta, Oversight and Investigations under Elliott Levitas, and Economic Development under Jim Oberstar. By and large, Howard is a noninterventionist in his dealings with these subcommittees. On the other hand, Howard—as former chair of the Subcommittee on Surface Transportation, and an enthusiastic and informed "player" in transportation policy—maintains a tight rein over subcommittee chair Glenn Anderson. Our interview source noted that Howard will not hesitate to "pull rank and yank a bill" away from Anderson if he disapproves of the handling.

A Democratic member of the Science and Technology Committee who also sits on one of our focal committees made an important point in an interview regarding the way in which external actors (interest groups) can affect the relationship between the full committee chair and the subcommittee chair. His example was that many representatives of the "scientific community" prefer to deal with committee chair Don Fuqua rather than with the chair of the subcommittee with jurisdiction over federal research and development programs. The subcommittee chair is treated politely and is consulted, but both Fuqua and the major spokespeople work to maintain their long-standing special relationship. In light of this, the iron triangle begins to look more like a rectangle.

One theme that emerged from our interviews and observations was that full committee chairs can still lead in the era of subcommittee government in two fundamental ways—administratively and substantively. Restated, this means that they can employ the procedural powers and budgetary powers, or they can exercise influence on policy through analytical and coalition-building activity. Our very distinct impression is that most chairmen of the day are reasonably adept at the former type of leadership, but relatively inept at the latter.

Peter Rodino, chairman of the House Judiciary Committee, has come in the last two years to be seen as a legislative "undertaker" specializing in the squelching of conservative policy initiative in such areas as busing, abortion, and school prayer. Rodino utilizes his subcommittee chairs to delay the bills or delete them from the agenda altogether (Cohodas 1984, 1097).

House Armed Services Committee Chairman Melvin Price stands as an example of one who has apparently lost control of both the full committee and the subcommittees, thus failing the test of leadership on administration and policy (Glennon 1984, 735–36). The personal fondness of many committee members for the chairman may be the critical factor in maintaining the appearance of control.

A senior Republican committee staffer was not optimistic that the next generation of committee chairs would be as capable as (let alone better than) the current crop. After providing his version of how the reforms of the 1970s and the changing nature of electoral politics have combined to jeopardize the legislative process, the veteran staffer said of the younger members, "Too many of them are just ticket punchers who don't understand or know how to use power. There are a lot of subcommittee chairmen now who are pretty sorry. And I don't think they are going to get any better at it when they take over as committee chairs." But a young subcommittee chairman took a drastically different tack on the same question, saying:

> Some of the older guys are so process-oriented that they don't have a good feel for certain issues—Central America, for example. I am pretty optimistic about issue-oriented subcaucuses developing around a core of subcommittee chairmen. Not exclusively chairmen, of course. One thing you can say for the current leadership is that once they see you know what you're doing, and you have the jurisdiction, they are willing to let you go to work. Maybe that's not leadership, but its probably preferable to what went on around here before the changes [House reforms of the 70s].

LEVERAGE FROM THE SUBCOMMITTEE CHAIR AND STAFF

As we turn our attention to the role of the subcommittee chair, we should begin by observing that the people occupying these posts must concern themselves with establishing independence from the full committee chair and with exercising influence over the other members of the subcommittee. It may or may not be the case that what serves the subcommittee chair well in one relationship will also serve him or her well in the other. We will discuss a few of the potential tools at the disposal of these leaders.

One Democratic Appropriations Committee member told us that subcommittees have an advantage in full committee proceedings and that the advantage stems from the fact that few members of the full committee will be aware of what the subcommittee is going to recommend until the moment the crucial documents are produced, which is often the last minute. HUD Subcommittee Chair Edward Boland was mentioned by two interviewees as the most secretive of the Appropriations chairs, so much so that many members of the subcommittee are left in the dark until the last minute. Nonetheless, Boland is also given very high marks for his competence and bill management skill. A Republican not on Boland's subcommittee said, "It's the only subcommittee that *really* works."

A few of the younger Appropriations subcommittee heads are more amenable to keeping colleagues apprised of developments on controversial or politically sensitive legislation. But it would seem that the extent of subcommittee secrecy and "proprietary" attitudes make little difference for the fate of the bill in full committee. A subcommittee chair mentioned that the norm of subcommittee autonomy is so pervasive and powerful that "nobody wants to upset the applecart. The full committee goes through little charades and courtesy debates about things that are faits accomplis."

Subcommittee autonomy has its limits even on Appropriations, however. The common example in interviews was Clarence Long, chair of the Foreign Operations Subcommittee. Two Democratic colleagues who profess fondness for Long expressed their belief that he simply cannot "get it together" to manage the Foreign Aid Bill any longer. One of the colleagues noted that the larger the forum, the greater Long's difficulties. Thus, he functions satisfactorily in the subcommittee context, even though he is accused by both Democrats and Republicans of behaving capriciously. (For example, he might rigidly enforce the five-minute rule in allowing subcommittee members to question the witnesses, but allow himself to continue with questions at great length.) As the action moves to the full committee and the intensity of the debate increases, Long's grasp of the bill's particulars is seen as inadequate. Hence more amendments are proposed in committee, and if they fail there, they may rise again on the floor of the House, where Long is in greatest need of assistance, which is, it should be emphasized, willingly provided by supportive colleagues. As one of these colleagues put it, "Doc [Long] is still the chairman, after all, and damn it, he means well and he tries."

Although certain liabilities of other Appropriations subcommittees were mentioned, none seems as poignant and pertinent as the Long case. Quite possibly on a committee with less commitment to the norm of subcommittee autonomy, a Clarence Long would have by now been ousted as the chairman.

The proprietary attitude of subcommittee chairs is by no means limited to Appropriations. Consider what a Public Works Democrat told us about the style of Water Resources chairman Bob Roe: "He holds 'seances' with the subcommittee staff before the bill is brought up. Roe will know every dot and iota of the legislation, but he will be the only one [on the subcommittee] who knows it. His idea of consulting with you is to tell you how much good he is doing for you in the bill, even if you don't know it. It drives a lot of us up the wall."

What such cases as this teach us is that knowledge is power. This is a wonderful maxim, but it must always be followed by Michael Malbin's query, "Yes, but whose knowledge and whose power?" We would be surprised indeed to find very many members of today's House who do not understand all too well the political uses of superior knowledge. Therefore, they will not long be inclined to let subcommittee chairs (or anyone else) monopolize essential information.

Once one has the desired information, one must know what to do with it. A superb example of how the character of the knowledge can be an asset is the Health and Environment Subcommittee of Energy and Commerce. A Democratic member of the subcommittee told us that he could think of no other subcommittee whose professional staff enjoyed the kind of edge that the biomedical policy specialists do in dealing with members. The terminology and technical detail is so formidable that newcomers and amateurs cannot penetrate it. Whether this translates into an advantage for subcommittee chair Henry Waxman is hard to say. We suspect that the answer to that question depends upon the nature of the relationship between Waxman and the key subcommittee staffers.

One question that we asked of everyone interviewed pertained to the image and characteristics of a good subcommittee chairman. Although we heard many and varied answers to the question, we can say without hesitation that the responses did not differ in any systematic fashion according to which committee or subcommittee the respondent came from. The most commonly cited leadership traits were: (1) fairness; (2) intelligence, knowledge of the policy area; (3) ability to articulate, present; and (4) knowing how to develop compromises. We do not have a sufficient number of respondents to allow committee-by-committee comparison, but even if we did have more data we tend to believe that the variations among committees would be minor. The most likely exception would be Government Operations in particular and all of the oversight and investigations panels in general. Government operations staffers and members seem to share a consensus around the belief that to do well on the committee you have to like genuinely digging, probing, and interrogating. As one Government operations subcommittee chair expressed it, "The work is reminiscent of trial proceedings; if you enjoyed the courtroom you should feel at home in this committee." Thus, we suspect that a subcommittee head here must have a strong appetite for adversarial, even antagonistic, interactions.

Our final illustrative example of subcommittee chair leverage is what we call the pragmatic test. A Veterans' Affairs member told us that even a maverick subcommittee chairman can acquire leverage with a committee chair who disapproves of the subordinate's style or agenda. The key is to succeed (in terms of public relations benefits or production of a piece of legislation or a hearing that actually produces happy results). No matter how resistant the chairman may originally have been, a maverick sub-committee chair who brings credit to the full committee gains new influence. Conversely, independent or maverick activities such as highly controversial bills or embarrassing hearings that create negative press and "go nowhere" can serve to reduce the subcommittee chair's leverage both above and below (with subcommittee colleagues who feel ill served). A reporter mentioned the hearings on "Debategate" and stolen Carter 1980 campaign documents that were conducted by Donald Albosta's Post Office and Civil Service Subcommittee on Human Resources as a possible example of a high risk–low yield project.

If anything has become clear to us concerning the effectiveness of subcommittee chairs it is that they have something to lose. They must face the same array of challenges, albeit on a smaller scale, that full committee chairs face. They must learn to be good leaders, good followers, and good partners—sometimes simultaneously. And even those of lustrous reputation can suffer. Consider the plight of Tim Wirth, chair of the Subcommittee on Telecommunications, Consumer Protection, and Finance of the Energy and Commerce Committee. In 1983 one of the many controversial issues before Wirth's subcommittee was a proposal to deregulate the television industry. Wirth disliked the legislation and refused to move it. At the same time, he promoted his own idea of a mandatory "spectrum fee" that broadcasters would have to pay in order to use broadcast frequencies. Three of Wirth's subcommittee colleagues were so incensed by his obstructionism that they devised a plan to bypass the subcommittee and introduce the deregulation bill as an amendment in full committee to a pending authorization bill. Chances for passage in full committee were considered good, and Wirth was thus induced to make concessions to his pro-deregulation colleagues in order to recapture jurisdiction over the bill. The *Washington Post* story on the controversy quoted a committee staffer as saying, "This will be a victory of process over autocracy" (Schrage 1983, G11). A broadcasting industry lobbyist indicated to one of us in the summer of 1983 that "Wirth has lost control of the subcommittee on these issues. We are dealing with [subcommittee member Al] Swift more and more." Although Wirth's political demise was exaggerated by the lobbyist, the fact remains that his experience illustrates some of the perils of having subcommittee power.

CHOOSING AND CHANGING SUBCOMMITTEES

Movement by holdover members from one subcommittee to another within the same committee has not previously been studied, as best we can discern. The significance of such transfers for the operations of subcommittee government is apparent. If expertise comes with experience, and autonomy and influence flow from expertise, then experienced and stable subcommittees should be better off than inexperienced and fluid ones.

Bach (1984) provides us with a full record of aggregate subcommittee membership turnover by committee from the Eighty-eighth through the Ninety-eighth Congresses. From him we learn that House Appropriations subcommittees as a whole typically have high return rates (over 60 percent in eight of the eleven Congresses), while Commerce has ranged from 47 to 60 percent since the Ninety-fifth Congress. In the Ninety-eighth Congress, the return rate of Government Operations subcommittees was 28 percent; of Public Works, 43 percent; and of Veterans' Affairs, 37 percent. These are very useful figures in comparing the committees, but they do not tell us much about which subcommittees are experiencing various degrees of turnover.

Although we have not completed our study of subcommittee transfers over time for each committee, we are prepared to discuss what we have found for one committee in one Congress: Energy and Commerce in 1983. Our purpose in so doing is to outline the approach we expect to follow.

Of the twenty Democratic holdovers from the Ninety-seventh Congress, thirteen (65 percent) changed their subcommittee assignment package in some way. Similarly, none of thirteen (75 percent) of the Republican holdovers changed some feature of their assignment(s). Among the Democrats, only one retained his prior subcommittee and added an assignment. None added and changed as well. Three retained a prior subcommittee and also deleted one. Seven Democrats simply substituted a new subcommittee for an old one. Finally, two Democratic holdovers both deleted and substituted. (For example, one member left both Energy Conservation and Power *and* Fossil and Synthetic Fuels, while joining Telecommunications.)

Among Republican holdovers, none were retain-and-adds; six were simple deletions (largely owing to the less favorable ratio of Republicans to Democrats on the full committee); two were simple substitutes; and one was a delete-and-substitute.

Whether the changes in configuration were voluntary or involuntary, the fact remains that certain subcommittees ended up looking quite different in 1983 than they had looked in the previous session. Energy Conservation and Power (described by a committee staffer as a subcommittee with a growing reputation for being unable to move legislation) was halved in size (from twenty-two to eleven), and five Democratic seats were eliminated. Two subcommittee members who left the parent committee altogether made it possible for two new names to be added to the ECP roster: full committee holdover Thomas Luken and freshman John Bryant. The Republicans were forced to relinquish six seats on the subcommittee, of which three were held by departing members. Four committee holdovers gave up their seats, thus allowing the appointment of one new member of Congress: Dan Coats of Indiana.

Thus, in January 1983, the Energy Conservation and Power subcommittee was decidedly smaller than it had been the year prior, and it retained only eight (six Democrats and two Republicans) of its twenty-two members from 1982.

By way of contrast, Health and Environment gained a seat, lost two committee departees, lost one subcommittee switcher (Jim Florio) to Oversight and Investigations, and ended up needing three new Democratic appointees. Two Republican seats were eliminated, two departees left the committee, and thus no new faces were needed. All in all, Health and Environment was substantially similar in 1983 and 1982.

If all of this seems like an analytical briar patch, we are inclined to agree. The movements of individuals among committees are terribly cumbersome to track and difficult to interpret. The sheer volume of intra-committee churning is in itself a suggestive indicator. And the implications of new personnel, both in numbers and in types, cannot be ignored. It seems to us that an experienced subcommittee chair surrounded by a cast of *parvenus* is apt to face very different challenges than an experienced chair surrounded by a seasoned and stable subcommittee.

Our recommendation is that data on membership stability and inter-subcommittee mobility should be merged with data on conflict, productivity, and success in full committee, as well as with case studies of specific subcommittees at work. Naturally, the phenomenon of movement between subcommittees could be more properly explored if we had access to data on the subcommittee bidding that members engage in at the start of each new Congress. The data we currently have can tell us only who moved from where to where and who did not move; it cannot tell us who wanted to move where but *could not* do so.

We were told repeatedly by both members and staffers that the choice of subcommittee assignments is often hard to fathom. Nearly all respondents agreed that their committees had subcommittee "pecking orders" in terms of desirability to members. But everyone also believed that the pecking order (*a*) does not apply to every member and (*b*) changes over time.

One Appropriations Committee member informed us that today's new members try to gauge their subcommittee assignments on the basis of district needs to a much greater extent than was true ten or twenty years ago. Now seats are weighed for "visibility and policy-making opportunities." Once having chosen subcommittee seats, Appropriations members are less likely to switch than people on other committees, since seniority accumulates within the subcommittees of Appropriations but not in other committees. And although Appropriations subcommittee chairs are elected by the full caucus, seniority remains a key criterion.

Several Energy and Commerce staffers produced nearly identical subcommittee pecking order, with Telecommunications at the top, followed by Health and Environment, Fossil Fuels (on the wane in the age of plentiful gasoline), Oversight, Energy Conservation, and Commerce, Transportation, and Tourism. An interesting comment on the latter subcommittee by a staffer from the full committee was that "if the chairman (Jim Florio) knew how to capitalize on his jurisdiction over 'commerce generally' the subcommittee could become a hotbed of activity."

A senior Democratic staffer from Government Operations told us that the jurisdictional lines of the subcommittees were drawn in such a way as to make each subcommittee "equally attractive," subject to members' interests and needs. In other words, each subcommittee has plenty of meaty oversight opportunities attached to it. Chairman Brooks discourages the subcommittee chairs from serving on any subcommittee other than the one they chair. This unusual practice is intended to open more good seats up to junior members.

The pecking order of Public Works is a bit more ambiguous, except that all observers considered Public Buildings the least attractive subcommittee. Water Resources, Surface Transportation, and Economic Development rate much higher for most members, while Aviation is especially appealing to those whose districts have airports of any size.

Veterans' Affairs subcommittees, according to two members and the one staffer who would approach the issue, can be ranked as follows: Hospitals and Health Care first, with the other four tied for second.

Just as members seek appointment to standing committees for a multiplicity of reasons, some obvious, some obscure, so do they bid for subcommittees. As certain issues get "hot," certain subcommittees acquire appeal (Telecommunications because of telephone company breakup and the whole deregulation trend; energy issues in the late 1970s and into 1981 enhanced the appeal of Fossil Fuels). As issues wane and members' political circumstances change, the original subcommittee may or may not lose its lure. The prospect of acceding to a chairmanship may be just enough to induce an individual to stay put. One Appropriations Committee member admitted in his interview that he changed a subcommittee assignment because he thought he might have a better chance of eventually achieving a chair elsewhere. Another Appropriations member made a change because he was looking for more conflict and challenge than his subcommittee was giving him.

The research agenda on this subject is a particularly intriguing one. We need to do for subcommittees what was done more than a decade ago in the mining of committee preference data (Rohde and Shepsle 1973). And we must attempt to determine the extent to which subcommittee chairs themselves try to stack their subcommittees with their own favorites. An offhand remark by an Energy and Commerce staffer to the effect that Henry Waxman had "gone too far in loading his subcommittee with liberals" precipitated our interest in this particular matter.

SUBCOMMITTEE STRUCTURE, MEMBERSHIP SIZE, AND INTEGRATION

A quantitative measure of perhaps the more informal coordination that exists among the subcommittees of the five full committees under examination involves the reconnaissance of Democratic members' subcommittee assignment patterns. (The majority party is used as a barometer for the whole committee.) As previously noted, the "norm of subcommittee autonomy" derives much of its vim from the insulation provided by the lack of familiarity with another committee's jurisdictional issues. Conversely, if a large percentage of full committee members possess multiple subcommittee assignments, we would expect, particularly on the smaller committees, that the degree of autonomy derived from lack of familiarity, would be abated. If a significant number of members have two or three subcommittee assignments on a committee with only five or six subcommittees, then it would be accurate to conclude that at the least, *informal* coordination of the committee's subcommittees is the by-product. To facilitate this examination, we have employed cross-tabulations similar to the one in table 6-4 for each committee and for each Congress from the Ninety-third through the Ninety-eighth.

In each fraction the number (a) represents the total number of members assigned simultaneously to these two subcommittees. The denominator (b) represents the sum total of the seats available to Democratic members on these subcommittees (the combined total membership).

The measurement that we have developed for the purpose of bringing order out of the thirty separate committee matrices (five committees × six Congresses) is MCM percentage, or mean combined membership of all subcommittee pairs as a percentage of total committee membership. A committee with a large MCM is, in our view, one in which subcommittee responsibilities generate integrative opportunities. Lower MCM

Table 6-4. Example of Integration Cross-Tabulations: Veterans Affairs Committee, Democrats, Ninety-third through Ninety-eighth Congresses

	93d Congress				
	O&I	*H&HC*	*ET&E*	*CP&I*	*H&MA*
Oversight and Investigations	X	X	X	X	X
Hospitals and Health Care	4/12	X	X	X	X
Education, Training, and Employment	2/10	3/12	X	X	X
Compensation, Pension, and Insurance	1/8	6/10	0/8	X	X
Housing and Memorial Affairs	0/8	4/10	3/8	2/6	X

percentages suggest a higher degree of compartmentalization within the committee family.

Figure 6-1 graphically depicts the MCM percentage of each committee from the Ninety-third through the Ninety-eighth Congress. If subcommittee autonomy has increased during this period (as virtually every observer of Congress believes it has), perhaps a decline in integration will be reflected in lower MCM percentages.

For example, the Committee on Public Works and Transportation had an MCM of 139 in the Ninety-third Congress. This means that the average combined membership of the subcommittee pairs was 39 percent larger than the full committee's Democratic membership. With large subcommittee memberships relative to the size of the committee, Public Works exhibited a structural form capable of producing a great deal of informal coordination. By the time of the Ninety-eighth Congress, the Democratic MCM percentage of the committee had slipped sharply to 67. This decrease of 72 MCM percentage points may be one indication that the compartmentalization of subcommittee delegations is at least a correlate if not a cause of certain alleged pathologies of subcommittee government. We are not oblivious to the effects that chamber, party caucus, and committee rules changes about numbers of subcommittees, numbers of assignments to committees and subcommittees, limits on chairmanship opportunities, party ratios, and committee sizes might have on the MCM percentage data. Undoubtedly we could reconstruct committee changes over the six Congresses that would help us to understand why the MCM percentage lines move as they do.

We see that both the committees on Government Operations and

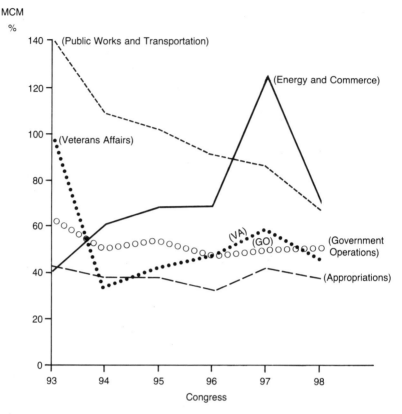

Figure 6-1. Democratic Mean Combined Membership Percentage, Ninety-third through Ninety-Eighth Congresses

Veterans Affairs exhibited a significant decline in the informal subcommittee coordination represented by the MCM percentage rating. In the Ninety-third Congress the average size of any two Veterans Affairs subcommittees was nearly equal to the size of the Democratic full committee membership. Because the Democratic subcommittee on the average is one-half the size of the Democratic full committee membership, the average Veterans Affairs member thus serves on half the subcommittees of the full committee. Clearly, with full committee members involved, at any one time, with half of all the committee's subcommittee activity, the degree of informal coordination was likely extensive. But like the Public Works and Transportation Committee, Veterans Affairs, by the Ninety-eighth Congress, had dropped 52 rating points to a 44 MCM percent. And Government Operations, which was moderately integrated during the Ninety-third Congress (62 MCM percent), fell to 49 MCM percent by the Ninety-eighth Congress. Again, this indicates that the informal integration provided by multiple assignments and members' familiarity with a variety of subcommittees declined.

The next two committees, Appropriations and Energy and Commerce, exhibit quite different MCM percentage patterns from the previous three committees. The Appropriations committee's trend shows little variation in the committee's degree of integration throughout the specified period. This revelation is not startling, nor is it surprising that throughout the six Congresses (except for the Ninety-fourth Congress), the Appropriations Committee consistently had the lowest MCM percentage score of the five committees. Traditionally, as the committee for which the phrase "norm of subcommittee autonomy" was coined, Appropriations has been the least integrated, most autonomous (in terms of subcommittees) House committee. Therefore, Appropriations' stable and low MCM percentage rating serves to confirm both the decentralized, compartmentalized nature of the committee and the validity of MCM percentage as a measurement of subcommittee integration.

More difficult to explain, however, is the MCM percentage pattern exhibited by the Committee on Energy and Commerce. Unlike Government Operations, Public works and Transportation, and Veterans Affairs, Energy and Commerce's measure of informal integration has climbed steadily from the Ninety-third to the Ninety-sixth Congress, increased sharply between the Ninety-sixth and Ninety-seventh Congresses, and tapered off by the Ninety-eighth Congress at a level significantly higher than the MCM percentage during the Ninety-third Congress. The Committee on Energy and Commerce, alone of all five committees, experienced an increase in integration during the six Congresses reviewed. The only tenable explanation for this phenomenon is that committee members, captivated by the "hotness" of the issues that Energy and Commerce reviews, have demanded an increasing number of subcommittee assignments. As a result, there has been a shift toward larger subcommittee memberships and, thus, greater integration. Traditionally, committees expand because members seek multiple assignments (Whiteman 1983).

Candidly, the MCM data cannot be presented as refined and valid measures of integration within the full committees. Obviously there is a qualitative dimension to integration that hinges upon how well people get along and how much they share the same values and objectives. Simply because there is a larger network of member contacts through the subcommittee system does not mean that it is a productive collaboration. At bottom, MCM can give us a hint of the extent to which individual members are likely to be impelled to adopt the broader perspective on the issues before the committee. If you, the liberal Democrat, and I, the conservative Democrat, are to serve together on three separate subcommittees, it is certainly best that we give some thought to the implications of our agreements and disagreements in one setting for our relationship in one of the other settings. We may be far apart on energy issues but relatively close on railroad policy and auto emissions. Neither of us can know for certain what roles the other may have to play in a future coalition. Such a "tempering" effect is not trivial. And whether the degree of integration that flows from larger subcommittees and multiple memberships is intentional or unanticipated, the potential impact on the dispersionary tendencies of subcommittee government may be welcome.

CONCLUDING THOUGHTS AND SOME EMERGENT HYPOTHESES

What follows is not intended as a comprehensive statement of what we have thus far learned and where we expect to see the study of Congressional subcommittees go. Much of what we have learned is very tentative. There is yet so much to do empirically and theoretically that one blanches at the thought of, say, a propositional inventory. We shall say nothing about the need to expand the study to the Senate (as Smith and Deering have done).

H1   Larger subcommittees, relative to the membership of the full committee, are more likely to see their legislative products adopted in full committee than are relatively smaller subcommittees. Coalitional training grounds are more likely to exist in larger subcommittees.

H2   Consensus within the subcommittee (intra-and interparty) leads to greater success in full committee deliberations.

H3   Policy consensus in a subcommittee can be achieved in several distinct ways: (*a*) recruitment and self-selection of like-minded people, (*b*) coalition-building and persuasion by subcommittee leadership, (*c*) external pressures (electoral, interest groups). Only (*a*), is apt to yield persistent consensus, while (*b*) and (*c*) are more likely to produce episodic consensus around specific bills and projects.

H4   The quality of relationships between full committee chairs and subcommittee chairs can work to facilitate or prevent productive interunit relations. Especially valuable in this regard is a mentor-protégé relationship. When chairs and subcommittee chairs are drawn from the same age cohorts, such relationships are less likely to form.

H5   The resources of leadership (budgets, scheduling, hiring, willingness to share public credit) can serve as important centripetal forces in the context of subcommittee government, but only if they are used with prudence. Current institutional norms preclude the frequent authoritarian exercise of such powers.

H6   Recentralized control by full committee chairs chiefly takes the form of consultations initiated by subcommittee leaders. Even when subcommittees have formal capacity to proceed autonomously, they may defer and consult with the full committee chair.

H7   Full committee chairs may be assessed and compared in terms of their (*a*) dispositive and (*b*) facilitative capacities. Dispositive capacity refers to formal authority or imputed power to allocate pertinent costs and benefits to colleagues. Facilitative capacity refers to demonstrated potential of a chair to help others achieve policy or political objectives as a consequence of the chair's professional esteem, moral leadership, and position as a link with other institutions in and out of government.

H8   Subcommittee chairs exercise power within their own subcommittees in a great variety of ways. The most important factors are expertise, effort, resources base, interpersonal skills, staff utilization skills, and configurations of external group support and opposition.

H9   Subcommittees that experience low rates of chair, member, and key staff turnover are more successful in achieving objectives than are committees with high turnover rates. Most crucial of the three is chairperson tenure.

H10   Committees in which integration is achieved through extensive multiple exposures of colleagues to each other through subcommittees are least likely to need central control. Socialization effects and opportunities for logrolling facilitate the conduct of legislative business. Chairs can function as brokers.

It should be obvious that a number of the hypotheses above are potentially interactive with each other and could be formulated in such a fashion as to generate complex, contingent statements that cohere in the form of a model. We must demur from such an effort at this time because of a limited data base. Several of the hypotheses lend themselves to fairly straightforward tests (for example, numbers 1 and 9); most others require extensive interviewing and observation en route to much more precise reformulation; a few may not even deserve to be called hypotheses but are so central to an effort to understand the phenomena that they must be given consideration.

As this project has progressed and this study has been written, we have come to feel rather like very small lumberjacks amid some very large trees in the "forest" of congressional research about which Rieselbach (1983) has so perceptively written. Perhaps a collective scholarly effort will enable us to convert some of the fallen timber to a livable structure.

REFERENCES

Bach, S. 1984. "Membership, Committees, and Change in the House of Representatives." Paper prepared for delivery at Annual Meetings of the American Political Science Association, Washington, D.C.

Clausen, A. 1973. *How Congressmen Decide*. New York: St. Martin's Press.

Cohodas, N. 1984. "From Activist to Obstructionist: Peter Rodino Turns Judiciary into a Legislative Graveyard." *Congressional Quarterly Weekly Report* 42 (12 May): 1097–1102.

Davidson, R. 1981. "Subcommittee Government: New Channels for Policymaking." In *The New Congress*, edited by T. Mann and N. Ornstein. Washington, D.C.: American Enterprise Institute, 99–133.

Dodd, L. 1983. "The Legislative Imperative: Building Broad-gauged Theory." Paper prepared for delivery at Annual Meetings of the American Political Science Association, Chicago.

Dodd, L., and B. Oppenheimer. 1981. "The House in Transition: Change and Consolidation." In *Congress Reconsidered*, 2d ed., edited by L. Dodd and B. Oppenheimer. Washington, D.C.: Congressional Quarterly, 31–61.

Fenno, R. 1966. *The Power of the Purse*. Boston: Little, Brown.

———. 1973. *Congressmen in Committee*. Boston: Little, Brown.

Glennon, M. 1984. "Democrats' Panel Defends More for Defense." *Congressional Quarterly Weekly Report* 42 (31 Mar.): 729–36.

Granat, D. 1983. "Byzantine World, Cramped Clubhouse: House Appropriations Panel Doles Out Cold Federal Cash, Chafes at Budget Procedures." *Congressional Quarterly Weekly Report* 41 (18 June): 1209–21.

Kingdon, J. 1981. *Congressmen's Voting Decisions*, 2d ed. New York: Harper and Row.

Malbin, M. 1980. *Unelected Representatives: Congressional Staff and the Future of Representative Government*. New York: Basic Books.

Maraniss, D. 1983. "Power Struggle Splits Democrats on Energy Panel." *Washington Post* 17 May, pp. A1, A8.

Ornstein, N. 1975. "Causes and Consequences of Congressional Change: Subcommittee Reforms in the House of Representatives." In *Congress in Change*, edited by N. Ornstein. New York: Praeger, 88–114.

Ray, B. 1982. "Committee Attractiveness in the U.S. House, 1980–1981." *American Journal of Political Science* 26 (Aug.): 609–13.

Rieselbach, L. 1983. "The Forest for the Trees: Blazing Trails for Congressional Research." In *Political Science: The State of the Discipline*, edited by A. Finifter. Washington, D.C.: American Political Science Association, 155–88.

Rohde, D., and K. Shepsle. 1973. "Democratic Committee Assignments in the House of Representatives." *American Political Science Review* 67: 889–905.

Schick, A. 1980. *Congress and Money*. Washington, D.C.: Urban Institute.

Schneider, J. 1979. *Ideological Coalitions in Congress*. Westport, Conn.: Greenwood Press.

Schrage, M. 1983. "Wirth Moves to Keep Control of TV Measure." *Washington Post*, 21 May, pp. G10–11.

Shepsle, K. 1978. *The Giant Jigsaw Puzzle*. Chicago: University of Chicago Press.

Sinclair, B. 1983. "Purposive Behavior in the U.S. Congress: A Review Essay." *Legislative Studies Quarterly* 8 (Feb.): 117–31.

Smith, S., and C. Deering. 1982. "Majority Party Leadership and the New House Subcommittee System, In *Understanding Congressional Leadership*, edited by F. Mackaman. Washington, D.C.: Congressional Quarterly, 261–92.

Smith, S., and C. Deering. 1984. *Committees in Congress*. Washington, D.C.: Congressional Quarterly.

Whiteman, D. 1983. "A Theory of Congressional Organization: Committee Size in the U.S. House of Representatives." *American Politics Quarterly* 11 (Jan.): 49–70.

Chapter 7

Committees

NORMAN J. ORNSTEIN,
THOMAS E. MANN,
and MICHAEL J. MALBIN

This chapter provides information on Congressional committees and chairmanships from 1955 to 1989. Tables 7-1 and 7-2 chart the ebb and flow in the number of committees and subcommittees. It should be noted that the number of subcommittees in a given Congress is a particularly nebulous figure. During any Congress, subcommittees are added or disappear, and some ad hoc or special units may be listed or omitted from the various directories. At least two sources were consulted for each Congress to obtain the number of subcommittees.

Tables 7-1 and 7-2 show an erratic but persistent growth in the number of House panels since the 1950s through the Ninety-fourth Congress (1975–76), with some stabilization and decline evident in the Ninety-sixth and Ninety-eighth Congresses. Since then, very little change has occurred, with the exception of a slight rise in the number of subcommittees. A very different recent pattern for the Senate is revealed in table 7-1. As a result of that body's successful committee reorganization in 1977, the number of panels, particularly subcommittees, was cut dramatically—from an overall 205 in 1975–76 to 130 in 1979–80. Whereas the House and Senate had an equivalent number of panels in 1975, the House in 1980 had a clear numerical superiority. In the Ninety-seventh Senate—controlled by Republicans—the number of panels rose from its

This chapter was originally published as "Committees," in Norman J. Ornstein, Thomas E. Mann, and Michael J. Malbin, eds., *Vital Statistics on Congress, 1989–1990* (Washington, D.C.: Congressional Quarterly, 1990), chap. 4. Several Senate tables have been omitted. It is reprinted by permission.

Table 7-1. Number of Committees in the House and the Senate,
84th–101st Congresses, 1955–1990

Congress	Senate	House	Total [a]
84th (1955–56)	133	130	242
90th (1967–68)	155	185	315
92d (1971–72)	181	175	333
94th (1975–76)	205	204	385
96th (1979–80)	130	193	314
97th (1981–82)	136	174	300
99th (1983–84)	137	172	299
98th (1985–86)	120	191	301
100th (1987–88)	118	192	298
101st (1989–90)	118	189	295

Sources: Charles B. Brownson, *Congressional Staff Directory* (Washington, D.C.:
Congressional Staff Directory, various years); *Congressional Quarterly Almanac*
(Washington, D.C.: Congressional Quarterly, various years); *Congressional Yellow Book*
(Washington, D.C.: Monitor Publishing Co., quarterly editions).
Note: "Committees" includes standing committees, subcommittees of standing
committees, select and special committees, subcommittees of select and special
committees, joint committees, and subcommittees of joint committees.
[a] Total is less than Senate and House combined because joint panels are counted
only once.

previous base, but the numbers declined in the Ninety-ninth and One
Hundredth Senates. The House-Senate gap, as shown in table 7-1, is
sharper now than it has been in more than three decades.

Table 7-3 displays the average number of committee assignments of
representatives for the period from 1955 to 1990. House committee and
subcommittee assignments have more than doubled since the 1950s. In
1989 representatives had an average of 6.8 assignments each. Senate
assignments were cut back considerably with the 1977 reorganization,
from 17.6 on average in 1975 to 10.4 in 1980, but rose again to 11.1
in 1989. Assignment inflation is a persistent phenomenon in the Senate;
note that even with the dramatic decrease since 1975, senators still average
nearly twice as many assignments as their House counterparts.

Table 7-4 examines chairmanships of committees and subcommittees
in the House. Table 7-4 shows that the proportion of majority party
House members with chairmanships of one sort or another rose steadily
in the 1960s and 1970s, and this figure has stabilized at about 50 percent
in the 1980s. The rise in the 1960s was a direct result of the increase in
the number of committees and subcommittees (see table 7-1).

Even though the number of panels declined between 1967 and 1971,
the number and proportion of Democrats chairing them increased. This
was the result of a 1971 Democratic reform that limited members to the

Table 7-2. *Number and Type of House Committees, 84th–101st Congresses, 1955–1990*

Congress	Standing Committees	Subcommittees of Standing Committees	Select and Special Committees	Subcommittees of Select and Special Committees	Joint Committees	Subcommittees of Joint Committees
84th (1955–56)	19	83	2	5	10	11
90th (1967–68)	20	133	1	6	10	15
92d (1971–72)	21	120	3	8	8	15
94th (1975–76)	22	151	3	4	7	17
96th (1979–80)	22	149[a]	5	8	4	5
97th (1981–82)	22	132	3	7	4	6
98th (1983–84)	22	130	3	7	4	6
99th (1985–86)	22	142	5	12	4	6
100th (1987–88)	22	140[b]	6	12	4	8
101st (1989–90)	22	138[b]	5	12	4	8

Sources: Brownson, *Congressional Staff Directory; Congressional Quarterly Almanac; Congressional Yellow Book.*

[a] Includes nine budget task forces and the Welfare and Pension Plans Task Force (of the Subcommittee on Labor Management Relations of the Education and Labor Committee).

[b] Includes panels and task forces only if committee has no subcommittees.

Table 7-3. *Committee Assignments for Representatives, 84th–101st Congresses, 1955–1990*

Congress	Mean No. Standing Committee Assignments	Mean No. Subcommittees of Standing Committee Assignments	Mean No. Other Committee Assignments [a]	Total
84th (1955–56)	1.2	1.6	0.2	3.0
92d (1971–72)	1.5	3.2	0.4	5.1
94th (1975–76)	1.8	4.0	0.4	6.2
96th (1979–80)	1.7	3.6	0.5	5.8
97th (1981–82)	1.7	3.4	0.4	5.5
98th (1983–84)	1.7	3.6	0.5	5.8
99th (1985–86)	1.8	4.0	0.8	6.6
100th (1987–88)	1.7	3.8	1.0[b]	6.5
101st (1989–90)	1.8	3.9	1.1[b]	6.8

Sources: Brownson, *Congressional Staff Directory*; *Congressional Quarterly Almanac*; *Congressional Yellow Book*.
[a] "Other" committees include select and special committees, subcommittees of select and special committees, joint committees, and subcommittees of joint committees.
[b] Includes task forces when committee has no other subcommittees.

chairmanship of only one subcommittee. The numbers of members with more than one chairmanship declined accordingly, and for the first time more than half the majority party members held chairmanships of one kind or another. The number holding multiple chairmanships of any sort fell somewhat through 1982, then rose substantially in 1983 and jumped again in 1985 and 1987. Apparently the norm against "stockpiling" chairmanships has relaxed.

Table 7-5 provides insights into the causes and consequences of seniority reforms in the 1970s, in the House of Representatives in particular. In the 1950s and early 1960s, Democrats from the Deep South constituted a near majority of their party, but they held an even greater share of committee chairmanships. Their overall strength in numbers, however, discouraged any challenge to the system of selecting chairmen by nonsoutherners who opposed the system's unrepresentative results. By the late 1960s, the South's share of the Democratic party in Congress was on the wane, but its hold on chairmanships of committees, especially the most powerful committees, was more tenacious. The declining number of southern members facilitated a change in the seniority pattern for the selection of chairman in 1971. After this reform and the dramatic ouster of three southern chairmen in December 1974, the figures changed mark-

Table 7-4. *Majority Party Chairmanships of House Committees and Subcommittees, 84th–101st Congresses, 1955–1990*

Congress	Party in Majority	No. Majority Party Members in House	No. Chairing Standing Committees and Sub-committees	No. with 2 or more Chair-manships	% Chairing Standing Committees and Sub-committees	No. Chairing All Committees and Sub-committees [a]	No. with 2 or More Chair-manships	% Chairing All Committees and Sub-committees [a]
84th (1955–56)	D	232	63	18	27.2	75	22	32.3
90th (1967–68)	D	247	111	32	44.9	117	38	47.4
92d (1971–72)	D	254	120	25	47.2	131	31	51.6
94th (1975–76)	D	289	142	24	49.1	150	28	51.9
96th (1979–80)	D	276	144	19	52.2	149	28	54.0
97th (1981–82)	D	243	121	16	49.8	125	26	51.4
98th (1983–84)	D	267	124	23	46.4	127	33	47.6
99th (1985–86)	D	253	129	27	51.0	131	37	51.8
100th (1987–88)	D	258	128	28	49.6	132[b]	42	51.2
101st (1989–90)	D	260	134	26	51.5	137	38	52.7

Sources: Brownson, *Congressional Staff Directory*; *Congressional Quarterly Almanac.*

[a] Includes standing committees, subcommittees of standing committees, select and special committees, subcommittees of select and special committees, joint committees, and subcommittees of joint committees.

[b] Includes task forces when committee has no other subcommittees.

Table 7-5. *Southern Chairmanships of House and Senate Standing, 1955–1989*

	House				Senate			
Year	No. Southern Chairmen	% Chairmanships Held by Southerners	% 3 Exclusive Committees [a] Chaired by Southerners	% Majority Party [b] from the South	No. Southern Chairmen	% Chairmanships Held by Southerners	% Exclusive Committees [a] Chaired by Southerners	% Majority Party [b] from the South
1955	12	63	67	43	8	53	50	46
1967	10	50	100	35	9	56	100	28
1971	8	38	100	31	9	53	100	30
1975	9	41	33	28	6	33	100	27
1979	5	23	33	28	4	27	50	28
1981	6	27	33	29	3	20	25	19
1983	7	32	67	30	3	19	25	20
1985	8	36	67	29	2	13	0	19
1987	7	31	67	29	7	44	75	30
1989	8	40	67	29	6	38	50	27

Sources: *Congressional Directory* (Washington, D.C.: Government Printing Office, 1955, 1971, 1975, 1979, 1981, 1983, 1985, and 1987); *Congressional Yellow Book.*

[a] In the House: Ways and Means, Rules, and Appropriations; in the Senate: Appropriations, Finance, Foreign Relations, and Armed Services.

[b] In 1981, 1983, and 1985 the Republicans were the majority party in the Senate. For all other years in the table, Democrats were the majority party in both the Senate and the House.

edly. By 1979 southerners were underrepresented in committee chair-manships, and while they have steadily regained power in the 1980s, southerners are far from the disproportionate share of House chairman-ships they held in the 1950s and 1960s.

Chapter 8

Congressional Committee Leadership, 1971–1978

JOSEPH K. UNEKIS
and LEROY N. RIESELBACH

"Leadership," James MacGregor Burns writes (1978, 2), "is one of the most observed and least understood phenomena on earth." Nowhere is this more the case than in the U.S. Congress and particularly in congressional committees. According to current conventional wisdom, the committees and their subcommittees are the preeminent legislative decisionmakers; yet very little is known about the ways committee leaders operate and the effects their actions generate. While there are some insightful case studies of particular legislative leaders (see, for example, Manley 1970, chap. 4, on Wilbur Mills), there have been few systematic, comparative analyses of committee leadership. We seek, in this chapter, to begin to fill this vacuum in the literature.

In the congressional context at least, leadership is a reciprocal relationship between leaders and followers. The former presumably initiate the contacts to impel, induce, cajole, persuade, beg, influence, force, or otherwise move the latter to behave in ways the leaders desire. The relationship is reciprocal because leaders cannot compel compliance from

This chapter was originally published in *Legislative Studies Quarterly* 8 (May 1983): 251–70. Copyright © 1983 by the Legislative Research Center. It is reprinted by permission. It is a revision of a paper presented at the Everett McKinley Dirksen Congressional Leadership Research Center—Sam Rayburn Library Conference, Understanding Congressional Leadership: The State of the Art, Washington, D.C., 10–11 June 1980. The authors gratefully acknowledge the valuable advice, to which they did not always consent, of Edward G. Carmines, Lawrence C. Dodd, and James H. Kuklinski. Kansas State and Indiana Universities generously supported the project of which this essay was a part.

their followers; they must, therefore, consider what the followers will accept. The famous "law of anticipated reactions" applies as leaders ask for things they have some reasonable expectation—given the followers' beliefs and independence—of achieving. Congressional committee leadership is, to use Burns's (1978) term, "transactional," involving an exchange which enables both leaders and followers to gain some acceptable result.[1]

Assessing committee leadership is all the more difficult because, as Fenno (1973; see also Price 1981) has taught us, committees vary considerably. They differ with respect to their members' goals, the environmental constraints within which they operate, the decision-making premises they develop, and (most important for present purposes) the decision-making structures they establish. Because they differ, committees limit their members, including their ostensible leaders, differently.[2] "Whatever [their] personal characteristics, temperamental or ideological, this context puts limits on the kind of behavior [they] can engage in and still retain . . . leadership, and it sets forth positive guidelines for . . . success and effectiveness inside the Committee" (Fenno 1973, 133).[3]

There are two linkages which, theoretically, need investigation. First, we want to know to what extent committee attributes are associated with committee leadership patterns. Are there identifiable antecedent conditions—the members' motives, the committee's environment, its decision-making rules—that incline committees to adopt particular leadership styles? Do, for instance, committees that operate in homogeneous environments (e.g., Ways and Means) display different forms of leadership than those that confront a more heterogeneous set of external forces (e.g., Education and Labor)? Second, we want to know whether committees with distinctive leadership patterns perform in distinctive ways. If there exist clear patterns of committee leadership, are there equally clear consequences for committee performance associated with particular patterns? Do committees with a given type of leadership win full House approval for the legislation they report more often or more easily than panels with contrasting leadership forms? A full theory of committee leadership would explain both the causes and consequences of leadership patterns. In this chapter, we begin to construct such a theory. We use committee roll-call data to identify the chairperson's place in the overall committee voting patterns, to chart the changes in leadership positions that occur over time, and to assess the relationship of leadership posture to committee performance.

PATTERNS OF COMMITTEE LEADERSHIP

We define first the place of the formal committee leader, the chairman,[4] in the factional structure of his committee. We want to know whether the chairman votes with major factions in committee or with major partisan, regional, or ideological groupings. Drawing on studies of political parties, we anticipate three possible patterns of committee leader behavior:

1. The Extremity Pattern. One leadership strategy is to mobilize a dominant majority party faction. Leaders will, according to this view, "tend to occupy the extreme ends of the ideological continuum" (Patterson 1963, 404; see also MacRae 1956). In the congressional setting, with Democratic majorities, the extremity hypothesis predicts that the chairman will rally liberal Democrats to his cause, to assemble a majority coalition that draws heavily on the liberal wing of his party. Conversely, this hypothesis predicts that the chairman will agree sometimes with any nonextreme voting blocs within his own party and seldom with the ranking minority member, members of ideologically opposed voting clusters, the opposition party generally, and conservatives.

2. The Partisan-Middleman Pattern. Truman's analysis (1959, chap. 6) of party leaders suggests a second pattern of committee leadership: chairmen may, by taking a centrist stance within their parties, try to unify members of their own party on the committee (for corroborative evidence, see MacRae 1958). Because the middleman tactic is still basically partisan, the committee leader who pursues it is likely to disagree often with the ranking minority member, members of the opposition (as individuals and in factions), and dissimilar ideologues.

3. The Bipartisan-Consensual Pattern. A third possibility (Fenno 1973, chap. 4) is leadership through consensus. Here the chairperson will try to build general support for committee positions, drawing votes from wherever they are available. In such circumstances, the chair may belong to a broad bipartisan faction or may avoid identification with any single bloc, preferring to work with all members. In addition, he should avoid commitment to any ideological element within the committee.

In searching for evidence of these leadership patterns, we cannot resolve a complex problem of causality. Roll-call data do not permit us to say whether leader behavior creates or reflects a committee's ways of conducting business. For example, it is entirely possible that some leaders take an extremist stance because their committees consist mainly of liberal members; that is, the leaders conform or adapt to ongoing committee patterns. Other chairmen may simply share an ideological perspective with the members; that is, their views naturally coincide with those of the committee majority. Still others may steer their rank and file toward liberal voting; that is, they actually lead the committee. Leaders may also assert their independence, voting consistently with no single set of committee members. In fact, there is in our data a clear relationship between leadership style[5] and committee liberalism. Partisan-extremist chairpersons presided over committees whose Democratic majorities averaged 18.8 on the Americans for Constitutional Action scale (see Appendix); Democrats on committees with partisan-middleman and bipartisan leadership were less liberal, averaging 28.8 and 37.6, respectively, on the ACA measure. All we can say is that leadership and member preference are related; we do not pretend to be able to specify cause and effect clearly. Nonetheless, in the absence of any systematic, comparative evidence about leadership styles, we believe that it is valuable, as a first step, simply to describe the extent to which chairmen vote with various rank-and-file elements on their committees, regardless of the direction that influence runs.

METHODS OF ANALYSIS

We have the data to establish these patterns because the Legislative Reorganization Act of 1970 mandated that congressional committees record and make available their roll-call votes. These votes provide a glimpse into the inner workings of individual committees: they permit definition of the factional structure of the committees, and if assessed separately for each Congress, they allow observation of change that external events, personnel change, or specific reforms may generate.[6] We describe our methods in detail in the Appendix but will do so briefly here. Using cluster-bloc procedures, we identify voting factions on each committee in each Congress. Next, using Pearsonian correlation coefficients (r) and interagreement (IA) scores, we define the chairperson's position with respect to these voting clusters as well as to party groups (all Republicans, all Democrats, and northern Democrats separately) and ideological groups (liberals, conservatives, and the Conservative Coalition). We also note the chair's agreement with the ranking minority member. These measures enable us to locate the committee leader within the committee's decision-making structure.

Each leadership pattern suggests a distinctive array of interagreement scores. The extremity pattern predicts strong agreement (interagreement scores that approach or exceed .40) between the leader and the groups that support him; it predicts low (generally negative) agreement between the leader and opposition elements on the committee. Voting on the House Education and Labor Committee in the Ninety-second Congress (table 8-1, column 1) illustrates clearly the extremity pattern. The panel chair, Carl Perkins (D., Ky.), belonged (IA = .50) to a thirteen-member, liberal[7] (Americans for Constitutional Action score = 11), Democratic bloc (cluster 1). He was associated (IA = .32) with a slightly more moderate (ACA = 14) group of three Democrats (cluster 3). His relations with potentially supportive factions on Education and Labor were cordial; his interagreement scores with all Democrats, liberals, and northern Democrats, were .42, .31, and .43, respectively. Conversely, Perkins disagreed (IA = −.26) regularly with the eleven-member conservative (ACA = 68) Republican bloc (cluster 2), with all Republicans (IA = −.24), conservatives (IA = −.18), the conservative coalition (IA = −.20), and Albert Quie (R., Minn.), the ranking minority member (IA = −.38). In short, Chairman Perkins and the liberal Democrats fought the conservative GOP contingent on an Education and Labor Committee polarized along partisan-ideological lines.

The partisan-middleman pattern also predicts distinctive voting alignments. Since the middleman strategy calls for mobilizing all the chairperson's partisans, the leader should display moderately positive agreement (IA scores of .20 to .35) with all his potential backers and moderately negative agreement (IA scores from −.10 to −.20) with the opposition. Compared with the extremist, the middleman should be more centrally located within his own party and less ardently opposed to the minority members. The House Interstate and Foreign Commerce Committee in the Ninety-fourth Congress presents a typical picture of the middleman pattern (table 8-1, column 2). Harley Staggers (D., W.Va.), the chair, joined a small (n = 3), moderately liberal Democratic bloc (cluster 3). He maintained positive relations with a large liberal Democratic faction (cluster 2) and with a smaller, more moderate group (cluster 4) of fellow partisans. In addition, he voted regularly with all Democrats, liberals, and northern Democrats. Simultaneously, he opposed the nine-member (cluster 1), conservative Republican bloc and voted against all Republicans, conservatives, the Conservative Coalition, and the ranking minority member—Samuel Devine of Ohio—more often than not. In sum, Staggers was a typical middleman: centrally placed in his own party, regularly but moderately opposed to the minority.

Finally, the bipartisan-consensual pattern presents a contrasting picture, which the House Government Operations Committee in the Ninety-second Congress typifies (table 8-1, column 3). The committee chair, Chet Holifield (D., Calif.), displayed the predicted nonpartisan posture: moderate, positive levels of agreement (generally, IA = .10 to .30) with

Table 8-1. Leadership Patterns and Voting Clusters for Selected House Committees

Variable	Extremity: Education and Labor (92d Cong.)			Partisan-Middleman: Interstate and Foreign Commerce (94th Cong.)				Bipartisan-Consensual: Government Operations (92d Cong.)					
	Cluster Number			Cluster Number				Cluster Number					
	1	2	3	1	2	3	4	1	2	3	4	5	6
Cluster attributes													
Size	13	11	3	9	13	3	4	12	7	8	2	2	3
Percentage of Democrats	100	00	100	00	100	100	100	25	100	75	00	100	100
Average ACA score	11	68	14	84	07	29	20	58	38	13	94	09	21
Chairman's average voting correlation with cluster	.50	−.26	.32	−.25	.27	.45	.25	.74	.12	.31	.14	−.46	.27
Chairman's average voting correlation with committee members who are:													
Democrats		.42				.24					.24		
Republicans		−.24				−.22					.52		
Liberals		.31				.26					.32		
Conservatives		−.18				−.19					.41		
Conservative Coalition		−.20				−.10					.38		
Northern Democrats		.43				.26					.30		
Ranking minority member		−.38				−.26					1.00		
Number of roll calls		99				105					13		

all committee groupings on both sides of the aisle. Specifically, he was a member of a large bipartisan (three Democrats, nine Republicans) moderate cluster (cluster 1). In addition, he regularly voted with a second bipartisan (six Democrats, two Republicans) but more liberal faction (cluster 3). Holifield also agreed more often than not with the major moderate Democratic faction (cluster 2), with a conservative Republican pair (cluster 4), and with a three-member liberal Democratic group (cluster 6).[8] He sided frequently, moreover, with each partisan and ideological grouping within the committee, with interagreement scores ranging from .24 to .52. And, emblematic of bipartisan harmony, Holifield and Florence Dwyer (R., N.J.), the ranking minority member, voted together on each Government Operations roll call (IA = 1.O). Overall, consensus that crossed party lines prevailed on the committee.

We search for the extremity, middleman, and bipartisan-consensual leadership patterns on the nine committees in the House that took a minimum of ten recorded roll calls in the first four Congresses after the 1970 Reorganization Act (the Ninety-second through the Ninety-fifth). This criterion provides sufficient roll calls for us to identify factional alignments within each. Moreover, it gives us a set of varied committees: two are exclusive (Rules; Ways and Means), five are semiexclusive (Agriculture; Armed Services; Banking, Finance, and Urban Affairs; Education and Labor; Interstate and Foreign Commerce), and two are nonexclusive (Government Operations; Post Office). Finally, and most important for present purposes, these committees include some on which leaders survived the decade (Education and Labor; Commerce), some characterized by "normal," evolutionary leadership change (Government Operations; Post Office; Rules), and some that experienced more violent leadership upheavals (Agriculture; Armed Services; Banking; Ways and Means).

We seek to define the chairman's voting stance within each of nine committees with reference to two kinds of data: (1) an empirically determined (with cluster-bloc techniques) set of committee factions and (2) a group of party, regional, and ideological categories commonly used in roll-call studies. These data are represented in the upper and lower portions of table 8-1, respectively. Space limitations preclude our presenting both sets of data for all nine committees in each of the four Congresses; because they provide a somewhat fuller portrait of the leader-follower voting agreement, we present in full (in table 8-2) the second kind. The relationship between chairman and bloc is, in every instance, consistent with the data we present and requires no qualification of the arguments we advance.[9]

FINDINGS: THE DISTRIBUTION OF LEADERSHIP PATTERNS

Empirically, these committees and their leaders fall readily into one or another of the three patterns previously identified. Table 8-2 presents our categorization of each committee and the interagreement scores between the chairperson and the groups defined by party and ideology on which that categorization rests. In thirty-four of the thirty-six cases (nine committees in each of four Congresses), the assignment of the chairperson to extremity, middleman, or bipartisan-consensual pattern is relatively straightforward. Only the Post Office and Civil Service Committee under David Henderson (D., N.C.) in the Ninety-fourth Congress did not display one of the hypothesized configurations. The Interstate and Foreign Commerce Committee, Ninety-second Congress, was excluded from the analysis because Chairman Harley Staggers voted on less than 60 percent of the roll calls (see Appendix). Subsequent discussion deals with the thirty-four assignable cases.

These data on the nine House committees suggest, once again, the rich variety of committee behavioral patterns, warning anew against easy generalizing about congressional committees. There are, over four Congresses, numerous instances of each of the specified leadership postures. Committee chairpersons display extremity (eight cases, 24 percent of the cases), middleman (fifteen cases, 44 percent), and bipartisan-consensual (eleven cases, 32 percent) positions relative to their committee colleagues. They may create these alignments through leadership or they may conform to existing configurations, but in any case they fit clearly into identifiable committee voting alignments.

In addition, these results reveal both the nonrandom distribution of leadership styles and the differential impact of change, intended or otherwise, on individual committees. Four panels—Armed Services, Banking, Education and Labor, and Commerce—displayed constant leadership patterns across the four Congresses. This is not unexpected for the latter two: their respective chairs, Perkins and Staggers, served throughout the period and seemingly adhered to consistent styles of leadership. But for Armed Services and Banking, change might well have been predicted. In the aftermath of Watergate, the Republicans suffered grievously at the polls in the 1974 midterm elections, and the seventy-five predominantly liberal freshman Democrats who took seats in the Ninety-fourth Congress contributed mightily to their party caucus's purge of three senior, southern committee chairmen (Hinckley 1976; Parker 1979). This stunning coup, a sharp break with the virtually inviolate seniority norm, claimed Chairmen F. Edward Hebert (D., La.) of Armed Services and Wright Patman

Table 8-2. Interagreement Scores: Committee Chairmen with Committee Groups

Committee, Congress, and Chairman	Leadership Style[a]	Committee Groups							
		DEM	REP	LIB	CON	CC	NDEM	RMIN	(N)
Agriculture									
92d, Poage	M	.52	−.08	.44	.16	.20	.44	−.21	(11)
93d, Poage	B	.21	.05	.10	.16	.16	.06	−.29[b]	(48)
94th, Foley	M	.11	−.17	.22	−.19	−.13	.25	−.19	(75)
95th, Foley	M	.33	−.18	.26	.06	.08	.31	−.10	(61)
Armed Services									
92d, Hebert	B	.28	.27	.23	.30	.29	.24	.72	(34)
93d, Hebert	B	.39	.42	.24	.49	.50	.18	.48	(25)
94th, Price	B	.09	.23	−.04	.23	.22	−.01	.06	(22)
95th, Price	B	.13	.07	.13	.09	.07	.17	−.04	(28)
Banking									
92d, Patman	M	.15	−.14	.15	−.10	.10	.18	−.04	(149)
93d, Patman	M	.28	−.04	.25	−.05	.03	.31	−.13	(117)
94th, Reuss	M	.25	−.09	.22	−.06	.01	.25	−.16	(80)
95th, Reuss	M	.18	−.09	.17	−.07	−.05	.21	−.06	(103)
Education and Labor									
92d, Perkins	E	.42	−.24	.31	−.18	−.20	.43	−.38	(99)
93d, Perkins	E	.35	.01	.27	−.06	.07	.35	−.12	(64)
94th, Perkins	E	.36	−.19	.31	−.12	−.14	.36	−.25	(44)
95th, Perkins	E	.33	−.26	.24	−.27	−.26	.33	−.31	(79)
Government Operations									
92d, Holifield	B	.24	.52	.32	.41	.38	.30	1.00	(13)
93d, Holifield	B	.20	.19	.21	.18	.19	.22	.75	(18)
94th, Brooks	E	.26	−.46	.22	−.31	−.23	.31	−.40	(16)
95th, Brooks	M	.18	−.19	.17	−.10	−.03	.18	.32	(38)
Commerce									
92d, Staggers[c]									(25)
93d, Staggers	M	.15	−.11	.14	−.07	−.03	.14	−.20	(51)
94th, Staggers	M	.24	−.22	.26	−.19	−.10	.26	−.26	(105)
95th, Staggers	M	.14	−.19	.14	−.18	−.11	.18	−.28	(65)
Post Office									
92d, Dulski	B	.34	.12	.34	.19	.19	.34	.10	(23)
93d, Dulski	M	.45	−.18	.37	−.04	−.06	.52	−.47	(19)
94th, Henderson	U	−.01	.09	.03	.01	.03	.02	.02	(16)
95th, Nix	M	.26	−.19	.20	−.14	−.07	.27	−.06	(59)
Rules									
92d, Colmer	B	.03	.28	.02	.22	.22	−.02	.32	(21)
93d, Madden	E	.31	−.34	.21	−.40	.07	.33	−.25	(86)
94th, Madden	E	.34	−.45	.30	−.53	−.08	.31	−.52	(99)
95th, Delaney	E	.32	−.40	.24	−.57	−.13	.32	−.52	(65)
Ways and Means									
92d, Mills	B	.21	.44	.22	.38	.34	.25	.43	(32)

Continued on next page

Table 8-2—Continued

Committee, Congress, and Chairman	Leadership Style[a]	Committee Groups							
		DEM	REP	LIB	CON	CC	NDEM	RMIN	(N)
93d, Mills	B	.15	−.01	.20	−.02	.01	.20	−.05	(75)
94th, Ullman	M	.28	−.19	.36	−.11	.07	.35	−.00	(235)
95th, Ullman	M	.21	−.08	.25	−.04	.03	.25	.05	(161)

[a] E, extremity, M, middleman, B, bipartisan, U, unclassified.
[b] Teague (Calif.) was replaced as ranking minority member by Wampler (Va.) during the Ninety-third Congress. Poage/Wampler correlation = .24.
[c] Staggers participated in less than 60 percent of the roll-call votes during the Ninety-second Congress.

(D., Tex.) of Banking as victims. However, their successors, Melvin Price (D., Ill.) and Henry Reuss (D., Wis.), assumed the same leadership postures—bipartisan-consensual and middleman, respectively—as their ousted predecessors. These two cases underscore the reciprocal character of committee leadership. Chairmen do not possess unrestricted influence. Rather, the leadership they exercise must be consistent with their members' goals and the committee's decision-making premises and structures; where these do not change, the chairman may find his opportunity to lead severely constrained.

Two committees show a single change over the 1971–78 period: in each case, a new leader, operating under conditions of reform-induced uncertainty and upheaval, adopted a leadership stance at variance with that of his predecessor and followed it faithfully thereafter. On Rules in the Ninety-second Congress, William Colmer (D., Miss.), the last of the southern conservatives to hold the chair, followed a bipartisan strategy. Following his retirement, in 1973, the chair fell into liberal hands. Simultaneously, the Speaker of the House won new powers that enabled him to harness the committee firmly to the party (Oppenheimer 1977). In consequence, the new chairmen—Ray Madden (D., N.Y.) in the Ninety-third and John J. Delaney (D., N.Y.) in the Ninety-fifth—assumed extremity positions, joining the committee liberals against the conservative committee minority.

The change on Ways and Means was equally dramatic. Wilbur Mills was the epitome of the bipartisan-consensual leader in the Ninety-second and Ninety-third Congresses, but even he was not immune to the reform fervor of the 1970s. The reformers, during this period, had begun to chip away at committee prerogatives; most importantly, the closed rule— long the protector of Ways and Means legislation—was modified. At the start of the Ninety-fourth Congress, after his fling with his femme fatale,

Fanne Fox, Mills declined to seek reelection as chairman, and the caucus cracked down on the committee. It transferred the party's committee assignment responsibilities to the Steering and Policy Committee, it enlarged Ways and Means from twenty-five to thirty-seven members and appointed freshmen where only seniors had served previously, and it required the committee to create subcommittees. The committee, under its new chairman, Al Ullman (D., Ore.) was unable to restrain partisanship; consensus eluded it. Instead, Ullman adopted a middleman position, attempting (with mixed success) to hold the committee Democrats together (see Rudder 1978). The Rules and Ways and Means experiences, in contrast to those of Armed Services and Banking, suggest that under some circumstances change—of chairmen, rules, and/or external conditions—may mandate altered leadership styles.

The remaining three committees reveal more variability still. Agriculture Chairman W. R. Poage (D., Tex.) abandoned a middleman position for bipartisanship in the Ninety-third Congress; but Thomas Foley (D., Wash.), who won the chair in 1975 following Poage's ouster, reverted to the former in the Ninety-fourth and Ninety-fifth Congresses. On Government Operations in the Ninety-fourth and Ninety-fifth Congresses, Jack Brooks (D., Tex.) tried both extremity and middleman strategies after the period of bipartisan consensus that had prevailed under Chet Holifield. And a succession of chairmen took middleman and bipartisan stances on Post Office during the 1970s.

In sum, these data reveal that identifiable extremity, middleman, and bipartisan-consensual leadership patterns regularly appear on House committees. Moreover, committees vary considerably in the extent to which their leaders adhere to particular patterns or alter their positions in response to changing committee circumstances. Leadership emerges as a complex and fluid set of interactions between chairman and rank-and-file members, interactions that reflect both factors peculiar to single committees and changes in the broader environment of the House and American national politics. At the very least, these varying patterns underscore the value of Congress-by-Congress, committee-by-committee analysis.

RESULTS: COMMITTEE LEADERSHIP AND COMMITTEE PERFORMANCE

Differing leadership patterns take on added significance to the extent that they help explain committee behavior. Does it really matter whether committee chairpersons adopt extremity, middleman, or bipartisan-consensual positions? Even a preliminary answer to this, our second question, is a complicated matter. External events (e.g., the "subcommittee bill of rights") and personnel turnover (e.g., the large, liberal class of 1974) may impinge on individual committees in different ways (Ornstein and Rohde 1977; Rohde and Shepsle 1978). Despite these complexities, we can formulate some expectations about the relationship between leadership style and committee performance, specifically between the chairperson's stance and committee partisanship, committee integration, and committee floor success (for our measures of these factors, see the Appendix). We test these expectations both with aggregate comparisons and with an examination of individual committees.

One obvious hypothesis links leadership and partisanship. The extremity posture and strong partisanship should be closely related. A chairman voting with partisan ideologues is likely to evoke strong reactions from the opposition; the committee should operate in an atmosphere of extreme partisanship. The middleman stance is also partisan, but because it is more moderate, encompassing a broader ideological range, it should be accompanied by less violent partisan animosity. Bipartisan-consensual committees, of course, mute party considerations and should be characterized by still lower levels of partisan conflict. In short, moving from extremity through middleman to bipartisan leadership styles should lead to a diminution of interparty cleavage.

Aggregate comparisons support this view. In the eight instances of leadership extremism (table 8-3, column 2), the level of party conflict averaged 77 percent. Comparable figures for the middleman panels (N = 15) and the consensual committees (N = 11) were 68 and 42 percent. Moreover, the student's t test for difference of means shows that these differences are statistically significant: extremist-middleman, $t = 4.30$, $p < .001$; extremist-bipartisan, $t = 10.94$, $p < .001$; middleman-bipartisan, $t = -8.68$, $p < .001$.

The data for individual committees also indicate a clear relationship between leadership style and committee partisanship (table 8-3, column 3). Committees with stable leadership patterns should see only marginal shifts in levels of partisanship from Congress to Congress; this appears to be the case for Education and Labor, Commerce, and Banking.[10] By contrast, changes in style and partisanship should covary: less extreme leadership (e.g., change from extremity to middleman, or from middleman to bipartisan patterns) should go with reduced partisan voting, and the converse should also be true. Government Operations, Post Office, Rules, Ways and Means, and Agriculture all perform consistently with the hypothesis. In short, the weight of the evidence strongly sustains the direct link between committee leadership patterns and committee partisanship.

We can also test a related hypothesis concerning committee party unity.

Table 8-3. Committee Leadership Style and Committee Performance

Committee, Congress, and Chairman	Leadership Style [a]	Committee Performance [b]			
		Partisan Votes (%)	Democratic Party Integration	Committee Floor Wins	
				(%)	(N)
Agriculture					
92d, Poage	M	55	.68	85	(27)
93d, Poage	B	52	.59	79	(42)
94th, Foley	M	68	.45	82	(34)
95th, Foley	M	70	.55	90	(40)
Armed Services					
92d, Hebert	B	12	.57	100	(36)
93d, Hebert	B	16	.46	91	(34)
94th, Price	B	23	.31	91	(33)
95th, Price	B	32	.30	94	(31)
Banking					
92d, Patman	M	61	.53	81	(31)
93d, Patman	M	44	.53	85	(53)
94th, Reuss	M	77	.66	89	(35)
95th, Reuss	M	50	.55	86	(51)
Education and Labor					
92d, Perkins	E	80	.66	71	(73)
93d, Perkins	E	69	.70	88	(91)
94th, Perkins	E	84	.76	89	(46)
95th, Perkins	E	75	.70	82	(88)
Government Operations					
92d, Holifield	B	77	.35	100	(8)
93d, Holifield	B	72	.60	92	(25)
94th, Brooks	E	100	.61	76	(21)
95th, Brooks	M	89	.57	91	(22)
Commerce					
92d, Staggers	—	—	—	—	—
93d, Staggers	M	78	.50	91	(96)
94th, Staggers	M	86	.63	85	(100)
95th, Staggers	M	83	.50	100	(48)
Post Office					
92d, Dulski	B	43	.61	100	(9)
93d, Dulski	M	74	.71	100	(15)
94th, Henderson	U	—	—	—	—
95th, Nix	M	66	.57	91	(33)
Rules					
92d, Colmer	B	48	.40	89	(56)
93d, Madden	E	71	.56	88	(123)
94th, Madden	E	76	.59	96	(95)
95th, Delaney	E	85	.64	96	(155)

Continued on next page

Table 8-3—Continued

Committee, Congress, and Chairman	Leadership Style [a]	Committee Performance [b]			
		Partisan Votes (%)	Democratic Party Integration	Committee Floor Wins	
				(%)	(N)
Ways and Means					
92d, Mills	B	34	.37	95	(22)
93d, Mills	B	55	.43	96	(23)
94th, Ullman	M	74	.46	84	(76)
95th, Ullman	M	62	.34	79	(62)

[a] E, extremity, M, middleman, B, bipartisan, U, unclassified.
[b] The measures for the committee performance variables are described in the Appendix.

For reasons analogous to those underlying the committee partisanship proposition, we predict that leadership style will relate to majority party (Democratic) cohesion. Extremity leadership seems to require a solid core of majority party ideologues, the middleman stance spans a wider partisan spectrum, and the bipartisan pattern actually crosses party lines. Moreover, the extremism pattern presupposes greater partisan polarization than others; this, in turn, should stimulate majority (and minority) unity. If so, then moving from extremity through middleman to bipartisan leadership styles should lead to decreasing Democratic party unity. Again, the aggregate data sustain the hypothesis: the Democrats on committees characterized by extremist leadership averaged an integration score of .65; those on panels where the chairman assumed a middleman posture averaged .51; and the majority of bipartisan panels averaged .46 on the integration measure.[11]

Here, too, the performance of individual committees provides evidence that sustains the proposition (table 8-3, column 4). The integration scores for consistent committees—Education and Labor, Commerce, and Banking—varied little from Congress to Congress.[12] Committee change also provides supporting evidence, but there are some exceptions. Rules presents the clearest case: the shift from Colmer's bipartisanship to the extremist stance of his more liberal successors was accompanied by the predicted rise in Democratic unity. The same tendency appears on other committees experiencing leadership change, particularly on Government Operations and Ways and Means, but also, with occasional deviation, on Post Office and Agriculture. The sum of the evidence strongly suggests a clear link between leadership style and committee integration.

A third hypothesis relates leadership to extracommittee performance, victory on the floor. Dyson and Soule (1970) find cohesive (integrated) committees to be the most successful on the floor, and we have suggested that leadership style is associated with party cohesion. It seems reasonable, in consequence, to infer that style may relate to floor performance on amendments and to final passage as well. If party conflicts are not resolved in committee, they may spill over onto the floor and lower the prospects for victory there. We predict, therefore, that partisan leadership—extreme or middleman variety—will be less successful on the floor than bipartisan strategies.

Once again, the aggregate figures tend to sustain our expectation: bipartisan committees have their position supported by a majority of the full House on 88.2 percent of all roll calls; the comparable figures for the committees with extremity and middleman leadership are 84 and 86 percent.[13] In addition, the Banking, Commerce, Armed Services, and Education and Labor Committees (those with invariant leadership patterns) had, as expected, quite stable records of floor success, although each of the latter two deviated once from the committee norm. Among committees that underwent change in leadership style, Government Operations and Ways and Means showed a concomitant drop in floor victories when they shifted to more partisan leadership. On the other hand, during the Congress in which the leadership of Agriculture or of Rules had a bipartisan pattern, those committees did not have more floor wins, as the hypothesis predicts. Again, though the evidence is certainly mixed, the relation of leadership to floor success seems worth serious consideration.

Overall, leadership seems related to committee performance on each of the three measures. Specifically, leadership style seems incontrovertibly linked to committee partisanship and at least related more than modestly to Democratic party integration on the committees and to the committees' success on the House floor. Leadership style, in short, tells us more than simply the relation of the chairperson to committee; it contributes to understanding various aspects of committee performance.

CONCLUSION

Conceptualizing leadership as a transactional relationship between leader and followers, we have suggested that congressional committees can be characterized by identifiable leadership patterns, or styles, that are associated with both committee attributes (e.g., member goals and committee norms) and committee performance (e.g., partisanship and floor success). Acknowledging the problems of establishing causality, we have used committee roll-call data to begin to define the place of leadership in committee politics. We have asked, first of all, whether there is any identifiable pattern of leader-follower relations on congressional committees. We have found clear evidence of three leadership patterns—extremity, partisan-middleman, and bipartisan-consensual—and discovered that chairmen can readily be assigned to them. Moreover, each style had a sizable number of practitioners. The availability of committee votes has enabled us to chart, from a new vantage point, the shape of committee leadership, and to provide valuable and independent perspective on committee terrain already surveyed, less systematically, through close and astute observation.

A second general question, the skeptics' "so what?" asks whether knowledge of committee leadership styles reveals anything about committee politics and performance. The data suggest an affirmative answer: leadership style seems directly related to committee partisanship and, with a few exceptions on a few committees, to majority party integration and committee success on the floor. Despite the difficulty in establishing definitively the direction in which influence flows as well as in distinguishing the impact of leadership from that of other forces that affect committees, these data, particularly those on change over time, permit the inference that leadership may help shape committee performance.

In addition, though we do not bring data directly to bear on the matter, our findings suggest, at least speculatively, that committee attributes and committee leadership are reciprocally related. On the one hand, member goals and committee norms and procedures may structure committee leadership. For example, on Armed Services and on Banking, new chairmen who were relatively liberal northerners replaced southern conservatives (Berg 1978) and adopted leadership styles identical to those of their predecessors. Similarly, where committee conditions change, leadership change may follow directly: on Ways and Means, dramatically restructured (especially by a greatly enlarged contingent of liberal Democrats), Al Ullman was unwilling or unable to continue Wilbur Mills's pattern of bipartisan-consensual leadership. On the other hand, Jack Brooks, succeeding to the chair on Government Operations, a committee only moderately influenced by broader change in the House, consciously abandoned Chet Holifield's bipartisanship (Ornstein and Rohde 1977).

In general, then, our results sustain the view that leadership in the congressional committee context is transactional and highly variable in form. Committee chairmen do have leadership resources—e.g., influence over subcommittee structures and recruitment of committee staff. But their success in securing their followers' support may well be limited by their own leadership skills and by the committee settings in which they seek to lead. Committee—specific factors—followers' personal goals, the aggressiveness of the now formally dominant majority party committee caucus, the committee's relations with actors in its environment, and the extant committee norms and decision process—all impinge on the leaders' opportunities. Individual chairmen, our data suggest, respond to these circumstances in distinctive ways; they may seek to lead within these constraints or they may conform to them. Most often, we infer, their leadership posture is severely limited by on-going committee processes.[14] However, the leadership style chairmen assume, whether by choice or necessity, appears to relate directly to committee performance. Finally, these relationships may alter as conditions change. If Wilbur Mills was the leader of Ways and Means, then Al Ullman, operating in a quite different committee setting, was much more a follower. Committee leadership is patterned, but the patterns are neither simple nor immutable.

Although much more must be learned about committee leadership, we hope that by identifying extremity, middleman, and bipartisan leadership types and by linking these styles to committee performance we have provided a starting point for further analysis of leadership, this "least understood" aspect of congressional committees.

APPENDIX

We identify the factional alignments within each committee, for each Congress, with cluster-bloc analysis. (For a discussion of the technique and its use in roll-call analysis, see Anderson et al., 1966, chap. 4.) The procedure uses vote correlations to build a first cluster of committee members to the point where adding members would produce a heterogeneous cluster. Second and subsequent clusters are then built until all individuals have been assigned or until the remaining members fail to meet the defined minimum correlation for being added to an existing cluster or for beginning a new cluster.[15]

To start a cluster, two variables (committee members) must correlate (vote together) at a level equal to or greater than a given minimum threshold (startmin). To enter a cluster, individuals must have an average correlation with the variables already in the cluster that is equal to or exceeds a specified minimum (endmin). To stay in the cluster, the individual's voting must correlate with those already in the cluster, at a level equal to or greater than a specified minimum (staymin). The choice of cutoffs, or minimum thresholds, is critical: cutoffs set too high will minimize clustering; those set too low will create either a multiplicity of small, virtually meaningless clusters or a single, all-encompassing bloc. Using these procedures, we obtained the clearest picture of committee factional structure when startmin = .50, endmin = .35, and staymin = .30.[16] These values mean that to be in a cluster members must have an average agreement of .35 with all others in that cluster and an agreement of at least .30 with each other member.

We have considerable confidence in the validity of the committee voting structures these methods produce, not only because they make sense intuitively but also because they are for the most part statistically significant. Willetts (1972 see also Garson 1976, 212–23) has devised a test that uses both the number of cases and the levels of agreement between individuals to assess the statistical significance of empirically defined cluster blocs. Applying his technique and interpretive criteria (see his table 2, 574) to our data reveals that 142 of the 160 clusters identified are significant at the .10 level.[17] The remaining 18 are significant at levels between .11 and .17 (i.e., the likelihood of their being chance agreements does not exceed one in eight), and most are ($N = 2$) factions marginal to the analysis.

The analysis is based on all nonprocedural roll calls taken in the nine committees in the Ninety-second through Ninety-fifth Congresses. Votes to close committee meetings, refer bills to subcommittees, raise points of order, postpone action on legislation, reconsider votes, or specify floor procedures may have had substantive significance but were treated as procedural and omitted from the analysis. What remains are substantive roll calls dealing with amendments to bills or with decisions to report legislation. This pool of votes is reduced further by eliminating all unanimous or near-unanimous votes (those on which 10 percent or fewer of the members took the minority position); one-sided roll calls distort the bloc structure the cluster technique identifies. Finally, all members who participated on fewer than 60 percent of a committee's roll-call votes are excluded from the analysis; widely varying numbers of votes distort the correlations that define the voting clusters.

Cluster-bloc analysis empirically defines voting blocs from the propensity of legislators to vote together on issues before their committees. It provides no clue, however, to the reasons why the blocs develop. To specify further the underlying nature of the factions the technique identifies, we explore the partisan and ideological bases of the blocs. We examine the following groups.

Partisan blocs
> Republicans: all committee Republicans
> Democrats: all committee Democrats
> Southern Democrats: all Democrats from the eleven states of the Old Confederacy, Kentucky, and Oklahoma
> Northern Democrats: all Democrats from the remaining thirty-seven states

Ideological blocs
  Conservatives: all committee members whose Americans for
    Constitutional Action (ACA) ratings are above 50 percent
  Liberals: all members with ACA scores of 50 percent and below
  Conservative Coalition: all Republican and southern Democratic
    members

These indices not only permit us to describe the voting clusters but also subsequently to locate the place of committee leaders within the committee structure. We use average interagreement scores,[18] reflecting agreement levels between each pair of committee members (see Anderson et al. 1966), to compare the committee chairperson with the voting factions and with the party and ideological groups within each committee. The interagreement (IA) scores range from 1.0 (voting agreement between the leader and each member of the criterion group on each roll call on which both participated) to −1.0 (disagreement with each member on each roll call).

To relate the leadership patterns to committee performance (table 8-3), we use the following measures.

Partisan votes: the percentage of committee roll calls on which a majority of Democrats opposed a majority of Republicans
Party integration: the "proportion of times each committee member agrees with every other committee member" (Dyson and Soule 1970, 633–35)
Floor wins: the percentage of roll calls on which majorities of the reporting committee and the full House agree

The measure of floor wins (or floor successes) includes votes on amendments and final passage. If a majority of the committee and the full House agree, we assume that the former are satisfied with the outcome. In fact, committee majorities oppose about three-fourths of all floor amendments, and their position prevails on more than 80 percent of the floor votes (see table 8-3). Each of the three measures of committee performance uses only those roll calls that meet the criteria (see above) for inclusion in the cluster-bloc analysis.

NOTES

1. For a full discussion of leadership, in general and in the legislative setting, see Burns 1978, chaps. 1 and 13.
2. We are well aware that the formal or nominal leader, the chairperson, may not be the "real" leader on any committee. For instance, Richard Bolling (D., Mo.) was clearly the de facto leader of the House Committee on Rules long before he became

the de jure leader by acceding to the chair in 1979. Yet there is ample precedent for treating formal (positional) leaders as the leaders (e.g., Peabody 1976); moreover, if the form of analysis we attempt works for the official leaders, it can be used with equal facility to study the informal leadership.

3. Fenno's generalization (for other versions, see Peabody 1976, 7; Jones 1981) is probably even more accurate in the postreform period in Congress—that is, since 1975, when the formal authority of full committee chairs was sharply curtailed (see, inter alia, Ornstein 1975; Welch and Peters 1977; Rieselbach 1978).

4. The use of the masculine form here intends no slight to women. It is simply realistic: all eighteen individuals who chaired the committees we consider were men.

5. We use "leadership style" in a restricted sense here, to refer to the voting alignment—extremity, middleman, or bipartisan—that links a committee's chairperson to its rank and file. We recognize fully that leaders who display the same style, as we use the term, may possess quite different personal qualities or quirks (Wright Patman and Henry Reuss on the Banking Committee come readily to mind). In addition, there may be intracommittee variation in leadership across different issues, with respect to particular subcommittee's products, or in consequence of the chair's relations with the ranking minority member. Yet our purpose, for now, remains limited: we want merely to map the patterns, the styles, of committee leadership in general and to explore some broad effects of such patterns on committee performance.

6. For a pioneering effort using these data, see Parker and Parker 1979. Our method of analysis differs from the Parkers'; we look at each Congress separately and therefore can include more members and chart change more precisely.

7. For expository convenience, we categorize blocs ideologically according to their members' mean Americans for Constitutional Action score (see Appendix) as follows: liberal, 0–33; moderate, 34–66; and conservative, 67–100.

8. In the single exception to Holifield's bipartisan leadership strategy, he disagreed sharply (IA = −.46) with an extremely liberal (ACA = 09) doublet (cluster 5). He was feuding with one of the pair, Benjamin Rosenthal (N.Y.) (see Ornstein and Rohde 1977, 210), but his relationship to the other dissenter, John Culver (Iowa), was also negative (IA = −.27).

9. For a full picture of the cluster-bloc analysis, see Rieselbach and Unekis 1981–82. The complete array of factional structure identifies individual bloc members and the level at which their votes correlate with the cluster to which they belong. We will provide the cluster-bloc data—the factional structures and the correlations of the chairman with them—for each of the nine committees in each of the four Congresses on request.

10. On Armed Services, however, when a new chairman took over there occurred a clear and persistent increase in partisanship.

11. The student's t tests demonstrate the statistical significance of these differences: extremist-middleman, $t = -8.5 \ 8$, $p < .001$; extremist-bipartisan, $t = -9.06$, $p < .001$; middleman-bipartisan, $t = 2.93$, $p < .004$.

12. Again, Armed Services does not quite meet expectations. Hebert and Price were both bipartisan leaders, but committee integration, higher than expected under the former, fell to more reasonable levels during the latter's tenure.

13. These are small differences, to be sure, but the range of variation across congressional committees is also small. Our data for the 1970s (table 8-3, column 5) show only four instances of committees that win fewer than eight of ten votes, and look very much like Dyson and Soule's (1970, tables 1 and 4) for the decade 1955–64. The data suggest that even the least successful committees can count on seeing

most of their legislation enacted. In addition, the t test for the difference between the bipartisan and the extremity leadership patterns is significant ($t = 1.94$, $p = .05$), while that for the bipartisan and middleman groups is in the right direction but fails to reach significance ($t = -1.29$; $p = .20$).

14. Elsewhere (Rieselbach and Unekis 1981–82), we have elaborated on this argument. An assessment of the four House committees that changed chairmen at the outset of the Ninety-fourth Congress—Agriculture, Armed Services, Banking, and Ways and Means—leads to the conclusion that only radical change (of the sort Ways and Means experienced) is likely to lead to fundamental alteration of the committee's customary modes of conducting business.

15. The OSIRIS program MDC was used to compute the Pearson product-moment correlation between each member's committee voting and that of each other member. The resulting correlation matrix was used, as input to the OSIRIS program CLUSTER. See OSIRIS III, vol. 1, 465–71, 679–86, and vol. 5, 29–37.

16. The Banking and Rules Committees were exceptions to this rule. The thresholds for these two committees were set at startmin = .40, endmin = .30, and staymin = .30 because clusters failed to form at the higher thresholds.

17. We will make a table of cutoff points, similar to the one Willetts provides, available to the interested reader on request.

18. The vote correlation matrix used to identify clusters contains additional information. Since each member's voting relationship with every other member is known, it is an easy matter to focus on particular sets of associations in which we have some interest. Thus, we can compare the committee chairperson with all Democrats (or any other group) simply by averaging the correlations between the chair and each Democrat on the committee. This average is the interagreement score.

REFERENCES

Anderson, Lee F., Meredith W. Watts, Jr., and Allen R. Wilcox. 1966. *Legislative Roll Call Analysis*. Evanston, Ill.: Northwestern University Press.

Berg, John. 1978. "The Effects of Seniority Reform on Three House Committees," In *Legislative Reform: The Policy Impact*, edited by Leroy N. Rieselbach. Lexington, Mass.: Lexington Books, 49–59.

Burns, James MacGregor. 1978. *Leadership*. New York: Harper and Row.

Dyson, James W., and John W. Soule. 1970. "Congressional Committee Behavior on Roll Call Votes: The U.S. House of Representatives, 1955–1964." *Midwest Journal of Political Science* 14:626–47.

Fenno, Richard F., Jr. 1973. *Congressmen in Committees*. Boston: Little, Brown.

Garson, G. David. 1976. *Political Science Methods*. Boston: Holbrook Press.

Hinckley, Barbara. 1976. "Seniority 1975: Old Theories Confront New Facts." *British Journal of Political Science* 6:383–99.

Jones, Charles O. 1981. "House Leadership in an Age of Reform." *Understanding Congressional Leadership*, edited by F. H. Mackaman. Washington, D.C.: Congressional Quarterly Press, 117–34.

MacRae, Duncan, Jr. 1956. "Roll Call Votes and Leadership," *Public Opinion Quarterly* 20: 543–58.

———. 1958. *Dimensions of Congressional Voting*. Berkeley and Los Angeles: University of California Press.

Manley, John F. 1970. *The Politics of Finance*. Boston: Little, Brown.

Oppenheimer, Bruce I. 1977. "The Rules Committee: New Arm of the Leadership in a Decentralized House." In *Congress Reconsidered*, edited by Lawrence C. Dodd and Bruce I. Oppenheimer. New York: Praeger, 96–116.

Ornstein, Norman J., ed. 1975. *Congress in Change: Evolution and Reform.* New York: Praeger.

Ornstein, Norman J., and David W. Rohde. 1977. "Shifting Forces, Changing Rules and Political Outcomes: The Impact of Congressional Change on Four House Committees." In *New Perspectives on the House of Representatives*, 3d ed., edited by Robert L. Peabody and Nelson W. Polsby. Chicago: Rand McNally, 186–269.

OSIRIS III. 1974. Vols. 1 and 5. Ann Arbor: University of Michigan.

Parker, Glenn R. 1979. "The Selection of Committee Leaders in the House of Representatives." *American Politics Quarterly* 7:71–93.

Parker, Glenn R., and Suzanne L. Parker. 1979. "Factions in Committees: The U.S. House of Representatives," *American Political Science Review* 73:85–102.

Patterson, Samuel C. 1963. "Legislative Leadership and Political Ideology," *Public Opinion Quarterly* 27:399–410.

Peabody, Robert L. 1976. *Leadership in Congress.* Boston: Little, Brown.

Price, David E. 1981. "Congressional Committees in the Policy Process." In *Congress Reconsidered* Lawrence C. Dodd and Bruce I. Oppenheimer, Washington, D.C.: Congressional Quarterly Press, 156–85.

Rieselbach, Leroy N., ed. 1978. *Legislative Reform: The Policy Impact.* Lexington, Mass.: Lexington Books.

Rieselbach, Leroy N., and Joseph K. Unekis. 1981–82. "Ousting the Oligarchs: Assessing the Consequences of Reform and Change on Four House Committees." *Congress and the Presidency* 9:83–117.

Rohde, David W., and Kenneth A. Shepsle. 1978. "Thinking About Legislative Reform," In *Legislative Reform: The Policy Impact*, edited by Leroy N. Rieselbach. Lexington, Mass.: Lexington Books, 9–21.

Rudder, Catherine. 1978. The Policy Impact of Reform of the Committee on Ways and Means." In *Legislative Reform: The Policy Impact*, edited by Leroy N. Rieselbach. Lexington, Mass.: Lexington Books, 73–89.

Truman, David B. 1959. *The Congressional Party.* New York: Wiley.

Welch, Susan, and John G. Peters, eds. 1977. *Legislative Reform and Public Policy.* New York: Praeger.

Willetts, Peter. 1972. "Cluster-Bloc Analysis and Statistical Inference." *American Political Science Review* 66:569–82.

PART III   *On the Floor*

The floor of the House, like its counterpart in the Senate, is the ultimate setting for activity on legislation. Once bills clear committees they are scheduled by the party leadership, usually working through the House Committee on Rules, for floor action. It is here that the formal equality of membership—one member, one vote—is most directly achieved. Steven S. Smith in his article, "Revolution in the House: Why Don't We Do It on the Floor?" reports on increases in amending activity on the floor since the 1950s and 1960s. He shows how changes in the procedures adopted in the early 1970s, most notably recorded and electronic voting, resulted in an expanded and increasingly complex legislative agenda in the 1970s and 1980s. One consequence has been more amendments offered on the floor with members of committees other than those of the original jurisdiction having a more favorable chance of having their amendments accepted.

Another way of looking at floor activity and the impact of roll call voting on legislative outcomes is set forth in a classic article by Barbara Deckard Sinclair, "State Party Delegations in the U.S. House of Representatives: A Comparative Study of Group Cohesion." This article explores the voting cohesion and information sharing of members of twelve state delegations in the Ninetieth and Ninety-first Congresses. State delegations, particularly those demonstrating a high cohesion, continue to have a major impact on voting behavior in the House of Representatives.

Chapter 9

Revolution in the House:
Why Don't We Do It on the Floor?

STEVEN S. SMITH

The process of decentralization in the U.S. House of Representatives during the last three decades has been well documented. More recently, treatments of developments in the 1970s and 1980s have emphasized the greater equality of the membership, the ability of noncommittee members to successfully challenge committee proposals, the creation of ad hoc groups and decision-making mechanisms, and the breakdown of jurisdictional or normative barriers to effective participation (Ornstein 1981; Smith 1985). While related to the process of decentralization, these developments are not synonymous with decentralization. Instead, they might be characterized as "collegial" developments in which members seek to overcome the constraints of structure, including a decentralized structure, in order to influence policy and political outcomes.

The ultimate barometer of these developments is the floor of the House. While party and committee structures inevitably limit and direct participation, the floor is the one location where the formal equality of membership can be enforced, at least in principle. Parliamentary procedure on the floor remains a constraint that advantages some and disadvantages others, of course, but that too can be modified on the floor. Understanding changing patterns of floor decision-making clearly is central to an understanding of the collegial aspects of House politics.

I have turned to the record of amending activity to examine the evolution in the role of the floor since the 1950s. My first purpose is simply

This chapter was originally published as a Brookings Discussion Paper in Governmental Studies, September 1986. It is reprinted by permission.

to describe the change in aggregate amending activity. Has it increased? How have outcomes changed? Has the contestedness of amending activity increased? Unfortunately, answering these questions is not as straightforward as one might think, for the voting procedures of the Committee of the Whole prior to the 1970s make it impossible to limit the focus to the convenient roll-call record. In the Eighty-fourth Congress (1955–56), for example, only fifteen of over four hundred amendments offered on the floor were subject to roll-call votes. Procedural reforms in 1971 and 1973 brought recorded and electronic voting to the Committee of the Whole, expanding the proportion of amendments subjected to recorded votes, but also making it difficult to compare pre- and postreform congresses. Thus, all floor amendments must be examined, and the reforms of voting procedures must be taken into account.

My second purpose is to more directly examine changing patterns of participation in amending activity. What was the timing and extent of the demise of traditional norms limiting participation? Who took advantage of new voting procedures? Who, if anyone, has become more successful on the floor? The answers to these questions will yield a picture of the political implications of the changing role of the floor for the two parties, both ideological extremes, junior members, and committees.

A third purpose is to explore the consequences of these changing patterns of amending activity for the treatment of committees on the floor. Which committees have been most affected? Has the balance of insiders and outsiders attacking committee proposals changed more for some committees than for others? The study gives us the first comprehensive look at committee floor experiences over time and provides a basis for assessing the consequences of the developments on the floor for the committee system.

Finally, I consider the place of the changing role of the floor in the pattern of evolution in House decision-making processes over the past two decades. The revolution in the use of the floor was an integral part of the reform period of the 1970s. And the new role of the floor stimulated other developments in the parties and the committee system. Most important, the process of decentralization was both reinforced and checked by the new role of the floor.

This study encompasses the floor amendments of seven congresses spanning the period from 1955 to 1980.[1] Three Congresses, the Eighty-fourth (1955–56), Eighty-eighth (1963–64), and Ninety-first (1969–70), predate the implementation of recorded teller voting in 1971. The Ninety-second (1971–72) brought recorded teller voting and the Ninety-third (1973–74) brought electronic voting for all recorded votes. The Ninety-fourth (1975–76) and Ninety-sixth (1979–80) are postreform

Congresses, with respect to most committee and party reforms as well as floor voting procedures. While examining only seven Congresses of the period imposes constraints on the interpretations that are possible, these congresses permit me to assess the general nature of the change that has occurred.

The change has been quite dramatic. Between the 1950s and the 1980s, the number of amendments offered to pending legislation in each Congress more than tripled. The percentage of all legislation subject to floor amendments more than quadrupled. The number of members offering amendments almost doubled. The norms of specialization, committee reciprocity, and apprenticeship met their demise during the 1960s and 1970s, and nearly all House committees faced many more floor amendments. These changes represent a transformation of the policy-making process in the House and of the institutional environment in which members pursue their political goals. With greater frequency members now ask each other, "Why don't we do it on the floor?"

SOURCES OF CHANGE

Nearly all forces of change in and out of Congress during the past three decades converged to push House members toward more amending activity on the floor. Reciprocal and reinforcing effects abound, making causal linkages among the forces of change difficult to establish empirically. Many of these forces are well known, but their effect on floor activity is seldom appreciated. A review of the factors involved will serve to demonstrate the weakness of countervailing forces and will help formulate expectations about the timing and type of change in amending activity since the 1950s. Four sets of factors stand out: (1) political environment and workload, (2) committee reform, (3) rank-and-file resources, and (4) rules governing floor debate.

Environment and Workload

The political environment, in and out of Washington, became more complex for members during the 1960s and 1970s. More issues and programs created more incentives for members to contribute to policy making at all stages of the legislative process. There have been astounding increases in the number, differentiation, and activity of interest groups placing demands on members (Salisbury 1983). More local newspapers cover members' Washington activity, partly as a result of new communications technology available to members and partly as a result of the growth of newspaper chains and Washington news services. Constituents also are more numerous—the average House district has grown from

345,000 to 520,000 since the 1950s—and more heterogeneous for most members. The cost of campaigns and competition for contributions have increased. These factors have both increased the demands on members by outsiders and created new opportunities for members to demonstrate responsiveness to outsiders whose support or opposition affects their political well-being.

A variety of indicators show an expanding and increasingly complex legislative agenda since the 1950s. Time in session shows dramatic growth, of course, but this is influenced greatly by the volume of amending activity as well as by the number and complexity of the bills brought to the floor. The number of bills considered on the floor has actually fallen by more than 40 percent since a peak in 1955–56, but since the 1950s the total number of pages in bills enacted into law has more than doubled and the number of pages per bill has more than tripled (see Davidson 1986). Some of the greater length of enacted legislation may be due to amending activity, but it also appears that larger, more complex bills stimulated more amending activity.

Concrete policy objectives played an important role. During the 1960s, a succession of issues—civil rights, poverty, the Vietnam War, pollution—excited intense activity among both liberals and conservatives in the House. For example, the Civil Rights Act of 1964 and the Voting Rights Act of 1965 stimulated dozens of floor amendments sponsored by southern Democrats. At other times, Democratic liberals were frustrated by conservative committee chairmen and appealed committee recommendations on the floor. Republicans, suffering their semipermanent minority status, sought to publicize the faults of the majority party on the floor. The Senate was showing the way, as more and more senators, especially new groups of liberals, turned to the floor in pursuit of their policy objectives in the early 1960s (Sinclair 1985).

The Role of Committees

The institutional context of floor decision making was evolving as well, especially with respect to decision-making processes within committees. Chairmen had less influence over the shape of legislation and fewer effective tools for maintaining cohesiveness among their committee colleagues. They could no longer withhold legislation from the floor single-handedly, self-selection was instituted as the method for making subcommittee assignments for majority party Democrats, and subcommittee chairmanships became elective. In the absence of dominating full committee chairmen, disputes within committees often were less manageable and more frequently spilled over to the floor. And on the floor bill management responsibilities were expected to be turned over to subcommittee chairmen, who usually lacked the experience and political tools of full committee chairmen of the previous era (Smith and Deering 1984, 194–95).

Opportunities to pursue policy interests at prefloor stages of the legislative process expanded greatly for most members. Per capita committee assignments grew from 1.3 to over 1.8 for majority party Democrats between the Eighty-fourth and Eighty-eighth congresses, and from 1.2 to 1.7 for Republicans. Opportunities at the subcommittee level expanded as well with a doubling in the number of subcommittees and a 30 percent increase in average subcommittee size between the 1950s and the mid-1970s. A Democratic Caucus rule limiting members to one subcommittee chairmanship yielded full or subcommittee chairmanships for nearly half of all House Democrats by the 1980s. In the smaller minority Republican party, nearly 60 percent typically serve as a ranking minority member of a committee or subcommittee in recent congresses. The result: more members could rely on committee membership and expertise as grounds for floor activism, and outsiders could draw upon more members as well-placed sponsors for their amendments.

Rank-and-File Resources

The staff resources of rank-and-file members also have increased. The cap on personal staff appointments, established in House rules, increased from eight to ten in 1965 and again to 18 in 1975. More members allocated casework and other constituency duties to district offices, freeing staff in Washington for more legislative activity (Schiff and Smith 1983). Members holding subcommittee chairmanships or positions as ranking minority members also gained staff assistance. In sum, more and more members gained the wherewithal to write amendments, prepare for floor debate, and garner support from colleagues.

Rules Governing Floor Debate

During the 1970–75 period, a number of House and Democratic Caucus rules were adopted that affected floor amending activity. Three sets of rules are worth brief review: (1) previously noticed amendments and special orders, (2) recorded and electronic voting, and (3) multiple referral. These rules directly shape the incentives and disincentives, the opportunities and constraints, perceived by prospective amendment sponsors.

Previously Noticed Amendments and Rules. Beginning in 1971, members placing amendments in the *Congressional Record* a day in advance of the debate were guaranteed consideration. The rule protects members who otherwise might find it difficult to gain the recognition of the chair for the purpose of offering amendments and creates the possibility of filibusters by amendment when the amendments are not anticipated by the Rules Committee.

The Rules Committee, of course, must first grant a special order, or "rule," for major legislation to reach the floor. The rule often waives the right to previously noticed amendments by limiting amendments. Unhappiness with closed rules, especially those for Ways and Means' legislation, led the Democratic Caucus in 1973 to require that the Rules chairman notify the House in advance of the committee's intention to report a closed rule. The caucus also granted itself the power to instruct the Rules Democrats to make particular amendments in order. The immediate effect was to virtually eliminate closed rules in the Ninety-third and Ninety-fourth Congresses (Bach 1981a, 43). Eighteen closed rules were reported in the Ninety-fifth and Ninety-sixth Congresses, but they seldom involved major bills of much controversy.

The Rules Committee has adapted by writing more "complex" rules— that is, rules that are not simply open or closed but that limit amending activity in some other way (Bach 1981b). Such rules may limit amendments to those published in the *Record* in advance, identify particular amendments that will be in order, specify the order of amendments, waive certain points of order against amendments, limit amending activity to some certain parts of legislation, or otherwise structure the amending process in the Committee of the Whole. About half of these rules have expanded amending opportunities beyond what the rules of the House would allow otherwise. More than 20 percent of rules have been complex rules in recent congresses, up from 2 or 3 percent in the late 1960s.

Recorded and Electronic Voting. Recorded and electronic voting played a major role in the expansion of amending activity, as we will see. Amendments offered in the Committee of the Whole prior to 1971 were subject to a voice vote, division vote, or teller vote; House rules did not provide for a recorded vote. Recorded votes (the "yeas-and-nays") could be requested by one-fifth of those present, as provided in the Constitution, after the legislation was reported to the House from the Committee of the Whole. Prior to the Ninety-second Congress teller votes could be requested by twenty members in the Committee of the Whole (one-fifth of a quorum); the new rule in the Ninety-second stated that a *recorded* teller could be requested by twenty members. In the Ninety-third Congress, electronic voting supplanted teller voting. All electronic voting, whether in the Committee of the Whole or in the House, is now commonly called "roll-call" voting.

The sponsors of the recorded voting reforms hoped that vote outcomes would change (*Congressional Record*, 27 July 1970, 25797). It was argued that attendance would increase and thus change the composition of the voting membership on critical issues, and that some members' votes would be cast differently if their votes were made public. Liberals later claimed that recorded voting was vital to stopping the supersonic transport program and finally cutting funding for the Vietnam War. While some concern was expressed in 1970 about the prospect of members spending more time on the floor to cast recorded votes, the chief sponsor of the reform dismissed the complaints by saying that recorded votes would be demanded on only a handful of issues in each Congress. No concern was expressed at the time about the possibility that more amendments would be offered. Moreover, when the issue of electronic voting was settled two years later, no significant concern about more amending activity was expressed. Efficiency and accuracy in recorded voting were the themes. In fact, supporters of electronic voting produced estimates showing great savings in floor time for a membership accustomed to milling around the House floor waiting for their names to be called and teller votes to be counted. These estimates went unchallenged.

By mid-1973, just a few months after electronic voting began, many members were complaining that the number of recorded votes was forcing them to spend much more time on the floor, with many complainants noting an increase in the number of minor amendments. It appeared that the incentives to put oneself on the record, or to force others to go on the record, stimulated a significant number of amendments. Amendments often permit members to vote for a policy position more closely tailored to their political needs than final passage votes, thus providing some political cover for unavoidable difficult votes. At other times, recorded voting may strip away the political cover of anonymous voting, thereby enhancing outsiders' influence and countering the influence of powerful insiders. In any case, recorded voting increased attendance and so affected members' calculations about the costs and benefits of sponsoring amendments. And by cutting the time consumed by recorded voting, electronic voting also reduced the antagonism engendered by individual requests for recorded votes.

In response to the complaints, a Rules subcommittee sought to increase the number of members who must call for a recorded (electronic) vote before one is ordered. A proposal to do so was defeated on the floor by a coalition of Republicans, who enjoyed putting the majority on the record, and liberals, who wanted to protect their "sunshine" reform. A modest change increasing the number required from twenty to twenty-five was adopted in 1979 at the start of the Ninety-sixth Congress.

Multiple Referral. Referral of legislation to multiple committees by the Speaker was authorized in 1974 and quickly became a well institutionalized process as committees routinely laid claims to legislation. Multiply referred legislation as a percentage of all passed legislation has increased steadily since 1974, rising from 1.5 percent in the Ninety-fourth Congress to 5.1 in the Ninety-sixth and to 7.0 in the Ninety-eighth (Oleszek, Davidson, and Kephart 1986, 41). By expanding the number of members who have been involved with an issue, multiple referral increases the odds that policy conflicts, complicated by jurisdictional jealousies, will be pushed to the floor. Floor amendments often are the only vehicles available for settling differences between committees that have a stake in the legislation. The last House Select Committee on Committees reported that bills subject to multiple referrals in the Ninety-fifth Congress (1977–78) faced an average of four amendments, compared to 1.2 amendments for singly referred bills (cited in Oleszek, Davidson, and Kephart 1986, 60).

Counterbalancing Developments

Developments counterbalancing the multiple forces for more amending activity in the House are few in number. One change in the House rules that has a clear constraining effect concerns the use of the Suspension Calendar (see Oleszek 1984, 101–2). Legislation passed under suspension of the rules requires a two-thirds majority and may not be amended, although amendments to the legislation may be included in the suspension motion itself. In 1975 and 1977, House Democrats imposed rules changes that doubled, and then quadrupled, the number of days in which suspension motions are in order. The latest version permits the Speaker to entertain suspension motions every Monday and Tuesday the House is in session.

The rule changes produced a surge in suspension motions in the late 1970s (Bach 1986a). The number of suspension motions nearly doubled from the four Congresses of the 1965–73 period to the four Congresses of the 1977–84 period (Bach 1986a, 62). Once offered, suspension motions usually pass. In the Ninety-eighth Congress (1983–84), for example, more than 96 percent (408 of 423) of suspension motions were adopted. Criticism from Republicans and within the ranks of the majority party led the Democrats in 1979 to prohibit the use of suspension for bills involving sums of money over $100 million, except by vote of the party's Steering and Policy Committee. This constraint may have restrained even more frequent use of the suspension mechanism to bypass the amending process of the Committee of the Whole.

There are other countervailing forces. For example, the increased burdens on members' time since the 1950s—more trips home, more committee meetings and hearings, and so on—probably distract members from floor activity. But these countervailing forces have been overwhelmed by the tremendous forces generating more floor activity. Political incentives for floor participation have increased, many procedural and structural obstacles to floor participation have been removed, and resources to support floor participation have improved. The evolutionary direction in the factors influencing floor decision-making is clear.

AMENDMENTS ON THE FLOOR

Measuring the location and extent of substantive decision-making in the modern Congress is a difficult problem. I have opted to use floor *activity* measures as indicators of substantive decision-making. While I draw upon several measures of floor activity, I emphasize *volume, contestedness*, and *outcomes* of floor *amending* activity. Both volume and contestedness seem to be necessary, though probably not sufficient, conditions for the presence of significant substantive decision-making, at least when viewed in the aggregate. In the extreme case, the absence of contested amendments suggests an absence of substantive decision-making and a routine ratification of committee recommendations. As the frequency and contestedness of amendments increase, the evidence that more substantive decisions are made on the House floor would be very strong, although not conclusive.[2] The evidence would be more conclusive if, at the same time as the frequency and contestedness of amendments increases, the number of successful amendments increases.

Volume of Amending Activity

The volume of amending activity increased dramatically between the 1950s and 1970s. Several elements of this change are worth special emphasis. First, the level of amending activity was increasing before the adoption of teller and electronic voting reforms in the early 1970s. Only one in twenty bills on the House floor was subject to amendment attempts in 1955–56, while nearly one in five measures was subject to amendment attempts in 1969–70 (table 9-1). The number of amendments offered on the floor doubled between the mid-1950s and the late 1960s (table 9-2).

Second, there is no evidence that the move to recorded voting *per se* was sufficient to stimulate more amending activity. The previously noticed amendment rule and recorded tellers were implemented in the Ninety-second Congress (1971–72) with no discernible effect on the number of amendments. In fact, the Ninety-second does not even show the continuing trend of more amending activity that is suggested by the pattern

Table 9-1. *Percentage of Legislation Subjected to Amendment*

Congress	Number of Amendments Offered					
	None	1	2	3–4	5–9	10+
84th (1955–56)	94.2	2.9	0.9	0.8	0.7	0.4
88th (1963–64)	89.6	3.6	2.1	2.1	1.9	0.7
91st (1969–70)	81.8	8.3	2.1	3.2	2.7	1.9
92d (1971–72)	78.2	11.2	2.6	2.3	3.8	1.9
93d (1973–74)	72.1	10.7	4.6	4.4	3.9	4.3
94th (1975–76)	75.9	6.3	4.0	3.8	5.7	4.3
96th (1979–80)	77.4	8.3	2.6	2.9	3.7	5.1

Each cell is a percentage of all bills and joint resolutions passed by the House in that Congress. A small number of bills and resolutions considered on the floor are not passed (roughly 2%) and may have been subject to amendment.

of the Eighty-fourth, Eighty-eighth and Ninety-first Congresses. The dip in the congressional workload, as judged by the number of bills and pages enacted into law (Davidson 1986, 52), may explain the lull in amending activity. Perhaps learning to take advantage of the new political opportunities took some time, although parliamentary ignorance does not seem a likely explanation.

Third, a dramatic increase in amending activity occurred with the advent of electronic voting in the Ninety-third Congress (1973–74). The number of amendments increased by 78 percent from the Ninety-second to the Ninety-third. For amending activity only, about 80 percent of the projected savings in regulation voting time for recorded votes was not realized because of the growth in the number of amendments subject to recorded votes.[3] This estimate would be much higher if it included the time spent on amendments not subject to recorded votes that may have been by-products of amendments subject to recorded votes, time devoted to recorded votes on procedural motions related to amendments, and the time members spent running to and from the floor.

The increase in amending activity in the 1970s occurred just before the upswing in the use of suspension motions to circumvent the amendment process. In 1979–80, for example, nearly 60 percent of the bills not facing amendments on the floor were passed under suspension of the rules. The timing of these changes suggests that the increased vulnerability on the floor led more bill managers to look to suspension as a source of protection, an option made even more attractive in the absence of closed rules. The majority party leadership also appeared to be looking for ways to streamline consideration of noncontroversial bills at a time when other bills were consuming more floor time.

Fourth, with recorded voting in the Ninety-second Congress, more

Table 9-2. *Method of Final Disposition of House Floor Amendments*

Congress	Voice Vote	Division Vote	Unrecorded Teller	Recorded	Total
84th	60.5	25.9	9.9	3.7	100.0
	(245)	(105)	(40)	(15)	(405)
88th	60.1	23.1	15.8	1.0	100.0
	(369)	(142)	(97)	(6)	(614)
91st	64.4	22.6	11.1	1.9	100.0
	(565)	(198)	(97)	(17)	(877)
92d	56.9	18.3	0.03	24.5	100.0
	(451)	(145)	(2)	(194)	(792)
93d	62.0	13.2	N.A.	24.7	99.9
	(880)	(188)		(351)	(1419)
94th	58.4	14.3	N.A.	27.2	99.9
	(798)	(196)		(372)	(1366)
96th	66.0	8.5	N.A.	25.6	100.1
	(911)	(117)		(353)	(1381)

The first number given is a percentage; the number in parentheses is the number of amendments. The "recorded" column includes recorded teller votes, yea-and-nay votes, and electronic votes on amendments, as is appropriate for each Congress. As elsewhere, the table excludes amendments subject to a successful point of order, withdrawals, and other nonvote outcomes. N.A. = not applicable.

amendments were pushed to the most advanced form of voting in the Committee of the Whole; electronic voting did not further increase the proportion subject to the most advanced form of voting. That is, recorded voting encouraged members to exhaust their parliamentary options, even though it did not spur amending activity itself. These developments are shown in table 9-2, which indicates the voting method used to dispose of amendments. Recorded and electronic voting led to the demise of the division vote as a method for disposing of amendments. In the prereform Congresses, attendance was modest for division votes (table 9-3), which were not announced by the House bell system. While it improved when the bells rang for follow-up unrecorded teller votes, it remained fairly low. As a result, the outcome usually was not likely to change by calling for a teller vote (which happened only 15 percent of the time in the Eighty-fourth). Attendance for both divisions and tellers was even worse in the Ninety-first, when the volume of amending activity was much larger. But with recorded teller voting in the Ninety- second overall teller vote turnout increased by 86 percent over the previous Congress (figures not shown) and turnout for recorded votes remained high thereafter.

Fifth, attendance at pre-roll-call stages of debate on amendments has declined markedly, despite the greater turnout for deciding votes on amendments. This is reflected in the two-thirds drop in turnout for

Table 9-3. *Mean Turnout on Votes for Amendments on Which Both a Division Vote and a More Advanced Vote Were Taken*

Congress	Division Vote Attendance	Unrecorded Teller Vote Attendance	Recorded Vote Attendance
84th	183.5	217.1	—
88th	173.6	224.6	—
91st	120.4	162.7	—
92d	128.6	—	362.6
93d	107.3	—	386.9
94th	73.1	—	384.8
96th	56.0	—	392.0

division votes between the Eighty-eighth and Ninety-sixth Congresses (table 9-3). The drop in attendance during debate is due, no doubt, to the increasing burden of committee and other duties and, perhaps, to the devaluation of the policy significance of typical amendments. Thus, while attendance on roll-call votes in recent Congresses far exceeds the attendance on unrecorded tellers in earlier Congresses, the quality of participation on the typical amendment probably has declined. Interaction between members on the floor is now more frequent and diverse but probably has lost some of its richness. This inference suggests that the weakening of personal relationships among members in the 1970s, as has been noted occasionally, may be due to the institutional context of their interaction as much as to changing political personalities.

Sixth, the upsurge in the Ninety-third Congress was not limited to amendments subject to a recorded vote. The number of amendments handled by voice vote nearly doubled between the Ninety-second and Ninety-third Congresses (table 9-2). Factors other than voting procedure per se were obviously at play as the floodgates of amending activity opened in the Ninety-third. Recorded, electronic voting helped to create a new environment in which even members satisfied with voice vote outcomes became more active. It appears that the complainants of 1973 probably were wrong in thinking that the number of amendments would drop if the number required for a recorded vote was increased. Members may have been called to the floor less frequently, but it is not likely that amending activity would have contracted simply by making a recorded vote marginally more difficult to obtain.

Finally, measures subject to multiple referral faced more amendments on the floor of the House. In the Ninety-sixth Congress, the only Congress included in which a significant amount of multiply referred legislation reached the floor, singly referred bills faced an average of 1.4 amendments and multiply referred bills faced 2.9. Disregarding bills passed by suspension of the rules, the averages were 2.3 and 5.8, respectively.[4] These figures do not control for the policy or political significance of the legislation, unfortunately. The figures are consistent with the pattern in the Ninety-fifth Congress, which was noted above.

The pattern evolving in the House is one of increasing polarization in the manner in which legislation is handled on the floor. In the 1950s, few measures faced amendments on the floor and many of those that would have faced amendments were protected by closed rules. In the 1970s, most legislation is either amended on the floor or is immunized from amendments procedurally. On the one hand, legislation going to the floor unprotected by closed rules, which now are seldom available, faces more amending activity than it did in the 1950s and 1960s. Complex rules often limit the number of amendments, but they also make explicit the intention to entertain certain amendments. On the other hand, more and more legislation has been passed under suspension of the rules, thus avoiding the amendment process. Suspension motions have not compensated for the expansion of amending activity since the Ninety-third Congress, but, along with restraining rules, suspension motions have suppressed some of the increase that would have occurred otherwise. The net effect appears to be that the House has reached an equilibrium between the incentives and opportunities to offer amendments and the procedural and time constraints working against amending activity.

Contestedness of Amending Activity

Tables 9-1 and 9-2 also provide clues about the level of contestedness in floor decision-making. With the implementation of recorded voting in the Ninety-second, more measures faced numerous floor amendments and more amendments were subject to the most advanced available voting mechanism. Moreover, table 9-4 indicates that the number of amendments subject to a close division, teller, or recorded vote increased in two leaps timed with the advent of recorded tellers and electronic voting. By all three indicators, then, the volume of contested amendments has increased since the 1950s, with the voting procedure reforms coincident with important increases in contestedness. But the proportion of frivolous or symbolic amendments may have increased as volume increased, reducing the proportion of amendments that were contested. This did not occur. The percentage of amendments subject to a close vote shows no trend since the 1950s, as in the Senate (Sinclair 1985, 5).

Outcomes of Amending Efforts

Overall success rates have not changed systematically with the advent of recorded or electronic voting, although there was an inexplicable increase

Table 9-4. Contested Amendments

Congress	Number of Contested Amendments	Contested Amendments as Percentage of All Amendments	Total Amendments
84th	77	19.0	405
88th	117	19.1	614
91st	126	14.4	877
92d	152	19.2	792
93d	226	15.9	1419
94th	232	17.0	1366
96th	186	13.5	1381

An amendment is "contested" if it is subject to a division, teller, or a recorded vote *and* the outcome was split 60–40 or closer on at least one teller or recorded vote.

in the Ninety-sixth Congress (table 9-5). As for contested amendments, a reasonable expectation might have been that increasing amending activity would have been accompanied by a decrease in the proportion of successful amendments. Instead, the success rate of amendments has not changed systematically with the increase in amending activity. If anything, there has been a slight increase in the overall success rate. The pattern in the success rate therefore reinforces the conclusion that a dramatic increased substantive decision-making on the floor occurred during the 1970s.

Two pieces of evidence indicate that the reformers were right when they asserted that the move to recorded votes would change outcomes, even in the aggregate. First, amendments subject to roll-call votes in the 1970s generally were 10 percent more likely to pass than were their teller vote ancestors (table 9-5). Second, more division votes were overturned when appealed to recorded votes in the postreform period than were overturned when appealed to tellers in the prereform period. The percentages of appealed division outcomes that were overturned in the pre- and postreform periods were 15.9 and 28.7, respectively (for the Congresses in this study). Not surprisingly, the percentage of division votes that were appealed was higher in the postreform period (33.3 versus 22.4).

Finally, the number of frivolous amendments probably increased in the 1970s. This is indicated by the lower success rate for amendments considered by voice vote. Frivolous amendments tend to receive such an overwhelming negative vote that it is pointless to ask for a division or recorded vote, or they are so insignificant to their sponsors that it is not worth pursuing them beyond a voice vote. The increase in truly minor

Table 9-5. Amendment Outcomes by Method of Final Disposition (Percentage Adopted)

Congress	Voice Vote	Division Vote	Unrecorded Teller	Recorded	All
84th	98.3	21.0	25.0	*	62.9
88th	99.1	9.9	29.9	*	56.4
91st	100.0	19.7	19.6	*	62.3
92d	94.0	24.1	100.0	29.1	58.2
93d	75.9	26.1	N.A.	39.6	58.3
94th	97.1	29.6	N.A.	34.4	65.2
96th	91.2	34.2	N.A.	39.9	72.4

N.A. = not applicable.
* Very small Ns. The success rates for the 84th, 88th, and 91st in the recorded vote column are 47.7%, 33.3%, and 64.7%, respectively.

amendments comports with the observations of many members and suggests that the 1970s brought greater variation in the political character of the amendments considered on the floor.

The Changing Character of Amending Activity

To fully grasp the meaning of the expansion of amending activity for the House and its members, an appreciation of the daily schedule is required. Table 9-6 reports the daily and hourly amendment rates for House floor sessions. The average number of amendments in a day's session more than doubled between the 1950s and 1970s, despite a 30 to 40 percent increase in the number of session days. The daily rate was increasing prior to the reforms but jumped by nearly two amendments per day after electronic voting was in place. The higher rate of amending activity is even more impressive in the case of the hourly rate: with the help of electronic voting, the House managed nearly one amendment per hour for the nearly 1,500 hours of the Ninety-third Congress. The pace dropped thereafter, but remained at a remarkably high level of three amendments every four hours through the Ninety-sixth.[5]

Thus, the density of substantive decision-making on the floor increased greatly during the 1970s. The burdens of floor decision-making probably forced members to become more dependent on decision-making shortcuts. Cue taking and political habit probably became even more important as methods of choice in the postreform period. The increase in amending activity forced typical members to react to a wider variety of policy proposals and to interact with more colleagues, as superficial as that interaction sometimes may be. Unfortunately, the two major studies of individual decision-making on the floor appeared just as the revolution on the floor occurred (Clausen 1973; Kingdon 1973).

Table 9-6. *Daily and Hourly Rates of Amending Activity*

Congress	Amendments per Day	Amendments per Hour
84th	1.76	.43
88th	1.84	.49
91st	2.51	.54
92d	2.66	.55
93d	4.46	.95
94th	4.39	.76
96th	4.24	.74

Days and hours in session taken from Ornstein et al. 1982, 130.

MEMBERS ON THE FLOOR

Volume increases need not have been accompanied by increases in the number of amendment sponsors, but they were. The number of House members sponsoring amendments increased by 76 percent from the mid-1950s to the late 1970s. In the Eighty-fourth Congress, 189 members sponsored amendments, in contrast to 254 in the Ninety-second, 327 in the Ninety-third and 333 in the Ninety-sixth. As table 9-7 indicates, the number of amendments per member more than tripled from the 1950s to the 1970s, with the typical member of the 1970s offering at least three amendments in a Congress. When compared to the typical senator, floor participation for the average representative remains very low. In the Ninety-sixth Congress, for example, representatives averaged only one amendment for every 102 days of floor sessions. Nearly a quarter of the House sponsored no floor amendments in the Ninety-sixth. In contrast, 89 percent of the Senate offered amendments that were subject to a roll-call vote and senators averaged one such amendment every 54 session days (calculated from Sinclair 1985, table 6, and Ornstein et al. 1982, 131, 133). But given the size and time constraints of the House, which are severe, the breadth of participation in floor decision-making is now quite remarkable.

Floor participation in the amending process has increased for nearly every obvious category of members. The pattern of change is not even, though, and the political uses of the floor have changed in important ways. I focus on three aspects of changing patterns of amendment sponsorship: (1) party and regional differences; (2) activism among junior members; and (3) the importance of committee position.

Party and Region

The most striking change in party differences in amending activity is that the Republicans took disproportionate advantage of electronic recorded voting. In three of the four preelectronic Congresses, including the Ninety-second, when recorded tellers were used, the typical Democrat offered more amendments than the typical Republican (table 9-7). The upsurge in amending activity in the Ninety-third occurred disproportionately among Republicans, giving Republicans the per capita edge in the Ninety-third, Ninety-fourth, and Ninety-sixth. In the latter two Congresses, the typical Republican offered over 40 percent more amendments than the typical Democrat. Democrats continue to sponsor a majority of all floor amendments, but the typical Republican is now significantly more likely to go to the floor with an amendment than the typical Democrat.

Explaining definitively the pattern of change in party differences is not possible within the scope of this paper. Several factors are worth noting. Prior to the reforms, when teller voting was time consuming and public attention to floor proceedings was minimal, control of the floor by a presiding officer of the majority party worked to the disadvantage of Republicans. Recognition by the chair for the purpose of offering an unfriendly amendment sometimes was difficult to attain, and the majority closed many important bills to any amendment. Republicans suffered under severe staffing constraints as well, making it more difficult for them to devise timely amendments. Nevertheless, recorded voting was of great interest to the minority party. Minority party members, often frustrated by their inability to shape committee decisions, used the floor as an appeals court. And Republicans were generally more willing to exhaust their parliamentary options than Democrats, no doubt because they were more likely to be unsatisfied with previous results. As table 9-8 demonstrates, Republican sponsors pushed a disproportionate number of their amendments all the way to a teller vote in the Eighty-fourth and Eighty-eighth Congresses.

The introduction of electronic voting reduced the obstacles to minority party participation, and Republicans began to offer amendments to nearly every significant bill reaching the floor. Republicans again pushed amendments to the most advanced form of voting out of proportion to their numbers. Their success rate—which was below that of Democrats throughout the period under study—did not change much, but they suddenly were able to build a public record for themselves and against Democrats even in losing.

Starting in the late 1960s, liberals—those with a conservative coalition support score of 20 or less—were the most active amendment sponsors, despite the overall Republican advantage over Democrats. Liberals had reached average postreform levels of amending activity in the late 1960s. More generally, from the Ninety-first Congress onward, liberalism is

Table 9-7. Amending Activity by Party and Region, Seniority, and Ideology (Amendments per Capita)

Congress	All House Members	Party				Seniority				Ideology		
		Democrats			Republicans	1 Term	2 Terms	3 Terms	More Than 3 Terms	Liberal	Moderate	Conservative
		All	North	South								
84th	0.9	1.1	1.0	1.2	0.7	0.7	0.6	0.7	1.1	0.8	1.0	0.9
88th	1.4	1.3	0.9	2.1	1.6	0.8	1.4	1.2	1.6	1.0	1.6	1.7
91st	2.0	2.5	2.8	1.8	1.4	1.0	1.8	1.9	2.3	2.9	1.8	1.5
92d	1.8	2.2	2.6	1.4	1.3	1.3	1.3	1.3	2.1	3.0	1.7	1.0
93d	3.3	3.2	3.6	2.5	3.3	1.9	3.7	2.9	3.6	4.1	3.1	2.7
94th	3.1	2.9	3.2	2.1	3.7	3.0	2.2	3.4	3.4	3.3	3.1	3.0
96th	3.2	2.9	3.3	2.2	3.6	2.0	3.3	3.1	3.6	3.8	3.3	2.4

Table 9-8. The Use of Recorded Voting by House Republicans

Congress	Republicans in House (%)	Amendments Sponsored by Republicans (%)	Unrecorded Teller Amendments Sponsored by Republicans (%)	Recorded Vote Amendments Sponsored by Republicans (%)
84th	46.7	37.0	52.5	—
88th	40.5	46.9	61.9	—
91st	44.1	31.6	38.1	—
92d	41.4	28.9	—	37.2
93d	43.0	43.8	—	50.1
94th	33.1	39.1	—	49.2
96th	36.3	41.1	—	51.3

positively related to amending activity, with clear liberals more active than moderates and moderates more active than clear conservatives. Liberals' activism was not always matched by success, particularly in the Ninety-first and Ninety-second Congresses (table 9-9). Their frustrations with committee products and lack of success on the floor served as important stimuli for the reforms of the early 1970s.

Seniority

One of the enduring truths about the prereform House is the importance of apprenticeship as a norm governing rank-and-file participation. New members were expected to devote a period of time to learning House politics and policy substance before participating actively in decision-making (Asher 1973). If the norm applied to committee activities, as it did, it surely applied to the floor. The norm reinforced the seniority system and protected the dominance of full committee chairmen and their close allies, thereby enhancing the significance of formal position and structure for policy-making. We are led to expect precious little amending activity by junior members prior to the 1970s and very little indeed in the 1950s. Table 9-7 yields some clues about the timing and extent of the demise of the apprenticeship norm.

Junior members—those in their first, second, or third term—were distinctly less likely to sponsor floor amendments in the 1950s and 1960s than more senior members. The differences were not as large as one might expect, largely because senior members offered few amendments as well. Junior members also were far less successful than more senior members (table 9-9). Overall, junior members were only a little better than half as successful as more senior members prior to 1973. The substantive content of junior members' amendments cannot be judged, unfortunately,

Table 9-9. Success Rate of Amendments by Party and Region, Seniority, and Ideology (Percentages)

Congress	All House Members	Party				Seniority				Ideology		
		Democrats			Republicans	1 Term	2 Terms	3 Terms	More Than 3 Terms	Liberal	Moderate	Conservative
		All	North	South								
84th	51.9	55.7	50.4	60.4	45.3	33.3	54.5	52.6	53.7	43.0	58.9	41.8
88th	42.5	50.9	55.1	47.1	33.0	26.4	28.8	22.7	50.0	53.8	42.8	32.5
91st	45.8	48.7	43.4	63.3	39.7	14.0	32.8	24.8	54.6	26.4	59.7	45.4
92d	47.1	50.3	46.7	62.9	39.3	22.9	24.6	43.8	52.5	37.6	54.4	48.4
93d	52.1	59.5	57.6	64.6	42.6	48.9	44.8	47.0	54.4	51.5	53.8	47.8
94th	54.7	61.2	59.8	65.9	44.6	46.4	51.4	54.3	57.9	56.3	57.2	46.0
96th	69.1	74.1	72.0	81.2	61.9	65.3	59.8	66.8	72.9	69.9	72.9	58.2

but it appears that junior members were at a distinct disadvantage in their efforts to shape policy on the floor.

Differences between junior and senior members' floor activity and success continued in the 1970s as both junior and senior members became far more active. Junior members, like others, showed greater activism in the 1970s, but, as a group, they did not reduce the gap between themselves and more senior members. In fact, the gap between freshman and senior members was greatest in the postreform Ninety-third and Ninety-sixth Congresses. The freshman participation rate in the Ninety-sixth reflected a general settling in aggressiveness since the late 1970s.

The pattern of change among successive cohorts during the period of reform is instructive as well. Each freshman class from the Ninety-first to the Ninety-third increased its amending activity in its sophomore year. Each succeeding freshman class during the reform period also exhibited more activity than the preceding freshman class. But the class of 1974, the freshman of the Ninety-fourth, stands out above the rest. These "Watergate babies" moved immediately to near the mean in the Ninety-fourth and above the sixty-five sophomores of that Congress.

The success rates of junior members improved markedly in the 1970s, although they did not quite match senior members' rates. We can speculate that expanded resources and opportunities at prefloor stages affected junior members' success rates. It is also likely that the breakdown of the apprenticeship norm made an independent contribution. As senior members and other junior members became more tolerant of junior members' floor participation, we would expect fewer negative votes cast out of spite and more assistance to be forthcoming from resourceful senior members.

Thus, the Ninety-third Congress proved to be a watershed Congress for junior members as well, in terms of both participation and success. For most junior members, participation, though substantially higher, continued to lag behind that of senior members. Floor success for junior members also continued to lag slightly behind that of senior members in the 1970s. The evidence, then, supports the view that the apprenticeship norm disappeared in the 1970s as an independent external constraint on junior members' participation, although the disadvantages of inexperience, fewer resources, and lack of institutional position continued to constrain many junior members.

Committee Position

The norm of apprenticeship was closely related to the norms of specialization and intercommittee reciprocity. Members' apprenticeship was served within the confines of their committee assignments, providing a basis for specialization and the rationale of expertise for deference to the policy recommendations of committees by outsiders. Apprenticeship, specialization, and intercommittee reciprocity made the informal seniority system and the formal committee system a coherent whole. To the extent that the apprenticeship norm was no longer observed, a recognized specialty became more difficult to develop and the rationale for deferring to committee members was undermined. The seniority and committee systems were weakened as more junior outsiders dared to challenge committee and subcommittee chairmen on the floor. The obliteration of apprenticeship in the early 1970s suggests a similar demise for the specialization and intercommittee reciprocity in floor decision-making.

Committee membership was a powerful force shaping floor participation throughout the period under study. With very little variance, members of the committee(s) of origin sponsored about half of all floor amendments in each of the seven Congresses (table 9-10). In contrast, committee sizes averaged only 8 or 9 percent of the chamber. The disproportionate floor activity of committee members was unaffected by the reforms of the early 1970s. The unavoidable conclusion is that specialization by committee assignment continued to shape floor participation in the 1970s.

At first blush, the stability of this pattern may seem to undermine the proposition that the norms of specialization and intercommittee reciprocity have weakened in the House. However, this pattern must be viewed in the context of the changing absolute level of amending activity. Sponsorship patterns for the Eighty-fourth and Eighty-eighth Congresses were consistent with both norms. Neither members of the originating committee(s) nor nonmembers were actively amending legislation on the floor, as the low absolute frequency of amendments for both groups in these congresses indicates. Generally, committee members supported their committees on the floor and nonmembers deferred to the committee specialists. In the early 1970s, both committee members and outsiders increased their rates of participation at about the same time and to the same degree. As table 9-10 indicates, the absolute number of amendments increased for nearly all members, both committee members and nonmembers, when the upsurge occurred in the Ninety-third. The 1970s appear to have brought a sweeping change that undermined both committee cohesiveness and intercommittee reciprocity. Nonmembers became less deferential to committee products just as those products were challenged increasingly by committee members. Committee members, with their advantage of interest, expertise, and staff support, continued to be represented disproportionately among amendment sponsors.

The norm of intercommittee reciprocity waned in terms of outcomes as well. As nonmembers became more active they also became relatively

Table 9-10. Committee Position of Amendment Sponsors

Congress	Committee Members						Non-Committee Members					
	Full Committee Ch	Subcommittee Ch	Full Committee RMM	Subcommittee RMM	Other	All	Full Committee Ch	Subcommittee Ch	Full Committee RMM	Subcommittee RMM	Other	All
84th	6.9 (28)	9.4 (38)	7.7 (31)	3.7 (15)	23.5 (95)	51.1 (207)	5.2 (21)	9.1 (37)	3.5 (14)	5.2 (21)	25.9 (105)	48.9 (198)
88th	6.2 (38)	12.9 (79)	2.6 (16)	10.3 (63)	20.5 (126)	52.4 (322)	2.1 (13)	7.2 (44)	1.8 (11)	13.5 (83)	23.0 (141)	47.6 (292)
91st	6.8 (60)	12.1 (106)	1.9 (17)	7.1 (62)	23.7 (208)	51.7 (453)	2.6 (230)	11.7 (103)	1.5 (13)	7.3 (64)	25.2 (221)	48.3 (424)
92d	4.0 (32)	11.1 (88)	1.6 (13)	6.9 (55)	24.5 (194)	48.2 (382)	2.0 (16)	10.6 (84)	2.3 (18)	6.7 (53)	30.2 (239)	51.8 (410)
93d	3.5 (50)	10.1 (143)	3.1 (44)	12.9 (183)	21.9 (311)	51.5 (731)	2.0 (29)	10.9 (154)	3.8 (54)	6.9 (98)	24.9 (353)	48.5 (688)
94th	2.2 (30)	12.4 (169)	2.6 (36)	12.2 (167)	22.8 (311)	52.2 (713)	1.5 (20)	12.9 (176)	3.1 (43)	9.1 (124)	21.2 (290)	47.8 (653)
96th	3.6 (50)	13.1 (181)	1.7 (24)	11.4 (157)	20.1 (277)	49.9 (689)	2.9 (40)	12.5 (173)	3.4 (47)	12.2 (169)	19.0 (263)	51.1 (692)

Ch = chairman; RMM = ranking minority member. The first number given is a percentage; the number in parentheses is the actual number of sponsors.

more successful (table 9-11). The difference between members and non-members was cut in half with the advent of electronic recorded voting in the Ninety-third. A 20 percent gap was reduced to 10 percent from the 1960s to the 1970s. Nonmembers' activism and success were mutually reinforcing developments, no doubt.

Beyond committee membership alone, holding a majority party committee leadership position is strongly related to floor amendment success. Full committee and subcommittee chairmen (of a committee of origin) had success rates far above average in all seven Congresses. Full committee chairmen were successful more than 90 percent of the time, and subcommittee chairmen were successful over 80 percent of the time. In contrast, ranking subcommittee Republicans generally were successful less than half of the time. On the other hand, full committee chairmen became less conspicuous, relatively speaking, on the floor in the 1970s. Subcommittee chairmen maintained a stable share of floor amendments, not demonstrating the increase one might have expected with the intra-committee reforms of the early 1970s.

The success of majority party committee leaders is not due to the resources associated with position alone, of course. Committee and subcommittee chairs have the advantage of numbers as members of the majority party. Moreover, they often introduce amendments representing postcommittee decisions on behalf of their committees, decisions that frequently represent an evolving consensus on previously unresolved issues. Perhaps we should be surprised that they lose as often as they do.

The most significant increase in amending activity occurred among the ranking minority members of House subcommittees (of committees of origin). Unfortunately, the data do not permit us to determine whether a sponsor comes from the *sub*committee of origin. Ranking subcommittee Republicans made up a highly disproportionate part of the Republican upsurge in the Ninety-third and held their own thereafter, matching their majority party counterparts. These midlevel Republicans may have been among the most suppressed members with respect to amending activity prior to the reforms. Their success within their committees was limited, and their resources to pursue floor amendments were limited as well. The early 1970s brought minority party staffing to many committees for the first time, and the opportunities and incentives of electronic recorded voting opened the door for their participation.

In general, then, committee position remains a distinct advantage in floor amending activity, although its significance is not as great as it was in the 1950s and early 1960s. The most successful amendment sponsors, by a substantial margin, are full committee and subcommittee chairmen of the originating committees. Nevertheless, the norms of committee

Table 9-11. *Success Rates of Amendments by Committee Position (Percentages)*

Congress	Committee Members						Non–Committee Members					
	Full Committee Ch	Subcommittee Ch	Full Committee RMM	Subcommittee RMM	Other	All	Full Committee Ch	Subcommittee Ch	Full Committee RMM	Subcommittee RMM	Other	All
84th	89.3	73.7	64.5	60.0	47.4	61.4	57.1	43.2	50.0	42.9	36.9	41.9
88th	89.5	80.8	60.0	44.3	28.7	53.1	53.8	31.8	27.3	33.7	26.6	30.8
91st	95.0	80.0	62.5	45.2	31.9	54.3	78.3	43.7	30.8	37.5	29.4	36.8
92d	100.0	90.7	45.5	39.6	43.5	58.4	31.3	48.8	22.2	39.6	33.1	36.6
93d	96.0	84.6	65.9	32.8	51.3	57.0	72.4	52.6	42.6	45.9	43.4	46.8
94th	100.0	80.5	52.8	48.5	50.0	59.3	95.0	58.0	48.8	39.5	45.9	49.6
96th	94.0	88.4	66.7	65.6	65.0	73.4	85.0	63.6	57.4	57.4	68.3	64.7

Ch = chairman; RMM = ranking minority member.

specialization and intercommittee reciprocity weakened substantially in the 1970s. Non–committee members were more active and more successful than they were previously, and committee members demonstrated much less respect for the work of their own committees.

The Changing Character of Amendment Sponsors

Amendment sponsorship is now spread broadly in the House. Extreme activism on the floor, in the style of many senators, remains uncommon in the House. Even in the hyperactive Ninety-third Congress, only eight representatives offered fifteen or more amendments. Only about thirty members (less than 7 percent) sponsored ten or more amendments in the postreform Congresses, although that is up from the ten to fifteen members typical of the early 1960s. Those members that are more active than most are self-selected and generally respected for their legislative skills or policy expertise. The House is a more tolerant institution and is more appreciative of the advantages of collegial decision-making processes.

The breadth and speed of the expansion of amendment sponsorship in the early 1970s represented a revolutionary change in the use of the floor by rank-and-file members. While predictable distinctions in participation and success rates remain, few members ignore the floor as a place for pursuing personal policy initiatives or addressing grievances carried over from committee deliberations. Freshmen now regularly look for the right opportunity to make their amendment debut on the floor, minority party members often consider the floor their best chance at influencing policy, and committee members and outsiders alike appeal decisions made at prefloor stages. Effective floor participation now reinforces, and is reinforced by, effective participation in party and committee forums for most members.

COMMITTEES ON THE FLOOR

In the face of the sweeping changes in floor amending activity in the 1970s, it should not be surprising that nearly all House committees faced greater uncertainties on the floor. The degree of change this represented varied considerably among committees, however, and there are significant systematic differences in the pattern of change among committees. Especially important is the possibility that committees with large, salient jurisdictions might have been able to insulate themselves from amending activity, thereby minimizing the significance of the changes on the floor. Because space and good judgment do not permit a detailed treatment of each committee here, only broad generalizations about the changing floor experiences of committees can be offered. I do so in two categories: substantive decision-making on the floor faced by each committee, and the committee membership of the amendment sponsors faced by each committee.

Facing Decisions on the Floor

Committees vary in many ways that are related to their floor experiences (Dodd 1972; Dyson and Soule 1970; Fenno 1966, 1973). Most of these ways are grounded in differences in jurisdictions and, perhaps more importantly, in their active policy agendas (Smith and Deering 1984). Generally speaking, incentives are greater for members to pursue floor amendments where committees' policy agendas are larger, more salient, and more controversial. This truism suggests two propositions. First, committees with the largest, most salient, and most controversial policy agendas have experienced the greatest change in floor experience during the period of revolutionary change of the early 1970s. Such committees may have always faced more amending activity on the floor, but the new opportunities for antagonists to pursue their legislative fights on the floor affected these committees disproportionately. And second, increases (decreases) in the size, salience, and controversy of a committee's policy agenda enhance (reduce) the effects of the expanded amending opportunities of the early 1970s.

To explore floor decision-making experiences for committees, I again turn to the volume, contestedness, and outcomes of amending activity. The number of amendments associated with each committee can be determined from table 9-12, where amendments are divided between committee members and nonmembers. Unfortunately, good quantitative measures of agenda size, salience, and controversy are not available, especially for the entire period under investigation. Instead, I take advantage of some informed judgment available in previous work (Smith and Deering 1984, chap. 3). The now familiar committee categories (prestige, policy, and constituency) will help structure the discussion (Bullock 1976; Fenno 1973; Smith and Deering 1984).

The cross-sectional assumption is supported by the historical record: committees with large, salient, and controversial agendas are associated with the most substantive decision-making on the floor. If a fairly stringent standard is applied—that a committee be above the median for the number of amendments, the number of contested amendments, and the number of successful amendments—nine committees meet the standard for the prereform Congresses and eight for the postreform Congresses. All are above average in the size, salience, and controversy in their policy agendas. Appropriations stands out above the rest in both periods. The scope and

Table 9-12. *Amendment Sponsors by Committee, Members and Nonmembers*

	84th		88th		91st		92d		93d		94th		96th	
	M	NM	M	NM	M	NM	M	NM	M	NM	M	NM	M	NM
Prestige committees														
Appropriations	38	57	18	55	60	87	58	116	84	135	101	112	110	223
Rules	4	—	1	8	5	55	3	4	9	18	10	13	15	4
Ways and Means	3	2	2	3	8	7	2	4	2	5	31	33	29	20
Budget	—	—	—	—	—	—	—	—	—	—	15	14	27	40
Policy committees														
Banking	14	7	16	6	53	34	20	23	58	53	48	24	56	59
Commerce	7	6	14	8	57	37	26	25	98	70	111	88	139	110
Education and Labor	22	3	43	23	40	28	60	51	76	78	45	39	44	10
Foreign Affairs	6	8	32	28	30	14	16	15	39	49	31	72	100	83
Government Operations	3	0	5	6	1	2	7	3	35	36	24	23	18	23
Judiciary	12	23	73	68	45	19	34	22	42	17	59	51	66	53
Constituency committees														
Agriculture	19	14	32	19	13	18	16	18	45	45	51	19	37	24
Armed Services	10	28	13	14	27	29	32	28	26	14	25	16	35	27
Interior	22	10	36	16	17	5	35	20	112	51	61	48	50	36
Merchant Marine	2	2	0	0	2	7	9	11	1	0	6	14	35	9
Public Works	15	7	3	8	7	20	25	33	43	25	12	10	54	35
Veterans' Affairs	5	6	0	0	5	3	2	0	4	0	1	0	0	1
Science	—	—	5	1	3	9	0	3	13	16	14	16	41	18
Others														
Atomic Energy	12	4	1	0	1	0	2	10	5	14	14	21	—	—
District of Columbia	7	0	7	7	41	13	16	6	24	11	2	2	2	2
House Administration	1	0	3	1	1	8	13	13	7	6	15	11	4	1
Post Office	5	21	18	15	37	25	5	4	9	13	30	25	35	16
Small Business	—	—	—	—	—	—	—	—	—	—	—	—	3	2

M = committee members; N = Nonmembers.

frequency of appropriations legislation has long made it the target of floor amendments. Five policy-oriented committees — Banking, Commerce, Education and Labor, Foreign Affairs, and Judiciary — are substantially above the median on the three measures for both periods as well.[6] Three constituency-oriented committees (Agriculture, Armed Services, Post Office) are above the median on all three measures in the prereform Congresses but only Agriculture meets the standard in the postreform period. Interior, whose environmental legislation made it very similar to the policy-oriented committees in the 1970s, meets the standard for the postreform Congresses.

The first proposition that the reform period affected the committees with large, salient, and controversial agendas disproportionately also is supported. Of the twenty committees that can be compared, Appropriations and the five policy committees account for over 46 percent of the increase in the number of floor amendments between the Ninety-second and Ninety-third Congresses. As a group, their proportionate increase also was slightly larger than that of other committees. Nearly 62 percent of the increase in contested amendments over those two Congresses occurred on these six committees, although the committees vary greatly inside and outside of this group. Finally, the six committees account for 56 percent of the increase in the number of successful amendments. In absolute terms, then, Appropriations and the five policy committees exhibited a greater increase in the substantive decision-making they faced on the floor than other committees.

Ways and Means felt the dramatic affect of amending activity in 1975–76 (see Rudder 1977). Without the protection of closed rules, the committee suddenly became vulnerable to floor amendments. In February 1975, liberal Democrats employed their new power to force floor consideration of amendments and imposed a deletion of the oil depletion allowance on the committee. Ways and Means found itself about on par with Education and Labor in the number of amendments (and the number of successful amendments) it faced on the floor.

The second proposition is more difficult to evaluate because of the absence of good measures of agenda salience and controversy over time. Two pairs of committees offer good illustrations, however (Smith and Deering 1984, chap. 4). Both Commerce and Interior were directly affected by the rise of two issues, first environmental protection and then energy, that greatly increased member interest in membership on these committees and heightened the political significance of their decisions in the late 1960s and early 1970s. They experienced the greatest increases in amending activity between the Ninety-second and Ninety-third Congresses in the House. The number of floor amendments rose from 51 to 168 for Commerce and from 55 to 163 for Interior. Issues such as energy conservation and strip mining attracted dozens of amendments on the floor. On the other hand, the agendas of Education and Labor and Judiciary declined in size, salience, and controversy from the mid-1960s to the early 1970s. Divisive labor-management and civil rights issues lost their dominance on the congressional agenda by the early 1970s. Education and Labor had a below average increase from 111 to 154 floor amendments between the Ninety-second and Ninety-third and dropped to 84 in the Ninety-fourth and 54 in the Ninety-sixth. Between the Ninety-second and Ninety-third Judiciary saw only three more amendments on the floor. Thus, it appears that both cross-sectional and longitudinal variation in amending activity is related to committees' policy agendas.

Finally, it is worth noting that the variation in floor experiences among committees has increased fairly steadily since the mid-1950s. This is true for volume, the number of contested amendments, and the number of successful amendments.[7] The change is greatest in the variation in the number of successful amendments. The increasing means for all three factors make room for greater variation, of course, but the pattern represents a genuine increase in the disparity among committees in the difficulties and uncertainties faced on the floor. The homogenizing influences of rules and norms are gone, connecting floor experiences much more directly to the nature of committee policy agendas and member interest than they once were.

Sponsors and Committees

As might be expected, all committees with any significant level of amending activity on the floor experienced an increase in the number of committee members and non members offering amendments (table 9-12). Two distinct patterns deserve notice. First, the five active policy-oriented committees of the prereform period exhibited a highly disproportionate level of amending activity by committee members. For only Foreign Affairs and Judiciary in the Eighty-fourth Congress did more nonmembers than members sponsor amendments. This supports the findings of previous research that the members of policy-oriented committees cared less about committee cohesiveness than members of prestige or constituency committees and were less inhibited about pursuing their policy preferences on the floor (Fenno 1973; Smith and Deering 1984).

The pattern holds less well in the 1970s for the policy-oriented committees. Indeed, a disproportionate part of the increasing activity of nonmembers affected these committees. As committees with large, salient agendas and histories of incohesiveness on the floor, it should not be surprising that newly active outsiders would take special interest in their legislation and would not be inhibited about amending their bills.

Second, Appropriations is the only committee in the prereform Congresses that consistently faced more amendments from outsiders than from committee members. The pattern confirms the uniqueness of Appropriations as described in Fenno's *Power of the Purse* (1966). Fenno noted that Appropriations' members prized committee cohesiveness on the floor: "Every section of the book has revealed the Committee's own conviction that its floor success depends on its ability to present a united front. . . . Unity is the one key variable over which Committee members can exercise some control, and they bend every effort to do so" (460). At the same time, Appropriations' broad subject matter and its tendency to run into conflict with authorizing committees encouraged a large number of outsiders to offer floor amendments. The net result was a lower than average success rate for amendments to Appropriations bills. The success rate mean for the three prereform Congresses included in this study was 34.8 percent for Appropriations amendments, well below the 52.6 percent for all amendments.

Appropriations lost much of its advantage in the 1970s (Bach 1986b). In the three postreform Congresses, both committee members and non members were more active on the floor on Appropriations bills. Floor unity was much less in evidence as Appropriations' members averaged nearly two amendments to committee bills in the Ninety-fourth and Ninety-sixth Congresses. The declining loyalty to the committee on the floor reflected the changes within Appropriations that undermined the power of the full committee chairman, created greater individualism, and undermined the strong norm of committee support (Schick 1980, 424–36). Nevertheless, outsiders still outnumbered members in the postreform period, and the success rate of amendments to a Appropriations bills still lagged behind amendments to other committees' legislation. In those three Congresses, just less than half of a Appropriations amendments passed, while just over 60 percent were adopted for the typical committee. One explanation offered by participants for the lower success rate is that the budget process imposed special constraints on Appropriations bills not faced as directly by most other legislation (but see Schick 1980, 469).

The relationship between the proportion of committee members challenging their committee with floor amendments and the success rate of amendments remains an important one. With the declining differences in the success rates of members and nonmembers, one might have expected the ratio of members to nonmembers to be more weakly related to success rates in the 1970s. It was not. The relationship between the percentage of amendments offered by committee members and the success rate (across committees) is strong and positive in six of the seven Congresses examined.[8] Moreover, it is generally stronger in the 1970s than in the earlier Congresses. Committee members retain distinct advantages in resources and external support over nonmembers and may have the first pick of viable amendments.

In sum, the committees affected the most by the changing role of the floor were those that had the most to lose. If Appropriations, Ways and Means, and the five policy-oriented committees had not been so affected, the substantive impact of the changes would not have been meaningful.

SOME LESSONS

In several respects, conventional wisdom has been supported by a closer look at floor amending activity. The advent of electronic recorded voting was a major stimulant of amending activity. Voting procedures affect outcomes. The norms of apprenticeship, specialization, and intercommittee reciprocity declined as constraints on floor participation. Liberals were the most active ideological group in the 1970s. Committee position mattered in the House in the 1950s and 1960s. The prestige committees, Appropriations and Ways and Means, fell on hard times on the floor in the 1970s.

Not-so-conventional wisdom also has been given a boost. Amending activity was already increasing before the 1970s. More than just recorded-vote amendments multiplied in the 1970s. Roll-call votes do not tell the whole story, even for floor voting. Multiple referral is positively related to amending activity. Minority party Republicans took advantage of the new amending opportunities of the 1970s disproportionately. Junior and non–committee members still lag slightly behind senior committee members in their floor activism and success. Committee position still matters in the House. The policy-oriented committees of the House faced continuous amending activity on the floor during the 1970s.

What do the developments on the floor mean for broad interpretations of House decision-making processes? Unfortunately, treatments of the House in the 1970s and 1980s are plagued by vague and confusing terminology. There is a plethora of related but not synonymous terms, which are often used interchangeably: democratization, decentralization, atomization, fragmentation, diffusion of power—to name a few. Many studies of change in Congress slur differences in meaning and therefore ignore important implications for congressional politics. Care in terminology is critical here, for it yields an important qualification on most interpretations of House decision-making processes in the 1970s and 1980s.

The diffusion of power away from full committee chairmen during the early 1970s occurred in many directions. Decentralizing change took the form of devolution of the power of full committee chairmen to subcommittees and their chairmen. Smaller groups of members in more numerous decision-making units assumed primary responsibility for devising legislation within committees. Decentralization in this way tended to fragment jurisdiction and responsibility when it was not checked by counterbalancing change at earlier or later stages of decision-making. Less dramatic but notable centralizing reform came with the reinvigoration of the powers of the Speaker, both as a leader of the majority party and as the presiding officer of the House.

Underlying both sets of reforms was the assertion of a greater voice in policy-making by rank-and-file members. The diffusion of power away from full committee chairmen occurred in a way that limited the autonomy of committees, subcommittees, and formal leaders. Committees retained great independence in setting their own agendas and devising legislation in the 1970s, but their decisions were less likely to go unchecked. To the extent that committees, subcommittees, and formal leaders became more accountable to rank-and-file members, the reforms had a democratizing effect. That much is fully appreciated.

But the term "democratization" does not capture the full meaning of the developments in the House. Standard criteria for democracy, at least within the majority party, could have been met by reforms enhancing rank-and-file control of the selection of committees and their leaders. Indeed, norms restraining participation on the basis of deference to expertise are not inherently inimical to the responsiveness expected from periodic elections. It is a matter of the bounds of expected responsiveness and the time frame within which responsiveness is judged. But accountability and the responsiveness it might produce were not enough. More extensive change was sought. Many members wanted direct and frequent influence over policy outcomes. Some wanted to expand the range of interests reflected in policy outcomes. At a minimum, they wanted a greater voice in shaping the policy alternatives from which they must choose, which required greater participation at earlier stages in the process. For some, participation itself was highly valued, quite apart from its implications for policy or career advancement. Such a role involves going beyond voting on policy alternatives; it involves participating in a process of discussion and deliberation. In pure or ideal form, it might be labeled "collegial" decision making, a process in which members are encouraged to participate because they are assumed to have valuable and legitimate contributions to offer. In short, the egalitarianism emerging as a norm governing interpersonal relations yielded a preference for collegial mechanisms of collective choice.

Collegial decision-making serves as an alternative model to the more common centralized and decentralized models in which House decision-making is usually conceived.[9] Norms that impose artificial constraints on participation—such as apprenticeship or even party loyalty—are inconsistent with collegial decision-making. The related jurisdictional lines and party structures also interfere with collegial decision-making in ideal form. But like truly centralized and decentralized systems, collegial decision-making cannot be realized in the House. The size and workload of the House dictate an intricate division of labor and provide incentives for a decentralized structure that run contrary to the premises of collegial decision-making. Moreover, the lack of intense, broad interest in most issues supports decentralization by default. Yet, the new role of the floor and related developments can only be understood by recognizing this alternative direction of change. Two implications of this direction of change are particularly significant.

First, the developments on the floor were integral to the changes within House committees. Most obviously, the expansion of amending opportunities and the advent of recorded voting made it easier for committee members to challenge their chairmen on the floor. The reforms did not strip chairmen of all power. Chairmen retained day-to-day control of committee agendas, large staffs, and a reservoir of expertise and political relations. As a result, rank-and-file members, especially minority party members, often require extracommittee sources of bargaining leverage to be effective participants within their committees. In some cases, then, a viable floor option enhanced the collegial character of decision-making within committees. Occasionally, extracommittee leverage proves important to subcommittee chairmen as well. The reforms created independent but not autonomous subcommittees. Subcommittees are challenged frequently in full committee, and full committee decisions, which go against subcommittee recommendations with some frequency, are then appealed to the floor. The political competitiveness of many subcommittee chairmen would suffer in the absence of a viable floor option. Thus, in certain circumstances, collegial or democratic reforms supported decentralization within committees.

Second, moves in the direction of collegial decision-making served to check the extent of decentralization in the House. In a direct way, floor amending activity undermined the autonomy of all standing committees, regardless of the degree of decentralization within them. It changed the strategic setting in which committee members operate by expanding the range of interests involved, enlarging the scope of conflict, and adding new uncertainties. The new uncertainties on the floor also often created difficulties in molding bargaining positions in anticipation of a conference with the Senate.

Expanding amending activity also played a role in other developments that serve indirectly to undermine the autonomy of committees. As the floor became a more important location for substantive decision-making, members looked for ways to exploit their new opportunities. Much of the growth of single-issue caucuses, party caucus and committee activity, and ad hoc groups of other kinds has occurred because of opportunities to pursue policy interests on the floor. Many of these innovative organizational forms are explicitly vehicles for organizing support for floor amendments.[10] Others, such as leadership task forces, represent efforts to manage the potential chaos of floor activity through accommodation and cooptation. Within the majority party, the more frequent use of whip and caucus meetings reflects the intensity of interest among rank-and-file members in floor strategy, as well as leadership efforts to learn about their concerns and accommodate them in advance of floor debate. All of these developments encouraged participation outside of the traditional bounds of formal committee and party structures.

Furthermore, the enhanced role of the floor encourages continual formation and reformation of modes of participation and decision-making. Traditional reliance on the committee system and supportive norms tended to insulate policy outcomes from change in the House at large, whether in the intensity and breadth of interest in an issue or in the strength of factions. Adaptations that did occur in the short run had to come from committees and their chairmen, who, protected by seniority and reappointment norms, could slow or minimize the adjustments. The new role of the floor encourages swifter adaptation by committees in the face of nonmembers who rapidly seek to exploit or defend against changes in the chamber. How to devise strategy and policy—who should be involved, at what time, with what decision rule—is taken for granted less frequently. Solutions suitable in one setting may not be suitable in the next.

Despite the clear thrust of these developments in the House, opportunities for truly collegial participation are still greatly outnumbered by those structured by the committee system. As has been noted, the committee system has adjusted internally in ways consistent with the demands for more meaningful participation. Moreover, some of the pressure for extracommittee forms of participation has been relieved by the routinization of committee assignments and subcommittee self-selection (Gertzog 1976; Smith and Ray 1983). These practices have permitted most members, in the majority party at least, to gravitate to committees and subcommittees of special interest to them. Nevertheless, the demands for extracommittee modes of participation continue. Substantive decision-making on the floor is likely to continue at a high rate for the foreseeable future.

Acknowledgments. I would like to thank Judy Newman and Emily Zimmerman for their extraordinary research assistance. Jim Gold, Radhika Karmarker, Don Kennedy, Ben Page, and Karen Vogler also provided superb assistance. Without their diligence, patience, and good humor, this study would not have been possible. For allowing me access to some of their data on multiple referrals and suspensions, I thank Stanley Bach, Roger Davidson, and Tom Kephart.

NOTES

1. All four types of amendments are included: first-degree amendments, amendments to pending amendments, substitute amendments, amendments to substitute amendments. Excluded from the study are motions to "strike the enacting clause," pro forma amendments such as those "to strike the last word," previously noticed amendments not actually offered on the floor, amendments withdrawn by their sponsors, amendments ruled out of order, and committee amendments.

Amendments were identified by using the Index to the bound *Congressional Record*. Each member's floor amendments are listed in the Index with the bill or resolution number and page number in the Record. The amendments were sorted by page number, and the *Record* was examined to determine whether the amendment was in fact offered, whether more than one amendment was offered, and the outcome. The compilation is dependent on the accuracy of the Index.

2. Identifying the location of substantive decision-making is difficult in a multistage legislative process, at least in the aggregate and over time. Ideally, assessing the location of substantive decision-making would rest on a content analysis of decisions made at each stage of the legislative process. Both data and methodological limitations make that impossible. A second-best strategy would be to follow amending activity at each stage in order that floor decision-making could be viewed in the context of earlier and later stages. But even that is impossible for more than just a few recent Congresses.

The focus on amending activity ignores other parliamentary forms in which decisions are made on the floor. Most obviously, final passage decisions, motions to strike the enacting clause, motions to recommit, and similar forms are ignored. On rare occasions, important legislation is defeated in these ways. A count for the Ninety-fifth and Ninety-sixth Congresses showed that about two percent of all legislation considered on the floor was defeated (Bach 1981b, 573). In many cases the legislation was revived and passed later, sometimes after alteration. Other floor decisions, such as votes on rules and presidential vetoes, also are ignored.

3. This estimate is based on the number of recorded tellers in the Ninety-second Congress and the number of electronic votes in the Ninety-third, assuming that recorded votes in the Ninety-second took thirty minutes each and that electronic votes took fifteen minutes each.

4. These estimates are based on the number of measures passed on the floor as reported in the *Daily Digest* of the *Congressional Record*. The adjusted figures are based on measures passed that were not passed by suspension of the rules, but include measures (eleven) that were debated under a closed rule.

5. Figures for recorded-vote amendments are similar but not as dramatic. The daily rates for the Ninety-second and Ninety-third are 0.65 and 1.10, respectively. The hourly rates are 0.14 and 0.24, respectively.

6. Only Government Operations is not on the top of the list among the policy-oriented committees. Members gained an interest in pursuing personal policy interests as fraud and waste in government became popular issues in the early 1970s. The

committee still handled far fewer bills than the other policy-oriented committees in the 1970s.

7. For the Eighty-fourth, Eighty-eighth, Ninety-first, Ninety-second, Ninety-third, Ninety-fourth, and Ninety-sixth Congresses, the standard deviations in the number of amendments are 21.4, 35.0, 43.6, 39.5, 69.4, 64.8, and 81.4, respectively. The standard deviations in the number of contested amendments are 5.8, 7.3, 5.5, 3.3, 6.8, 8.0, and 4.1, respectively. The standard deviations in the number of successful amendments are 10.8, 12.9, 15.1, 17.6, 32.7, 32.6, 59.6, respectively.

8. The Pearson r's between the percentage offered by members and the success rate for each of the seven Congresses are, in order, .44, $-.06$, .21, .59, .64, .42, and .34. Only the coefficients for the Eighty-eighth and Ninety-first Congresses are not significant at the .05 level.

9. Similar notions are discussed in recent literature; see Cooper 1970; Maass 1983; Mansbridge 1983. As Cooper points out, what I have labeled collegial decision-making is close to the standard applied by members of the early Congresses.

10. In the Ninety-ninth Congress, for example, Chairman Les Aspin faced numerous outsiders offering amendments to the defense authorization bills reported from the House Armed Services Committee. In the first session, the amendments were offered in the typical ad hoc fashion on the floor. Some were adapted, but were dropped in conference, stimulating an outcry from their supporters. In the second session, in response to demands for a voice from committee outsiders, Aspin created task forces of outsiders, provided committee staff assistance, and promised to support their recommendations on the floor. A large package of procurement reform proposals was adopted this way.

REFERENCES

Asher, Herbert B. 1973. "The Learning of Legislative Norms." *American Political Science Review* 67:499–513.

Bach, Stanley. 1981a. "Special Rules in the House of Representatives: Themes and Contemporary Variations." *Congressional Studies* 8:37–58.

———. 1981b. "The Structure of Choice in the House of Representatives: The Impact of Complex Special Rules." *Harvard Journal of Legislation* 18:553–602.

———. 1986a. "Suspension of the Rules in the House of Representatives." Congressional Research Service, 12 May 1986.

———. 1986b. "Representatives and Committees on the Floor: Amendments to Appropriations' Bills in the House of Representatives, 1963–1982." *Congress and the Presidency* 13:40–58.

Bullock, Charles S., III. 1976. "Motivations for U.S. Congressional Committee Preferences: Freshmen of the 92d Congress." *Legislative Studies Quarterly* 1:201–12.

Clausen, Aage R. 1973. *How Congressmen Decide: A Policy Focus*. New York: St. Martin's Press.

Cooper, Joseph. 1970. *The Origins of the Standing Committees and the Development of the Modern House*. Houston: Rice University Studies, vol. 56.

Davidson, Roger H. 1986. "The Legislative Work of Congress." Paper delivered at the 1986 annual meeting of the American Political Science Association, Washington, D.C.

Dodd, Lawrence C. 1972. "Committee Integration in the Senate: A Comparative Analysis." *Journal of Politics* 34:1135–71.

Dyson, James W., and John W. Soule. 1970. "Congressional Committee Behavior on Roll Call Votes: The U.S. House of Representatives." *Midwest Journal of Political Science* 14:626–47.

Fenno, Richard F. 1966. *The Power of the Purse: Appropriations Politics in Congress.* Boston: Little, Brown.

———. 1973. *Congressmen in Committees.* Boston: Little Brown.

Gertzog, Irwin N. 1976. "Routinization of Committee Assignments in the U.S. House of Representatives." *American Journal of Political Science* 29:693–713.

Kingdon, John W. 1973. *Congressmen's Voting Decisions.* New York: Harper and Row.

Maass, Arthur. 1983. *Congress and the Common Good.* New York: Basic Books.

Mansbridge, Jane J. 1983. *Beyond Adversary Democracy.* Chicago: University of Chicago Press.

Oleszek, Walter J. 1984. *Congressional Procedures and the Policy Process*, 2d ed. Washington, D.C.: CQ Press.

Oleszek, Walter J., Roger H. Davidson, and Thomas Kephart. 1986. "The Incidence and Impact of Multiple Referrals in the House of Representatives." Congressional Research Service, July 1986.

Oppenheimer, Bruce I. 1977. "The Rules Committee: New Arm of Leadership in a Decentralized House." In *Congress Reconsidered*, edited by Lawrence C. Dodd and Bruce I. Oppenheimer. New York: Praeger, 96–116.

Ornstein, Norman J. 1981. "The House and Senate in a New Congress." In *The New Congress*, edited by Norman J. Ornstein and Thomas E. Mann. Washington, D.C.: American Enterprise Institute.

Ornstein, Norman J., Thomas E. Mann, Michael J. Malbin, and John F. Bibby. 1982. *Vital Statistics on Congress.* Washington, D.C.: American Enterprise Institute.

Rudder, Catherine E. 1977. "Committee Reform and the Revenue Process." In *Congress Reconsidered*, edited by Lawrence C. Dodd and Bruce I. Oppenheimer. New York: Praeger, 117–39.

Salisbury, Robert H. 1983. "Interest Groups: Toward a New Understanding." In *Interest Group Politics*, edited by Allan J. Cigler and Burdett A. Loomis. Washington, D.C.: CQ Press.

Schick, Allen. 1980. *Congress and Money.* Washington, D.C.: Urban Institute.

Schiff, Steven H., and Steven S. Smith. 1983. "Generational Change and the Allocation of Staff in the U.S. Congress." *Legislative Studies Quarterly* 8:457–68.

Sinclair, Barbara. 1983. *Majority Leadership in the U.S. House.* Baltimore: Johns Hopkins Press.

———. 1985. "Senate Styles and Senate Decision-Making." Paper presented at the 1985 annual meeting of the American Political Science Association, New Orleans, La.

Smith, Steven S. 1985. "New Patterns of Decisionmaking in Congress." In *The New Direction in American Politics*, edited by John E. Chubb and Paul E. Peterson. Washington, D.C.: Brookings Institution.

Smith, Steven S., and Christopher J. Deering. 1984. *Committees in Congress.* Washington, D.C.: CQ Press.

Smith, Steven S., and Bruce A. Ray. 1983. "The Impact of Congressional Reform: House Democratic Committee Assignments." *Congress and the Presidency* 10:219–40.

Sullivan, Terry. 1984. *Procedural Structure.* New York: Praeger.

Chapter 10

State Party Delegations in the U.S. House of Representatives: A Comparative Study of Group Cohesion

BARBARA SINCLAIR

Congressional scholars, in recent years, have shown an increasing interest in state party delegations in the House of Representatives. David Truman's[1] findings concerning voting cohesion among the members of state party delegations have been confirmed in recent studies by Donald Matthews and James Stimson[2] and by Aage Clausen.[3] While differing in approach and method, these studies show that many state party delegations display considerable voting cohesion, and the authors all infer that this cohesion is, in part, the result of interaction and cue-giving within the delegation. Using data obtained from interviews and observation, Alan Fiellin[4] and John Kessel[5] showed that the delegations they studied, the New York Democratic delegation and the Washington delegation respectively, are, in fact, face-to-face groups in which the members serve as sources of information and as allies for one another. Work by Charles Clapp[6] and by Randall Ripley[7] also indicates that some state part delegations are sociological groups that influence the behavior of their members.

These studies suggest that some state party delegations, through the effect they have on their members' behavior, do influence the political process in the House. The studies also indicate that delegations vary

This chapter was originally published in the *Journal of Politics* 34, no. 1 (1972):199–222 and is reprinted by permission of the author and the University of Texas Press. It is based upon the author's Ph.D. dissertation, "State Party Delegations in the House of Representatives" (University of Rochester, 1970). Special thanks are due to Richard F. Fenno for his help and encouragement at every stage in the research project.

considerably in voting cohesion and in the extent to which they function as face-to-face groups. The purpose of this paper is to explore this latter variation and attempt an explanation. An explanation of this variation in group cohesiveness should clarify the role of delegations in the House and increase our understanding of political behavior in Congress. The existence of the delegation as a categorical group is merely a function of electoral outcomes; its existence as a sociological group is, however, dependent upon the decisions of its members.

HYPOTHESES

The basic framework of analysis is derived from small-group theory. The limitations of the data prohibit a use of the more sophisticated ideas and theoretical relations of that literature. A few basic principles will be used to suggest hypotheses, but no attempt will be made to use or test all of the possible small-group findings that might in fact be relevant to our task. This is an explanatory study, and the author's interest centers on the politically significant behavioral indicators and consequences of cohesiveness, not on cohesiveness as a theoretical notion.

Cohesiveness is the central concern of small-group theory. "Theoretically, cohesiveness is the essential small-group characteristic. This 'stick togetherness' or member attraction at once characterizes a small group and differentiates it from other social units."[8] While the literature is too voluminous to review,[9] there is general agreement that cohesiveness is a function of the attractiveness of the group to its members. The characteristics of the group and the characteristics of the member together determine attractiveness. The attractiveness of many informal groups derives from the psychological and social rewards they provide their members. But, because of the time pressures under which the congressman works, it seems reasonable to assume that a group must also provide him with political benefits if it is to be worth the time it costs him.

Previous studies provide considerable information on the problems the congressman faces.[10] The freshman congressman must learn a complex new job before he can become an effective participant in the political process in the House. Getting a good committee assignment—one that will help him win reelection or prestige in the House and preferably both—is an extremely important step in the congressman's House career. Whether he is a freshman or a several-term member who wants to change committees, he must have someone to speak for him in this party's Committee on Committees. All congressmen, the most senior as well as the freshmen, are faced with a perpetual need for information at as cheap a cost in time as possible. Even a senior man has a direct share in the making of only a small fraction of all House decisions. Allies can give a member a voice in committees other than his own. In bargaining with committee or party leaders or with the executive branch, allies are helpful to the senior man and essential to the junior member. The only task that delegations have been assigned is that of channeling their members' committee preferences to the party Committee on Committees. Fiellin's and Kessel's studies show that some delegations also help their members with the problems of socialization, information, and allies.

Delegations can perform a number of useful functions for their members. But since attractiveness depends upon the characteristics of the member as well as those of the group, the value placed upon the aid the delegation can provide may vary among congressmen. While all congressmen do need allies and a cheap source of information and thus will find very useful a delegation that provides these aids, this usefulness must be weighed against the time cost of participation. The congressman is most likely to perceive the benefits of participation as greater than the costs if the functions the delegation can perform are directly related to his primary political goals. To the man who aspires to a position of influence in the House, the functions a state party delegation can perform are central. Even after he has learned the ways of the House and has obtained a good committee assignment, he still needs a cheap source of information and allies. Both are essential for the attainment and effective use of a position of influence. If, however, the congressman's goal is higher office, the delegation can do little to help him directly. He must satisfy the demands of the desired office's constituents. These demands come from outside the House and much of the behavior required to satisfy them must take place in the constituency of the desired office. Because the congressman must apportion his limited time so as to maximize the probability of attaining his primary goal, he may well consider the time cost of group membership prohibitive. Furthermore, the delegation may contain a number of potential rivals.

Since the value of a cohesive delegation is a function of the congressman's goals, the first hypothesis concerns the distribution of goals within the delegation: *The greater the proportion of delegation members interested in making the House their career, the more likely it is that the delegation will act as a group.* The second hypothesis concerns the stability of the delegation: *The more stable the delegation—that is, the lower the rate of membership turnover—the more likely it is to act as a group.* The importance of stability has been overwhelmingly demonstrated in small-group and organizational studies,[11] so little need be said in explanation or justification. High turnover increases the cost of delegation membership for senior members by increasing the time that must be spent in the socialization of new members. Further, it directly reduces the benefits since new members, lacking expertise, influence, and friends, can initially contribute little to the group.

Because reelection is a prerequisite to influence in the House, the effect of constituency similarities or differences upon delegation cohesion must be considered. Clearly a congressman will not participate in a group that requires him to act in a manner that would reduce his probability of reelection. Thus one would expect differences in the constituency demands made upon the members to affect the activities a delegation undertakes. If the members of a delegation perceive their constituents as making clear and different voting demands upon them, they will not vote as a bloc and thus not bargain with votes. If, on some matter, the members of a delegation perceive their districts' interests as conflicting, they will not work together. Mere diversity of district interests seems less likely than a traditional sectional rivalry in the state to result in perceptions of mutually exclusive district interests. Thus joint delegation action is limited to those areas in which the members perceive their constituents' demands as not in conflict. Nevertheless, such differences need not prevent the sharing of information, nor will such differences be relevant to many matters on which members could act as allies for one another. The picture of the congressman as pragmatist, which most studies convey, makes it seem unlikely that congressmen will let conflicts in one area prevent mutually advantageous cooperation in another. The final hypothesis states that *neither ideological nor district homogeneity is a necessary condition for delegation cohesion.*

Clearly many of the data to test these hypotheses could only be obtained through interviews with members of state party delegations in the House. It was therefore necessary to select certain delegations for study. The decision to concentrate on the larger delegations[12] was based on the expectation that the larger number of members interviewed from each would provide a check on the accuracy of the data. Both party delegations from New York, California, Pennsylvania, and Illinois were studied, as were the Texas Democratic, Wisconsin Republican, North Carolina Democratic, and Massachusetts Democratic delegations.[13]

COHESION

Given the size of the sample necessary and the consequent impossibility of combining participant-observer and interview techniques, a simple operational definition of cohesion was necessary. The rate of interaction among the members is the major indicator used, but since only politically significant groups are of interest the operational definition of cohesion cannot be based solely on the rate of communication among the members of a delegation; the definition must have political content. Group behavior patterns can be considered as being of two types—interaction, and joint action directed at actors outside the group. Interaction is a necessary but not sufficient condition for joint action. Rate of interaction and the internal consequences of interaction will be used as indicators of cohesion. In terms of the functions discussed above, the internal consequences used as indicators are the extent to which the members of a delegation share information and the extent to which they help socialize their new colleagues.

Rate of Interaction

Within four state party delegations, the rate of interaction is very high. The California Democratic delegation meets weekly for breakfast. Attendance is high. The staff member in charge of delegation matters said the normal attendance is about fifteen, that this tends to drop toward the end of the session, but that the scheduled discussion of an important subject usually brings out the full membership. Her figures agree with the estimates given by the congressmen. Only two said that they often do not go, one attributing his low attendance—"about half the time"— to the early hour of the meetings. He added, "I make damn sure to be there when patronage is discussed." Intradelegation contact is not restricted to these weekly meetings. The members sit together on the floor, and they often have lunch together.

The level of face-to-face contact among the Texas Democrats is also high. One member expressed it thus:

> It's said around here that the Texans don't associate much. They just have coffee together in the morning, eat lunch together, sit together on the floor, and go to the same cocktail parties—but aside from that they don't associate much.

The Texas delegation has met for lunch every Wednesday in the Speaker's dining room for the past twenty-five years. Luncheons to which the congressmen bring constituents and other guests alternate with meetings confined to members. The occasional Texas Republican used to be included, but now the luncheons are restricted to Democrats. The Democratic senator attends, as did Lyndon Johnson when vice-president and, for a time, as president. According to the congressmen interviewed, attendance is high; only one man said he did not often attend, but even he had attended or had heard about the two meetings prior to the interview.

Intradelegation contact is not restricted to the Wednesday luncheons.

In the private members' dining room there is a round table in one corner that is informally reserved for the Texans. Here a shifting group of Texans lunch together. Although not everyone comes every day and, in fact, the table can accommodate only ten or twelve at a time, almost everyone seems to attend fairly frequently. One busy senior member said that, because he was holding hearings, he had been able to join the group only once that week, aside from having attended the Wednesday luncheon.

Although the Massachusetts Democratic delegation does not hold regularly scheduled meetings, the rate of interaction among members is very high. The members sit together on the floor, and many have breakfast together every morning. The members are personal friends; they see each other socially. The whole state delegation meets approximately once a month.

Within the Illinois Democratic delegation the rate of interaction is highest among eight of the nine Chicago members. While formal delegation meetings are infrequent, these men sit together on the floor and often eat breakfast and lunch together. As one man said, "We see each other every day." Although the three downstate members do associate frequently with the Chicago men, the really high rate of interaction is among the Chicago members who numerically dominate the delegation, and it is for that reason that the delegation is included in the high-interaction category.

These four delegations are further distinguished from the others studied by the way in which the congressmen spoke about their delegations. The members of these delegations more often referred to the delegation as "we." Unlike the members of other delegations, they often described their delegation as "tight-knit" or "cohesive." Many expressed pride in the close, friendly relations that exist within their delegations. Two Californians commented as follows:

> The meetings are nice for the camaraderie, the friendship. We're the most cohesive delegation in the House.

> The California delegation is the best-organized political unit I've ever seen. The delegation is the most cooperative in the House.

Many Texas Democrats described their delegation as "tight-knit":

> We have close-knit, personal relationships, more than other delegations. In some, one member will hardly talk to another. [He then mentioned the round table.] No other delegation does that.

> We're a close delegation socially—we know each other's views and children and visit with each other.

The Massachusetts Democrats described their state delegation as well as their party delegation as cohesive:

> The Massachusetts delegation is very close, we're friendly. In some they don't even speak to each other.

> No one would think of having a cocktail party without inviting all the other Massachusetts members, and not as Democrats or Republicans, but as friends. We're by far the closest delegation in the House. Anyone will tell you that. No other delegation is so friendly.

Two Illinois Democrats commented as follows:

> We're close. I don't think there is any other delegation in which you will find the mutual respect we have for each other. It's a fine delegation.

> We're close. We work and go as a unit.

Within six delegations the rate of interaction is fairly high, although appreciably lower than that in the four delegations discussed above. The Illinois, Pennsylvania, and Wisconsin Republican delegations meet at irregular intervals but at least once a month. Within each, there is considerable informal contact; the members frequently sit together on the floor and sometimes eat lunch together. The California Republicans, although they meet formally only four or five times a year, keep in close touch with one another by telephone and sit together on the floor. The North Carolina Democratic delegation meets weekly but other interaction among the members is less frequent than that within the first four delegations discussed. The Pennsylvania Democrats seldom hold formal meetings but often have informal caucuses on the floor. The rate of interaction among the five Philadelphia men is very high. They meet almost daily and see each other in their home city as well as in Washington. The rate of interaction among these men is as high as that among the members of the first four delegations discussed. They comprise a minority of the delegation, however, and the rate of interaction of the whole state party delegation was used for classification.

The rate of interaction within two delegations is low. The New York Democratic and the New York Republican delegations meet two or three times a year. Both delegations are split. In the New York Democratic delegation, a number of junior members see themselves as "liberal activists" and their seniors as "old-line," "old-guard," "machine" Democrats:

> I don't see anything of people like Rooney and Delany. The younger men just have nothing in common with them.

This feeling is reciprocated by some senior men. Asked if he worked with the junior members, one said, "Some are too leftist. I don't even talk to them." The New York Republican delegation is also "fragmented." There are two loose groupings in which the members differ in party loyalty and in type of district represented. In both delegations, informal contact among members occurs primarily within these subgroupings. None of these subgroupings, however, can be properly called a group. The members do not meet or even sit together regularly on the floor.

Thus, on the basis of interaction, the twelve delegations can be tentatively classified as follows: the California, Texas, Massachusetts, and Illinois Democratic delegations are highly cohesive; the Pennsylvania and North Carolina Democratic delegations and the Pennsylvania, Illinois, Wisconsin, and California Republican delegations are cohesive; the New York Democratic delegation and the New York Republican delegation are not cohesive.

Information Sharing

The first question asked of the more senior members of each delegation (usually those serving their third or subsequent terms) concerned their sources of information. The question contained no mention of delegations and was asked first to avoid suggesting the delegation as an answer. The great majority of the members of the four highly cohesive delegations replied that their delegation colleagues were a major source of information. The Texas and the California Democrats usually explained about the weekly delegation meetings and said that the sharing of information which takes place is the single most useful aspect of the meetings:

> You get the technicalities explained. It gives us a preview. We know what to look at when we get the report. We don't have to read it all. It saves time.

For the Massachusetts Democrats, the daily breakfasts serve the same function. Senior congressmen and other governmental officials stop by to talk with the Speaker, thus making a wide range of information available:

> You find out what is going on in other committees, the plans of the leadership, about general problems.

The time spent waiting on the floor is also used for information exchange as a Texan explained:

> Texas has good [committee] spread. I'll be in hearings this morning. Poage will be in Agriculture hearings; there are Judiciary hearings. If you go to the House at noon you'll see a lot of people milling around on the floor.

But really I go up to Poage and see what's happened in the Ag. hearings, ask Jack Brooks about reapportionment.

The members of these delegations emphasized that, because of the work-load, a congressman must rely upon his colleagues: "There's such a large number of bills that you can't keep up any other way." Two Illinois Democrats explained:

We have good committee spread. The man on the committee takes the lead, keeps the rest of us informed about what's going on. We get pretty good intelligence that way.

We don't always go along but I'd say we vote together ninety percent of the time. You'll say, "That's not right. Where's your independence?" But they've done the work, studied the bill. They know what's good for the city.

In each of these delegations, one of the major purposes of interaction is the sharing of information. A result of the high rate of interaction is that these delegations serve as the primary source of information for their members. No member of any of these delegations, unlike their counter-parts in less cohesive delegations, mentioned staff work or other groups as a major source of information.

A smaller number of the members of the six cohesive delegations mentioned their delegation in reply to the first question and some of these men do belong to other informal groups in the House. When asked if they rely upon their delegation colleagues for information most said, "Yes, certainly," and many added that a congressman really has to do so.

We're so busy we have to find shortcuts. If you talk to someone on the delegation, you can find out the inside things—which parts were contro-versial and who was on which side. The workload is impossible.

These delegations do hold meetings to discuss legislation of major im-portance:

We meet when something important comes up, like the surcharge. I was asked to give a presentation of about ten minutes on it. Another member who was going to vote against it was also asked to speak.

Like the members of the highly cohesive delegations, these men reported that much swapping of information takes place on the floor and during other informal intradelegation encounters:

I see the California Republicans on the floor. I sometimes check with them about what's going on on the floor. It only takes a few moments, but it's important.

Thus, in each of these delegations, the members are an important source of information for one another. Because the rate of interaction is lower, however, the extent to which these delegations serve as sources of information for their members is somewhat less than was the case in the first four delegations discussed.

Neither the New York Democratic nor the New York Republican delegation is a major source of information for its members. Asked how they keep up with what is going on in other committees, none of the members mentioned the delegation. Staff work, informal groups such as the Acorns and the Democratic Study Group, and informal relations with other members were most frequently mentioned. After some probing, the majority said that they occasionally do use some of their delegation colleagues as sources of information.

> I will ask Conable and McEwen how they're going to vote—they're both in the Eighty-ninth Club. I'll ask Goodell about the party position. We see each other on the floor of the House, but we don't sit together.

> You talk to people you know and trust. Reuss and Udall are people I often talk to. It's not necessarily other New Yorkers.

The sharing of information that does take place occurs within loose subgroupings in both delegations. There is little contact between subgroups:

> The old-timers and the young liberals have nothing in common. It's like two different states. I wouldn't call Rooney for anything, anymore than I'd call a conservative southerner.

> Why, I'm not sure I know what committees they're [the other New York Republicans] on. . . . ———and I represent adjacent districts but I don't ask him about legislation.

The junior men especially find the information problem onerous:

> I don't handle it very well. I read. Occasionally I call people.

> I just hired a girl to keep up on the other committees. If a constituent writes asking about a bill that I know nothing about, I'll call the staff people on the committees. I just don't have time to read the record.

Socialization

"The House must be a pretty confusing place to a new man. How did you learn your way around when you first came?" was the first question asked of the more junior members of each delegation. The members of the four highly cohesive delegations usually mentioned their delegation colleagues without prompting from the interviewer, and when asked directly all said they had received invaluable aid:

Everyone's been very helpful. They'll give you advice. Even someone as busy as Mr. Mahon. I've often called him about some financial matter. He's taken the time to explain how things work . . . or Wright Patman, well you can go right down the line. They've all been as helpful as they can be.

When Eddie and I first came down here in '52, well, every afternoon McCormack goes to cocktail parties. Well, he'd say, "Why don't you come along? There are people you'll want to meet." That way we met people we'd never have had the chance to meet otherwise. I know he did the same for Burke. It opens an awful lot of doors that wouldn't be open otherwise.

The six cohesive delegations also help their junior members learn the job. The rate of interaction in these delegations, however, is lower than within the four highly cohesive delegations, and the assistance the freshman receives is somewhat less:

[I learned my way around] by trial and error. That's not quite accurate but it pretty well describes it. . . . And last but not least, there were Laird and Byrnes and Davis, they were very helpful. They told me to come to them with questions and were always willing to help.

Well, to be honest, no. [The other Pennsylvania Republicans were not helpful.] The congressman here is pretty much an entity unto himself. I don't mean they weren't at all helpful. If you went to them and asked them a question they would answer it, but they didn't come and offer help.

The freshman New York congressman receives very little help from his delegation colleagues. Asked how they had learned their way around, two New York Democrats replied:

By the "bump-your-nose" procedure. It can be pretty agonizing.

By stumbling. . . . In the morning I used to wander around the halls introducing myself to other congressmen.

A New York Republican said:

The interest of the other New York Republicans was uneven. Some did a little something, others seemed totally uninterested in getting a new colleague. I'd say they were *under*whelmed.

None of the delegations studied make an organized group effort to socialize their freshmen. Members of cohesive delegations do try to help the new men on an individual basis, and freshmen are encouraged to call their seniors for information and advice, but socialization is primarily a by-product of delegation interaction. The new member of a cohesive delegation interacts frequently with his senior colleagues. By asking questions and by observation he learns what is expected of him; he learns which modes of behavior are considered acceptable and which are most likely to result in success.

Clearly the extent to which the members of a delegation rely upon one another for information, and the extent to which they socialize their new members, are closely related to the delegation's rate of interaction. Thus the tentative classification of delegations into cohesion categories will now be considered final.

MEMBERSHIP STABILITY

The need for socialization is, of course, directly related to the delegation's membership stability. As table 10-1 shows, three of the delegations have recently experienced major membership changes.

The instability of the New York Republican delegation is the result of a severe reduction in size and the loss of the delegation's leadership. For both the California and the New York Democratic delegations, instability took the form of a sudden large increase in membership. The 1962 election increased the size of the California Democratic delegation from sixteen to twenty-four and brought ten freshmen Democrats to the House. But most of these new members did not arrive in Washington as complete strangers. Seven of the ten had served in the assembly. It was often mentioned that new members knew each other and some of the more senior delegation members as well from earlier service in the state legislature. These men agreed that their senior colleagues had been helpful:

> Of course the members of your delegation are the most helpful—to varying degrees. George Miller spent an hour spontaneously one day. He took me over to the Senate side—on the floor. I didn't even know we were allowed to do that. McFall took me to lunch.

The 1964 election increased the size of the New York Democratic delegation from twenty to twenty-seven. Nine new men were elected. The men first elected in 1964, all of whom were reelected in 1966, differed appreciably in background from the senior members. Four of the nine had attended prestige universities rather than the city colleges typically

Table 10-1. Delegation Stability, Eighty-seventh to Ninetieth Congresses

| Delegation | Percentage of Freshmen[a] | Variance[b] | |
		Newcomers	Seats
Low regular turnover			
Massachusetts Democrats	0	0	0.18
Pennsylvania Democrats	8.9	0.69	0.50
Illinois Democrats	9.8	2.69	1.25
North Carolina Democrats	10.8	0.50	1.19
Texas Democrats	11.6	0.25	0.75
Wisconsin Republicans	12.5	0.29	0.50
High regular turnover			
Illinois Republicans	17.4	1.50	0.25
California Republicans	18.3	1.69	1.50
Pennsylvania Republicans	20.3	1.19	1.25
High sudden turnover			
New York Republicans	14.1	2.25	10.69
California Democrats	17.8	11.19	15.50
New York Democrats	17.8	10.11	7.15

[a] Total number of newcomers/total number of seats = percentage of total terms served by delegation members that were served by freshmen.
[b] Variance in number of newcomers, and in number of seats held, per Congress for the Eighty-seventh to Ninetieth Congresses.

attended by representatives elected previously; a smaller percentage were lawyers. Three had held appointive positions in Washington or with the United Nations. Only two were elected from New York City and both had unseated regular Democratic incumbents in bitter primary fights. Senior delegation colleagues made little attempt to assist the new men. "Only the Democratic Study Group really went out of its way to be helpful," an administrative assistant said. The different responses of these two delegations to a similar problem suggests that the extent to which the newcomers are similar to their senior colleagues is as important for stability as is the number of newcomers.

GOALS

To ascertain the congressmen's goals, the men interviewed were asked if their delegation colleagues were interested in making the House their career. If the congressman said that he was interested in another office or if at least two of his colleagues attributed such an interest to him, he was classified as having higher office as his goal. Every congressman who replied that he was interested in another office was mentioned by at least two of his colleagues. The reverse was not true.

The number of delegation members mentioned as actively interested in higher office clearly distinguishes two classes of delegations. A third or more of the members of three delegations are interested in another office. But if the hypothesis is to be tested, some further distinctions must be made. The congressman's satisfaction with the job provides another indicator.

When answering the question about goals, members of some delegations often complained about the job. It seems reasonable to suppose that the congressman who is unhappy with certain aspects of the job is less fully committed to staying in the House, whatever his immediate plans may be.[14]

The two indicators yield the following categorization:

1. Few interested in other office: Massachusetts Democrats, Texas Democrats, California Democrats, California Republicans, Wisconsin Republicans, Illinois Democrats

2. Few interested in other office but many unhappy with job: Pennsylvania Democrats, Pennsylvania Republicans, North Carolina Democrats

3. One-third or more interested in other office: Illinois Republicans, New York Republicans, New York Democrats

CONCLUSIONS

The delegations have now been placed into three ordinal categories on each of the variables—cohesion, interest in a House career, and stability. The hypothesis states that cohesion varies directly with both independent variables. The sample is small and was not randomly selected. Thus the usual statistical tests are inapplicable. But if the relation is strong, inspection of the data should reveal its existence. First some definite predictions[15] must be made, and the following, I believe, are cautious as well as explicit. A delegation that falls into the first (third) category on both independent variables should be highly cohesive (noncohesive). It seems reasonable to assume that the "distance" between the categories *noncohesive* and *cohesive* is greater than the "distance" between the categories *cohesive* and *highly cohesive*. Thus a delegation that falls into the first category on one independent variable and into the second on the other, as well as a delegation that falls into the second category on both independent variables, should be cohesive. As table 10-2 shows, nine of the twelve delegations are consistent with the predictions. There are no extreme deviations. The author does not claim that the hypothesis has been fully verified. The number of cases is too small, and the data are not sufficiently precise. But within these limitations, the fit between

Table 10-2. Cohesion as a Function of Stability and Interest in a House Career

		Interest in a House Career	
Stability	1	2	3
High cohesive			
1	*Massachusetts Democrat* *Texas Democrats* *Illinois Democrats*		
2	California Democrats		
3	Wisconsin Republicans		
1		*Pennsylvania Democrats* *North Carolina Democrats*	
		Pennsylvania Republicans	
Cohesive			
2	*California Republicans*		
3			Illinois Republicans
Noncohesive			
1			
2			*New York Democrats*
3			*New York Republicans*

Note: Delegations italicized are consistent with predictions

223

hypothesis and data is close. If one were to place twelve delegations into three cohesion categories randomly, the probability of correctly placing at least nine of the twelve is less than .004.

A subsidiary hypothesis states that neither ideological nor district homogeneity are necessary conditions for cohesion. Limitations of space prohibit a rigorous examination of the relation between delegation cohesion and ideological homogeneity. But since the hypothesis states that ideological homogeneity is not a necessary condition for delegation cohesion, one counterexample is sufficient to falsify the alternative hypothesis. On the basis of both roll-call[16] and interview data, the highly cohesive Texas Democratic delegation is the least ideologically homogeneous delegation studied. The following comments illustrate the members' awareness of the delegation's heterogeneity and something of the manner in which they cope with it.

> We're a close group, tight-knit, even though we have different views, probably because we don't try to force agreement. There's no friction— there would be if we did. We have everything from liberal to conservative— some would say ultraliberal to ultraconservative. . . . And the spread is getting wider.

> There's never any attempt to get people to vote a certain way. . . . We have a wide range of opinions—a diversity of districts, everyone's independent. We respect each other.

As the above comments suggest, heterogeneous delegations do not attempt to bargain with votes. The Texas Democratic delegation has, in fact, developed norms prohibiting ideological arguments and attempts at pressure. Strict observance of these norms probably is, as the members believe, a necessary condition for the continued existence of the group. All cohesive, ideologically homogeneous delegations seek to "stick together" whenever possible but the intensity of such efforts varies greatly among delegations. Ideological homogeneity is a necessary but not sufficient condition for a delegation's attempts to bargain with votes.

It was hypothesized that district heterogeneity is not directly related to cohesion but that it will limit the range of joint action. The term *district heterogeneity* is used to refer to the perception on the part of the members of a delegation that the interests of their districts are, in general, different. District heterogeneity is defined in terms of perceptions to provide a more stringent test. Any index constructed from district census data can be criticized on the ground that the characteristics included may not be those important to the congressman. The members of a delegation may see the interests of their districts as different without, however, interpreting these differences as conflicts. It was hypothesized that a regional rivalry in the state is the most likely basis for perceptions of conflicting interests.

A pronounced regional rivalry does exist in three of the states studied. The congressmen from California, Illinois, and New York are quite aware of the cleavages within their home states. But only the New York congressmen consider the regional rivalry sufficiently devisive to prevent joint action. The congressmen from Texas and Pennsylvania emphasized the diversity of their states. These men perceive the interests of their districts as different but not as conflicting. The congressmen from Massachusetts, Wisconsin, and North Carolina mentioned no major or divisive differences among their districts.

Table 10-3 summarizes these findings. If district heterogeneity were used to predict cohesion, the six delegations off the main diagonal would be misclassified. Clearly district heterogeneity is not a necessary condition for cohesion. Both noncohesive delegations are from a state with a regional rivalry, but three of the four highly cohesive delegations are from states with either a regional rivalry or considerable district diversity. Furthermore, district heterogeneity does not appreciably limit joint action on the part of a cohesive delegation. The members of all cohesive delegations act as allies for one another on district projects and problems and in the committee assignment process.

Of the possible determinants of cohesion that were examined, stability and the proportion of delegation members interested in a House career are most closely related to cohesion. Because of limitations of data, the findings are tentative. Still they seem to justify certain methodological and substantive observations. When one studies professionals in their area of professional competence (in this case professional politicians in a political arena) the assumption that professional goals will dominate behavior seems sufficiently realistic to lead to significant predictive accuracy about behavior. This implies that one can assume that professionals, again in their area of professional competence, will act rationally in the commonsense use of that term. In studies of congressional behavior, it may soon be possible to progress from the use of "bits of theory" to an explicit and integrated theoretical framework based upon these assumptions.

Substantively, this study reconfirms the findings of previous studies concerning the congressman's sources of information. Congressmen do rely heavily upon one another for information. Within cohesive delegations, fellow members are the single most important source of information. The complaints made by members of noncohesive delegations indicate that intradelegation sharing of information may well be the least

Table 10-3. Cohesion and District Heterogeneity

Source of Perceived Heterogeneity	Noncohesive	Cohesive	High Cohesive
Regional rivalry	New York Democrats New York Republicans	Illinois Republicans California Republicans	California Democrats Illinois Democrats
Diversity		Pennsylvania Democrats Pennsylvania Republicans	Texas Democrats
None mentioned		Wisconsin Republicans North Carolina Democrats	Massachusetts Democrats

time-consuming way of handling the problem. Since time is crucial, the member of a fairly large cohesive delegation does have an advantage over other congressmen. The cohesiveness of his delegation probably affects the congressman's performance and may well have some effect on his career goals. Certainly, for the member of a cohesive delegation the job of congressman is less hectic than it is for his less-fortunate colleagues.

Membership in a cohesive delegation is clearly useful to the congressman, but what are the effects of such groups on the political process in the House? Cohesive delegations seem to play an important system-maintenance role. Throughout the interviews it was found that a certain amount of impatience with the decision-making process in the House is typical of most junior members. Those delegations with a vigorous group life temper it through the socialization process and by enabling their junior members to exert a certain amount of indirect influence through their senior delegation colleagues. In return for keeping their expressions of impatience within House limits of tolerance, the junior men receive help from their seniors with committee assignments and district projects. Further, cohesive delegations, especially heterogeneous ones, do reinforce House norms of courtesy and compromise. By giving structure to the mass of party members, they expedite communication and facilitate bargaining. But cohesive delegations also reduce their members' dependence upon the party leadership. The members of such delegations serve as an important source of information for one another and are thus less dependent upon other sources of information; as a group, they have much more bargaining strength than they would have as individuals. Without cohesive delegations and other informal groups, and the structure and coordination they provide, the decision-making process in the House might well break down. At the same time, the existence of such groups, by proliferating centers of influence, increases decentralization and decreases the party leadership's chances of dominating even postcommittee decision-making.

Epilogue
STATE DELEGATION INFLUENCE

The dispersion of influence that resulted from the reforms of the 1970s increased the value of the services state delegations can perform for their members. As the amount of legislative activity rose and the identity of key actors became less predictable, good sources of information became even more important. As the opportunities for influencing outcomes spread beyond the most senior members on the committee with juris-diction, allies became even more valuable.

Members continued to use their state delegations as sources of infor-mation and allies; in addition, they created a large number of informal groups, built in part upon the state delegation model, to serve these purposes. Some of these congressional caucuses are based upon ideolog-ical and policy like-mindedness—the Arms Control and Foreign Policy Caucus, for example. The majority are related to a constituency interest; thus the Automotive Caucus, the Northeast-Midwest Congressional Co-alition, and the Rural Caucus provide organizational structures for mem-bers with similar constituency interests to share information and to work together.

During the 1980s, huge budget deficits heightened competition for scarce district-project dollars and made joint efforts all the more necessary. Members have continued to work through their delegations and through caucuses. The recent contest to obtain the superconducting supercollider, a major scientific installation that will bring the winning state jobs, dollars, and prestige, saw a number of large state delegations, including Texas, Illinois, and California, both cooperating to ensure funding for the project and competing to obtain the site. All the states in the competition launched major bipartisan efforts involving House members, senators, and the states' governors. The success of Texas, close observers said, was the result of that delegation's long tradition of effective joint action as well as the individual clout of a number of its members.

In sum, House members have developed a broad array of groups that provide them with great flexibility in obtaining the information and allies needed to influence outcomes in the more demanding environment of the 1980s. In the contest to obtain district benefits, the state party del-egation is nevertheless often the group of choice, and those delegations that do work as a unit continue to be advantaged.

NOTES

1. David B. Truman, "The State Delegation and the Structure of Voting in the United States House of Representatives," *American Political Science Review* 50 (Dec. 1956): 1023–45.

2. Donald R. Matthews and James A. Stimson, "Decision-Making by U.S. Rep-resentatives: A Preliminary Model," in Sidney Ulmer, ed., *Political Decision-Making* (New York: Van Nostrand, 1970), 14–43.

3. Aage R. Clausen, "Home State Influences on Congressional Behavior" (Paper delivered at the Sixty-sixth annual meeting of the American Political Science Asso-ciation, Los Angeles, 2–6 Sept. 1970).

4. Alan Fiellin, "The Functions of Informal Groups: A State Delegation," in the 1st ed. of this work (Chicago: Rand McNally, 1963), 59–78.

5. John H. Kessel, "The Washington Congressional Delegation," *Midwest Journal of Political Science* 8 (Feb. 1964):1–21.

6. Charles L. Clapp, *The Congressman: His Work as He Sees It* (Garden City, N.Y.: Doubleday, 1964), 41–50.

7. Randall B. Ripley, *Party Leaders in the House of Representatives* (Washington, D.C.: Brookings Institution, 1967), 169–75.

8. Robert T. Golembiewski, *The Small Group* (Chicago: University of Chicago Press, 1962), 149. Also see Darwin Cartwright and Alvin Zander, eds., *Group Dynamics: Research and Theory* (Evanston, Ill.: Row, Peterson, 1960), 72.

9. See Golembiewski, *Small Group,* and Cartwright and Zander, *Group Dynamics.* Also T. M. Newcomb, R. H. Turner, and P. E. Converse, *Social Psychology: The Study of Human Interaction* (New York: Holt, Rinehart, and Winston, 1965).

10. See among others Clapp, *The Congressman.*

11. See Lewis A. Froman, Jr., "Organization Theory and the Explanation of Important Characteristics of Congress," *American Political Science Review* 62 (June 1968):518–26.

12. In the Ninetieth Congress twenty state party delegations had seven or more members. Of the 435 U.S. representatives, 58 percent were members of these twenty delegations.

13. The author interviewed 111 congressmen and a number of staff members during the Ninetieth and the first two months of the Ninety-first Congress. The number of congressmen interviewed from each delegation were: N.Y.—D., 13 of 25; R., 10 of 15; Calif.—D., 10 of 21; R., 8 of 17; Pa.—D., 7 of 14; R., 7 of 13; Ill.— D., 8 of 12; R., 7 of 12; Tex.—D., 19 of 21; Mass.—D., 4 of 7; N.C.—D. 4 of 8; Wis.—R., 6 of 7.

14. The political necessity of belonging to the Tuesday through Thursday Club was the most frequent cause for complaints. Spending at least every weekend in the district is immediately expensive in terms of time and money. It also reduces the probability that the congressman will attain personal influence in the House because he is considered a part-time congressman by other members and has less opportunity to make friends in the House. The Chicago Democrats are the only congressmen interviewed who do not consider membership in the Tuesday through Thursday Club onerous. The Illinois Democratic delegation is also the only delegation studied that regularly bargains with votes. These men may consider membership in the Tuesday through Thursday Club no problem because they make use of a type of influence that is not dependent upon their fulfillment of House norms.

15. These predictions state sufficient conditions for various levels of cohesion. Since each of the two independent variables can take three values, there are nine possible combinations. Predictions are made for only five of these nine. Given the imprecision of the data, further predictions would be of dubious validity. Thus for a delegation with any of the other four combinations of values on the independent variables no predictions are made. These are, within limits of consistency, indeterminant cases but, to increase the rigor of the test, they are treated as violations of the theory. Also for rigor, the predictions are treated as if they stated necessary and sufficient conditions for various levels of cohesion.

16. Using the Rice index of voting cohesion on the *New Republic*'s twelve key votes as an admittedly crude indicator of ideological homogeneity, the Texas Democratic delegation, with an index score of 40.4, ranked lowest of the twelve delegations studied. The scores of the other delegations ranged from 94.4 (Massachusetts Democrats) to 49.4 (New York Republicans).

PART IV

Leadership

Article I, Section 2, of the U.S. Constitution specifies that "the House of Representatives shall choose their Speaker and other officers." All the major leadership positions other than the Speaker—floor leaders, whips, and the chairmen of various party organizations such as policy committees, caucuses, and conferences—came into being rather slowly and informally, mostly in response to the increasing organizational pressures of the late nineteenth and the twentieth centuries.

In "Joseph G. Cannon and Howard W. Smith: The Limits of Leadership in the House of Representatives," Charles O. Jones compares the trials and tribulations of an early twentieth-century Speaker and a mid-twentieth century chairman of the House Committee on Rules. For Jones, the 1910 revolt and the 1961 rules enlargement controversy illustrate the constraints that even the most powerful leaders must confront in a decentralized institution such as the House.

Nelson W. Polsby examines the forces that decided the selection of Carl Albert (D., Okla.) over Richard Bolling (D., Mo.) in "Two Strategies of Influence: Choosing a Majority Leader, 1962." Internal factors, especially one-on-one persuasion, proved to be more decisive than external forces, including lobbying by outside interests and media endorsements.

"How and Why Do Leadership Institutions Change?" asks David T. Canon in an informative, synthesizing essay. Focusing upon such key institutional variables as durability, boundedness, internal complexity, and universal norms and rules of congressional leadership, he finds House Democrats of the 1970s and 1980s to be the most institutionalized of the four congressional parties and Senate Republicans to be the least institutionalized.

Finally, Lynne P. Brown and Robert L. Peabody, in "Patterns of Succession in the House Democratic Leadership, 1989," study a series of majority leadership contests. The first cluster in 1986 led to the selection of James C. Wright of Texas as Speaker, Thomas S. Foley of Washington as majority leader, and Tony Coelho of California as the first elected whip. In 1989—the main thrust of this research—the focus was upon the resignations of Wright and Coelho after charges of ethics violations, with Foley advancing to Speaker, and House Democrats turning to Richard A. Gephardt of Missouri and William H. Gray III of Pennsylvania as majority leader and whip. *Patterns* of succession, the practice of advancing from lower to higher positions of leadership, became more volatile, but holding a position seemed strengthened as a prerequisite to higher leadership.

Chapter 11

Joseph G. Cannon and Howard W. Smith: The Limits of Leadership in the House of Representatives

CHARLES O. JONES

That the House of Representatives is characterized by bargaining has been well established by many scholars of that institution[1] and suggests that leaders of that body must be skilled negotiators. Ultimately each representative, even the freshman, has some bargaining power (at minimum, his vote). It is on this basis of bargaining that the "middleman" thesis of congressional leadership has been developed.[2] Rightly or wrongly, House leaders must attend to their majorities.

Two types of majorities in the House are of interest here—procedural and substantive. Procedural majorities are those necessary to organize the House for business and maintain that organization.[3] They are formed at the beginning of the session. Leaders are selected and provided with a number of bargaining advantages so that the House may perform its functions in the political system. Normally, membership of procedural majorities and minorities coincides with that of the two political parties.[4]

Substantive majorities are those necessary to pass legislation in the House. Whereas procedural majorities are relatively stable in membership, the makeup of substantive majorities may well differ issue to issue, since many substantive measures cut across party lines. Leaders are expected

This chapter was originally published in the *Journal of Politics* 30 (1968):617–46 and is reprinted by permission of the author and the University of Texas Press. Financial support was provided by the American Political Science Association's Study of Congress, Professor Ralph K. Huitt, Director, and the Institute of Government Research, University of Arizona. I wish to acknowledge the comments of Richard Cortner, Conrad Joyner, John Crow, Phillip Chapman, and Clifford Lytle.

to build substantive majorities—employing the many bargaining advantages provided by their procedural majorities. They are not expected, nor do they normally have the power, to force members into substantive majorities.

House leaders must take care not to lose touch with any sizable segment of their procedural majorities. On most issues they will find the basis for substantive majorities in their own party. Obviously, party members have views on the substantive matters before the House. If he wishes to remain in office, a leader must hold himself accountable to his procedural majority when building substantive majorities and accommodate important substantive changes among segments of his procedural majority. House leaders have latitude in their behavior, to be sure, and the process of defeat and/or reform is often painfully slow, but the leader who maintains himself in a responsible position of authority over a long period of time must be adaptive, communicative, accommodating, and accountable.

What if a House leader fails to behave in this way? In the short run, it probably will not make much difference. In the long run, however, aberrant behavior is bound to cause trouble for the leader with segments of his procedural majority. If it is a case of a leader exceeding the authority given to him, or failing to meet the expectations of his followers, he may simply be removed. But what if he has developed sources of power which make him independent of his procedural majority? That is, he is exercising authority which is real—it is incorporated into the position he holds—but is contextually inappropriate because it violates the bargaining condition in the House. Under these circumstances removing the leader is not the whole solution. One may expect some House members to be concerned enough about the potential of divorce between the procedural majority and its leader to press for reform. One may further expect that in these situations the House will define the limits of leadership in that body as it debates reform.

There are two spectacular cases of "excessive leadership" in the House in this century. Joseph G. Cannon, as Speaker, had become an exceptionally powerful figure in American politics. He had a wide variety of sanctions available, and he used them all. Nearly fifty years later, Howard W. Smith, as chairman of the Committee on Rules, also had an impressive array of prerogatives—all of which he used to his advantage. The purposes of this essay are to examine the authority of these two men, how they exercised this authority in relationship to their procedural majorities, and the reaction and ultimate loss of their majorities. The findings not only tend to support the "middle-man" hypothesis but provide a clearer indication of its meaning as defined by the members themselves.

THE CASE OF UNCLE JOE CANNON

The House leadership situation in 1910 should have satisfied many of the responsible party scholars. There was no question that the Speaker was responsible for leading the House. Since his election in 1903, Speaker Joseph G. Cannon had enjoyed rather substantial procedural majorities and due to the growth of the speakership and Cannon's interpretation and use of his powers, a procedural majority carried with it awesome authority. He could appoint committees—including the chairmen—determine the schedule of business, recognize members on the floor, appoint members to conference committees, dispense favors of various kinds.

Cannon's Exercise of Power

Particularly significant was Speaker Cannon's power as chairman of the Committee on Rules. The committee was small—never over five members prior to 1910. The three-to-two edge of the Republicans was potent, however, since the Speaker appointed the members carefully—insuring that they agreed with his views.[5] Champ Clark's view of the committee was widely shared: "I violate no secret when I tell you the committee is made up of three very distinguished Republicans and two ornamental Democrats. [Laughter] . . . There never would be a rule reported out of that committee that the Speaker and his two Republican colleagues do not want reported."[6]

During Speaker Cannon's reign, four Republicans served on the Committee on Rules in addition to the Speaker himself—John Dalzell (Pa.), Charles Grosvenor (Ohio), James S. Sherman (N.Y.), and Walter I. Smith (Iowa). These members had considerable seniority (overall the average number of terms served by committee members was approximately three times that of other House Republicans) and therefore also were high ranking on other important standing committees.

A second center of power which the Speaker dominated was the Committee on Ways and Means. It was the custom to have the chairman of Ways and Means serve as the majority floor leader. Sereno Payne, New York, served Cannon in these two important posts during his speakership. There was considerable overlapping membership between Rules and Ways and Means. Between 1903 and 1907, Dalzell and Grosvenor were second- and third-ranking Republicans on Ways and Means. Dalzell remained in both positions throughout Cannon's speakership.[7]

The list of grievances against Cannon and his lieutenants on Rules and Ways and Means lengthened with each year of his speakership. A frequent complaint was that Speaker Cannon abused House rule X, which gave him the power to appoint the standing committees. He had made some spectacular appointments and adjustments prior to 1909—selecting Tawney (Minn.) as chairman of Appropriations in 1905, even though Tawney had never served on that committee; Overstreet (Ind.) as chairman of Post Office and Post Roads in 1903, even though Overstreet had never served on that committee; and Scott (Kans.) as chairman of Agriculture in 1907 over Henry (Conn.), whom Cannon removed completely from the Committee, and Haughen (Iowa). In 1909, however, Speaker Cannon appeared to shift assignments about at will. Though seniority was not an inviolable rule at this time, it was relied on as a significant factor in committee assignments.[8] Twelve Republicans had not voted for Cannon for Speaker in 1909, and seniority was certainly no protection for them. Table 11-1 provides some examples of actions taken by the Speaker in the Sixty-first Congress.

Speaker Cannon was not above delaying the appointment of committees until his wishes on legislation had been met. In the famous Sixty-first Congress, he appointed the important Rules and Ways and Means Committees on 16 March, the second day of the session. Most of the remaining appointments had to wait until the Payne-Aldrich tariff bill was in the conference committee—nearly five months after the session began.[9]

Joe Cannon did not limit himself to managing committee appointments. He also managed the output of the House. George Norris describes one of his early experiences on the House Committee on Public Buildings and Grounds. The committee discussed drafting a public building bill, and Norris soon learned that the Speaker would ultimately decide whether the committee should proceed or not. "The senior Democratic member of the committee, Representative Bankhead of Alabama, . . . actually made a motion that the chairman of the committee should seek a conference with the Speaker and ascertain whether or not we should be allowed to have a public building bill at that session."[10]

There were many examples of the frustrations of the insurgents in dealing with Speaker Cannon's Committee on Rules during the debate in 1910 to remove the Speaker from that committee. One involved a first-term congressman from New York, Hamilton Fish. He had unsuccessfully sought to get a hearing before the committee on a resolution which called on the Committee on Post Office and Post Roads to inquire into the feasibility and the desirability of establishing a parcel post system. The colloquy between Fish and Walter I. Smith (Iowa), a member of the Committee on Rules, is worth recording here as an example of how various senior members would treat a freshman.

Table 11-1. *Examples of Violations of Seniority Principle in Committee Assignments, Sixty-first Congress*

Member	Committee and Rank, 60th Congress	Committee and Rank, 61st Congress	Comments
Cooper, Wis.	Insular Affairs, chair	Elections #3, 2d Foreign Affairs, 10th	Cooper had been chairman since 56th Congress.
Fowler, N.J.	Banking & Currency, chair Reform of Civil Service, 2d	Insular Affairs, 11th Reform of Civil Service, 2d	Fowler had been chairman since 57th Congress. Vreeland, N.Y., made chairman. Not on Banking & Currency before. Was lowest on Appropriations in 60th.
Haugen, Iowa	Agriculture, 2d War Claims, 2d Expenditures in Interior Dept., chair	Agriculture, 4th War Claims, 3d	Haugen had been passed over in 60th in Agriculture. In 61st two lower-ranking members moved ahead of him. Same on War Claims—thus denying him chairmanship.
Lovering, Mass.	Coinage, Weights & Measures, 4th Interstate & Foreign Commerce, 5th	Coinage, Weights & Measures 4th Manufacturers, 4th	Lovering had previously been removed from Banking & Currency (59th).
Morse, Wis.	Indian Affairs, 10th War Claims, 9th	War Claims, 4th Manufacturers, 6th Private Land Claims, 4th	
Murdock, Kans.	Post Office and Post Roads, 9th	Post Office and Post Roads, 12th	Six new members plus one who was below Murdock in 60th were placed ahead of him.
Norris, Nebr.	Election of Pres., V. Pres. & Reps., 3d Public Bldgs. & Grounds, 6th Labor, 7th	Coinage, Weights & Measures, 7th Private Land Claims, 2d Revision of the Laws, 6th	

Sources: Various volumes of the *Congressional Directory* and Paul D. Hasbrouck, *Party Government in the House of Representatives* (New York: Macmillan, 1927).

> *Mr. Smith.* I deny that a hearing has ever been refused.
>
> *Mr. Fish.* Mr. Speaker, I have the evidence in writing that I asked a hearing and none has been granted me.
>
> *Mr. Smith.* Well—
>
> *Mr. Fish.* I will ask the gentleman, in the six weeks that the resolution has been before the Committee on Rules, why he has not answered my request and given me the privilege of a hearing?
>
> *Mr. Smith.* Does the gentleman ask that question?
>
> *Mr. Fish.* Yes; why have you not given me a hearing?
>
> *Mr. Smith.* I wrote the gentleman in person that while I did not approve of a parcel post myself I was opposed to suppressing any measure, and that I was willing to give him a hearing and report the bill adversely.
>
> *Mr. Fish.* I would ask the gentleman, then, why he did not give me a hearing?
>
> *Mr. Smith.* The gentleman never appeared and asked for a hearing.
>
> *Mr. Fish.* But I have written time and time again asking for it.
>
> *Mr. Smith.* Oh, written—[11]

Fish's subsequent question to John Dalzell, also a member of the Rules Committee, regarding how a member extracted a bill from a committee which did not wish to report it, went unanswered.

Managing the work assignments of congressmen, managing their work, and managing the rules by which their work would be done—such were the powers of the Speaker. Yet still other sanctions were available to him. Speakers have always had a number of temporary and honorary appointments which they can make. In some cases these are much sought after—for publicity, prestige, or some other special purpose. Norris reports one such appointment which he sought. William C. Lovering (Mass.), a close friend of Norris and an early insurgent congressman, died 4 February 1910. Norris wished to be appointed to the committee representing the House at the funeral.

> I hoped the Speaker, recognizing my close ties with Mr. Lovering, would accord me the privilege of paying my respects to a very dear friend, as a member of the House committee. Without seeing the Speaker about it personally, I had one or two friends approach him; and they reported he refused absolutely to approve my selection. It was a long time before the deep resentment which this aroused in me disappeared.[12]

This awesome list of powers exceeded that exercised by any previous Speaker. It was exceedingly difficult for the insurgent members to "force" the Speaker to accommodate their views because (1) he had so many sanctions available and could discipline not only them but any members who might otherwise be enticed to join them, and (2) the insurgent Republicans did not want to defeat Cannon so as to elect a Democratic Speaker, who would likely be no more accommodating to their views. Thus, Cannon had a considerable advantage and could ignore the changes occurring within his own procedural majority—he had developed a certain amount of independence from that majority.

The Warning Signals

Speaker Cannon and the regular Republicans had ample warning of the unrest among their more progressive brethren during the Sixtieth and Sixty-first Congresses. In fact, members made no effort to hide their dissatisfaction in speeches on the House floor. Twelve insurgents refused to vote for Cannon for Speaker at the opening of the special session in 1909 called by President Taft to consider the tariff. And a combination of insurgents and Democrats defeated the motion to adopt the rules of the preceding Congress. Minority Leader Champ Clark followed this victory with a resolution which would have increased the size of the Committee on Rules, removed the Speaker from the committee, and taken from the Speaker his power of appointing all committees except Ways and Means. With insurgent support, the stage was set for revolution at that moment, but John J. Fitzgerald (D., N.Y.) and twenty-two bolting Democrats voted with the majority of Republicans to defeat Clark's move, and Cannon was saved. Fitzgerald then offered a compromise motion of his own which established a unanimous consent calendar and a motion of recommital (for use by the minority) and increased the majority necessary to set aside Calendar Wednesday.[13]

Calendar Wednesday itself had been adopted at the close of the Sixtieth Congress, and though it did not meet the reform standards of the insurgents, there were strong hopes that it would limit Cannon's power. These hopes were dashed rather soon and rather decisively. A call of standing committees every Wednesday allowed committee chairmen to take bills which had been reported off the calendar for House consideration. With the changes as a result of the Fitzgerald compromise, the procedure could be dispensed with only by a two-thirds majority. A variety of devices were used to neutralize the procedure—adjournment required only a simple majority and was used to avoid Calendar Wednesday; bills of great length and complexity were called up and debated on successive Calendar Wednesdays (all nine Calendar Wednesdays were devoted to one bill in the third session of the Sixty-first Congress).[14]

The Consent Calendar was more of a victory for the rank and file. There was a unanimous consent procedure in existence wherein any member could move consideration of a bill. The Speaker, theoretically, had no greater power of objection than any other member. In practice, however, the Speaker required advance notice of a unanimous consent request before he would recognize it. Thus, members had to clear such requests with Cannon before they could even be recognized on the floor.[15] The rules change created a Calendar for Unanimous Consent. The Speaker's consent was no longer required for a unanimous consent motion.

It was unlikely that these reforms would satisfy those members who were increasingly alienated from their own party. The 1908 elections resulted in a further reduction of the size of the House Republican majority. Cannon had a slim 29-vote majority in his first term as Speaker. Roosevelt's election in 1904 brought with it a 114-vote majority for Republicans in the House. This was reduced to 58 in 1906 and to 47 in 1908. Many of the new Republicans elected in 1906 and 1908 were from states in the Middle West and were soon to join veteran insurgents like Henry Cooper (Wis.), Gilbert Haugen (Iowa), and George Norris (Neb.). Thus, not only was Cannon's majority being reduced, but regular Republicans were being replaced by members who were potential threats to Cannon's leadership. The result was that if enough members absented themselves on crucial votes, the insurgents would hold the balance of power. For the insurgents the time had come. Speaker Cannon would be taught some fundamental lessons about leadership in the House of Representatives. Though he had developed impressive power as Speaker and found that he didn't have to make accommodations to a changing procedural majority in the short run, there were other alternatives available to the insurgents. They could always take their one bargaining advantage—the vote—and join the Democrats to curb the powers of the Speaker.

The Revolt

The full-scale revolt against Cannon began on 16 March 1910. Though the details of the revolt are adequately recorded in a number of sources,[16] a brief résumé of pertinent facts is necessary. The day was Calendar Wednesday. Mr. Crumpacker (R., Ind.) called for the consideration of House Joint Resolution 172 on the 1910 census.[17] Mr. Fitzgerald (D., N.Y.) made the point of order that a call of the committees was in order, under the Calendar Wednesday procedure. Speaker Cannon overruled the point of order, noting that "a certain class of business, like election cases, like matters arising in impeachment, and like legislation relating to apportionment or the taking of the census as to the population, have invariably been admitted as involving *constitutional privilege,* presenting a privilege higher than any rule of the House would give."[18] Fitzgerald appealed the ruling of the chair to the House. Crumpacker moved that the matter be postponed until Thursday—thus postponing the appeal to the chair as well. Fitzgerald objected. Cannon overruled his objection, but the House supported Fitzgerald and refused to allow the matter to be postponed. After some debate, the appeal to the House was voted on and Cannon was defeated, 112 to 163, as 42 Republicans voted with the Democrats. Cannon then made the dramatic announcement: "The decision of the chair does not stand as the decision of the House."[19]

On 17 March, Crumpacker again attempted to bring his resolution before the House. Cannon refused to rule. He put the question to the House: "Is the bill called up by the gentleman from Indiana in order as a question of constitutional privilege, the rule prescribing the order of business to the contrary notwithstanding?"[20] The House, in no mood to let the Speaker snatch victory from defeat, responded negatively. The House then passed the following revised version of the question, as put by Oscar W. Underwood (D., Ala.): "Is the House joint resolution called up by the gentleman from Indiana in order now?"[21] Note that no mention was made of the Constitution in the Underwood resolution. It simply asked if the Crumpacker resolution were in order "now." William R. Gwinn, in his account of the overthrow, observes that the House had "endorsed the proposition that his [Crumpacker's] resolution was privileged under the Constitution"[22] and, as is discussed below, George Norris later so argued. Technically, however, the House never did rule that the Crumpacker resolution was privileged.

Following the debate on House Joint Resolution 172, Norris pulled from his pocket a resolution to change the rules of the House. In his autobiography, Norris observes: "I had carried it for a long time, certain that in the flush of its power the Cannon machine would overreach itself. The paper upon which I had written my resolution had become so tattered it scarcely hung together."[23] Norris announced: "Mr. Speaker, I present a resolution made privileged by the Constitution." In Crumpacker's effort to have his census resolution considered on Calendar Wednesday, Norris found a way to circumvent the House Committee on Rules for effecting a rules change. His "privileged" resolution would reorganize the Rules Committee by increasing its size, having members selected by groups of state delegations, and removing the Speaker from the committee. Norris argued that his resolution was privileged under the Constitution because in Article I, Section 5, paragraph 2, it stated, "Each House may determine the rules of its proceedings." The Speaker ordered the clerk to read the resolution. "The moment the reading clerk saw it he smiled, for he recognized the fact that the great fight on the rules of the House was on."[24]

The turnabout was a strange one indeed. Speaker Cannon had ruled that Crumpacker's resolution was privileged but was overruled by the House. Norris had voted against the Speaker. On 17 March the House *voted against* Cannon's question, which explicitly stated that the resolution was in order *under constitutional privilege* but voted in favor of the more ambiguous motion, which simply stated that the Crumpacker resolution was in order. Norris waltzed through all of this with the head-spinning logic that his resolution was privileged because the Crumpacker resolution was in order. And there was no difference between the two resolutions resulting from the fact that Crumpacker's had been in committee and Norris's had not (a critical fact if his resolution was to survive).

> If it [Crumpacker's] was privileged it was privileged because the Constitution made it so, and having decided that it was privileged, because the Constitution made it privileged, its privileged character was not added to by the fact that it had been referred to a committee and a report made by the committee.[25]

As indicated here, there is considerable doubt that Crumpacker's resolution *was* ruled by the House to be privileged. If it was not, then Norris and Cannon might well be faced with a complete reversal of positions — Cannon denying Norris's request because the House had not allowed the Crumpacker resolution to be privileged matter, and Norris arguing that the Crumpacker resolution had been ruled as privileged, even though Norris had not agreed that it should be.

Cannon, in his book written by L. White Busbey, argues that Norris was right. Not because Norris's resolution was as privileged as Crumpacker's but rather because "the House having made itself ridiculous in the space of two days and publicly declared that it was bound by no rules and had no regard for logic and consistency, why should it not continue to maintain the record?"[26]

The Cannon forces stayed with their original position, however — that the Crumpacker resolution was privileged. They then proceeded to argue that the Norris resolution was not. The difference was in the wording of the two relevant sections of the Constitution. "The actual enumeration *shall be made*" (Article I, Section 2, clause 3), but "Each House *may* determine the rules." One was interpreted to be compelling, and thus privileged; the other was a right, could be accomplished at any time, and was not privileged.

Thus began the debate which was to terminate on March 19 with important rules changes that would have a serious impact on party government in the House of Representatives. There were six unsuccessful attempts to recess throughout the evening, on into the night, and the next morning. At 2:02 P.M. on 18 March, a motion to recess until 4:00

P.M. was finally approved. The House had been in session over twenty-six hours. The House again recessed at 4:00 P.M. until 19 March at noon. Speaker Cannon then ruled that "the [Norris] resolution is not in order." Norris appealed the decision of the chair, and the Speaker was overruled (162 Republicans supporting Cannon, and 34 Republicans voting with 148 Democrats against him). An amended version of the Norris resolution then passed the House 193 to 153. A total of 43 insurgent Republicans crossed over on this key vote to defeat the Speaker. Speaker Cannon then invited a resolution which would declare the Speakership vacant and call for an election. Such a resolution was introduced by Burleson (D., Tex.) and was overwhelmingly defeated. Only eight insurgents voted against Cannon.

Defining the Limits of Leadership

In debate the Cannon forces set forth the following argument—basically a party responsibility position with important modifications. The people had elected a majority of Republicans to the House of Representatives. That majority had selected a leadership group which acted for the party and therefore for the country. There is a necessary coincidence between electoral majorities, procedural majorities, and substantive majorities which must not break down. That is, no member may leave the majority without severe penalty. Those members who reject the party leadership are rejecting the Republican party and its mandate from the people to manage the House and its work. The leadership would provide mechanisms whereby individual members could make their opinions known. Mr. Fassett of New York spoke for the Cannon forces:

> We are robust partisans, every one of us. . . . I take it that no Democrat was elected to cooperate with our party nor was any Republican elected to hand over the Republican control of this House to our political opponents. . . . A man ought to have opinions and convictions. He ought not to be a political chocolate eclair. . . . In my judgment, the place to adjust differences of opinion on unimportant questions, and on important questions of public policy and party policy is not in public, where one minority uniting with another minority may make a temporary majority; but in the family caucus.[27]

Mr. Gardner of Michigan noted the importance of two parties which put the issues before the people in debate and the threat caused by actions of the sort contemplated by Norris.[28] Mr. Nye of Minnesota observed that "Parties are a necessity, and the great power and effectiveness of the Republican party has been largely its cohesiveness. Its followers have stood shoulder to shoulder and fought the battle against a political foe.[29]

But it was left to Speaker Cannon, following his defeat, to summarize the position most eloquently.

> *The Speaker.* Gentlemen of the House of Representatives: Actions, not words, determine the conduct and the sincerity of men in the affairs of life. This is a government by the people acting through the representatives of a majority of the people. Results cannot be had except by a majority, and in the House of Representatives a majority, being responsible, should have full power and should exercise that power; otherwise the majority is inefficient and does not perform its function. The office of the minority is to put the majority on its good behavior, advocating, in good faith, the policies which it professes, ever ready to take advantage of the mistakes of the majority party, and appeal to the country for its vindication.[30]

After his defeat, Cannon surprised both his friends and his enemies by entertaining a notion to declare the office of the Speaker vacant so that the new majority could proceed to elect a new Speaker. It was a perfectly consistent maneuver on his part—consistent with his notion of party leadership in the House of Representatives. If a new majority had formed, and the recent vote indicated to him that such was the case, then that new majority "ought to have the courage of its convictions, and logically meet the situation that confronts it." Though Cannon's action was consistent with his notions of party leadership, it is likely that this move was less honest consistency than it was impressive strategy. If he felt strongly about the logic of his theory of party leadership, he could have easily resigned. He did not resign, however, because, in his words, he declined "to precipitate a contest upon the House, . . . a contest that might greatly endanger the final passage of all legislation necessary to redeem Republican pledges" and because resignation would be "a confession of weakness or mistake or an apology for past actions."[31] Neither reason is convincing. A lengthy and divisive contest could as easily ensue as a result of declaring the office vacant. Cannon himself noted that he was entertaining the motion so that the new majority could proceed to elect another Speaker. There was no reason to think that Cannon would be the only nominee. Further, if Cannon was consistent with the party responsibility theory, he would have resigned, not because of his analysis of his personal weakness or strength or because of his view of whether he had made mistakes or not, but due to the simple fact that on a paramount issue, *he had been defeated.* Other considerations were irrelevant.

In short, Cannon, and probably his cohorts, believed more in strong, personal party leadership with limited accountability to party membership, let alone the nation as whole, than they did in the classic party responsibility position. There is abundant evidence for this interpretation in their behavior before 1910, in the actions of the cabal before the debate in 1910, and in the Cannon maneuver following his defeat. He chose the strategy of entertaining the motion to declare the office vacant so that he might regain control of the situation. At the time, it looked very much as though he might succeed. As he proudly notes in his autobiography: "I was given more votes than at the beginning of Congress and when I went back to resume the Chair I received a demonstration from both sides such as the House has seldom witnessed."[32]

It was precisely this "limited accountability" interpretation of party leadership in the House which defeated Cannon. It was not, and is not, consistent either with the structure of the House as noted above or in the "middleman" concept of leadership which is fostered by this structure. The insurgents articulated an interpretation much more consistent with the structure of the House. Whether theirs was a good or bad theory, whether it was well articulated or not, are not relevant to the present argument. Though their position was much less tidy, and required considerable painful unraveling in the 1910 debate, it was more in the mainstream of the traditions of party leadership in Congress.

The insurgents argued that Cannon and his supporters had simply gone too far. Each congressman is an individual who is potentially part of a majority—procedural or substantive. On substantive issues, the insurgents argued, the Republican leadership was not attuned to new attitudes among Republicans. Leaders were using sanctions provided by procedural majorities to force—rather than build—substantive majorities. Leaders who do not attend to new opinions, and recognize their force, must face the consequences of losing their procedural majorities. Mr. Lindberg of Minnesota argued the case for the insurgents as follows:

> When I look back over the proceedings of this House, and when I know, and the entire country knows, that by indirection the will of this House has been thwarted time and time again, then I say, when we have a resolution before us, which proposes to do by direction the will of the House, it is time now and here on this occasion to manifest our power, to enforce the rule of the majority, in the language that has frequently been expressed by the able Speaker of this House. I say now and here, in the light of what has occurred over and over again, in defeating, in holding back, in preventing bills that have been introduced in this House, which were in accord with the wish of the entire country at large—I say, when those bills have time and time again been pigeonholed by select committees, that now . . . the House can by a direct vote do directly the will of the House.[33]

John Nelson of Wisconsin also stated the insurgents' case vigorously. He observed that their duty was unpleasant—but that theirs had been an unpleasant experience in the House for some time. They had foregone the many privileges of the "regulars"—e.g., patronage and power—for the sake of principle. Their punishment was severe for failing to "cringe or crawl before arbitrary power of the Speaker and his House machine." Nelson then discussed the problems of majorities, rules, leadership, and representation.

> The eloquent gentleman from New York [Mr. Fassett] says the majority must control, but what is the majority? Speaker Reed emphatically said: "There is no greater fallacy than this idea that majority and minority are predicated on political parties only." Why should the subject of the rules be a party matter? At what convention did the Republican party adopt the present rules of the House? The Speaker says he represents the majority. But how? He and his chief lieutenants—favorites or personal friends, a small minority within the majority—call themselves the party and then pass the word on to the rank and file of the Republican membership to line up or be punished. What is the controlling force? Party principles? No. The Speaker's power under the rules. . . . We are no less Republicans because we would be free Members of Congress. We do not need to be kept on leading strings. We are free representatives of the people, and we want freedom here for every Member of every party.[34]

It seems quite clear that Nelson's remarks may be interpreted in line with the analysis suggested here. Cannon's exercise of power was inconsistent with the bargaining condition in the House and therefore "free representatives" would form a new majority which would change the sanctions available to the Speaker.

The argument of the Democrats was very much like that of the insurgents. Oscar W. Underwood was led to conclude that leadership in the House should not be centered in the speakership—at least as it was exercised by Cannon. The Cannon "system" had to be overthrown.

> We are fighting a system, and that system is the system that enables the Speaker, by the power vested in him, to thwart and overthrow the will of the majority membership of this House. We recognize to-day that there has to be leadership; that some man must be the leader of the majority and some man must be the leader of the minority, but we say the place for that leadership *is not in the Chair*.[35]

In summary, the insurgent Republican members were led to take the drastic action of leaving their party to join the Democrats on a major procedural change because they were convinced that the Speaker's authority had allowed him to ignore segments of his procedural majority. They were unable to reach him directly in pressing for representation of their views. As their numbers grew, they merely waited for the right moment—primed to take action sometime to make the Speaker more accountable. Mr. Norris's resolution served as the catalyst for action.

THE CASE OF JUDGE SMITH

In 1961, the House voted 217 to 212 to enlarge the Committee on Rules from twelve to fifteen members. By this action, the House took the first of a series of steps to curb the power of the committee and its chairman, Howard W. Smith of Virginia. The Committee had, since 1937, developed an antiadministration nature. Southern Democrats and Republicans joined to defeat presidential proposals. There was considerable evidence to suggest that these actions more often than not had the tacit support of a bipartisan majority in the House. As Lewis J. Lapham concluded:

> It is perfectly true that a very good case can be developed for supporting the proposition that the Rules Committee, though out of sympathy with the majority party program as defined by the President and his supporters, did in fact faithfully represent majority sentiment in the House.[36]

Adolph Sabath (D., Ill.) chaired the committee every Congress, except the Eightieth, between 1939 and 1952. Though he personally supported Democratic presidents and their programs, he was extremely weak and ineffective as chairman. Lapham observed that "the *Congressional Record,* since 1939, is replete with candid admissions by Mr. Sabath that he was 'helpless' in the face of an obstinate majority on the Committee which he could not control."[37]

In 1953, conservative Republican Leo Allen (Ill.) again chaired the committee, as he had in the Eightieth Congress. And in 1955, after the Democrats recaptured control of Congress in the 1954 elections, Howard W. Smith became chairman. Smith had been influential on the committee before his accession to the chairmanship. He and Eugene E. Cox of Georgia were the principal leaders of the southern Democratic–Republican coalition during Sabath's long tenure as chairman. Smith was first appointed to the committee in 1933—over the objections of the then-Speaker, Henry T. Rainey of Illinois. As chairman, Smith was free to exercise his considerable powers to stifle legislation which he and his southern Democratic and Republican colleagues opposed. In some cases the legislation was part of President Eisenhower's program—in other cases, attempts by the Democratic majority in the House to enact their own legislation.

Smith's procedural majority was of a different sort than that provided Speaker Cannon. Whereas Cannon was elected to office, Smith achieved his position of leadership through seniority. Thus, in accepting seniority as a procedure for committee chairmanships, the Democrats had to accept Howard W. Smith as chairman of the Committee on Rules. To "defeat" Smith, the Democrats would have to strike a blow against a whole seniority system. Thus, Smith, like Cannon, had a considerable advantage. He had a certain amount of independence from his procedural majority. Up to a point, he could afford to ignore it in exercising the considerable reservoir of power in the Committee on Rules. He proceeded to do just that.

Chairman Smith's Exercise of Power

How did Smith develop and use his powers? Two careful students of the House Committee on Rules, James A. Robinson and Walter Kravitz, have examined the influence of the committee on legislation during this period.[38] Both indicated the wide variety of powers available to the committee at the height of its influence. The more overt actions were to refuse to grant a hearing for a rule and to refuse to grant the rule. During the Eighty-fourth Congress, Robinson found that only four requests for hearings were refused and eleven rules were denied. During the Eighty-fifth Congress, twenty requests for hearings were refused and nine requests for rules were denied. In addition to these more obvious exercises of power, the committee could force changes in the legislation as a condition for granting a rule, it could delay granting a rule until the mood of the House changed for some reason, it could grant a rule with conditions for debate which the authors did not want, it could threaten to refuse a rule. All of these tactics were relied on during the Eighty-fourth and Eighty-fifth Congresses. And, as is indicated by both Robinson and Kravitz, the legislation which was affected was often important legislation—the doctors' draft, housing, statehood for Alaska and Hawaii, aid to education, civil rights, depressed areas aid, presidential disability, absentee voting, appropriations measures, federal judgeships.

Warning Signals Again

In 1958, the Democrats won a sweeping victory throughout the nation. They increased their margin in the House by forty-nine seats and their margin in the Senate by seventeen seats. A number of Democratic liberals in the House went to the Speaker and proposed that the party ratio on the Committee on Rules be changed from eight Democrats and four Republicans to nine and three. They further pressed for the return of the twenty-one-day rule. Speaker Rayburn convinced them that they should not press for changes. He assured them that legislation would be brought out of the committee.[39]

The 1958 elections were of considerable importance to Chairman Smith and his power base. It was at this time that his procedural majority began to change drastically. There were forty-eight congressional districts in which Democrats replaced Republicans. What was the significance of this trade for Chairman Smith? The *Congressional Quarterly* provides economy support and opposition scores for the Eighty-fifth Congress and for the first session of the Eighty-sixth Congress.[40] The forty-eight House Republicans who were replaced by Democrats in 1958 had an average economy support score of 42.9 and an average economy opposition score of 42.0 in the Eighty-fifth Congress. Their Democratic replacements in the Eighty-sixth Congress, first session, had an average economy support score of 9.3 and an average economy opposition score of 86.3. Obviously this new group of congressmen was considerably more liberal than the Republicans who left Congress in 1958, and markedly less dependable for Chairman Smith.

If Chairman Smith wished to retain his position of power in the long run, several developments made it evident that he would have to make some accommodations during the Eighty-sixth Congress. Speaker Rayburn had given the reformers his assurance that important legislation would not be delayed and thus had put his prestige on the line. The new Democrats were anxious to develop a legislative record for the 1960 presidential elections. Criticism of the chairman and his committee had continued to mount during the Eighty-fifth Congress. And the new Democrats had served notice of their intentions with their reform suggestions during the early days of the Eighty-sixth Congress (much as the progressive Republicans had placed Speaker Cannon on notice fifty years earlier).

The record shows, however, that Chairman Smith continued to block legislation. He relied on the same techniques as before, despite the fact that a new, restive majority was emerging in the House—a majority which ultimately could deprive Chairman Smith of much of his influence through procedural changes. During the Eighty-sixth Congress, the Committee on Rules denied thirty-one requests for hearings and eleven requests for rules. As before, the committee was a major factor in practically all significant legislation to come before the House—either by preventing its consideration on the floor or by influencing the substance of the legislation. But the most controversial action of the committee was that taken in 1960 to defeat the first broad-scale federal aid to education bill since the Morrill Act of 1862. Following the passage of the bill in both houses, the Committee on Rules invoked its power to deny the request for a rule allowing the House of Representatives to agree to a conference so as to resolve the differences between the House and Senate versions of the bill. The result, of course, was to kill the bill. By this action, the Committee on Rules seemed to place itself above majority action by *both* the House and the Senate. It became obvious to the liberal and moderate Democrats that Chairman Smith was not going to make accommodations. They concluded that their only alternative was to curb the power of Chairman Smith and his Committee on Rules.

The Limits of Leadership Reemphasized

The 1960 elections brought to the White House an energetic young president of the twentieth century. He had campaigned on a platform of "action." Though his majority in the House was twenty less than the Democratic majority of the Eighty-sixth Congress, it was still sizeable and it was made up of many members who were extremely critical of the Committee on Rules. If the president's program was to receive favorable consideration in Congress, it would have to receive favorable consideration in the Committee on Rules. Unless changes were made, it was unlikely that the committee would be so cooperative.

The results of the power struggle between the young president, his Speaker, and Chairman Smith have been well chronicled and thus only the sequence of events needs repeating here.[41] Our interest is not in the details of what happened but rather in the arguments which were made, since these arguments should provide clues in defining the limits of power for leaders in the House. A brief sequence of events is provided in table 11-2.

As might be expected there are parallels between the debate in 1910 and the debates during the 1961–65 period (of which the 1961 debate was the most crucial). As in 1910, those who pressed for change in 1961 argued in favor of leadership accountability to the majority. The Committee on Rules was a roadblock to the majority. It was not allowing the House to vote on measures which a majority in the House wished to vote on. Despite the fact that the majority party had a two-to-one majority on the committee, Chairman Smith and second-ranking Democrat, William Colmer (Miss.), would frequently vote with the four Republicans on important legislation to prevent it from coming to the floor. John A. Blatnik (D., Minn.), head of the Democratic Study Group, and therefore a principal leader in adopting the rules changes, stated the case as follows:

Table 11-2. *Sequence of Events in Decline of Power of House Committee on Rules,*
1961–1965

Event	Date	Vote
Enlargement of committee from 12 to 15 for 87th Congress	31 January 1961	217–212 GOP: 22–148 Dem: 195–64
Permanent enlargement of committee from 12 to 15	9 January 1963	235–196 GOP: 28–148 Dem: 207–48
Reinstitution of the 21-day rule and transfer of power regarding sending bills to conference.[a]	4 January 1965	224–201[b] GOP: 16–123 Dem: 208–78

[a] The second change permitted the Speaker to recognize a member to offer a
motion to send a bill to conference.
[b] On a motion to close debate. Rules changes actually passed by voice vote.

My constituents did not cast a free ballot for the office of U.S. Representative to Congress to have the functions of that Office limited by one or two or even six other Members. They understand that in a body as large as this the majority shall be established in caucus and put forward in the form of legislation by the leadership chosen by the majority. It is difficult to explain to them how 2 members of the majority [Smith and Colmer] can desert the majority's program, join with 4 members of the minority and among them determine the course of action of 431 other Members of this House. . . . Does their judgment supersede the cumulative judgment of the legislative committees? Do they have some inherent right . . . to determine the course of legislation . . . ? It would appear that they at least think so.[42]

Thus, though Blatnik, and others who pressed for change, agreed that any leader or any leadership committee had latitude in exercising power, they also agreed that there should be limits beyond which leaders are not permitted to go. To the reformers, the Committee on Rules ultimately should be a part of the majority leadership. That meant something very specific. For example, to Paul J. Kilday (D., Tex.), it meant:

The Committee on Rules is an arm of the leadership of the majority party. . . . One who assumes membership on the Committee on Rules must be prepared to exercise a function of leadership. His personal objection to the proposal is not always sufficient reason for him to vote to deny the membership of the whole House the opportunity to express its approval or, equally important, the opportunity to express its disapproval.[43]

Speaker Rayburn expressed much the same sentiment:

> I think that the Committee on Rules should grant that rule whether its membership is for the bill or not. I think this House should be allowed on great measures to work its will, and it cannot work its will if the Committee on Rules is so constituted as not to allow the House to pass on those things.[44]

Frequent references to 1910 were made. At the time "too much control was centered in the Speaker." "Today . . . we fight a system which has deposited too much power in the Committee on Rules,"[45] according to Sidney R. Yates (D., Ill.). What is the definition of "too much power"? It is that situation when leaders have been permitted to exercise greater authority than was intended by the procedural majority in the House.

The Limited Accountability Theory Restated

The arguments of Smith and his supporters also bore the characteristics of the 1910 debate. Speaker Cannon believed in limited accountability and so did Smith. Though their positions of leadership were different, and therefore one would not expect exact parallels between the two situations, the two had similar views of leadership and accountability. To Chairman Smith, the whole effort to enlarge the committee was both unnecessary and premature. In a series of circumlocutions (some of which were contradictory), Smith and his cohorts argued as follows:

1. The committee has been wrongly charged—it does not block important legislation which requires "emergency action." As Clarence Brown (R., Ohio), ranking Republican on the Committee on Rules and close colleague of Chairman Smith, noted: "In my nearly quarter of a century of service here, I have never known of a single instance when the House leadership desired a bill to be brought to a House vote, that such measure was not voted upon."[46]

2. The committee will delay on measures which are not "emergency" measures, but "nothing is lost and much is gained by delay. . . . 'Haste makes waste.' . . . John Nance Garner . . . once was reported to have said, 'The country never suffers from the things that Congress fails to do.'"[47]

3. The majority can always work its will—it can go around the Committee on Rules by relying on Calendar Wednesday discharge petition, and suspension of the rules.

4. Much more legislation is killed in other standing committees than in the Committee on Rules.

5. How can the president know that his program will not be enacted? He has just arrived on the scene. It would be better to leave the "packing"

resolution on the calendar for two years and then assess the situation when the evidence is in.

6. The chairman is willing now to insure that "no obstacles" would be interposed "to the five major bills that the President has publicly announced as his program for this session."

This example of a Smith accommodation is very revealing and brings us to an analysis of his broader view of his position of leadership. He did not consider it necessary generally to work with his party leaders and membership in passing legislation, but he was willing to allow five major bills to reach the floor. This offer was considered "audacious" by the reformers. Blatnik expressed their views:

> Who else would have the audacity and arrogance to even suggest that in exchange for our agreeing to the status quo they would permit us to consider five pieces of legislation said to be the cornerstone of the new administration's domestic program? This offer was an insult to the House and its Members. The fact that it was a bona fide and sincere attempt only heightens the frightening picture of two men telling a nation that they will permit five bills to pass if they can reserve their right to kill off any others that do not meet with their approval.[48]

How could this type of proposal be offered by Smith? Clearly, he saw it as a definite concession. "All of the five bills which the President has announced as his program for this session . . . are five bills that I am very much opposed to."[49] Smith did not consider that he had an obligation to support his party's legislation just because he chaired the committee which scheduled that legislation.

> When I made this pledge to the Speaker and to the Members of this House, it is a pledge I made when I first became chairman of the Rules Committee. That is, *I will cooperate with the Democratic leadership of the House of Representatives just as long and just as far as my conscience will permit me to go.*[50]

The convenience of holding oneself accountable to "conscience" is that only the individual himself is involved in defining accountability. This self-interpretation was the very thing that was objected to by the reformers. It meant that the majority could not be assured of cooperation from one of their leaders. Speaker Rayburn, among others, expressed his concern: "The gentleman from Virginia says that he is not going to report anything that violates his conscience and then winds up his talk on the floor by saying you have nothing to fear from the action of the Committee on Rules."[51]

In 1963 the Committee on Rules was permanently expanded to fifteen members. Many of the same arguments were invoked but the political situation had changed. The reformers could now defend their experiment—pointing out that the dire predictions of those opposed in 1961 had not come true. Even the Republicans seemed to accept the fifteen-member committee, though they tried to have a party division changed from ten Democrats and five Republicans to nine Democrats and six Republicans. The best the opponents of a fifteen-member committee could do was to reiterate their earlier arguments and note that the committee's performance in the Eighty-seventh Congress was little different than before—it, too, blocked legislation.[52] For Judge Smith's part, he focused his attention on southern Democrats, warning:

> This matter of packing the Rules Committee affects more closely our area of the country than anywhere else. . . . I hope that none of my southern friends are going to be complaining around here when certain measures come up, and come up quite promptly, if the Committee on Rules is packed again. . . . I hope that at least those Members who voted against the packing before will see fit to do the same thing again, because I believe *it is vital to the interests of their States.*[53]

The chairman also addressed the new members of the Eighty-eighth Congress. He warned them that unwise fiscal legislation would soon be introduced.

> Are you going to yield up every little leverage or every little weapon you may have to defeat measures so unsound? Are you going to yield some of your prerogatives and privileges here today that are going to adversely affect your people for the next twenty years? If you do, *that is your business and none of mine.*[54]

Howard W. Smith proved himself to be an unintentioned prophet. By a margin of thirty-nine votes (see table 11-2), the House did make an attempt to clarify the distinction between its business and that of Judge Smith. Thus occurred the second important increment in the decline of the chairmanship of the Committee on Rules.

The third increment came in 1965. With very little debate, the House reinvoked the twenty-one-day rule[55] and took away the Committee on Rules' power, when any member of the House objected, to grant rules to send a bill to conference (or to agree to the Senate version). In both instances, the powers of the Speaker were increased. To Clarence Brown (R., Ohio) this raised the specter of the all-powerful Speaker before 1910. In a colloquy with Speaker McCormack, he observed:

> You are too nice a fellow. But I am thinking about some dirty dog that might come along some other time and say here is a nice little wrinkle in

the rule which we can use to block this legislation.

In other words, should we give that power to every Speaker in the future? We gave that power to "Uncle Joe" Cannon and Tom Reed as the gentleman recalls. We gave them too much power.[56]

Ironically, Brown failed to perceive that his colleague, Howard W. Smith, also had been given more power than was compatible with the structure, organization, and composition of the House of Representatives. Smith had developed independence from those who ultimately had provided him with this position of authority. Smith's refusal to heed the warning signals of substantive shifts in his procedural majority resulted in changes which forced him to be more dependent on this majority or face a serious loss of influence in the process of building substantive majorities.

CONCLUSIONS

In 1910 and 1961 the House of Representatives acted to curb the power of two generally well-loved and admired leaders—Joseph G. Cannon and Howard W. Smith. These men had realized the full potential of the authority inherent in their respective positions in the House. Though in different ways, they both had become virtually independent of their procedural majorities. Defeating them would not have solved the problems raised by their exercise of power. Thus, the House took the more drastic action of making procedural changes to guarantee the predominance of the condition of relatively free bargaining, with leaders acting as "middlemen."

Though it is not possible as a result of this inquiry to set forth a handbook for successful leadership in the House, it is possible to draw some inferences concerning the limits which must be observed by the "middleman" type of leader. First, the procedural majority is of major significance for House leaders since the sanctions it allows determine the limits on leaders in forming or thwarting substantive majorities. In order to protect his position, the House leader must be exceptionally protective of this procedural majority—developing techniques which will inform him as to substantive changes which have occurred within various segments of the majority, and making a requisite number of adaptations.

Second, there are cases, as noted here, where leaders have developed, over a period of time, the authority of the position to the extent that they seemingly are independent of the procedural majority. Their exercise of power eventually leads some members to the conclusion that procedural changes are necessary to prevent a recurrence of such independent action.

If there are enough members of the majority who perceive violations of bargaining behavior on the part of leaders over a period of time, they may take extreme action to force compliance with their expectations. These instances are of major significance for the study of the House since they provide important clues as to how that body defines leadership for itself.

Third, all House leaders have considerable latitude in using the sanctions provided by procedural majorities in building substantive majorities. In the short run, therefore, leaders thwart the emergence of new majorities. Furthermore, leaders are normally given ample warning of dissatisfaction before action is taken. If the leader persists in ignoring these signs (or in simply failing to read them properly), he will be defeated. If, in addition, he has assumed so much power that he is protected from his procedural majority, the reform condition is set and changes will be made eventually.

Fourth, both cases cited here suggest that leadership positions of great, absolute authority in the House of Representatives are contextually inappropriate. Congressional political parties are coalitions of members, each of whom has some bargaining power. Thus, conditions in the House are not conducive to the exercise of power with such limited accountability to major segments of the procedural majority, as in the two cases cited here.

Fifth, one is inevitably led to inquire whether Speaker Cannon and Chairman Smith could have avoided the consequences which ultimately developed. If the analysis of this essay is accurate, the answer must be "yes." They could have avoided the reforms by accepting the conditions of leadership in the House and behaving accordingly. Had they been more flexible, they would likely have not only avoided being "reformed" but also have preserved more power for themselves in the long run. Speaker Sam Rayburn, the model "middleman," could have counseled them both on such matters.

NOTES

1. For a sample of this literature see David B. Truman, *The Governmental Process* (New York: Knopf, 1951); Bertram M. Gross, *The Legislative Struggle* (New York: McGraw-Hill, 1953); the 1st ed. of this work (Chicago: Rand-McNally, 1963), and particularly Robert L. Peabody, "Organization Theory and Legislative Behavior: Bargaining, Hierarchy, and Change in the U.S. House of Representatives" (Paper delivered at the Annual Meeting of the American Political Science Association, New York, 1963).

2. The "middleman" thesis of congressional leadership is discussed in David B. Truman, *The Congressional Party: A Case Study* (New York: Wiley, 1959). See also

Samuel C. Patterson, "Legislative Leadership and Political Ideology," *Public Opinion Quarterly* 27 (Fall 1963):399–410.

3. Richard F. Fenno, Jr., has eloquently discussed the organizational problems of the House in his essay in David B. Truman, ed., *The Congress and America's Future* (Englewood Cliffs, N.J.: Prentice-Hall, 1965).

4. Lewis A. Froman, Jr., and Randall B. Ripley note that the two parties maintain the highest level of cohesion on procedural questions. See "Conditions for Party Leadership: The Case of the House Democrats," *American Political Science Review* (59 (Mar., 1965):52–63. Much of this essay tends to support their general argument.

5. Cannon allowed the Democrats to select their members, though he did not have to make this concession. He did so because he thought that by giving the minority leader this power, the Democrats would fight over committee assignments. See William R. Gwinn, *Uncle Joe Cannon: Archfoe of Insurgency* (New York: Bookman Associates, 1957), 97.

6. 17 Mar. 1910, *Congressional Record,* 61st Cong., 2d sess., 3294.

7. Cannon also preferred to have his whip on Ways and Means. James Tawney (Minn.), James Watson (Ind.), and John Dwight (N.Y.), all were on that committee while serving as whip under Cannon.

8. For discussions of seniority and its development, see George Goodwin, "The Seniority System in Congress," *American Political Science Review* 53 (June 1959):596–604; George B. Galloway, *History of the House of Representatives* (New York: Crowell, 1961); and particularly Nelson W. Polsby, "The Institutionalization of the U.S. House of Representatives," *American Political Science Review* 62 (Mar. 1968):144–68.

9. See Paul D. Hasbrouck, *Party Government in the House of Representatives* (New York: Macmillan, 1927), 37.

10. George Norris, *Fighting Liberal* (New York: Macmillan, 1945), 109.

11. 17 Mar. 1910, *Congressional Record,* 61st Cong., 2d sess., 3300.

12. Norris, *Fighting Liberal,* 144.

13. Hasbrouck, *Party Government,* 4–6.

14. The principal student of these changes is Joseph Cooper. See "Congress and Its Committees" (Ph.D. diss., Harvard University, 1961). See also Chang-wei Chiu, *The Speaker of the House of Representatives since 1896* (New York: Columbia University Press, 1928), chap. 6. Actually, for rather complicated reasons, the insurgents hadn't voted for Calendar Wednesday: see Cooper, "Congress and Its Committees," chap. 2.

15. Hasbrouck, *Party Government,* 126.

16. One can consult any number of sources on the 1910 revolt. Those highly recommended include Hasbrouck, *Party Government*; Chiu, *The Speaker*; Gwinn, *Uncle Joe Cannon*; Norris, *Fighting Liberal*; Kenneth Hechler, *Insurgency* (New York: Columbia University Press, 1941); George R. Brown, *The Leadership of Congress* (Indianapolis: Bobbs-Merrill, 1922); Charles R. Atkinson, *The Committee on Rules and the Overthrow of Speaker Cannon* (New York: Columbia University Press, 1911), plus the several biographies and autobiographies of those who participated. For a listing of the latter, see Charles O. Jones and Randall B. Ripley, *The Role of Political Parties in Congress: A Bibliography and Research Guide* (Tucson: University of Arizona Press, 1966).

17. Gwinn suggests that this move was prearranged between Crumpacker and Cannon. See *Uncle Joe Cannon,* 206.

18. 16 Mar. 1910, *Congressional Record,* 61st Cong., 2d sess., 3241. Emphasis added.

19. Ibid., 3251.

20. 17 Mar. 1910, *Congressional Record,* 61st Cong., 2d sess., 3287.

21. Ibid., 3289.

22. Gwinn, *Uncle Joe Cannon,* 207.

23. Norris, *Fighting Liberal,* 126.

24. *New York Times,* 18 Mar. 1910, p. 1.

25. 17 Mar. 1910, *Congressional Record,* 61st Cong., 2d sess., 3292.

26. L. White Busbey, *Uncle Joe Cannon: The Story of a Pioneer American* (New York: Holt, 1927), 254.

27. 17 Mar. 1910, *Congressional Record,* 61st Cong., 2d sess., 3302.

28. Ibid., 3305.

29. 19 Mar. 1910, *Congressional Record,* 61st Cong., 2d sess., 3430.

30. Ibid., 3436.

31. Ibid., 3437.

32. Busbey, *Uncle Joe Cannon,* 266.

33. 17 Mar. 1910, *Congressional Record,* 61st Cong., 2d sess., 3300.

34. Ibid., 3304.

35. 19 Mar. 1910, *Congressional Record,* 61st Cong., 2d sess., 3433. Emphasis added. Interestingly, Underwood later became the principal leader of the House during the Sixty-second Congress as majority leader. The Democrats were in a ticklish spot. They wanted to emphasize the internal divisions in the Republican party so as to win the 1910 elections, but did not want the Republicans either to get credit for reform or to reunite after reform. One news story suggested that the Democrats wanted Cannon to win, so as not to lose an issue in 1910 (*New York Times,* 19 Mar. 1910). The Democrats also had to consider the problems for themselves of a drastic change in the Speaker's power, should they gain control of the House in 1910.

36. Lewis J. Lapham, "Party Leadership and the House Committee on Rules," (Ph.D. diss., Harvard University, 1954), 137.

37. Ibid., 123.

38. See James A. Robinson, *The House Rules Committee* (Indianapolis: Bobbs-Merrill, 1963), and the several useful unpublished research papers on the House Committee on Rules produced by Walter Kravitz of the Legislative Reference Service, Library of Congress. See also Christopher Van Hollen, "The House Committee on Rules (1933–1951): Agent of Party and Agent of Opposition" (Ph.D. diss., Johns Hopkins University, 1951).

39. See *Congress and the Nation* (Washington, D.C.: Congressional Quarterly, 1965), 1425. See also William MacKaye, *A New Coalition Takes Control: The House Rules Committee Fight 1961* (New York: McGraw-Hill, 1963).

40. *Congressional Quarterly Almanacs,* vols. 14, 15 (Washington, D.C.; Congressional Quarterly, 1958, 1959).

41. Note in particular, in addition to Robinson, *Rules Committee* and MacKaye, *New Coalition,* the two articles in the 1st ed. of this work—one by Peabody ("The Enlarged Rules Committee") and one by Peabody and Milton C. Cummings, Jr., ("The Decision to Enlarge the Committee on Rules: An Analysis of the 1961 Vote") and Neil MacNeil, *Forge of Democracy: The House of Representatives* (New York: MacKay, 1963), chap. 15.

42. 31 Jan. 1961, *Congressional Record,* 87th Cong., 1st sess., 1582–1583.

43. Ibid., 1574.

44. Ibid., 1579.

45. Ibid., 1581.
46. Ibid., 1575.
47. Ibid., 1577.
48. Ibid., 1583.
49. Ibid., 1576.
50. Ibid. Emphasis added.
51. Ibid., 1580.
52. Particularly noted was the defeat of the federal aid to education bill in the committee in 1961. Though a bargain had been struck between pro- and anti-parochial-school-aid members, the parochial-aid proponents were not convinced that they would get what they wanted. Thus, a liberal, Democratic, Catholic member of the Committee on rules, James Delaney of New York, voted with the conservatives to kill the bill. See H. Douglas Price, "Race, Religion, and the Rules Committee," in Alan F. Westin, ed., *The Uses of Power* (New York: Harcourt, Brace, 1962) and Robert Bendiner, *Obstacle Course on Capitol Hill* (New York: McGraw-Hill, 1964).
53. 9 Jan. 1963, *Congressional Record*, 88th Cong., 1st sess., 18. Emphasis added.
54. Ibid. Emphasis added.
55. The twenty-one-day rule had been implemented during the Eighty-first Congress and abandoned in the Eighty-second Congress. It has since been abandoned in the Ninetieth Congress.
56. 4 Jan. 1965, *Congressional Record*, 89th Cong., 1st sess., 22.

Chapter 12

Two Strategies of Influence: Choosing a Majority Leader, 1962

NELSON W. POLSBY

Political scientists seem to be fond of debating whether traditional political theory in America is dead or only sleeping.[1] Either way, there is no argument that the speculations which occupied thinkers of other days have been little used to illuminate current political behavior. The argument, when there is one, concerns whether it is even possible to use traditional political theory in this way. Regrettably, optimists on this point have not always demonstrated that they were right in supposing that traditional political theory could contribute to the understanding of present-day politics. But this does not mean that they are wrong.

A major obstacle to the use of traditional political theory in modern political science has been theory's long-standing concern with prescriptive statements. Prescriptions are not necessarily the best instruments for organizing information about the empirical world, since the preferences which they assert may not correspond to any observed (or even observable) events. However, prescriptions may in fact point to quite interesting and genuine dilemmas in the real world. In these circumstances, we have

This chapter was originally presented at the annual meeting of the American Political Science Association, Washington, D.C., 1962. Copyright © 1962 by the American Political Science Association. It is reprinted by permission. Several members of Congress, who I am sure would prefer to remain anonymous, read an early draft and made many useful comments. I should also like to thank Lewis A. Dexter, H. Douglas Price, and Robert L. Peabody. Others who have been helpful include Aaron B. Wildavsky, Lewis A. Froman, Jr., Norman O. Brown, Luigi Einaudi, Joseph Cooper, Alan L. Otten, and Neil MacNeil. Research assistance was provided by a Ford Foundation grant to Wesleyan University.

the option of converting the language of prescription to that of description if we desire to put traditional political theory to more modern uses.

The possibilities of this device have lately been explored by a group of students of the legislative process, using as their text the celebrated speech to the electors of Bristol by Edmund Burke.[2] In this speech, on the occasion of his election as member of Parliament from Bristol, it will be recalled that Burke undertook to state and resolve a recurring dilemma of the representative:

> Certainly, gentlemen, it ought to be the happiness and glory of a representative to live in the strictest union, the closest correspondence, and the most unreserved communication with his constituents. Their wishes ought to have great weight with him; their opinion high respect; their business unremitted attention. . . . But his unbiased opinion, his native judgment, his enlightened conscience he ought not to sacrifice to you. . . . Your representative owes you, not his industry only, but his judgment. . . . Government and legislation are matters of reason and judgment, and not of inclination; and what sort of reason is that, in which the determination precedes the discussion; in which one set of men deliberate and another decide? . . . Parliament is not a *congress* of ambassadors from different and hostile interests . . . but . . . a *deliberative* assembly of *one* nation. . . . We are now members for a rich commercial city; this city, however, is but part of a rich commercial nation, the interests of which are various, multiform, and intricate. . . . All these widespread interests must be considered; must be compared; must be reconciled if possible.[3]

Six years after Burke spoke these words, he stood for election once again, and on the same topic said:

> I could wish undoubtedly . . . to make every part of my conduct agreeable to every one of my constituents. . . . But . . . do you think, gentlemen, that every public act in six years since I stood in this place before you— that all the arduous things which have been done in this eventful period, which has crowded into a few years' space the revolutions of an age—can be opened to you on their fair grounds in half an hour's conversation? . . . Let me say with plainness . . . that if by a fair, by an indulgent, by a gentlemanly behavior to our representatives, we do not give confidence to their minds, and a liberal scope to their understandings; if we do not permit our members to act upon a *very* enlarged view of things, we shall at length infallibly degrade our national representation into a confused and scuffling bustle of local agency.[4]

A brief historical detour will suggest certain empirical problems related to Burke's position. Shortly after the second speech quoted here, Burke withdrew his candidacy, feeling he could not win. He and his constituents had disagreed over several matters, in particular his vote to free Irish trade from restrictions operating in favor of Bristol. Burke remained in Parliament, however, representing a pocket borough thereafter.[5] Although acting on his principle of independence from constituent pressures was costly to him, Burke was clearly in a position to take a more luxurious stand on such a question than another member could who did not have the protection of a pocket borough and the party list.

This raises still a more general empirical point: Under what conditions will the representative be more likely to respond to the demands of "local agency"? When is he more likely to respond to a political situation as it appears to him in the light of his experience at the seat of government? Under what conditions will attempts to influence the representative through his constituency bring better results than attempts to influence him through the network of loyalties and affiliations he has built up through service in his deliberative body—and vice versa?

The United States House of Representatives is one laboratory for the exploration of questions such as these. Indeed, where the stakes are as high as they often are in House decision-making, it is not surprising that full-scale campaigns are mounted in order to sway sometimes no more than a handful of marginal votes. But are these votes swayed from the inside or the outside? Do constituencies matter more or less than colleagues?[6]

Sometimes the answer is reasonably clear and unequivocal. Here are examples of *inside* influences at work:

Representative Cleveland Bailey is a genuinely dedicated opponent of reciprocal trade. . . . [He] is unusual among members—probably unique— in that protection is *the* most important issue to him and that he creates a sense of having a deep-felt conviction on the subject. In 1953 to 1954 he went around and pled individually with a number of members to vote against reciprocal trade and for the West Virginia miners. One member put it, "He was rough, real rough. . . . I had to be rough with him." Another said, "In the 1954 vote, Cleve Bailey was worth fifteen votes to his side easily."[7]

The morning of one of the key votes on reciprocal trade [1955], Speaker Sam Rayburn attended a breakfast of the freshman Democrats in the House. I asked one of the congressmen who was there about it. He chuckled: "Oh, you heard about that? . . . We'd just invited Mr. Sam to this breakfast. He turned it into a sort of speech and said he'd observed that *generally the new members got along better who went along*, but he didn't make any particular application—of course you could guess what he had in mind."[8]

On the other hand, it is sometimes possible to detect *outside* influences. The following examples comes from the January 1961 battle over the size of the House Rules Committee:

> It was learned that Representative Howard Smith, southern leader and Rules Committee chairman, has held several meetings in his office in recent weeks with representatives of the most powerful conservative lobbies in the country, trying to shape a campaign to beat Rayburn by applying pressure on members from home. The groups included the National Association of Manufacturers, the United States Chamber of Commerce, the American Medical Association and the American Farm Bureau. . . . Some members have reported heavy mail from business interests in their home districts. . . . On the other side, northern Democrats have sent out an appeal to organized labor for help. Yesterday, Andrew J. Biemiller, chief AFL-CIO lobbyist, was at the Capitol trying to line up votes.[9]

> During the aid to education debate [a Roman Catholic congressman] threatened to kill the public school measure by tagging on to it a parochial school amendment. [Presidential Assistant Lawrence] O'Brien appealed to [the congressman's home district party leader], who immediately telephoned [the congressman]. "Who sent you there, me or the Bishop?" he growled. "And who's going to keep you there, me or the Bishop?"[10]

At other times strong inside and outside influences are blurred together quite inextricably:

> A newspaper correspondent told me: "Oh yes, you know those two boys [congressmen]. . . . Well, you know why Jack voted against the leadership? Just to oblige Joe, to whom he's very close; Joe was afraid he'd be the only fellow from the state to vote against the leadership and he'd get into trouble with the leadership and the party organization so Jack went along with him to prevent his sticking his neck out all alone."[11]

> The whip from the area told me, . . . "Tom rather wanted to go along with the leadership, but he found Dave and Don and four other guys from surrounding districts were against the leadership, and he decided he'd better go along with them, because after all he's hearing a lot from his district against it, and how could he explain his being for it and Dave and Don and the rest being against it?"[12]

The recent contest for the majority leadership of the House provides, as it happens, a rather good contrast between the two strategies of influence. In turn, the close examination of this case may begin to suggest answers to some of the questions posed above.

I

On 10 January 1962, the Democratic members of the House met in caucus in the House chamber and nominated John McCormack as their candidate for Speaker. Immediately following the conclusion of this business, Richard Bolling of Missouri asked that the agenda of the caucus be expanded by unanimous consent to include the selection of a majority leader, and Carl Albert of Oklahoma, his party's whip and the only congressman put in nomination, was elected to that post. Thus ended a period of skirmishing for the majority leadership that had principally engaged Bolling and Albert from the time of Speaker Rayburn's death on 16 November of the previous year.

Most newspaper coverage of this event gave the impression that the battle between these two men was drawn on liberal-conservative lines. In Bolling's press conference on 3 January announcing his withdrawal from the race, newsmen repeatedly suggested that the contrast between them was predominantly ideological. A newspaperwoman asked, rhetorically, "Don't the liberals *ever* win around here, Mr. Bolling?" Another widely quoted colloquy went:

> *Reporter.* Mr. Bolling, do you regard your withdrawal . . . as a defeat for liberalism?
> *Bolling.* Well, I consider myself a liberal, and at the moment I certainly feel defeated.[13]

Close observation suggests that the liberal-conservative distinction has only a limited kind of utility for understanding the Bolling-Albert fight for the majority leadership.[14] It is not necessary to base this conclusion on a *Congressional Quarterly* tabulation showing that Albert supported the Kennedy program 91 percent of the time in the first session of the Eighty-seventh Congress and Bolling 94 percent—a fact continually cited by liberal supporters of Mr. Albert.[15] Equally significant are the facts, first, that Albert indeed had a great deal of support among members with impeccably liberal records of long standing and, second, that he was regarded at the White House as a genuine friend of the Kennedy program.[16]

If, then, the outcome of the Bolling-Albert contest cannot be explained by the usual ideological arithmetic one uses in analyzing the House, how can one explain what happened? In part, an explanation can be based on the strategies each of the main actors pursued. These strategies were in turn largely dictated by their respective positions and roles in the House during the final years of the Rayburn speakership.

Often great differences in resources between political actors are largely nullified by the fact that resources are generally employed at low levels of intensity and with indifferent skill. In this case, however, resources on both sides were employed with considerable skill and finesse, and hence the outcome comes closer to reflecting a commonsense notion of the logic of the situation than might otherwise have been the case. It makes sense to describe the "cards" that each man held because, in this instance, the man who held the better cards made no more mistakes than his opponent, and, in the end, he won.

It is worth stressing that only part of the explanation can be given by referring to the roles and strategies of the main participants and to the different ways in which their demands were communicated to other House members. Two other significant variables can be sketched in only very crudely. This battle took place in the very core of an institution about whose habits and practices precious little is known, and, second, it engaged the participation of a great many more facets of the human personality than political decisions in the House normally do. The mysteries of how men interact with one another, of what leads people into enmity, jealousy, friendship, all seem to me to have played a very significant part in this contest. Obviously, the extent to which the outside observer can detect and extract meaning from these relationships is extremely limited, and this must inevitably weaken the plausibility and also the generality of the case I am about to construct, using, for the most part, more readily accessible materials.

II

The realization that Speaker Rayburn's health was failing seriously dawned on different members of the House at different times during the summer of 1961. That summer happened to have been an extremely hot and humid one in Washington. The House stayed in session continuously through the summer, one of the longest, bitterest, and most grueling sessions in the memory of veterans on Capitol Hill.[17] Over the course of this period, many members and observers, especially those who were close to the Speaker, could not help but notice the wasting of Mr. Rayburn's solid, imposing figure, the occasional, uncharacteristic wandering of his attention from the business of the House, his increased susceptibility to bouts of fatigue and irritability, the slowing of his gait.

The House is, in the words of one of its members, a "Council of Elders." It honors age and places much power and trust in the hands of its most senior and oldest men. One consequence of this fact is the necessary, calm preoccupation of members—especially those just below the top rungs of power—with the inevitable occurrence of death. To that large fraction of members for whom the House is a career and a vocation, the longevity of members above them in the many hierarchies of the House—not the entirely predictable congressional election returns in their home districts—is the key to the political future. This is not to say that members habitually rub their hands ghoulishly or enjoy the prospect of losing valued friends, but only that the norms and the rules of the House bring due rewards to men who accept the world as it is, who prudently make their plans and bide their time.

On the other hand, informal norms of the House also put constraints on members based on commonly accepted notions of decent behavior, decorum, and good taste. Hence it is impossible for an outsider to say when Mr. Albert and Mr. Bolling began thinking in any concrete way about the next step in their careers within the House. However, it seems safe to make two assumptions: First, that they each had entertained some general thoughts on the question of the majority leadership well in advance of the occurrence of an actual vacancy (on 9 January) or probable vacancy (on 16 November) in the position. Second, both men knew Speaker Rayburn well, and both undoubtedly guessed earlier than most members that his health had permanently disintegrated.

III

On Saturday, 18 November, Sam Rayburn was buried in Bonham, Texas. Mr. Albert reports that he had planned to wait until the following Wednesday to begin his campaign for majority leader. "I was in my office in McAlester on Sunday night," Mr. Albert said, "when Charlie Ward [his assistant] came in and said, 'Bolling has announced for majority leader.' I heard it on the radio that night and saw a copy of the press release from my hometown paper before I announced myself. It was an Associated Press report, and Bill Arbogast [who covers the House for AP] wrote the story."

As a result of this turn of events, Mr. Albert got into the race sooner than he had intended. Mr. Bolling had thrown down a challenge which he could ignore only at his peril. In addition, Mr. Bolling's action offered Mr. Albert an opportunity to run a campaign against him, rather than against any of the more popular or more senior members who had been mentioned for leadership positions.

To each side it appeared that the other had begun to make plans well before Mr. Rayburn's death. Observers partial to Mr. Albert noted that as long before as the previous spring, Mr. Bolling was being referred to in public as a prominent contender for a leadership post.[18] It was easy to infer that, at least in part, these references had been suggested or "inspired" by Mr. Bolling. On the other hand, observers partial to Mr. Bolling thought an alliance between Mr. Albert and the Speaker-to-be, John McCormack, was being announced when Mr. Albert, as his chief deputy, led the tributes on 26 September 1961 in honor of Mr. Mc-Cormack's twenty-one years as majority leader.[19]

It seems plausible to suggest that the signs and portents friends of both men were reading did not reflect conscious efforts by either man to organize a premature campaign for the majority leadership. Rather, each man appealed particularly to slightly different publics: Bolling to the press corps, Albert to various groups within the House itself. These groups may, without encouragement from either man, have initiated activity designed to facilitate their chances of advancement. "After Mr. Rayburn went home to Texas," Mr. Albert reported, "I had fifty or sixty members pull me aside and say to me, 'He's not coming back. Don't sit there and be done out of what you're entitled to.' But I refused to discuss the matter with them." Several members mentioned that they had volunteered their support to Mr. Albert, and some, apparently, had attempted to persuade him to run for Speaker. "I would never do that against John McCormack," Mr. Albert said. "Mr. Rayburn and Mr. Mc-Cormack picked me and made me whip, and to run against Mr. Mc-Cormack would have been the act of an ingrate."

Two groups were especially partial to Mr. Albert: his deputy whip organization and colleagues in the Oklahoma delegation. "We make a fetish of the fact that if you scratch one Okie you've scratched all of 'em," one member told me. As soon as Mr. Albert announced that he would run for majority leader, the members of the delegation did whatever they could to help his candidacy. The deputy whips gave Mr. Albert a party after Mr. Rayburn had gone to Texas and attempted, without success, to induce Mr. Albert to begin work on his candidacy at that time.

Mr. Albert's announcement to the press followed the report of Mr. Bolling's by several hours. As soon as the announcement was made, Mr. Albert sent off a telegram to all members asking for their support and began telephoning each of them individually. "I bet you he was on the phone four days running," one member said.

Mr. Albert's intensive telephone campaign began with the West Coast members. "James Roosevelt [congressman from Los Angeles] was the first man I called outside my own delegation," he said. By the end of the first day of telephoning, Mr. Albert thought he had all but five westerners committed to him. "If I wasn't sure of a senior man in a delegation,"

Mr. Albert said, "I started with the most junior men and asked them directly to support me. Then I'd work my way up the line so that when the senior man said, 'I'll have to check with my delegation,' I would have something to report to him. Of course on a thing like this, you call your friends first, but I had no set, written-out plan. I don't work that way."

The reasons members gave for supporting Mr. Albert are quite illuminating. They reflect two dominant themes, both of which illustrate the "inside" quality of his influence. On the one hand, Mr. Albert was his party's whip. Although there is no tradition which dictates that the whip shall be advanced to the majority leadership (as there is in promoting the majority leader to Speaker) many members felt that Mr. Albert nonetheless was "entitled" to the job by virtue of his six years' service in the leadership hierarchy of the House. Some of them said:

> [*A liberal leader*]. I made a commitment to Carl based on his years of service as whip and the fact that he was in line for this job from the standpoint of his long service as whip.

> [*A southwesterner*]. Because I feel that he was entitled to it by reason of his effective part in the leadership of the House along with the Speaker and Mr. McCormack, I promised him my support.

> [*The elderly dean of a large delegation*]. I am a firm believer in the rule that has governed the House for over one hundred years, and that is that of seniority. If Congressman McCormack is to be promoted to the Speakership of the House on the premise of his seniority and being in line position, then obviously the majority leader and whip should pursue the same course.[20] I have had the honor of being a member of this great body for [many years] . . . and while I would be reluctant to say that the seniority process does not have some imperfections, nevertheless if any other procedure were to be applied, I am inclined to believe that rather a chaotic situation would immediately be evident.

A second theme illustrates Mr. Albert's personal popularity in the House. Many members could cite warm personal ties they had developed with Mr. Albert. The late John Riley of South Carolina said:

> Carl Albert married a girl from Columbia, you know, and so he is practically a constituent of mine.

> *A northern liberal*. I'm in something of a special situation with Carl, since we're the only two members of the House who [belong to an exclusive, honorary organization].

A congressman from a border state. In all good conscience, I had to agree to support Carl because of his great help and encouragement to me [on a pet bill].

A southwesterner. As one of his deputy whips, I feel committed to Carl Albert.

A southerner. I committed myself to Carl Albert, who is my neighbor in the House Office Building.

Another southerner. My association with Carl Albert has been extremely intimate.

Three men who served with Mr. Albert on committees said:

Carl and I have sat side by side on [our] committee for fifteen years.

Carl has been very kind to me in the committee work and has done several things for me which have been very important for my people.

I sit right next to Carl Albert. . . . We have been close personal friends due to our connection on the committee.

Another member said:

Ordinarily I'm slow to make commitments, but due to a friendship with Carl which began when we were in the . . . army together, I told him quite a while back that should he seek the position of Democratic leader, I would support him.

And some members, not unexpectedly, combined the themes. For example:

He is not only my neighbor but a member of my committee, and with it all a fine, able, conscientious man who has been doing the dirty work for the leadership for a long time.

It was characteristic of Mr. Albert's "inside" strategy of influence that he used the telephone energetically and extensively himself to make personal contacts with members as quickly as possible. As whip, he was the custodian of a complete set of home, office, and district telephone numbers for each member.[21] One member said:

Albert got on the phone and tracked me down in the frozen wastes of northern Rockystate the first day after the speaker was buried. You wouldn't think politicians would fall for that, but many of them did. They were impressed by the fact that he'd called them first. As a result he was able to line up a lot of the members, including many northern bleeding-heart liberals, in the first few days.

The principal argument which Mr. Albert used in asking the support of almost all the members I spoke with was the fact that he had already received a large number of commitments. This is instructive, because it evokes the almost obsessive preoccupation of congressmen with "getting along" and not sticking their necks out unnecessarily. "This House gives out no medals for individual bravery," said one congressman, "except posthumously."

Mr. Albert had an important further asset—the apparent backing of John McCormack. "I have heard McCormack say again and again that we have got to have a team player," one congressman said. "I guess he means by that a member of his team, and I suppose he favors Carl Albert." I asked a newspaperman who was following the situation closely to tell me who the most important congressman on Mr. Albert's side was, and he replied, "John McCormack." However, I could find no evidence that Mr. McCormack gave Mr. Albert any public endorsement.

Describing his campaign, Mr. Albert said:

> I didn't want to hurt Mr. Bolling's feelings. I never once threw knives or wrote mean things, although plenty of knives got thrown at me. I never once got on television. The sum total of my national publicity was a release when I got into the race and a release when I got up to Washington saying I thought I had enough votes to win. I refused to go on television although I was invited to go on most of the news and panel shows. I never mentioned Bolling's name at all. I never mentioned issues or anything.

IV

Mr. Bolling's campaign, in contrast, followed an "outside" strategy of influence. As in the Rules committee fight at the opening of the Eighty-seventh Congress and on numerous other occasions where he had planned legislative strategy and tactics, he held aloof from direct contact with most members. "I seldom try to persuade people directly," he said. "Our districts persuade us—if we are going to be persuaded at all."

Bolling had an uphill battle on his hands. He was severely handicapped at the start by his unwillingness to do anything in his own behalf until well after the Speaker had died. "It's a funny thing that Dick was so dilatory," a friend said. Although he leaked an announcement of his candidacy for the majority leadership to the press on 19 November, the day after the Speaker's funeral, it was not until 28 November that he sent a strikingly diffident letter to each of the Democrats in the House. This letter said:

> Just a note to confirm that I am running for Democratic floor leader and am seeking the support of my Democratic colleagues for that position. Reports during the past week have been encouraging and I am in this contest all the way.
>
> I am running on my legislative record and experience and hope that you will give my candidacy your consideration on that basis.

Several of his supporters expressed surprise at the mildness of this approach. The letter asked for "consideration," not support, and was not followed up by an energetic telephone campaign. Furthermore, Bolling had waited twelve precious days after the Speaker's death before making his move. Why?

Answers to a question of motive such as this one—even the answers given by Mr. Bolling himself—are bound to verge on speculation. My guess is that Mr. Bolling's hesitancy had something to do with the relationship he had had with Speaker Rayburn. According to the reports of numerous observers who had no axes to grind, Mr. Bolling and the Speaker had built a bond of affection between them that went well beyond the usual political alliance.[22] Mr. Sam, who had no immediate family, was well known for his habit of adopting political protégés with whom he could develop a relationship of warmth and trust similar to that found in the family situation. This was, apparently, Mr. Rayburn's way of overcoming the loneliness that otherwise might well have overtaken any elderly bachelor.

The need to overcome loneliness was strongly ingrained in Mr. Rayburn from childhood. Mr. Rayburn is quoted as saying:

> Many a time when I was a child and lived way out in the country, I'd sit on the fence and wish to God that somebody would ride by on a horse or drive by in a buggy—just anything to relieve my loneliness. Loneliness consumes people. It kills 'em eventually. God help the lonely.[23]

Mr. Rayburn's advice to Presidents Truman, Eisenhower, and Kennedy reflects the same theme. As he reported afterward on a conversation with Mr. Truman just after the latter had become president:

> "You've got many hazards," I said. "One of your great hazards is in this White House," I said. "I've been watching things around here a long time, and I've seen people in the White House try to build a fence around the White House and keep the various people away from the president that he should see."[24]

His biographer and research assistant, D. B. Hardeman, says, "Mr. Sam was . . . annoyed by inactivity. When he could think of nothing else to do at home in Bonham he would get out all his shoes and polish them. He dreaded holidays and Sundays because visitors were few."[25]

Mr. Rayburn found it particularly congenial to work with younger men. D. B. Hardeman says, "Lyndon Johnson once confessed, 'The Speaker and I have always been very close but if we are not as close as we were once, it is because I'm almost fifty. If you notice, he never has older men around him.' "[26]

"I always liked the House the best," Mr. Rayburn said. "There're more people there, usually they're younger people, and as I've advanced in years, I've stepped back in my associations, boys, young people ten, twenty years younger than I. Their bodies are not only resilient but their minds are too. They can learn faster than the fellow advanced in years."[27]

One of the things which no doubt drew Mr. Rayburn to Mr. Bolling was the exceptional resiliency and quickness of the latter's mind. On this quality, friends and political enemies of Mr. Bolling agreed. He is an extremely "quick study," and had several other things in common with the Speaker:

"Bolling loves the House," a judicious, slow-spoken southern congressman who knows him rather well told me. "He loves it and has studied it. He has read everything that has been written about the House and has studied its power structure. He has a brilliant mind."

Although nearly thirty-five years separated them, both Mr. Rayburn and Mr. Bolling were strongly committed emotionally to many liberal programs. Bolling refers to himself quite frankly as a "gut liberal"; *Time* magazine has aptly characterized Rayburn as a "liberal of the heart."[28] In addition, both men shared a high sense of rectitude in their work, treating the majority of their colleagues with reserve and judging them rather severely. This social distance which both men maintained was no doubt related in some complex way to the intensity of their feelings about political issues. It is instructive in this connection to note the tendency of both men to become laconic in public when dealing with problems with which they had great personal involvement. Compare Bolling's prepared statement of withdrawal from the majority leadership race in 1962 with Rayburn's statement of withdrawal in 1934 from an unsuccessful race for the Speakership.[29]

In 1934 Rayburn said, "I am no longer a candidate for Speaker. There are no alibis. Under the circumstances, I cannot be elected."[30]

In 1962 Bolling said, "I am withdrawing from the race for leadership of the House. Developments of the last few days have convinced me that I don't have a chance to win."[31]

Bolling privately expressed an unwillingness amounting to an inca-
pacity either to "do anything" until after a "decent" time had elapsed
after the Speaker's death,[32] or to canvas for votes in his own behalf. The
major portion of this burden within the House was carried by Representative Frank Thompson of New Jersey and a group of four or five
others. The brunt of Bolling's campaign was, however, carried on from
outside the House.[33] Initially, he had to decide whether to run for Speaker
or majority leader—which no doubt also contributed to the quality of
hesitancy in his campaign.

Factors pointing to the Speakership included the relative unpopularity
of Mr. McCormack (1) with members, and (2) at the White House; but
against this had to be weighed (1) Mr. McCormack's generally blameless
voting record (from the standpoint of a proadministration Democrat),
(2) his long service in the second position, (3) the weight of a tradition
which strongly favored the elevation of a majority leader, (4) Mr. Bolling's
own relatively junior position, (5) the fact that Mr. McCormack, if he
lost the Speakership, would remain as a majority leader not especially
favorably disposed toward the program of an administration that had
just done him in politically, and, (6) the fact that opposing Mr. Mc-
Cormack would unavoidably exacerbate the religious cleavage in the
House and the country which the fight over school aid in the last session
had revealed.[34]

And so, Mr. Bolling decided to run for majority leader against the
extremely popular Mr. Albert. In a straight popularity contest, Mr. Bolling
knew he was "born dead." His role in the House had been quite unlike
Mr. Albert's; indeed, several congressmen contrasted them starkly.

A close friend described Mr. Albert's approach to the job of whip:

> The whip is more the eyes and ears of the leadership than anything. On
> controversial matters, they like to know what the chances of success are.
> . . . So the deputy whips count noses, and the whip's job is to evaluate
> the count—especially to assess the doubtfuls. . . . Albert developed quite
> a genius for knowing what people would do. . . .
>
> Another service he performed endears him to people. Carl's the kind
> of a guy everybody could find. He would talk to the leadership for [rank-
> and-file congressmen].
>
> A lot of these eastern guys have a Tuesday through Thursday club. The
> whip takes the duty on of telling them if the signals change so they can
> get back here if they're needed.
>
> He's done so many things for people. They trust him. They think of
> him, "Here's a man I can talk to when I need help." When the members
> go about picking a leader, they want personal services, not intellectuals.[35]

I dare you to find a member of Congress who said Bolling had lifted a finger for him.

A supporter of Mr. Bolling's (for whom Bolling had, according to this member's testimony, lifted many a finger) saw the roles of the two principals in much the same light, although his evaluation of their roles was quite different:

> Albert's approach to legislative matters is, well, everybody ought to vote his own district. . . . He brings his friends and his enemies in [to vote] both. . . . Why the hell get [a certain southern congressman] out [to vote]? He doesn't vote with us on anything. And he's a deputy whip! It's ridiculous. . . . The function of the whip [under Mr. Albert] is room service to members.
>   Albert was the whip, but Bolling was doing the whipping. . . . When the heat was being put on in the Rules Committee and all the other fights, it was Bolling putting it on, and he wasn't making any friends doing it.[36]

Mr. Bolling was, as a friend of his described it, a "hatchet man" for Speaker Rayburn. This entailed a variety of activities on the Rules Committee, including monitoring the attendance of friends and foes, arranging for the disposition of bills, and keeping track of the intentions of the various (and numerous) factions in the House with respect to important legislation in behalf of the Speaker. Occasionally, Mr. Bolling's job included putting the finger on members who were open to (or vulnerable to) persuasion, and he often had a crucial part in the process of persuading them—not always a pleasant task.[37]

Although Mr. Bolling is entirely in sympathy with policies espoused by liberals in the House, his position close to the Speaker precluded his joining in any formal way in the activities of the Democratic Study Group, the House liberal organization. As a friend of his put it, "Dick was aloof from the uprisings of the peasants."

"Bolling's got a sort of chip on his shoulder," another member said.

"The thing you have to realize about Bolling," said an Albert backer, "is that he never bothers to speak to anyone else. I don't think Bolling understands politics."

Mr. Bolling's aloofness was, as I have suggested, probably something more than simply a reflection of his peculiar institutional position. A second friend of Bolling's said, "Despite a good deal of charm, Bolling just does not have a personality that inspires loyalty and friendship among men.[38] He's not a backslapping, how-the-hell-are-you type of guy. Bolling is personally quite pleasant, but reticent."

The late Clem Miller of California said, "Congress is a World War I rather than a World War II operation. You have to move huge bodies of men a few feet at a time. . . . Dick's spent the last few years divorcing himself from a base of fire. His job was right-hand man to the Speaker. He came to Democratic Study Group meetings but always identified himself as an observer, not as a participant. He came in a sense to lecture us like small children rather than lead us in our councils. There was a good deal of hostility toward him in the study group as a result of that. The study group was set up as a foil for the leadership. You can't have your foot in both camps, and so Dick alienated the base of support that he needed in the House."

Another member, often allied with Mr. Bolling, characterized him as "totally unfriendly."

Mr. Bolling's personal situation within the House was further complicated by a common enough phenomenon. As a relative newcomer, as an extremely able member performing difficult tasks well, and as an intimate of the Speaker, Mr. Bolling was, in the opinion of several observers, the victim of a certain amount of jealous resentment.

"Jealousy is a big factor," one congressman said. "Liberals have several characteristics that tend to make them ineffective, and vanity is one of them. They tend to be prima donnas."[39] Another said, "Dick is not a popular man in the House, no doubt a surprise to newsmen. For one thing, he's resented because of his ability."

Liberals were clearly not the only group of congressmen susceptible to jealous feelings toward Mr. Bolling. His relative youth was offensive to some of his seniors. Mr. Bolling had risen very fast in the House and had been given many advantages by his friend, the Speaker. The record he had made thus far also suggested that, if elected, he would take many more initiatives than Mr. Albert and would more decisively challenge the powers of committee and subcommittee chairmen to control the flow and content of legislation—in behalf of programs for which many of these leaders had no particular liking.

Even to the superficial observer, Mr. Albert and Mr. Bolling are quite contrasting figures. Mr. Albert was fifty-three years old, exactly on the House median; Mr. Bolling was only forty-five. Albert is physically probably the shortest man in the House and looks nothing like the collegiate wrestler he once was. He has a softly lined, friendly, gentle face which, says a colleague, "always looks faintly worried." Bolling is a tall, husky, quite handsome and imposing-looking man who gives the appearance of great self-confidence and looks very much like the collegiate football player he was. Mr. Albert in conversation is homespun, soft-spoken, emotionally unengaged, and low pressure. A colleague says, "You could vote impeachment of the president, and it wouldn't bother Carl." Mr. Bolling in conversation is articulate, expansive, sophisticated, intense; in short, one would surmise, a rather more threatening figure to someone of average inclinations than Mr. Albert.

Mr. Bolling has far greater acceptance in the higher echelons of the "downtown" bureaucracies and surely in the press corps than almost any other congressman, including Mr. Albert. Mr. Bolling is far more likely to spend his leisure hours among pundits, diplomats, and subcabinet officials than with congressmen, a pattern which Mr. Albert reverses. Mr. Albert prides himself, in fact, in spending a greater proportion of his time on the floor of the House than any other member, where he is continually accessible to his colleagues.[40]

To a great extent, Mr. Bolling understood that a variety of institutional and personal "inside" factors were working against him, and so he launched an "outside" campaign.

V

Bolling's task, as he saw it, was divided into several phases of activity. First, he had to stall the Albert bandwagon. Then he had to receive enough commitments to win himself. His primary targets were the big state delegations of New York, California, Illinois, and Pennsylvania. Secondary targets included getting a firm grip on his home-state delegation and going after younger, liberal congressmen and congressmen who had substantial labor and civil-rights-minded constituencies.

His strategy for accomplishing these ends had two major features. First, he intended to draw as sharp a contrast as he could between himself and Mr. Albert on issues and sell the contrast as hard as he could through the mass media. Second, he set about "pulling strings" on members, a process which he had practiced before in legislative battles.[41] This entailed identifying the men and interest groups favorable to his candidacy who for various reasons could reach and persuade members of Congress. Naturally, the foremost among these would have been the president, but at no time was presidential aid offered, and none was requested by Mr. Bolling.

The position of the White House in this battle was a complex one. While the mass media, on the whole, bought Mr. Bolling's contention that substantial differences in public policy separated him and Mr. Albert, the White House never did. It regarded both men as good friends of the Kennedy program, each having personal and political strengths and weaknesses. To intervene in behalf of one friend would have meant sacrificing another. For the White House to intervene and lose would have been disastrous for its prestige and legislative program. To intervene and win would have been more satisfactory but still would have involved (aside from the making of enemies) great exertion, the distribution of indulgences, and the "cashing in" on favors owed, all of which could otherwise be employed to improve the chances for passage of controversial reciprocal trade, medical aid, tax reform, and education bills. Several members of the president's official family were close to Mr. Bolling and were almost certainly partial to him, but none participated in the fight.

Mr. Bolling and his backers in the House concurred in the White House policy of nonintervention and in the reasoning behind it. The major inside advantage of their side, as they saw it, was a professional ability to predict outcomes accurately and to recommend appropriate strategies. They understood fully that the risks to the White House were great, the probabilities of success dubious. If they could come close to winning on their own, within perhaps five or ten votes, then their recommendation might change, since the White House could then probably put them over the top. But it is not at all certain that even then the White House would have been ready to move.

If the administration was inactive, other keenly interested bystanders were not. The AFL-CIO backed Mr. Bolling strongly and performed several notable services in behalf of his candidacy. Labor lobbyists made a complete canvass of possible supporters in the House and, in several cases, made representations in Mr. Bolling's behalf with members. The NAACP was also active. Roy Wilkins, national chairman, telegraphed 153 selected branches of his organization, "Bolling right on twenty-six civil rights votes, Albert wrong. Wire, write or call your Congressman. This could affect civil-rights legislation for years to come." The Democratic Reform Clubs of New York City were also interested in Bolling's candidacy, as were some local and national political leaders around the country and at least one farm organization.

An example of indirect influence in Mr. Bolling's behalf was described by an Albert supporter, "I heard that President Truman, a neighbor of Bolling's and a loyal Missourian, called Mayor Wagner of New York to try and get the New York delegation to support Bolling."

Mr. Bolling was especially successful in enlisting the aid of the mass media. Since the civil rights battle of 1957, when he anonymously kept newsmen briefed on the confusing tactical situation within the House, Mr. Bolling has been extremely popular with the Washington press corps.[42] He is asked to appear on broadcasts and telecasts much more often than the average member. He counts many Washington correspondents, including several famous ones, as close personal friends.

Hence, it is not altogether surprising that he was able to gain the endorsement of the *New York Times* as early as 11 December. On Sunday,

24 December, the *Times* reiterated its stand, saying, "The conservative coalition of southern Democrats and northern Republicans would find it much more difficult to exercise its suffocating veto over forward-looking legislation with the imaginative and hard driving Mr. Bolling as majority floor chief."[43]

Five days previously, on 19 December, James Wechsler, editor of the *New York Post,* gave a strong endorsement to Mr. Bolling, in which he printed a long verbatim extract of a letter endorsing Carl Albert which Bolling had received from Judge Howard W. Smith, leader of conservative southerners in the House.[44] Wechsler commented, "This is not to say Albert has faithfully followed Smith's gospel. He is a moderate, pleasant man whose voting record might be far more impressive if he came from a state more congenial to the advance of civil rights and less dominated by the natural gas interests. Despite their differences on a variety of matters, Smith is plainly confident that he can handle Albert; he is equally convinced that Bolling spells trouble."[45]

On 29 December, Marquis Childs[46] and Edward P. Morgan both urged the selection of Mr. Bolling, referring once again to the Smith letter and to issues separating the two candidates. Mr. Morgan was especially vigorous in his commentary:

> Where Bolling has been consistently for them, Albert has been basically against civil rights legislation, federal aid to education, full foreign aid and regulation of the oil and gas industry. It is reliably reported that one Texas congressman told a southern colleague that "with Albert in there, oil will be safe for twenty years."[47]

What of the outcomes of these activities? The relations between outside "pressures" and congressmen have been variously described in popular and academic literature. There is an old tradition which regards these relations as essentially nefarious.[48] Descriptively, the congressman is sometimes thought to be a relatively passive creature who is pulled and hauled about according to the play of pressures upon him and whose final decision is determined by the relative strength of outside forces.[49] More recently, political scientists have become preoccupied with the qualities of reciprocity in the relations of interest groups and politicians. This literature calls attention to mutually beneficial aspects of the relationship and lays stress on the ways in which politicians may act to govern the outside pressures placed on them.[50]

My information on the impact of Bolling's outside campaign is necessarily incomplete. It is apparent at a minimum that a sufficient number of congressmen were never reached by this campaign. One congressman said:

Bolling's best hope was forces outside the House—labor and civil rights groups. But I received not one communication in his behalf from anybody. There was nobody campaigning for him. Nobody knew if he was serious or not. Where was the heat?

Another congressman, from a heavily populated area, said:

> Our delegation was never put on the spot. Bolling never tried to wage a campaign in our delegation. Apparently he tried to get labor leaders to pressure Cautious [the state party leader] to put pressure on our congressmen. This is OK, but you really have to put the pressure on because if you know Cautious, he won't ever move unless he's really in a box.

In other cases, congressmen were able to quite easily to *resist* pressure. "The word got around," one liberal congressman said, "that this wasn't like the Rules Committee fight, where there was a legitimate issue. Rather, it was all in the family, and any outside interference, even from the White House, would be resented."

Harlem's Representative Adam Clayton Powell, announcing his support of Albert, charged that some organized labor representatives were putting pressure on some Democratic members of his committee. He added, "I can't understand why labor union leaders would do this. Frankly, this is Democratic party business, not labor business."[51]

On the other hand, Bolling's campaign from the outside made several converts. Representative Leonard Farbstein of New York City, for example, announced that he would vote for Mr. Bolling on the basis of Mr. Wechsler's column.[52]

Another congressman, a conservative veteran, wrote Bolling and detailed the substantial political disagreements between them, concluding, "But Famous Farmer tells me he is supporting you, and if he is supporting you, I am supporting you."

A leader of another interest group, in another part of the country, wrote, "I have just been informed by Congressman Dean Delegation's home secretary that Dean will be supporting you for majority leader. If there are any particular targets in [this state], I'm still available to apply whatever other pressures I can."

In aggregate, however, the impact of this campaign was not sufficient to accomplish Mr. Bolling's major goal. Edward Morgan commented with some asperity on the failure of Mr. Bolling to consolidate his support on an ideological basis, and at the same time, he renewed the plea that the battle be defined in ideological terms:

> If they voted . . . in support of their constituencies' needs for protection on gas prices, housing, civil rights, and the like, the big city and industrial

area representatives would have to come down almost unanimously for Bolling over Albert on their voting records alone and the man from Missouri would have it cinched. But he doesn't have it cinched. . . . At least one Massachusetts congressman has already committed himself to Albert in writing. . . . Adam Clayton Powell is looking south. . . . So are a couple of New Jersey representatives. . . . Most surprisingly, perhaps, two leading California congressmen, Holifield and Roosevelt, have not dashed to Bolling's aid.[53]

Over the long New Year's weekend, Bolling, Thompson, and Andrew Biemiller of the AFL-CIO met and assessed Bolling's "hard" strength at between sixty-five and seventy votes. Perhaps fifty more would have joined them if Bolling were going to win, but otherwise, they faded. A Bolling lieutenant said, "Everybody wanted to know, 'What's his chances?' The typical response was, 'I'll lie low. I'm with you if you've got a chance; otherwise, nix.'"

By the most realistic calculations, however, Mr. Bolling fell short of the 130 or more votes that he needed. He decided to withdraw his candidacy rather than embarrass his supporters in their state delegations and possibly jeopardize their future effectiveness in Congress.

VI

It is possible to identify at least four reasons why Mr. Bolling's attempt to win from the outside failed. The first two have already been mentioned: Mr. Albert's extreme popularity and Bolling's relative isolation provided little incentive for individual members to seek outside excuses of their own accord to do what they could more conveniently do for inside reasons. Second, the hands-off policy of the White House deprived Mr. Bolling's campaign of what would have been a major outside weapon had the president chosen to come in on Mr. Bolling's side.

The third major obstacle to the success of the outside campaign was the fact that, through no fault of Mr. Bolling's, a few of his supporters unwittingly blunted one of his principal weapons, the ideological contrast between himself and Mr. Albert. Just before the opening of the second session of the Eighty-seventh Congress, and at the same time the struggle over the majority leadership was going on, a group of liberal congressmen proposed that a policy committee be created in the Democratic party to be elected by the members from each of the eighteen whip zones. This committee was to advise and counsel with the leadership, and it was contemplated that it would be "more representative" (and presumably more liberal) than the leadership, unaided, would be.

Congressmen favoring this proposal circulated it among their Democratic colleagues in an attempt to get the fifty signatures necessary to place it on the agenda of the caucus which was to elect a new Speaker. Several liberals favoring Mr. Albert promptly signed, thus furnishing themselves with an excellent alibi, if they were challenged on ideological grounds by constituents and interest groups. They could claim that the fight over the majority leadership was not really significant since Bolling and Albert were, in their voting records, so close. But on the basic issue, on the institutional structure of leadership in the House, they were, as always, for liberalization.

This proposal went through several stages. At one point, it was seriously proposed that Mr. Bolling accept the chairmanship of this committee as the price for withdrawing his candidacy for the majority leadership. This proposal implied that the new Speaker had accepted the policy committee in principle.[54] Mr. Bolling was himself dubious about the chances that such a committee could perform the tasks its supporters envisaged for it. Counterproposals and negotiations buzzed back and forth about the possibility of putting "teeth" into the committee and about prior agreements as to its membership. At another level, Mr. Bolling and Mr. Thompson had to avoid being mousetrapped by the petition to put the policy committee on the agenda. To have signed the petition might have looked to Albert-McCormack forces like a proposal of terms and an acknowledgement of defeat. The fact that supporters of the Bolling candidacy were leading the fight for the policy committee was compromising enough as it was.

In the end, the whole idea came to nothing.[55] The proposal never received enough signatures to gain a place on the agenda, and at John McCormack's first press conference upon his nomination for the speakership, he said, "A policy committee is out."[56] But the policy committee plan served one significant purpose. It softened and blurred Bolling's attempt to define the issue between himself and Mr. Albert in such a way as to embarrass liberals who were not supporting him.

The fourth reason for the failure of the outside campaign is probably the most important. It has to do with the conditions under which the actual choice was going to be made. Normally, a congressman has considerable leeway in the casting of his vote because the issues are complex and technical, because the ways in which they are framed sometimes inspire no sharp cleavages of opinion, because interest groups are often disinterested and inattentive. But when an issue heats up and reaches the final stages of the legislative process, leeway dissipates. Interest groups become active. The mail begins to pour in.[57] Newsmen appear on the scene. Congressmen stick close to the floor, listen to debate, mill around, stand ready to answer quorum calls or to vote on amendments.

There are four procedures for voting in the House: voices, standing, tellers, and roll call, in the order in which they expose members to public view. In the Committee of the Whole House, only the first three types of votes are taken. A diligent reporter or lobbyist can, however, even without benefit of a roll call, usually find out how a given member votes. The procedure is not foolproof, but, from the gallery, an outsider can always keep his eye fixed on one or a few congressmen whose votes are of interest to him. Corroboration, if any is needed, can be obtained by asking around among other congressmen.

The caucus at which voting for majority leader was to have taken place provided no such opportunities for outside surveillance. No spectators were admitted. Congressmen were even protected from the scrutiny of their colleagues; Representative Francis Walter, chairman of the caucus, sent word that the balloting for majority leader, when the time came, would be secret. The rules of the caucus say nothing about a secret ballot; rather, general parliamentary law governs the caucus meetings, and there is a special provision that "the yeas and nays on any question shall, at the desire of one-fifth of those present, be entered on the journal"—all of which did not alter the fact that the balloting would be secret.

In spite of the interest which Mr. Bolling had stirred up among outside groups, these groups were operating under an insuperable handicap. The voting procedure maximized the chances that a congressman cross-pressured between the demands of a "local agency" and his own personal feelings would vote his private preferences with impunity.

VII

What does this case suggest about the general relations between inside and outside influences in the decision-making processes of the House?[58] Several things. First, it shows the extent to which inside and outside strategies tend to encourage different modes of communication among members and to evoke different definitions of the decision-making situation. The inside strategy is likely to define situations as "family matters," and to feature face-to-face interaction among members. The outside strategy is likely to evoke a more ideological, issue-oriented definition of the situation. Interaction among members is more likely to take place through third persons, lobbyists, and the press. Second, this case suggests conditions tending to promote the success of each strategy of influence. Inside strategies are favored when: (1) the matter to be decided can be rationalized as in some sense procedural rather than substantive; (2) there are great differences in the inside strengths of the two sides, but their outside strengths approach equality; and (3) members are protected from surveillance by outsiders. Outside strategies are favored, presumably, when these conditions are reversed.

Additional conditions bearing on the effectiveness of inside and outside strategies may be imagined. Presumably, the autonomy of a representative from constituent pressures diminishes as his constituency approaches unanimity in its preferences *or* as the intensity of preference for a given alternative by any substantial portion of his constituency increases. We know that few decisions before Congress are likely to unite constituencies in this way or to inflame their passions to such a great extent. In addition, Congress takes routine steps to insulate its decision-making from certain kinds of outside influences.

One such device is the consideration of business in the Committee of the Whole, where substantial revisions of legislation can be made on the floor without binding congressmen to a record vote. The committees — whose composition and behavior sometimes reflect outside interests[59] and sometimes inside distributions of influence[60] — mark up bills and vote on them in executive sessions only. A third device favoring inside distributions of influence in the House is the Rules Committee. One of the prerequisites for appointment to service on this committee is ability to "take the heat" and resist constituency pressures to report out bills which the House leadership wants killed.[61]

The enumeration of these devices hints at some of the problems facing two significant groups of outsiders: presidents of the United States and political scientists. The president has a never-ending battle of converting decisions in the House choices from inside ones to outside ones. Most of his attempts to influence decisions are direct, but his efforts to dramatize issues before relevant publics may also be interpreted as attempts to activate interest groups and unify constituencies so as to make the employment of inside strategies of influence in the House difficult.

For political scientists, the lesson is clear. In order to understand the context within which decisions in the House are being made sufficiently well so that we can identify the goals in terms of which outcomes may be seen as "rational," it will be necessary to study the House at close range. On the whole, political scientists have taken a somewhat Olympian view of congressional behavior. We have tended to organize our conceptions of rationality and legitimacy around presidential goals and presidential party platforms.[62] This has operated to obscure the constraints on the behavior of those in the House who share the policy preferences these political theories imply. It has also, I think, bred a kind of impatience with the study of strategies and tactics of House decision-making, which study, I believe, is a necessary step in understanding why the House operates as it does.

NOTES

1. The phrase "traditional political theory" refers in this context to the history of political thinking rather than to any specific political doctrines. See, for example, David Easton, *The Political System* (New York: Knopf, 1953); Harry V. Jaffa, "The Case against Political Theory," *Journal of Politics* 22 (May 1960): 259–75; Robert A. Dahl, "The Science of Politics, New and Old," *World Politics* 7 (Apr. 1955):479–89; Dahl, "Political Theory, Truth and Consequences," *World Politics* 11 (Oct. 1958):89–102; Norman Jacobson, "The Unity of Political Theory," in R. Young, ed., *Approaches to the Study of Politics* (Evanston, Ill.: Northwestern University Press, 1958), 115–24.

2. Heinz Eulau, John C. Wahlke, Leroy C. Ferguson, and William Buchanan, "The Role of the Representative: Some Empirical Observations on the Theory of Edmund Burke," *American Political Science Review* 53 (Sept. 1959):742–56.

3. "Speech to the Electors of Bristol," 3 Nov. 1774, *Works* (London: Oxford University Press, 1906), 2:164–66.

4. "Speech at Bristol," 6 Sept. 1780, ibid., 3:2, 3, 4.

5. Ibid., and F. W. Raffety, "Preface" in *Works,* 2:xiv–xv.

6. One approach to some of these questions was made by Julius Turner, who used the analysis of roll calls as his major source of data in *Party and Constituency: Pressures on Congress* (Baltimore: Johns Hopkins University Press, 1951). See also David B. Truman, *The Congressional Party* (New York: Wiley, 1959).

7. Lewis Anthony Dexter, "Congressmen and the People They Listen To" (Cambridge: Center for International Studies, MIT, 1956, Mimeographed), chap. 2, 14; chap. 8, 7.

8. Ibid., chap. 5, 4–5.

9. Richard L. Lyons, "Pressure Rises as House Moves to Vote on Rules," *Washington Post,* 31 Jan. 1961.

10. *Time,* 1 Sept. 1961, 14. The congressman is not identified here, as he was in the *Time* article, first because he denies the conversation took place (29 Aug. 1961, *Congressional Record,* 87th Cong., 1st sess., 16318) and second, because the *Time* reporter's source for the quote told me that he had deliberately left ambiguous the identity of the congressman, and, while the event really happened, the *Time* reporter was misled about whom it happened to.

11. Dexter, "Congressmen," chap. 8, 4.

12. Ibid., 4–5.

13. The best news coverage by far of this press conference that I saw occurred in the *Baltimore Sun,* 4 Jan. 1962: Rodney Crowther, "House Race Dropped by Bolling."

14. Pursuit of this line of thinking at a McCormack-Albert press conference, 9 January, visibly irked Mr. McCormack. "A reporter . . . caught [Mr. McCormack] at the door of the Speaker's lobby and asked him if he had asked for complete support of President Kennedy's program. The new Speaker drew back indignantly. 'I'm not trying to put words in your mouth,' said the reporter. 'Yes you are,' said Mr. McCormack, 'I've been voting for progressive legislation for thirty years. I'm not a one-

year man. Why don't you wake up?'" Mary McGrory, "McCormack Speaks as His Own Master," *Washington Star,* 10 Jan. 1962.

15. *Congressional Quarterly* 19 (24 Nov. 1961):1893–94. This tabulation also shows that throughout their careers in Congress, the voting records of these men were quite close by several criteria.

16. These statements, and many others throughout this paper, are based on interviews and observations gathered during the summer of 1961 and from December 1961 to February 1962 in Washington. During these months I spoke on matters connected with the subject of this paper, to over one hundred congressmen, congressional aides, newspapermen, and others, and during the latter period, I conducted interviews with twenty-six Democratic congressmen from all sections of the country on the leadership selection process then going on. Quotations are from notes taken during these interviews and are occasionally slightly altered so as to preserve the anonymity of the respondent. My work in the summer of 1961 was supported by a grant-in-aid from the Social Science Research Council, whose assistance is gratefully acknowledged.

17. The session lasted 277 days, the longest in ten years. Late one especially debilitating August afternoon, an elderly southern congressman shuffled over to where I was standing just outside the Speaker's lobby and confided that he was going to sponsor a bill that would abolish the final month of each session of Congress.

18. For example, Mr. Bolling was introduced to a large public meeting at the Midwest Conference of Political Scientists on 11 May 1961 as "the next Speaker of the House of Representatives."

19. Mr. Albert's tribute on this occasion was much more elaborate than that tendered by any other member—save by Mr. McCormack's Massachusetts colleagues. See 26 Sept. 1961, *Congressional Record,* 87th Cong., 1st sess., 20084–96.

20. Mr. Albert entered the House in 1947, Mr. Bolling in 1949, making them thirtieth (tied with nine others) and thirty-ninth (tied with nineteen others) in seniority respectively in the Democratic party in the House—not a very great difference. Mr. McCormack, on the other hand, was the beneficiary of a long tradition of advancement from majority leader to Speaker and, in addition, after the death of Speaker Rayburn, was third in seniority. He had never served as whip, incidentally, before his election as majority leader, nor had Speaker Rayburn. Both Mr. McCormack and Mr. Rayburn had held office for so many years it is highly probable that most members were unaware of the differences in the customs pertaining to the advancement of the majority leader and the whip.

21. Mr. Albert's administrative assistant said that this list happened to be in the Washington office while the telephoning was being done from McAlester, Oklahoma, where only the House telephone directory issued to all members was readily available.

22. Friends of Mr. Albert note that Mr. Albert was Speaker Rayburn's personal choice for whip in 1954 and further suggest that Mr. Albert was also a close personal friend of Mr. Rayburn's. One influential congressman said, "Mr. Sam thought the world of Carl Albert." But this same congressman indicated that he thought Mr. Bolling's relationship with the Speaker was unique. Without excluding the strong probability that Mr. Rayburn had a high personal regard for Mr. Albert (and, one supposes, several other members as well), the testimony of several knowledgeable and apparently unbiased observers was quite unanimous in indicating that for several years preceding his death Mr. Rayburn was particularly close to Mr. Bolling.

23. David Cohn, "Mr. Speaker: An Atlantic Portrait," *Atlantic Monthly* (Oct. 1942):

73–78. The quoted portion appears on p. 76. Mr. Cohn was a personal friend of the Speaker's. He comments on the quoted passage, "As he spoke, Rayburn relived the long, lean, lonely years of his childhood, and it was clear that he wished other children might be spared the bleakness of his youth."

24. CBS News, "Mr. Sam: A Personal and Political Biography," telecast, 16 Nov. 1961.

25. D. B. Hardeman, "The Unseen Side of the Man They Called Mr. Speaker," *Life*, 1 Dec. 1961, 21.

26. Ibid.

27. CBS News, "Mr. Sam."

28. *Time*, 10 Feb. 1961, 12. What is significant here, I think, is not the placement of either man on an ideological spectrum so much as the high degree of personal engagement which the references to parts of the body suggest.

29. I was a witness to the events surrounding the composition of Bolling's statement of withdrawal and am quite convinced that Bolling had no knowledge of Rayburn's statement. Rather, the striking resemblance between the two seems to me to illustrate a remarkable similarity in the styles of the two men, not conscious imitation.

30. Bascom N. Timmons, "Rayburn" (n.d., Mimeographed), pt. 4, 1. This series was supplied to certain newspapers at the time of Speaker Rayburn's death. Mr. Timmons is a newspaperman accredited to the House Press Gallery from a string of newspapers in the Southwest. He is a Texan and was a friend and contemporary of Mr. Rayburn's.

31. Rodney Crowther, "House Race Dropped." The psychologically minded would also no doubt find it relevant that Mr. Bolling's father died when he was in his early teens. However, anyone concluding from data such as have been presented here that either Mr. Bolling or Mr. Rayburn gave indications in their behavior of being emotionally crippled or lacking in control could not possibly be further from the mark. The point here is simply that certain easily verified events and patterns in the lives of each man may well have predisposed him to like the other.

32. Mr. Bolling's imputation of indecorousness (the news of which was communicated in such places as "Bitter Withdrawal," *Time*, 12 Jan. 1962, 12) was resented in the Albert camp. In their view, Mr. Bolling had himself precipitated the battle by first permitting word to leak to the newspapers that he was a candidate for majority leader.

33. One index of this is the apparent fact that Mr. Thompson is generally not too popular in the House (a fact of which both he and Mr. Bolling are aware). Mr. Thompson is an able and gifted man with extremely good political connections outside the House, both "downtown" and in his home state. (See Richard L. Lyons, "Thompson Decision to Retain Seat Gives House Liberals Needed Lift," *Washington Post*, 31 Jan. 1961.) But inside the House, he has a reputation for being sharp-tongued, supercilious, and too witty for his own good. He has a way of hanging nicknames that "stick" on friend and foe alike—to the delight of the former, the great chagrin of the latter. One political ally of Mr. Thompson's said, "He has got the reputation that whenever he is in favor of a bill, it is bound to lose. . . . Thompson is one of Bolling's major liabilities. I hear how the guys talk at the back of the room there [in the aisle behind the seats in the hall of the House]. They say, 'Whose amendment is that? Thompson's? That guy? To hell with that.' And they vote it down." Another ally of Thompson's said, "Frank's always trying to talk silly with you when you're talking serious, and trying to talk serious when you're talking silly."

34. See H. Douglas Price, "Race, Religion, and the Rules Committee" in Alan

Westin, ed., *The Uses of Power* (New York: Harcourt, Brace & World, 1962), 1–71.

35. Mr. Albert's friend may, in reflecting unfavorably on Mr. Bolling, have done Mr. Albert a slight injustice. Mr. Albert was an honors graduate of the University of Oklahoma and a Rhodes Scholar—neither of which makes him an intellectual, but they clearly don't disqualify him either.

36. There are now several accounts of the 1961 battle over the Rules Committee in print, including a treatment of the episode in Price, "Race, Religion, and Rules"; the analysis of the vote by Milton C. Cummings, Jr., and Robert L. Peabody, "The Decision to Enlarge the Committee on Rules: An Analysis of the Vote," in the 1st ed. of this work (Chicago: Rand McNally, 1963), chap 7, 167–94; a long chapter by Neil MacNeil in *Forge of Democracy* (New York: McKay, 1963), 410–88; and William MacKaye, *A New Coalition Takes Control: The House Rules Committee Fight of 1961* (New York: McGraw-Hill, 1963).

37. See *Time*, 10 Feb. 1961; William S. White, "The Invisible Gentleman from Kansas City," *Harper's*, May 1961; Neil MacNeil, "The House Confronts Mr. Kennedy," *Fortune*, Jan. 1962, 70–73.

38. Statements such as this one obviously are not intended to be taken with strict literalness. Most social scientists are agreed that personal "qualities" of leaders vary according to the situation.

39. Cf. a similar comment on Senate liberals by Tristam Coffin, "The Well-Tempered Politician," *Holiday*, Apr. 1962, 107.

40. See John M. Virden, "Little Giant from Bug Tussle," *Saturday Evening Post*, 24 Mar. 1962, 94–97; Paul Duke, "Albert's Soft Sell," *Wall Street Journal*, 6 Mar. 1962; "Carl Albert, Nose-Counter from Bug Tussle," *Time*, 12 Jan. 1962, 13.

Certain other characteristics place Mr. Albert closer to the rank and file of congressmen than Mr. Bolling. Mr. Albert was a small-town boy, the son of a farmer and laborer, educated in public schools; he is a Methodist. Mr. Bolling was born in New York City, the son of a well-to-do physician. He grew up in comfortable circumstances and socially prominent circles in Huntsville, Alabama, after his father's death went to Exeter and the University of the South, has a master's degree from Sewanee, did further graduate work at Vanderbilt, and is an Episcopalian. If the script for this contest had been written by C. Wright Mills or one of his followers, Mr. Albert would have been the more "liberal" candidate and wouldn't have had a chance. (See Mills, *The Power Elite* [New York: Oxford University Press, 1956]). Mills carefully excludes Congress from his discussion of "the power elite" for reasons which seem to this reader designed to protect his thesis from evidence which would reject it.

41. An example of this process was given in *Time*, 10 Feb. 1961, at the time of the Rules Committee fight: "*Time* Correspondent Neil MacNeil listened as two Rayburn lieutenants were running down the list of doubtful members. On one: 'The General Services Administration ought to be able to get him.' On another: 'The Air Force can take care of him.' A third? 'If you can get the Post Office to issue that special stamp for him, you've got him.' And a fourth? 'The United Mine Workers can get him.' And a fifth? 'Hell, if we can't get him we might as well quit. Go talk to him.' A sixth? 'No, but I'll fix that bastard.' " *Time* gives the strong impression that the two lieutenants are Bolling and Thompson.

42. A Washington correspondent commented: "[Bolling] was a good news source and popular among newsmen from the time he first got on the House Banking Committee and became even more popular when he was moved to Rules as Rayburn's obvious protégé."

43. *New York Times*, 24 Dec. 1961.

44. This letter was sent in response to Mr. Bolling's 28 November request for "consideration" from each Democrat. Supporters of Mr. Albert were dismayed by the fact that while they had not solicited Judge Smith's support and Mr. Bolling had, the Smith endorsement was being used by Mr. Bolling against Mr. Albert with the press.

45. James Wechsler, "Hill Battle," *New York Post*, 19 Dec. 1961. Mr. Bolling's constituency is the Fifth District of Missouri, which includes most of Kansas City. Mr. Albert represents the thirteen counties of Oklahoma's Third District, an area known as "Little Dixie." This district is predominantly rural and is somewhat depressed economically. Its major products are timber, peanuts, cotton, and livestock. Several Albert supporters suggested that a generally liberal record such as Mr. Albert had made in the House was in some ways a more creditable performance for a man from a district of this kind than for a man from a big city. Although this argument has some plausibility, it should also be noted that several of the most respected southern liberals and moderates in the House have come from districts very similar to Mr. Albert's. Sam Rayburn himself was one such example. Others would be Carl Elliott of Alabama, Frank Smith of Mississippi, and James Trimble of Arkansas. This argument may, in other words, be an attempt to appeal to a popular stereotype which automatically classifies big-city districts as "liberal" and rural southern districts as "conservative." But it may be that on the vast majority of issues coming to a vote in Congress, representatives from southern, rural, economically depressed areas have constituencies as liberal as any in the country.

46. Marquis Childs, "The High Stakes in House Battle," *Washington Post*, 29 Dec. 1961 — and elsewhere.

47. "Edward P. Morgan and the News," American Broadcasting Company, 29 Dec. 1961. The documentation of this case has never, to my knowledge, been made. I suggest that at the least the reference to Mr. Albert's position on federal aid to education would be difficult to defend.

48. See, for examples of this tradition, H. H. Wilson, *Congress: Corruption and Compromise* (New York: Rinehart, 1951); Karl Schriftgiesser, *The Lobbyists* (Boston: Little, Brown, 1951).

49. An excellent example of this mode of thinking is contained in Max Lerner, *America as a Civilization* (New York: Simon & Schuster, 1957), 415 ff. and especially 424. More generally, see Arthur F. Bentley, *The Process of Government* (Evanston, Ill.: Principia, 1949); Earl Latham, *The Group Basis of Politics* (Ithaca, N.Y.: Cornell University Press, 1952); Oliver Garceau, "Interest Group Theory in Political Research," *The Annals* 319 (Sept. 1958), and David B. Truman, *The Governmental Process* (New York: Knopf, 1955). Truman explicitly rejects the notion that congressmen are wholly passive.

50. Dexter, "Congressmen"; "The Representative and His District," chap. 1 of the 3d ed. of this work (Chicago: Rand McNally, 1977), 3–25; and, "What Do Congressmen Hear?" chap. 1 of the present volume. See also Donald R. Matthews, *U.S. Senators and Their World* (Chapel Hill: University of North Carolina Press, 1960), esp. chaps. 8, 9.

51. Robert C. Albright, "Powell Backs Albert for House Post," *Washington Post*, 1 Dec. 1961. Powell, unlike the congressman just quoted, checked with the White House before he made his announcement, obviously taking the position that the president had a legitimate interest in the outcome.

52. *New York Post*, 21 Dec. 1961.

53. "Edward P. Morgan and the News," American Broadcasting Company (29

Dec. 1961). This account may be contrasted with a column put out by William S. White, a former Capitol Hill reporter. White's explanation of what happened is: "Whatever chance [Bolling] might have had, however, was sunk without a trace by the ultraliberals themselves. They rushed forward to gather him into their arms, through zealous endorsements by such too-gooder groups as Americans for Democratic Action. No man in a House which—like the country itself—is essentially moderate could possibly have survived such embarrassing public embraces. So Mr. Bolling had to withdraw his candidacy." *Washington Star,* 5 Jan. 1962—and elsewhere. I could discover little evidence which would lend credibility to this analysis. Regrettably, Mr. White offers none.

54. The rate at which tentative proposals and counterproposals of this sort fly around Washington is perfectly phenomenal. Theodore H. White rhapsodizes about the kinds of people who often act in the capacity of carrier pigeon: "Washington holds perhaps fifty or a hundred . . . men, lawyers all, successful all, who in their dark-paneled law chambers nurse an amateur's love for politics and dabble in it whenever their practices permit. Where, in the regions, cities, and states of the country, provincial lawyers love to counsel local politicians, promote names for the local judiciary, arrange the candidacies of lesser men, in Washington lawyers dabble in national politics, in appointments to places of high political destiny. Their influence, collectively, can never be ignored, because, collectively, they possess a larger fund of wisdom, experience, contacts, memories, running back over thirty years of national politics, than most candidates on the national scene can ever hope to acquire on their own" (*The Making of the President, 1960* [New York: Atheneum, 1961], 33.)

Newspaper people also quite often undertake this sort of activity, and occasionally lobbyists do, too.

Fortuitously, much of the activity described in this paper took place during the Christmas–Debutante–New Year's social season in Washington. As a result, many of the participants in these events kept running into each other at parties. Political science may some day catch up with the slick magazines and novels in comprehending the true significance of Washington parties. In this case, it appears that much of the negotiating on whether or not Mr. Bolling would join the leadership group as head of the policy committee took place on an informal basis, through intermediaries and without any soul-stirring confrontations of rivals such as are found in Allen Drury's *Advise and Consent.*

55. That is, it came to almost nothing. In mid-March 1962, three months after the events described here took place, the Democrats reactivated a "steering" committee along the lines of the "policy" committee proposed at the opening of the session. Mr. Bolling did not become a member. A leading Democrat in the House observed to me that the members of this committee, including James Davis of Georgia, William Colmer of Mississippi, Paul Kitchin of North Carolina, Clarence Cannon of Missouri, were likely, if anything, to be *less* liberal than the leadership they were supposed to advise. This was an outcome exactly opposite to the one envisaged by proponents of the policy committee idea.

56. For the story at various stages, see Robert C. Albright, "Drive Is Begun for Democratic Steering Group," *Washington Post,* 30 Dec. 1961; Mary McGrory, "McCormack Silent on Liberals' Plan," *Washington Star,* 31 Dec. 1961; Robert K. Walsh, "Party Harmony Setup Seen by House Liberals," *Washington Star,* 5 Jan. 1962; Richard L. Lyons, "Liberal Democrats Defer Demands," *Washington Post,* 9 Jan. 1962; Rowland Evans, Jr., "Democrats Unanimous," *New York Herald Tribune,* 10 Jan. 1962.

57. Dexter, "What Do Congressmen Hear?" makes the point that the mail usually comes too late to affect the substance of legislation. However mail is used here only as an index of attentiveness to issues on the part of publics.

58. Obviously, no real-world case will fit a typology perfectly. It may be well to remind the reader that the predominant strategies of the major actors were as I have indicated, but that Mr. Albert had some support from outside the House (such as from Senators Kerr and Monroney and Governor Edmondson of Oklahoma), and many of Bolling's supporters within the House backed him for reasons other than outside "pressures" which he might have been able to bring to bear on them. These included some members from the South whose position on civil rights was more accurately reflected by Mr. Albert.

59. As an example, the Agriculture Committee. See Charles O. Jones, "Representation in Congress: The Case of the House Agriculture Committee," *American Political Science Review* 55 (June 1961):358–67 (reprinted as chap. 8 of the 3d ed. of this work [Chicago: Rand McNally, 1977]).

60. There are numerous examples of this—e.g., the operation of the seniority system. See George Goodwin, "The Seniority System in Congress," *American Political Science Review* 53 (June 1959):412–36. On the influence of state delegations on committee assignments and the force of tradition in determining the allocation of seats, see in general, Nicholas Masters, "Committee Assignments in the House of Representatives," *American Political Science Review* 55 (June 1961):345–57.

61. On the Rules Committee, see Robert L. Peabody, "The Enlarged Rules Committee," in the 1st ed. of this work (Chicago: Rand McNally, 1963), chap. 6, 129–64, and the following articles by James A. Robinson: "Organizational and Constituency Backgrounds of the House Rules Committee" in Joseph R. Fiszman, ed., *The American Political Arena* (Boston: Little, Brown, 1962); "The Role of the Rules Committee in Regulating Debate in the U.S. House of Representatives," *Midwest Journal of Political Science* 5 (Feb. 1961): 59–69; "Decision-Making in the House Rules Committee," *Administrative Science Quarterly* 3 (June 1958):73–86; "The Role of the Rules Committee in Arranging the Program of the U.S. House of Representatives," *Western Political Quarterly* 12 (Sept. 1959): 653–69.

62. This comment may be anachronistic, judging from much of the recent work on the House. It agrees with Ralph K. Huitt's similar judgment in "Democratic Party Leadership in the Senate," *American Political Science Review* 55 (June 1961): 333 ff.

Chapter 13

The Institutionalization of Leadership in the United States Congress

DAVID T. CANON

Leadership in the U.S. Congress is constantly evolving. In the past century, "czarist" Speakers, a "King Caucus," and powerful committee chairmen ruled the House, and autocratic leaders, committee barons, and collegial leaders led the Senate. Since the mid-1970s, leadership has responded to increased individualism and decentralization in the House and Senate by becoming more inclusive and service-oriented but also more institutionalized. This chapter examines the dimensions of institutionalization and asks the more general question, How and why do leadership institutions change?

The theory of institutionalization employed by Polsby (1968), Hibbing (1988), and others provides an excellent basis for answering the "how" part of the question. It also permits a focus on changes in leadership institutions that transcend the importance of any given leader. Most leadership studies are reluctant to generalize because of the perceived importance of leadership style and personality (Mackaman and Sachs 1988, 16–17, 38–39). The theory does not fare as well in explaining why institutions change (Hibbing 1988, 707–10). Gradual historical forces, such as increased societal complexity, cannot explain the evolution

This chapter was originally published in *Legislative Studies Quarterly* 14 (August 1989):415–43. Copyright © 1989 by the Legislative Research Center. It is reprinted by permission. Research reported was supported by a grant from the Duke University Research Council. I thank John Aldrich, William Bianco, and Chuck Jones for their comments on an earlier version of this chapter.

of institutions, nor do they recognize the tensions between different aspects of change.

The central part of this chapter addresses the question of how leadership institutions change, with a focus on the 1970s and 1980s. Changes in House and Senate leadership before this period are well documented (Ripley 1967; Peabody 1976) and therefore will be discussed only to be placed within the framework of institutionalization theory. Differences between the two institutions are discussed throughout. In the conclusion, I speculate about the consequences of institutionalization and present a theory of why leadership institutions change.

COMPONENTS OF THE INSTITUTIONALIZATION OF LEADERSHIP

The institutionalization of leadership in the House and Senate is indicated by four vaguely hierarchical characteristics. The first, durability, is the most fundamental; institutions must survive in order to develop. The second and third—internal complexity and boundedness—evolve together during the second stage; as institutions become more complex they are more well bounded and autonomous. The fourth, the universal norms and rules employed by the leadership, are the last to develop because they tend to undermine strong leadership. I will discuss each in turn.

Institutional Durability

The only constitutionally prescribed officers of Congress are the Speaker of the House, the vice president (who serves as president of the Senate), and the president pro tempore of the Senate. The other leadership positions in the House and Senate survive by custom, inertia, and institutional need. Therefore, durability is not a foregone conclusion.

To be characterized as durable, leadership institutions must meet two conditions: first, clearly defined leadership offices must persist over time, and second, powers and duties must have institutional rather than personal definition. Evidence for the first condition is easily obtained, but distinguishing between institutional and personal power is more complicated. Dramatic changes in the patterns of leadership associated with leadership turnover would indicate personal, rather than institutional, leadership. Evidence presented in this section indicates that House leadership is highly institutionalized, while Senate leadership is less stable and more personalized, especially in the Republican party.

Durability of House Leadership. Both parties in the House have met the first condition of durability for more than half a century. The top three leadership positions have existed continuously since the turn of the century.[1] The next level of leadership—the whip system, the party caucuses (or conference, for the Republicans), the rules committees, and policy committees—have undergone changes in the twentieth century, but they too have had a continuous existence. However, until the 1970s, patterns of leadership often changed dramatically as a result of leadership turnover, thus violating the second condition of durability. Sam Rayburn did not use the whip system in the 1950s, breaking with past practices. Barbara Sinclair reports that the whip, Carl Albert, had nothing to do, and Hale Boggs, the deputy whip, had "double nothing to do" (1983, 55). The Republicans' whip system was more stable (Leslie Arends was whip from 1943 to 1974), but the role of their other party institutions, the Republican Conference and the Policy Committee, varied greatly. John Byrnes transformed the Policy Committee into a vital part of the leadership from 1959 to 1965, after which time the conference became more central (Jones 1970, 153–60).

Since the early 1970s, Democratic leadership has met the second condition for durability, exhibiting continuity through several leadership changes. The whip system was greatly expanded and activated by Tip O'Neill, but the trend continued under John Brademas, Tom Foley, and Tony Coelho. The Speaker's task forces, used by O'Neill to promote an inclusive leadership style, have been expanded under the leadership of Jim Wright. Similarly, the Democratic Congressional Campaign Committee (DCCC) was transformed into a money-making machine under Coelho, and the committee's practices were institutionalized by Beryl Anthony.

Leadership in the minority party tends to be volatile, responding more dramatically than majority party leadership to external events such as changes in the party of the president and electoral disasters. However, the Republican leadership in the House has been more durable in the 1970s and 1980s. The whip system was strengthened under Trent Lott, and in the early days of the 101st Congress it appeared that Dick Cheney would carry on his practices.[2] William Connelly concludes that the Policy Committee "has not changed fundamentally" in the past twenty years, despite membership and leadership change (1988, 26). The leadership of Robert Michel has also contributed to continuity; in the 101st Congress, he will become the minority leader with the longest continuous service.

The increased durability of the Democratic and Republican party leadership in the House does not mean that institutionalization obliterates the imprint of individual leaders. Jim Wright is more involved in policy than Tip O'Neill was, and Tony Coelho has a style different from Tom

Foley's. However, leadership discretion is constrained in an institution-alized setting (Smith 1985, 228). As leadership institutions become durable, as I define that quality here, they develop inertia and expectations among the rank and file that are difficult to change.

Durability of Senate Leadership. Senate leadership is not as durable as leadership in the House, especially in the Republican party. Party offices have fallen into disuse in various periods, and positions are defined by the skills and style of given leaders, rather than by the institution. There are several reasons for this lack of durability, each of which I will discuss in turn. First, there is not a long tradition of strong formal leadership in the Senate. While the House had a Speaker in the first Congress, the first floor leader in the Senate was elected in 1911 (Peabody 1976, 325–29). The first Senate whip was elected in 1913, but did not play much of a role until the 1950s. Lacking clearly defined purposes, lower party offices have been unstable. Second, Senate leadership changes readily in response to changing external conditions (primarily, changes in which party controls the presidency). Third, given its size, the Senate has always been more disposed to personal leadership.

The first condition of durability has not been met by either party during the twentieth century. While parties have continuously elected majority and minority leaders in this period, stability in the lower leadership offices is less evident. Peabody reports that Republicans did not even bother to elect a whip between 1935 and 1944, and some whips, such as Lister Hill (Democratic whip from 1941 to 1947), "voluntarily gave up the job because they did not feel the position was worth the effort" (1976, 331). A deputy whip and assistant whips were appointed by the Democrats in 1937 but were soon discarded (Oleszek 1985, 9). More recently, the Republicans abolished their whip system, which had grown to sixteen assistant whips by the Ninety-sixth Congress. This incident deserves brief discussion because it illustrates the instability of Senate leadership and the importance of external conditions in dictating change.

In 1981, when the Republicans took control of the Senate for the first time in twenty years, they disbanded their whip system. This move is counterintuitive: the responsibilities of being in the majority and having to pass an ambitious presidential agenda should create a greater need for a whip system. But a top leadership aide explained that the principal service provided by the whip system was floor coverage, and the presiding officer of the Senate, who was now a Republican, could play that role.[3] The other two important functions of the whip system—whip counts and the dissemination of information—are done through other channels.

Howard Green, the party secretary, handles whip counts, and the Policy Committee serves as the primary source of agenda and policy information. The Republicans abolished their whip system in part because the division of labor broke down. The system was underutilized, because the whips did not know what they were supposed to do. "Functions were fairly ill defined," the aide said. "There was not a clear sense of getting anything done, so the assistant whips did not feel they were having an impact. More basically, there just was not that much for them to do."[4]

The second condition, that leadership be institutionally defined, is less likely to hold in the Senate than in the House. For example, the roles of the Republican Policy Committee and the Democratic Conference have depended greatly on who led those groups. When Robert Taft or Styles Bridges chaired the Policy Committee, it was an important arm of leadership. However, because the leadership was not institutionally defined, the committee's role changed greatly under the guidance of Bourke Hickenlooper and John Tower. Similarly, Robert Byrd as secretary of the Democratic Conference transformed it into a valuable service organization, but he was unique in that regard. For others, there is an initial period of adjustment, before they put their own imprint on the office. Robert Dole, for example, initially exhibited institutionalized leadership by following past practices: "Not having served as Party leader of the Senate, Senator Dole concluded that instead of trying out some new procedures immediately, he would utilize selected established procedures until he had more time to examine and study the existing procedures" (Riddick 1985, 20). Within a few months, Dole had implemented his own brand of leadership, with his "quorum government" allowing him to be at the center of most negotiation (Deering 1986). This pattern typifies personalized leadership and is less likely to happen in an institutionalized system.

Another way of understanding the same point is that leadership institutions in the Senate are not strong enough to compel a reluctant to lead. Two successive Democratic whips, Russell Long (1965–69) and Edward Kennedy (1969–71), were not willing to make the personal sacrifices that are required of Senate leaders. Long complained that the whip's position is "a grueling, day-to-day, thankless, time-consuming job of being around when nobody else cares to be" (quoted in Peabody 1976, 366). Kennedy, who defeated Long in 1969, found that he did not enjoy the duties of the position any more than his predecessor.

Robert Byrd's actions as whip and floor leader are further evidence of the personal rather than institutional nature of leadership in the Senate. Byrd transformed the whip's office, becoming very active in scheduling and in the formation of complex unanimous consent agreements. But when he was elected majority leader, he continued to play the same role. Smith and Flathman (1989) show that in the Ninety-second Congress (Byrd's first year as whip) the majority whip sponsored sixty-six complex unanimous consent agreements on key vote measures, while the majority leader sponsored only thirty-seven. By contrast, in the Eighty-eighth Congress, the majority leader had sponsored twenty-three of the twenty-four unanimous consent agreements formed by the leadership. When Byrd became majority leader, he sponsored all seventy-one of the agreements formed by the leadership, while Cranston was relegated to a much smaller role as whip. In a durable leadership system, the tasks would have remained in the whip's domain, once they had been defined as tasks performed by that office.

Institutional Boundaries

Polsby defines a well-bounded institution as one that is "differentiated from its environment" (1968, 145). Well-bounded leadership systems are not permeable; they have career structures that promote leaders from within. Other defining characteristics include long apprenticeships before top leadership positions are attained, lengthy tenure in leadership, and careers that finish in leadership positions (Polsby 1968, 148–52). By these measures, the top level of leadership in the House was well bounded by 1900.[5] Institutionalization is well documented for the House Democratic leadership (Hinckley 1970; Sinclair 1983; Brown and Peabody 1987), but relatively little attention has been directed to leadership career paths in the other three legislative parties, where leadership boundaries have been less distinct, or to careers in the extended leadership systems. I will show that boundaries have become more clearly defined for Senate Democrats and House Republicans and that additional evidence of institutionalization may be gained from examining career patterns below the top leadership in all of the legislative parties.

When positions below the top leadership are examined, it is evident that a well-bounded leadership system emerges in four stages. In the first stage, newly formed leadership positions are not the objects of intense competition; the leadership is permeable and turnover is high. In the second stage of development, as the number of leadership positions expands, top positions will be hotly contested but lower-level positions will not. In the third stage, there is competition at all levels of the leadership structure, and lower positions emerge as stepping stones to high party office; apprenticeship in the institution becomes a requirement for movement into the leadership. Voluntary retirement from the leadership system is relatively rare, and careers in leadership tend to be long. Finally, in a fully institutionalized system, competition continues at lower levels in the structure, but the top position is uncontested as the heir apparent reaches the top of the ladder. The ladder extends deeper into the structure as the leadership becomes more institutionalized (in the One Hundredth Congress, neither Tom Foley nor Jim Wright was challenged for the top position in his party in the House).[6]

Establishing Boundaries in House Leadership. The House Democratic party is the most institutionalized of the legislative parties. Having held majority status continuously for thirty-six years, the House Democrats have developed long-term career expectations and stable institutions. Though the pattern of succession is not written in stone, recent experience indicates it has solidified for the top three positions (whip to majority leader to Speaker). This ladder is unlikely to be challenged in the near future. With the top leadership progression firmly in place, most career decisions are made lower in the system. Little is known, however, about career patterns in the extended leadership.

The whip system is now the training ground and incubator for aspiring leaders. The top three Democratic leaders in the 101st Congress—Jim Wright (Tex.), Tom Foley (Wash.), and Tony Coelho (Calif.)—all served in lower leadership positions. Other prominent Democrats who have competed for access to the leadership ladder have also been weaned in the whip system, including Norman Mineta (Calif.), Bill Alexander (Ark.), Dan Rostenkowski (Ill.), and Charles Rangel (N.Y.). However, not all leaders attempt to climb the ladder.[7] Three distinct career types were identified in an examination of the leadership structure from 1973 to 1988: dabblers, whippers, and ladder climbers. Examining the careers of these three types provides a picture of the boundedness of the leadership system. More institutionalized systems should have a larger proportion of ladder climbers and fewer members who voluntarily leave the system.

Dabblers are those who serve in the leadership for one or two terms and then leave. More than half of the forty Democratic dabblers remained in the House after leaving the whip system (57.5 percent); the others retired or were defeated (27.5 percent), or sought higher office (15 percent). Despite the relatively large number of members in this category, careers in the extended leadership do not resemble the revolving door of the nineteenth-century leadership (Polsby [1968] mentions Henry Clay's wild career as being indicative of the fluid congressional careers in that period). Only 4 of the 122 Democrats and 1 of the 70 Republicans in this fourteen-year period reentered the leadership structure after leaving.

Whippers are the relative few who continue as at-large or regional whips year after year (the coding rule was three terms or more). Some, such as John P. Murtha (Penn.) and Tom Bevill (Ala.), seem to enjoy the cajoling and persuading, while others perform the whipping function out of a sense of duty or loyalty to the party. These members do not aspire to move beyond this limited but valuable role, and often they are heavily involved in committee work and other legislative concerns. Democratic whippers are loyal; only five of the forty-three (11.6 percent) left the leadership voluntarily, and only two were defeated.

Ladder climbers aspire to the speakership. Generally they move from regional whip to at-large whip to deputy whip and wait their turn to compete for the top positions (occasionally the intermediate level is skipped).[8] Members are included in this group if they have served at least three terms in the whip system and have climbed at least one level. Of the thirty-nine in this category, twenty-one can be considered "super–ladder climbers," by virtue of having progressed at least to the level of deputy whip. None of the ladder climbers voluntarily left the leadership system, indicating their commitment to a leadership career and their intense ambition. Two—McFall and Alexander—dropped out of the leadership after being defeated for a higher party office, and five were defeated in reelection attempts, including Whip John Brademas in 1980.

For most of the twentieth century, the leadership of the House Republicans has not been as well bounded as the Democratic leadership. Republicans were much quicker to turn their leaders out of office when the times got tough, and they did not establish clear patterns of succession. House Republicans revolted four times in the twentieth century against incumbent floor leaders or heirs apparent to the top position (1919, 1931, 1959, and 1965).

The absence of well-defined boundaries is further illustrated by the different paths of the top Republican leadership. In contrast to the House Democrats, the Republicans do not use the whip system extensively as a stepping stone. Instead, they use the six positions below the floor leader as outlets for leadership ambitions. Trent Lott was elected whip in 1981 from the Rules Committee and the Research Committee, and neither Rhodes nor Ford served in the whip system. Ford used the Conference and Rhodes used the Policy Committee as a stepping stone to the top.

This career pattern undermines the incentive to serve in the whip system. If there is no long-term payoff of a high leadership position, ambitious members may not be willing to commit the time and energy to serve in the whip system. Consequently, Republicans are far more likely to leave the system voluntarily than are their Democratic counterparts, perhaps seeing little value in the ultimate prizes. More than a third of all "whippers" (those who serve for three terms or more as a whip) voluntarily left the leadership between 1973 and 1988 (eleven of thirty), but only 14.7 percent of the Democratic whippers did so. Only 18.6

percent of those in the Republican leadership can be classified as ladder climbers, but 32 percent of the Democrats can be so classified. Even fewer stay in the leadership long enough to climb several levels.

It is too early for conclusive statements, but the 1980s may indicate that Republicans are creating a more bounded leadership system. The top four Republican positions in the House were held by the same people from 1980 until Jack Kemp stepped down as conference chairman in June 1987. The Republicans resisted their tendency to change leaders in the face of electoral defeat in 1982, and the 1987 and 1989 successions were chapters from the Democratic escalator.[9] Despite the recent election of Newt Gingrich to the whip position, the patterns of Republican leadership in the 1980s seem to contradict Peabody's hypothesis that "the longer the period of minority status, the more prone the minority party is to leadership change through revolt" (1976, 297).

Recent patterns of leadership succession in the House indicate that both parties have reached the fourth stage of the establishment of leadership boundaries. Top leadership positions are filled by heirs apparent in smooth transitions; the competition occurs lower in the leadership structure. The whip system is the vehicle for ambition in the Democratic leadership, while for the Republicans the outlet is the plethora of lower-level leadership positions. The stages of development are most clear for the Republicans. In the period from 1955 to 1974, the three successions to minority leader occasioned two successful revolts against an incumbent and one defeat of an heir apparent. In this same period, there was little competition for lower leadership positions. In the next three elections (1975–79), there were no challenges to the minority leader, and competition increased for lower offices. Stepping stones began to emerge in lower offices: Bob Michel moved from campaign chair to Whip in 1975; two Research Committee chairs, Louis Frey and Bill Frenzel, attempted to move to Policy in 1977 and 1979; and Samuel Devine moved from conference vice chair to conference chair in 1979. Between 1981 and 1989 the Republicans reached the fourth stage. Michel moved unopposed from whip to minority leader in 1981, and the regular patterns of succession described above emerged in the lower offices.

Establishing Boundaries in Senate Leadership. Peabody begins his chapter on Senate leadership by wondering, "Why do so few Senators gravitate toward elected party leadership, while the vast majority choose to make their mark on public policy primarily through legislative specialization?" (1976, 321). The primary reason is that the legislative process is more open and the leadership more fluid than in the House. Senators do not have to be in the formal leadership to help shape legislation. Though

Table 13-1. The Establishment of Boundaries in the Senate: The Careers of Floor Leaders and Party Whips, 1911–1989 (in Number of Years)

Position	Period	In Senate before Election		In Leadership[a]		After Leadership until Death		
		Mean	Median	Mean	Median	Mean	Median	(N)
Democrat								
Floor Leaders	1911–49	8.5	7.5	6.3	4.0			6
	1949–89	10.0	10.0	8.0	8.0			5
Party Whips	1913–49	5.6	4.0[b]	5.1	6.0	3.5	1.5	7
	1949–89	7.3	8.0	4.4	4.0	18.0	14.5	9
Republican								
Floor leaders	1911–49	18.9	16.0	5.6	5.0	3.8	1.0	7
	1949–89	11.0	10.5	5.0	5.0	5.6	4.0	8
Party whips	1915–49	5.7	6.0	4.2	4.0			6
	1949–89	6.0	6.0	6.2	7.5			7

Sources: Peabody 1976, tables 11-1 and 11-2; Riddick 1985, table II; various editions of Congressional Quarterly Weekly Report, Politics in America, and the Almanac of American Politics.
[a] Includes leadership in the One Hundreth congress.
[b] J. Hamilton Lewis served two nonconsecutive terms (1913–19, 1933–39) and served all twelve years as whip. Thus Lewis is counted twice: the first time with zero years of prior experience in the Senate, the second time with six years.

informal leaders and "leaders without portfolio" have recently played a more prominent role in the House (Calmes and Gurwitt 1987; Hammond 1988), these players have always been central in the Senate. As a consequence, leadership ladders have not developed fully and the leadership is very permeable, especially in the Republican party.

The measures used by Polsby in his seminal work—the number of years in Congress before succeeding to a top leadership position, the number of years in the leadership, and the length of time out of Congress after retirement from the leadership—indicate that the boundaries have not become better defined for either the Democratic or the Republican leadership in the post–World War II period (see table 13-1). The mean years of prior service in the Senate have increased for Democratic leaders but have fallen dramatically for Republicans. The length of time in the leadership has increased for Democratic floor leaders and Republican assistant leaders but stayed about the same for Republican leaders and Democratic whips.[10] The most significant change is that Democratic and Republican floor leaders are much less likely to finish their careers in the Senate.

Although the traditional measures of well-boundedness do not provide clear evidence, the Democratic leadership is more institutionalized on several other dimensions of well-boundedness: membership is more stable for the Democrats, succession at top levels is more structured, and, until recently, patterns of contesting leadership positions indicated a higher level of development.

From 1977 to 1989, the same three individuals occupied the top positions in the elected Democratic leadership. This degree of stability was unprecedented in the Senate. The Republicans, during the same period, had two different floor leaders, two whips, four conference chairs, three conference secretaries, and two policy committee chairs. The pattern holds in lower leadership positions. Almost 40 percent of the Republican membership held an assistant whip position in the Ninety-sixth Congress; according to a top leadership aide, anybody who wanted the title of assistant whip could have it. Less than 20 percent of the Democratic membership is generally in the whip system, and the current figure is one in six. As might be expected, the less bounded system also has greater turnover. In its last year, the Republican whip system had a 50 percent turnover, whereas the Democratic system's membership remained unchanged from the Ninety-seventh through the Ninety-ninth Congresses, except for the loss of Walter Huddleston (Ky.) through electoral defeat in 1984. Such stability is not observed even in the highly institutionalized Democratic whip system in the House. The average tenure of Republican whips in the last year of their system was 1.9 years; for Democrats in the Ninety-ninth Congress it was 7.8 years.[11]

Both the Democrats and Republicans have gone through the first two stages of career ladder development in fits and starts. The cyclical low interest in leadership positions that was typical before World War II has now given way to generally intense competition for the top leadership positions. Neither party has evolved to the final stage, in which top positions are not contested, but the Democrats have come closer than Republicans to reaching the third stage, characterized by competition at all levels, with stepping stones emerging. Since 1949, the whip position has become a regular stepping stone to majority leader for Democrats. Before 1949, six of the seven incumbent whips who had an opportunity to become floor leader when there was a vacancy were passed over (Peabody 1976, 330–32). Between 1949 and 1988, all four incumbent Democratic whips who had an opportunity were elected floor leader. This pattern was broken in the 101st Congress, when Alan Cranston did not run for majority leader.[12] Republicans also had established a pattern, with three whips out of four succeeding to floor leader between 1947 and 1976; however, in 1976 Howard Baker was elected over whip Robert Griffin, and in 1984 Robert Dole won over whip Ted Stevens.[13]

Since the revolts against incumbent whips in 1969 and 1971, the contests for Democratic leadership positions have been relatively peaceful.

Frank Moss was unopposed in 1971 to fill Byrd's position as conference secretary, which he held for three uncontested terms. The next change in leadership was 1977, when Byrd moved up to majority leader with a brief challenge from Hubert Humphrey. Cranston and Inouye were unopposed for the numbers two and three positions. The only challenge to the leadership in the next twelve years was Lawton Chiles's race for majority leader in 1984, in which he gained only eleven supporters. In 1989, Wendell Ford challenged Cranston, winning twelve votes, but in general it seems the Democrats have moved away from their more rebellious days. A true leadership ladder has not emerged, but the system is not as permeable as the Republican leadership.

Senate Republicans exhibit a pattern of contesting leadership positions that does not fit neatly into the theory of stages of development presented above. Between 1955 and 1969, the Republican leadership was in a classic stage two: elections for the top three positions were all contested (seven successions), and there was little interest in the lower offices of conference chair and conference secretary. Milton Young was the only secretary through the 1950s and 1960s, and only three people occupied the conference chair between 1948 and 1972 (Milliken, Saltonstall, and Smith). In the 1970s and 1980s, competition for the top positions abated slightly (four of six successions contested), and the lower positions were hotly contested. In ten elections, Republicans elected six different conference chairs (four contested) and six different conference secretaries (three contested). This pattern would be consistent with third-stage development if lower positions became stepping stones to higher office, but the opposite happened. The tentative first step on the ladder that began to emerge in the 1960s and early 1970s (whip to floor leader) disappeared with the defeats of Griffin and Stevens, and lower offices did not develop patterns of succession.

Autonomy. Thus far, I have defined the boundedness of leadership by the patterns of careers within the leadership. Congressional leadership is also differentiated from its environment by the degree to which congressional parties are autonomous or distinct from national parties. Until recently, congressional parties had little autonomy in one important area: fund-raising. For example, John F. Kennedy used his considerable fund-raising power to help the congressional committees, but the cost to congressional leadership was a merger of the Democratic National Committee (DNC) and the DCCC and a complete loss of control. This relationship remained intact until 1968, though Lyndon B. Johnson exerted less control over the congressional committees than Kennedy had (Menefee-Libey, 1990).

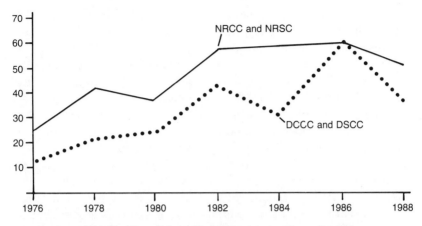

Figure 13-1. Campaign Funds Raised by the Legislative Party Campaign Committees as a Percentage of Total Party Receipts, 1976–1988.

For each party, the total party receipts are the sum of funds raised by the national party committee (the DNC or RNC) and by the Senate and House campaign committees (the DCCC and DSCC or the NRCC and NRSC). The points plotted are for two-year election cycles.

Source: Vital Statistics on Congress, 1987, table 3-13 (Washington, D.C.: Congressional Quarterly Press). Reprinted in Federal Election Commission Press Release, 3 November 1988, 2-3.

Recently, congressional parties have strengthened their fund-raising committees to gain autonomy.

In the early 1980s, the Republican congressional campaign committees surpassed the Republican National Committee (RNC) in total receipts, and the Democratic committees pulled even with the DNC, surpassing it in 1986 (see fig. 13-1). The increases are stunning, not only in relative terms but also in absolute terms. The Democratic Senate and House campaign committees raised their revenues from just under $2 million in 1976 to $25.7 million in 1986, while Republicans increased their totals from nearly $13 million to almost $126 million (Ornstein, et al. 1987, 99–101; Federal Election Commission Press Release, 3 Nov. 1988).

Increased financial power has allowed the congressional committees to become organizationally independent of the national party committees (Menefee-Libey, 1990), and it has influenced leadership ladders. Tony Coelho used his position as DCCC chairman to win the first election for Democratic whip in the House, and George Mitchell's chairmanship of the Democratic Senatorial Campaign Committee (DSCC) put him in good standing with the 1986 freshman class, who contributed to his election as majority leader of the Senate in December 1988. "Money, whether we like it or not, is a pretty powerful tool," commented W. G. Hefner, one of Coelho's opponents in the whip race. "He was the man who signed the checks," noted Charles B. Rangel, the other defeated candidate (Hook 1986, 3068).

Others who aspire to leadership positions recognize the power of money. Member political action committees (PACs) have become an increasingly popular tool for gaining favor with colleagues. Party leaders use PACs to solidify their position within the leadership and to strengthen party leadership generally. Others use PACs to win support in leadership races (Baker 1989). Lyndon Johnson was the first to systematically raise and distribute campaign funds within Congress for personal gain (though his activities were nominally under the auspices of the DCCC). In 1940, he became a "one-man national committee for congressmen" when he raised many thousands of dollars for marginal congressmen in desperate need of money (Caro 1982, 606–64). In the 1980s, there have been 111 PACs "associated with recognized individuals," ranging from Jerry Falwell's "I Love America Committee" to William Buckley's "BuckPAC" and Jim Wright's "Majority Congress Committee."[14] Seventy-six of these were still active at the end of the 1987–88 campaign cycle, and thirty-one are leadership PACs (those associated with congressional leaders or members who were campaigning for a leadership position). In 1980, there were only five leadership PACs, and these raised a total of $563,061 (for O'Neill, Wright, Rhodes, Dole, and Tower). In 1986, twenty-six leadership PACs raised $13.3 million; in 1988, twenty-six leadership PACs raised $10.1 million. The proliferation of leadership PACs indicates the attractiveness of leadership positions. Members would not be willing to spend so much time and money to be part of a leadership organization that was not well bounded.[15]

Internal Complexity

As leadership institutions become more highly developed, they delegate responsibility to lower party offices, devote more resources to the organization, and regularize patterns of communication and behavior. The degree of integration within the leadership—that is, the extent to which the various offices of the party structure are coordinated and utilized—is a new indicator of complexity that will be addressed here.

Internal Complexity in House Leadership. Democratic leadership in the House has become more internally complex. This development is most evident in the whip system, which has evolved slowly through the twentieth century. The first whips worked alone, but the Republicans greatly expanded their whip system in 1931, and in 1933 the Democrats expanded theirs. However, growth was not continuous. As Speaker, Sam Rayburn did not make much use of the whip system and instead "ran the whole thing out of his back pocket" (Sinclair 1983, 55). John Mc-Cormack moved toward institutionalized leadership by expanding the powers of the whip system in 1962 (Ripley 1967, 102), but he did not use the system extensively either (212). In 1969, the leadership used the whip system more aggressively because the president's liaison office was no longer in friendly hands.

The transition to a fully institutionalized House leadership system occurred between the Ninety-first and the Ninety-fourth Congresses. In the Ninety-second Congress the leadership disseminated whip packets, which contain the floor schedule, information on bills up for consideration, and copies of bills. Also, the division of labor became increasingly well defined: elected regional whips were responsible for headcounts and at-large whips for persuasion (Dodd and Sullivan 1983). In the Ninety-third Congress the leadership circulated whip advisories, which detailed the party's position on important legislation. The use of whip counts increased from seventeen counts in 1962–63 to fifty-three in the Ninety-third Congress (Dodd 1979, 37) to eighty in the Ninety-fifth and in the Ninety-sixth Congresses (Sinclair 1983, 56).

The Democratic whip system has also expanded. The number of at-large whips doubled from the Ninety-sixth to the Ninety-eighth Congresses and then doubled again in the next four years; the number of deputy whips tripled in that period (there were eighty-one members in the Democratic whip system in the One Hundredth Congress). The system was originally expanded to give more balance to the party leadership, but more recently appointive whips have been used as an arm of the top leadership and the leadership team has been better integrated.

Republican leadership in the House is not as internally complex as Democratic leadership. Charles Halleck attempted to activate the Policy Committee and to make extensive use of the whip system, but members complained of his leadership style, claiming there was too much whipping (Ripley 1967, 108). Under Gerald Ford, the Policy Committee was downgraded and there was not as much use of the whip system, but a hierarchical chain of command was implemented in the leadership. The goal, to develop policy alternatives to majority party proposals, met with some success. (The new breed of Republican activists in the House today has a colorful acronym for this minority strategy: CRAP—Constructive Republican Alternative Policies.)

John Rhodes and his successor, current minority leader Robert Michel, moved to integrate the leadership system and create a more active whip system. Trent Lott, the minority whip from 1980 to 1988, was a key player in this process. Under his active leadership, the Republican whip system evolved into an effective machine that rivals the Democrats in its ability to disseminate information, count heads, and build coalitions. He also integrated the whip system with the rest of the leadership through weekly whip meetings and good communication with Michel (personal interview). Recently, the Research Committee has become more important through the leadership of Jerry Lewis, Mickey Edwards, and Duncan Hunter. Most important, policy task forces, mimicking the Democratic counterpart, are now run from the Research Committee office.

A summary, albeit somewhat crude, measure of these various trends toward greater internal complexity is the allocation of resources to the leadership. The reports of the clerk of the House and the reports of the secretary of the Senate are the best available documents, but information is incomplete. As Polsby noted, "Reliable figures, past or present, on personnel assigned to the House are impossible to come by" (1968, 158). For example, through the 1960s, the minority party in the House had no separate authorization for its conference, Policy Committee, or Research Committee, but it did shift funds from individual members' staff allotments (Jones 1970, 177). Bearing these limitations in mind, the Clerk's Reports show that funds allocated to the leadership have increased greatly; from $47,825 in 1955, to $482,850 in 1968, to $2,343,225 in 1974, to $6,755,468 in 1986. This 141-fold increase is dramatically larger than the 21-fold increase in total legislative branch appropriations (both in nominal dollars), the tripling in the size of personal staff, and the 6-fold increase in the size of committee staff over this same period.[16]

Internal Complexity in Senate Leadership. Leadership is not as internally complex in the Senate as in the House, primarily because the Senate's smaller size makes institutions less necessary. The Senate is not easier to lead than the House; to the contrary, the highly fragmented and individualized nature of the body makes leading the Senate like "trying to push a wet noodle," according to a frustrated Howard Baker (Granat 1984, 3024). Cognizant of the difficulty of pushing wet noodles, the Senate has steadily increased its appropriations to the leadership: from $79,172 in 1956, to $388,064 in 1966, to $750,318 in 1974, to approximately $7 million in 1986. This 88-fold increase outpaced the growth in legislative branch appropriations reported above, the doubling of personal staff, and the tripling of committee staff during the same period. Thus, by this most simple indicator, Senate leadership has become more institutionalized.

Other measures of complexity—the division of labor, integration, and regular patterns of communication—reveal a mixed picture of institutionalization in Senate leadership. The division of labor appears to be more institutionalized in the Republican leadership because their secondary party positions—the chairs of the Republican Conference, the Policy Committee, and the Committee on Committees—are all held by different people. By contrast, the Democratic floor leader had also been chair of the Democratic Conference, the Policy Committee, and the Steering Committee through the 100th Congress. Two factors caution against drawing any conclusion from these divisions of labor. First, the Democrats dispersed power in the 101st Congress by making Daniel Inouye chair of the Steering Committee and Tom Daschle co-chair of the Policy Committee. Second, the lesser party positions have never been well integrated into the leadership in either party. Only the Republican policy chair and the Democratic conference secretary have ever assumed any importance (Peabody 1976, 332–33).

The number two leader in the Senate, the whip (or assistant leader, as the Republicans call him), gained a more prominent place on the leadership ladder but has generally not played a central role in leadership activities. The relatively weak position of the Republican whip is highlighted by the fact that Assistant Leader Alan Simpson is not authorized to conduct a whip count. That order must come from Minority Leader Dole. The previous Republican whip, Ted Stevens, also played a limited role in floor activity. One aide said that Baker was afraid to leave the Senate in Stevens's control because "he might get into fisticuffs with Metzenbaum or into some godawful parliamentary situation. He was always fighting with Metzenbaum."[17] Until recently, Cranston has not fared much better. According to two aides in the Republican Senate leadership, Alan Cranston's reputation as an integral player in the Democratic leadership[18] is exaggerated. One said, "Byrd likes to build him up in public, but Cranston is not the one who makes things run on the other side of the aisle. We never worked much with him, I'll tell you that much. Byrd runs the show." Integration is also a problem with the Democrats; Byrd and Cranston have never worked closely. Richard Cohen says, "There is not nearly so close a working relationship between Byrd and Minority Whip Alan Cranston of California, who has preferred to maintain his independence from Byrd and has been given few responsibilities. Their aides do not meet on an organized basis" (Cohen 1982, 1547).

The new majority leader, George Mitchell, has vowed to change all this. He says, "I want to try to get the whip and chief deputy whip involved and have them undertake meaningful assignments. . . . I've said

I do not intend to be a one-man band, and I've meant it" (*Congressional Quarterly Weekly Report* 3 Dec. 1988, 3423). The whip systems have shown some signs of increased internal complexity since the 1960s, especially on the Democratic side. In 1966, Majority Leader Mike Mansfield appointed four assistant whips, and Minority Leader Hugh Scott in 1969–70 nominated six regional whips (Oleszek 1985, 9–11). By 1981, the Democrats had eight regional whips and a chief deputy whip. Today there is another layer of four regional deputy whips in the system, with an assistant deputy whip under each of them. As was noted above, by 1979 almost 40 percent of Republicans were in the whip system (sixteen of forty-one), but the following year all assistant whip positions were abolished. Whip notices, which alert members to pending floor action and the timing of votes, have been used more frequently in recent years, expanding the visibility and importance of the office.

Another area in which patterns of behavior have become more institutionalized is the negotiation of complex unanimous consent agreements. With their increased use in the 1960s, Smith and Flathman (1989) note, senators began to demand a more institutionalized mechanism for receiving advance notice of unanimous consent requests. The informal procedure for informing the leadership of holds (objections to unanimous consent agreements) became institutionalized by Byrd's practice of circulating objection forms. This practice made scheduling easier and routinized the procedure for accommodating senator's desires.

Universalistic Practices

The tendency in institutionalized organizations to replace discretionary behavior with universalistic rules and norms undermines strong leadership. The seniority system (the main evidence of universalism in Polsby's account) constrains leaders' ability to promote sympathetic members to committee chairs, and the routinization of committee assignments precludes the aggressive use of assignments as a tool. Only rarely may leaders provide a prize assignments as a favor, strip a member of assignments (e.g., Phil Gramm in 1982), or deny an assignment (Loomis 1984). The most important norm limiting the power of leadership is that of allowing members to "vote their district," even when their vote conflicts with the interests of the party.

On a very mundane level, some universalistic or regularized patterns of behavior are evident: weekly leadership meetings, strengthened channels of communication, and a strategy of inclusiveness on important policy concerns. On the other hand, leadership naturally tends to resist universalistic practices, because strong leadership inherently involves the strategic and discretionary uses of power. Members obviously resist discretionary uses of power, so a compromise has been struck. Leaders maintain some discretionary power and adopt some universalistic practices, but both tend to support individual members' goals as the means to a collective goal of institutional maintenance.

The current use of party money in congressional elections is a good example: the collective goal is to maintain or expand the party's base in Congress, but the goal is achieved by supporting individual members' campaigns. A discretionary use of funds based on levels of party support would not be supported by the rank and file. Examples of discretionary uses of power that serve members' needs are the aggressive use of modified rules in the Rules Committee, the use of complex unanimous consent agreements in the Senate, Robert Byrd's masterful use of parliamentary tactics, and strategic use of multireferrals in the House and Senate.[19] In all of these instances, the commonly assumed tradeoff between individual and collective interests is avoided. Members' interests are served, but the leadership is permitted to set the ground rules and make important decisions.

CONSEQUENCES OF THE INSTITUTIONALIZATION OF LEADERSHIP

Though Polsby does not examine the point in detail, he argues that "along with the more obvious effects of institutionalization, the process has also served to increase the power of the House within the political system" (1968, 166). It is not so clear that the institutionalization of leadership has increased the power of leaders in Congress.[20] Powerful leadership is typically defined as the ability to pass a legislative agenda, an ability which is primarily shaped by external conditions (the presidency and the party system) and internal conditions (the partisan split in the legislature and the personal skills of the leaders). Powerful leaders have been those who have exerted personal control independent of constraining institutions. Therefore, institutionalization may seem marginally significant or even inimical to effective leadership. However, given the modern context of individualism and a weak party system, the institutionalization of leadership reveals that leadership is adaptive and can make the best of a difficult situation. Individual leaders are not as dominant in an institutionalized system, since the division of labor disperses authority, but the leadership team gains capacity to lead.

The institutionalization of leadership has also had an impact on the composition of leadership. A leadership structure that is well bounded and promotes from within is more likely to recruit ambitious, high-quality members than one that is open to outside challenges, because the thankless tasks of party whipping or floor coverage may have some payoff. A Howard Baker or a Robert Dole who is elected majority leader without "serving time" in a lower leadership position undermines members' incentive to sacrifice other options for a position that has no power and little prestige. Internally complex institutions will also be better able to recruit better members for low-level leadership positions because the tasks will be more meaningful and better defined. Ripley supports this conclusion: "These thirty-six men and women have made a commitment of time—which members of the House must necessarily hoard—to work for their respective parties within the House. Unless they felt that party work was worth doing, a sufficient number of commitments, of a desirable caliber, might not be forthcoming" (1964, 575). A top Senate leadership aide concurred: "The lack of clearly delineated lines to higher office undermined the attractiveness of assistant whip position [in the Republican system]. In the most highly developed whip system, that of the Democrats in the House, there is an expectation that you get a bit of a leg up in moving up the leadership system. This is clearly an incentive that didn't exist in our whip system, and this influences the type of member who is looking to serve in that position."

Well-bounded systems are also more likely to produce members who have shown their commitment to the party and to institutional maintenance. Speaker Jim Wright argues that leadership ladders produce "people who understand the institution and the problems, and who have seen Congress grapple with things, succeed and fail" (Calmes 1987, 6). Valuable skills are gained by serving an apprenticeship in the leadership. Furthermore, the automatic escalator avoids potentially divisive leadership contests. Though he expresses some reservations about the escalator, Peabody acknowledges that "it allows the House to get on with business" (Calmes 1987, 6). From an organizational standpoint, smooth leadership transitions are preferable to palace coups.

A THEORY OF LEADERSHIP INSTITUTIONALIZATION

This chapter has shown that leadership in the House is highly institutionalized on all dimensions. Both parties have established patterns of succession and autonomy in campaign finance. House Democrats now have membership on demand in the Speaker's task forces (Loomis 1988), a Rules Committee that services committee chairs (Smith and Bach 1988), an ever-expanding whip system, and flexible scheduling. House Republicans obviously do not play a central role in many of these leadership tasks, but they too have expanded their whip system and have an inclusive leadership style. Both parties in the House now have institutions that outlive the tenure of any single member.

The picture of the Senate is mixed. Senate Democrats have developed some boundedness in leadership careers and have increased autonomy in campaign finances, but personal leadership has limited the development of complex and durable institutions. Republican leadership in the Senate is the least institutionalized among the four legislative parties. In this concluding section, I explain why leadership systems develop at different paces in the two chambers and offer a more general theory of leadership institutionalization.

The large size of the House creates logistical problems for leadership in coalition building and communication. The decentralization of the House over the last two decades renders a Rayburn-style approach to these tasks impossible, so the leadership has adapted accordingly. The Senate, on the other hand, can survive with personalized leadership; indeed, members expect it. If the past is the best indicator, personal leadership is more effective than institutionalized leadership in the Senate. The three most effective Republican leaders in the post–World War II period—Dirksen, Baker, and Dole—and the best Democratic leader, Lyndon Johnson, all had highly personalized leadership styles. Existing leadership institutions were largely ignored, and new institutions were established to meet their needs. Elaborate institutional structures only get in the way in the Senate. As one aide put it, "Senators want direct access to the top. They don't want to deal with some regional whip."

A theory of institutionalization must do more than explain interchamber differences; it must explain why institutions develop. Four sets of factors must be considered: the stability in the partisan control of the chamber, external conditions, member goals, and the skills of individual leaders, primarily their ability to utilize existing institutions.

Partisan Stability

Democrats have controlled the House since 1954. This stability promotes institutionalization in both parties, as uncertainty about the future control of the chamber is reduced. This assertion runs counter to existing theory, according to which increasing frustration in the minority party could break down leadership institutions (Peabody 1976). The more volatile nature of partisan control and the size of party margins in the Senate make it more difficult to establish durable institutions.

External Conditions

Two factors are central here: the party of the president and the nature of the party system. First, the president has some impact on the institutionalization of leadership. If the president is relatively popular, the leaders' job of passing his agenda is aided by lobbying from the president and pressure from public opinion. Therefore, the need for strong leadership institutions may be more acute for the party that does not control the presidency. A more important factor is the weak party system, which requires each member of Congress to operate as an independent entrepreneur (Cooper and Brady 1981a). When members' electoral fortunes are only loosely tied to the party, the task of leadership is greatly complicated. Without control over the ultimate sanction, the party is unable to prevent each member from paddling his or her own political canoe in the legislature.

Member Goals

Members place individual and collective demands on the leadership. They want to vote as they wish, to go home when they wish, and to help form the legislative agenda when they have strong policy interests. Collectively, they want leadership that can mobilize coalitions to pass important legislation. Most aspects of today's service-based leadership meet these needs. The only component of institutionalized leadership that does not fit this picture is the leadership ladder, which forces members to sacrifice future career options.

Members are willing to support the ladder if the leadership is satisfying their current needs and if there is a reasonable expectation that collective goals will be met. Forming these expectations is not easy—information about the future behavior of candidates is at a premium in any election. Well-developed leadership institutions reduce information costs by allowing the rank and file to gain a clear picture of the leadership style of the candidate who is attempting to climb the ladder. In these cases, promoting from within becomes the low-risk alternative. Past leadership behavior allows members to make judgments about an "insider" candidate that may not be possible for an insurgent who has not served in the leadership. Edward Madigan's strong showing in the recent House Republican whip's race supports this observation. This decision context helps create leadership ladders.

Utilization

The skills and desires of individual leaders have a significant impact on the shape of leadership institutions; their actions determine whether institutions endure or fade away. When institutions become durable and highly complex, they develop a life of their own, but the process of evolution is highly unstable. Whether leaders maintain and develop existing institutions also has an impact on the emergence of leadership ladders. This link between durability, internal complexity, and the bound-edness of leadership can be presented as a hypothesis: leaders are promoted if they maintain and develop their current positions. If a leader is inef-fective in using the current office, it is not likely to become a springboard for higher office. Though a systematic test of this hypothesis is beyond the scope of this paper, anecdotal evidence supports the idea. Tip O'Neill, Tony Coelho, and Dick Cheney in the House and Robert Byrd, Lyndon Johnson, Robert Taft, and George Mitchell in the Senate all met this condition and climbed the leadership ladder. Ted Kennedy, Russell Long, Ted Stevens, and John McFall did not, and they were bumped off (though in McFall's case, personal scandal played a dominant role). Those who fall between these two extremes, such as Mansfield and Griffin in the Senate and Halleck and Carl Albert in the House, may or may not succeed or remain in office. In these cases, members who have already assumed a place on the career ladder will benefit from the institution building of their predecessors and be elected to the next rung on the ladder. If there is no ladder, other factors that are traditionally referred to—such as ideological diversity within the party, electoral losses, and personality—will predominate.

The theory describes tensions between individual and collective goals in Congress and the importance of external conditions: representatives pursuing individual goals, without a strong party system as an anchor, will continually press toward service-oriented, weak leadership. At the same time, leadership must be allowed to play an integrative role, to prevent legislative paralysis. If a balance is struck, institutionalized lead-ership can serve both individual and collective needs—a recipe for insti-tutional stability. If a compromise is not reached, institutional drift, or even chaos, may reign.

NOTES

1. The defeated candidate for Speaker has been recognized as the minority leader since 1883; the majority leader has been a distinct office since 1899 (prior to that, the Ways and Means Committee chair was considered the floor leader). The Repub-licans elected their first whip in 1897; the Democrats elected theirs in 1900 (Ripley 1967, 24–38).

2. Since this article was written, Dick Cheney became Secretary of Defense and Newt Gingrich was elected by a narrow 87–85 margin over Edward Madigan. This election appears to undermine my arguments that Republican leadership in the House has become more durable and, as I argue below, more well bounded. As a self-proclaimed "bomb thrower," Gingrich clearly intends to change the whip's duties, changes which would violate the second condition of durability. His lack of experience in lower leadership positions also violates the newly emerging boundedness of Re-publican leadership, which had observed rigid leadership ladders in the 1980s.

However, three factors reveal the highly idiosyncratic nature of this move. First, many Republicans believed they needed a strong spokesman to exploit the opportunities presented by Speaker Jim Wright's difficulties. As the initiator of the Wright investigation, Gingrich was the logical choice. Second, the Republicans had just gone through a leadership shuffle following Whip Trent Lott's election to the Senate. The newly elected conference chair, Jerry Lewis (Calif.), was urged by Bob Michel and others not to run, in order to minimize intraparty strife. "If he had, it would have set off another competition to succeed him and likely a chain reaction of lower-level leadership races. 'We would have spent the next two months rearranging the chairs of our leadership and not moving forward on our programs,' Lewis said" (*Congressional Quarterly Weekly Report* 18 March 1989, 563). Many insiders indicated to me that Lewis would have won had he run. Finally, some Republicans were not willing to vote for Madigan because of a regional imbalance (he and Michel are both from Illinois). That Madigan lost by only two votes is strong testimony to the institutionalization of leadership among House Republicans.

3. In July 1988, I conducted interviews with twelve top-level staffers and former staffers in the House and Senate leadership. Ten interviews were conducted in person and two over the phone; they ranged in length from 25 to 55 minutes. Unattributed quotes used in this article are from these interviews.

4. The whip system was reinstituted briefly in 1987 when the Republicans were back in the minority. A leadership aide said that each senator who volunteered (nine in all) became a regional whip. Once again, their duty was primarily floor coverage, but the system did not work because the regional whips were never there when Whip Alan Simpson needed them. The aide said, "When I would call the senators' offices to get them onto the floor for their four hour shift, their administrative assistant would often say, 'Oh, I didn't know he was a regional whip.' They didn't take the job too seriously."

5. Leadership in the nineteenth-century House was permeable, unstable, and transitory. There was no identifiable ladder, and prospective leaders did not serve long apprenticeships, to say nothing about training in lower leadership positions.

6. Development is not always linear. A leadership system may show signs of reaching the third stage only to sink back to the second (as with the Senate Republicans in the mid-1970s). For example, leadership positions become less desired as a party moves from being relatively competitive in the institution to being a small minority. On the other hand, the value of minority leadership increases when the president is of the same party.

7. With the expanded size of the whip system, only a small percentage of those who serve in the system win top positions. Of the 122 Democrats and 70 Republicans who served in the leadership from 1973 to 1988, fewer than a dozen held the positions of whip, floor leader, or Speaker.

8. The move from regional whip to at-large whip is clearly a step up the leadership ladder. In the past decade, ten have made the move in this direction and only one has made the opposite move.

9. In 1987, Dick Cheney moved without opposition from the number four (Policy Committee chair) to the number three position (Conference Committee chair), and Jerry Lewis, the "insider" candidate, moved from the number five position (Research Committee chair) to the number four position. The two top contenders for the Research Committee chair were ladder climbers from the whip system: Steve Bartlett of Texas, who had moved up from regional whip to deputy whip, and the winner, Mickey Edwards, who had moved up from regional whip to head regional whip of

the western and plains states. The "new stability" was supported again in the leadership shuffle following Whip Lott's election to the Senate in 1988. Michel and Cheney were unopposed for the top two spots, and Lewis and Edwards both moved up one notch (in the race for conference chair, Lewis defeated Lynn Martin, the former vice chair of the conference, 85–82; Edwards was unopposed for Policy Committee chair (*Congressional Quarterly Weekly Report*, 10 December 1988, 3474–75).

10. Although there is almost no difference in the length of time that members hold the top leadership positions in the House and in the Senate, there is large difference in the average length of apprenticeship for House and Senate leaders. Since 1900, House Democrats have served an average of 25.9 years before being elected Speaker and 18.9 years before being elected floor leader; for the Republicans, the averages were 22.4 and 16.8 years for those top two positions. The apprenticeship in the Senate is approximately half as long: Democrats had served an average of 9.2 years before being elected floor leader and 6.5 years before being elected whip; Republicans, 14.7 and 5.9 years.

11. The stability of the Democratic whip system changed in the One-Hundredth Congress, with only three whips carried over from the Ninety-ninth Congress and five new whips appointed. The dramatic difference in the tenure of Democratic and Republican whips can be explained by the practice in the Republican system of assigning all freshman senators to the whip system.

12. Nonetheless, the two top contenders for majority leader in the 101st Congress, Inouye and Mitchell, were third and fourth in the leadership hierarchy in the 100th Congress, respectively. At lower levels there is some indication of an escalator; for example, Inouye moved to the number three position, secretary of the conference, after serving several terms as an assistant whip. Byrd moved from conference secretary to whip and, in 1989, Alan Dixon was elected chief deputy whip after serving in the whip system since 1981.

13. Baker was a surprise winner over Griffin in 1976; he did not even announce his campaign until a day and a half before the election, according to one aide. Stevens, on the other hand, was not expected to win. An aide said, "We were as surprised as hell that he did as well as he did." Dole won the final tally 28–25 on the fourth ballot in a tight five-way race (*Congressional Quarterly Weekly Report*, 1 December 1984, 3025).

14. This information comes from an internal document of the Federal Election Commission (FEC) that my research assistant, Patrick Sellers, acquired through great persistence. The dollar figures reported here were tabulated from the FEC's figures for PAC receipts, disbursements, and cash on hand.

15. Of the total receipts from 1984 to 1988, 56.1 percent were from Dole's, Kemp's, and Gephardt's PACs; most of this money probably went for their presidential campaigns rather than congressional leadership activities. On the other hand, support for colleagues' campaigns by aspiring leaders is understated by the data on leadership PACs reported here. Some aspiring leaders do not establish separate PACs for these purposes. For example, in his campaign for chair of the Policy Committee in 1987, Duncan Hunter contributed $60,000 from his own campaign funds and campaigned for at least twenty members, activity that would not be reported in this FEC data (Hook 1987, 962; also see Sorauf 1988, 174–81).

16. Data collected by the author for the leadership; other figures from tables 5–9, 5–2, and 5–5 in Ornstein, et al. 1987. I am not entirely confident that the figures in the clerk's report and the secretary's report cover all the money appropriated to the leadership. For example, appropriations for the minority and majority leaders in the

Senate appear to have been included in the conference monies before 1973, at which point they become a separate line item. The accounting is further complicated by changes from annual to biannual to quarterly reporting.

17. The aide pointed out that Stevens's more important role was behind the scenes, especially in negotiations with the Republican committee chairs and the Democratic minority. He said, "Stevens is one, if not the only, person who can talk to Robert C. Byrd and get him to understand something that he doesn't want to understand or cut a deal with him." He also played a central role in improving communication with the Republican party in the House.

18. Robert Byrd called Cranston the "best nose counter in the Senate" (*Wall Street Journal*, 15 March 1977); also see Byrd's favorable comments in the *Congressional Record* S4496 (2 May 1980) and Robert Lindsay "Dark Horse from California," in the *New York Times Magazine*, 4 December 1983.

19. As Roger Davidson (1989) demonstrates, Senate leadership is far less likely to initiate multiple referrals and is more likely to ratify agreements already reached by committee chairs. On the other hand, the practice increased the powers of leadership in the House by "strengthening their role in centralizing and coordinating the House's workload." In both instances, a balance is struck between member and collective interests.

20. Others have also contested this assertion as it relates to the House as a whole (Cooper and Brady 1981a; Schmidhauser 1973).

REFERENCES

Baker, Ross K. 1989. "Growth and Development of Leadership PACs in Congress." Paper presented at the annual meeting of the Midwest Political Science Association, Chicago.

Brown, Lynne P., and Robert L. Peabody. 1987. "Patterns of Succession in the House Democratic Leadership: The Choices of Wright, Foley, Coelho, 1986." Paper presented at the annual meeting of the American Political Science Association, Chicago.

Calmes, Jacqueline. 1987. "The Hill Leaders: Their Places on the Ladder." *Congressional Quarterly Weekly Report*, 3 January.

Calmes, Jacqueline, and Rob Gurwitt. 1987. "Profiles in Power: Leaders without Portfolio." *Congressional Quarterly Weekly Report*, 3 January.

Caro, Robert A. 1982. *The Path to Power: The Years of Lyndon Johnson*. New York: Knopf.

Cohen, Richard E. 1982. "Nearly Anonymous Insiders Play Key Roles as Aides to Congress's Leaders." *National Journal*, 11 September.

Connelly, William F. 1988. "The House Republican Policy Committee: Then and Now." Paper presented at the annual meeting of the American Political Science Association, Washington, D.C.

Cooper, Joseph, and David W. Brady. 1981a. "Institutional Context and Leadership Style: The House from Cannon to Rayburn." *American Political Science Review* 75:411–25.

Cooper, Joseph, and David W. Brady. 1981b. "Toward a Diachronic Analysis of Congress." *American Political Science Review* 75:988–1006.

Davidson, Roger. 1989. "Multiple Referrals of Legislation in the U.S. Senate." *Legislative Studies Quarterly* 14: 375–92.

Deering, Christopher J. 1986. "Leadership in the Slow Lane." *PS* 19:37–42.

Dodd, Lawrence C. 1979. "The Expanded Roles of the House Democratic Whip System: The Ninety-third and Ninety-fourth Congresses." *Congressional Studies* 7:27–56.

Dodd, Lawrence C., and Terry Sullivan. 1983. "Majority Party Leadership and Partisan Vote Gathering: The House Democratic Whip System." In *Understanding Congressional Leadership,* edited by Frank H. Mackaman. Washington, D.C.: Congressional Quarterly Press.

Ehrenhalt, Alan. 1987. "Influence on the Hill: Having It and Using It." *Congressional Quarterly Weekly Report,* 3 January.

Granat, Diane. 1984. "Dole Elected Majority Leader; Simpson Wins GOP Whip Job." *Congressional Quarterly Weekly Report,* 1 December.

Hammond, Susan Webb. 1988. "Committee and Informal Leaders in the House of Representatives." Paper presented at the annual meeting of the Midwest Political Science Association, Chicago.

Hibbing, John R. 1988. "Legislative Institutionalization with Illustrations from the British House of Commons." *American Journal of Political Science* 32:681–712.

Hinckley, Barbara. 1970. "Congressional Leadership Selection and Support: A Comparative Analysis." *Journal of Politics* 32:268–87.

Hook, Janet. 1986. "House Leadership Elections: Wright Era Begins." *Congressional Quarterly Weekly Report,* 13 December.

Hook, Janet. 1987. "House Prepares for Leadership Shuffle." *Congressional Quarterly Weekly Report,* 16 May.

Jones, Charles O. 1970. *The Minority Party in Congress.* Boston: Little, Brown.

Loomis, Burdett A. 1984. "Congressional Careers and Party Leadership in the Contemporary House of Representatives." *American Journal of Political Science* 28:180–202.

Loomis, Burdett A. 1988. "Political Skills and Proximate Goals: Career Development in the House of Representatives." Paper presented at the annual meeting of the American Political Science Association, Washington, D.C.

Mackaman, Frank H., and Richard C. Sachs. 1988. "The Congressional Leadership Research Project: A Status Report." Paper presented at the annual meeting of the Midwest Political Science Association, Chicago.

Menefee Libey, David. 1990. "The Politics of Party Organization: The Democrats from 1968–1986." Ph.D. dissertation, University of Chicago.

Nelson, Garrison. 1977. "Partisan Patterns of House Leadership Change, 1789–1977." *American Political Science Review* 71:918–39.

Oleszek, Walter J. 1985. "History and Development of the Party Whip System in the U.S. Senate." Senate Document 98–45. Washington, D.C.: Government Printing Office.

Ornstein, Norman J., Thomas E. Mann, and Michael J. Malbin. 1987. *Vital Statistics on Congress, 1987–1988.* Washington, D.C.: Congressional Quarterly Press.

Peabody, Robert L. 1976. *Leadership in Congress: Stability, Succession, and Change.* Boston: Little, Brown.

Polsby, Nelson W. 1968. "The Institutionalization of the House of Representatives." *American Political Science Review* 62:144–68.

Riddick, Floyd M. 1985. "Majority and Minority Leaders of the Senate: History and Development of the Offices of Floor Leaders." Senate Document 99–3. Washington, D.C.: Government Printing Office.

Ripley, Randall B. 1964. "The Party Whip Organization in the United States House of Representatives." *American Political Science Review* 58:561–76.

Ripley, Randall B. 1967. *Party Leaders in the House of Representatives.* Washington, D.C.: Brookings Institution.

Schmidhauser, John R. 1973. "An Exploratory Analysis of the Institutionalization of Legislatures and Judiciaries." In *Legislatures in Comparative Perspective,* edited by Allan Kornberg. New York: David McKay.

Sinclair, Barbara. 1983. *Majority Leadership in the U.S. House.* Baltimore: Johns Hopkins Press.

Smith, Steven S. 1985. "New Patterns of Decision Making in Congress." In *The New Directions in American Politics,* edited by John E. Chubb and Paul E. Peterson. Washington, D.C.: Brookings Institution.

Smith, Steven S., and Stanley Bach. 1988. "Craftsmanship on Capitol Hill: The Pattern of Diversity in Special Rules." Paper presented at the annual meeting of the Midwest Political Science Association, Chicago.

Smith, Steven S., and Marcus Flathman. 1989. "Managing the Senate Floor: Complex Unanimous Consent Agreements since the 1950s." *Legislative Studies Quarterly* 14: 349–74.

Sorauf, Frank J. 1988. *Money in American Elections.* Glenview, Ill.: Scott, Foresman.

Chapter 14

Patterns of Succession in House Democratic Leadership: Foley, Gephardt, and Gray, 1989

LYNNE P. BROWN
and ROBERT L. PEABODY

> *Let no man arrogate to himself the almighty presumption of judging another's integrity—but let none shrink from the unforgiving mirror of his own.*
>
> *No other can pronounce with certainty whether your public career has been a faithful extension of yourself and what you most truly believe—or the extent to which you may have temporized with external truth, made a god of popularity, muted your message or defiled your dream.*
>
> *Nobody has to tell you. You know. In the quiet recesses of your soul, a still, small voice repeats the verdict in almost deafening tones. And no clamorous overplay of noisy self-justification can silence it.*
>
> —Jim Wright
> *Reflections of a Public Man*

"Let me give you back this job you gave to me as a propitiation for all of this season of bad will that has grown up among us" (*Congressional Record,* 31 May 1989, H2248). With these words, spoken to a packed and tense House chamber on 31 May 1989, James Claude Wright, Jr. (D., Tex.), became the first Speaker in the two-hundred-year history of the United States to be forced to resign his office.

This chapter is based on a paper prepared for delivery at the annual meeting of the American Political Science Association, San Francisco, 30 August–2 September 1990. Copyright © 1990 by the American Political Science Association. It is reprinted by permission.

319

Wright's announcement, expected for days, was the culmination of a year-long investigation into the ethics of the Speaker's financial dealings. Six weeks earlier, the House Committee on Standards of Official Conduct had charged Wright with sixty-nine possible violations of House rules. The charges centered on three areas of inquiry: Wright's relations with Texas businessman George Mallick; the terms under which Wright's wife, Betty, received a salary and other benefits from an investment corporation set up by the Mallicks and Wrights; and the Speaker's bulk sales of a paperback book of his speeches and writings, *Reflections of a Public Man* (1984) (Barry 1989; *CQ Almanac* 1989:36–40).

Wright's speech to the House of Representatives followed by five days the announcement by the third-ranking leader in the Democratic House hierarchy, Majority Whip Tony Coelho (D., Calif.), that he, too, was resigning from the House rather than face a possible prolonged investigation into a junk bond deal he had entered into with special interest support (Barry 1989). The resignations of two of the top three House Democratic leaders would result in a wholesale reordering of House majority leadership within twenty-two days. This upheaval was rare in congressional history, rarer still in the House of Representatives, where changes in Democratic leadership traditionally have followed an orderly and fairly predictable path (Peabody 1976; Nelson 1977; Brown and Peabody 1987).

How did the Democrats respond to the forced overhaul of their leadership? Who succeeded in advancing up the leadership ladder? Who failed and why? What do the House Democratic contests of 1989 reveal about the enduring and changing nature of congressional leadership? What are the longer-range consequences for the House of Representatives and legislative policy-making in a divided-government framework (Mayhew 1989)? These are the basic questions this chapter seeks to address.

PATTERNS OF LEADERSHIP SUCCESSION

Earlier works (Peabody 1967, 1976; Brown and Peabody 1987) have chronicled the tendency toward leadership stability, especially among majority Democrats, in the modern Congress. In his examination of changes in party leadership in the House and Senate from 1955 to 1974 and in subsequent studies, Peabody finds that incumbent leaders are rarely challenged, with two partial exceptions: House Republican minority leaders (Halleck versus Martin in 1959 and Ford versus Halleck in 1965), and Senate Democratic whips (Long in 1969 and Kennedy in 1971). In the event of a vacancy in any major congressional leadership position, the next ranking leader usually advances within the hierarchy to fill the empty post. From 1955 to 1974 at least, Republicans were more prone to contested leadership races in both Houses. The tendency for contests in all four congressional parties, however, may be enhanced if patterns of succession became more complicated in the postreform Congress (Ripley 1967, 1969; Jones 1970; Peabody 1976; Canon 1989).

Increasingly, leadership in the House of Representatives tends to run in cycles of six to ten years or longer. Speaker Sam Rayburn of Texas and Majority Leader John McCormack of Massachusetts hold the endurance record for sustained leadership: twenty-one years in tandem from 1940 to 1961. They led the majority for all but four of those years (the two Republican-controlled Congresses, the Eightieth from 1947 to 1948 and the Eighty-third from 1953 to 1954). After Rayburn's death, McCormack rose to the speakership and served from 1961 to 1970, to be succeeded, in turn, by his majority leader, Carl Albert of Oklahoma. Albert was the first Democratic leader to advance from whip to majority leader to Speaker. He served in the top leadership position from 1971 until his retirement in 1976. Thomas P. "Tip" O'Neill of Massachusetts was whip from 1971 to 1972 and majority leader from 1973 to 1976. He capped his lengthy leadership career with ten years (the longest continuous record of service) as Speaker from 1977 to 1986. At least until Jim Wright's performance in the One-Hundredth Congress, O'Neill was generally accorded the reputation of being the strongest Speaker since Rayburn.[1]

With this House Democratic pattern established, Democratic members of the House at the beginning of the One-Hundredth Congress (1987–88) widely assumed that their newly elected leaders, Speaker Jim Wright of Texas, Majority Leader Thomas S. Foley of Washington, and Majority Whip Tony Coelho of California, were launching another potentially decade-long cycle as the House majority leadership team (table 14-1). All three of these top lawmakers had won the clear support of the Democratic Caucus (Wright and Foley rising uncontested from their previous positions; Coelho winning the first elective whip race in a strong showing against two other candidates: 167 votes to 78 and 15 for the other two). At ages sixty-five, fifty-eight, and forty-five, Wright, Foley, and Coelho were considered to be in their political prime. They were highly esteemed by most of their Democratic colleagues and, in temperament and operating styles, complemented each other quite well.[2] The House Republican party, despite being headed by competent and proven leaders, especially Robert Michel of Illinois, minority leader since 1980, seemed destined to retain their minority status well into the 1990s, if not beyond.

The One-Hundredth Congress proved to be a highly productive one in which a great proportion of the legislative agenda was determined by

Table 14-1. *The Changing Democratic House Leadership*

	1986	1987	1988	1989
Speaker	Thomas P. O'Neill, Jr. (Mass.)	James C. Wright, Jr. (Tex.)	James C. Wright, Jr. (Tex.)	Wright/Foley (Wash.) [a]
Majority leader	James C. Wright, Jr. (Tex.)	Thomas S. Foley (Wash.)	Thomas S. Foley (Wash.)	Richard A. Gephardt (Mo.)
Whip	Thomas S. Foley (Wash.)	Tony Coelho (Calif.)	Tony Coelho (Calif.)	Williams H. Gray, III (Pa.)
Chief deputy whip	Bill Alexander (Ark.)	David E. Bonior (Mich.)	David E. Bonior (Mich.)	David E. Bonior (Mich.)
Caucus chair	Richard A. Gephardt (Mo.)	Richard A. Gephardt (Mo.)	William H. Gray, III (Pa.)	Steny Hoyer (Md.)
Caucus vice chair	Mary Rose Oakar (Ohio)	Mary Rose Oakar (Ohio)	Steny Hoyer (Md.)	Vic Fazio (Calif.)
DCCC chair	Tony Coelho (Calif.)	Beryl F. Anthony (Ark.)	Beryl F. Anthony (Ark.)	Beryl F. Anthony (Ark.)

[a]Wright announced his plans to resign on 31 May 1989; Foley was elected Speaker on 6 June 1989.

Democrats, with the Reagan White House and Republican minorities in Congress playing a diminished role (Sinclair 1989). In the Senate, Democrats had regained control in 1986 after being out of the majority for six years, and they, too, were led by a new, innovative leader, George Mitchell of Maine. Yet by the late spring of 1989, this promising picture of stable, assertive, and effective leadership had turned into a near nightmare for the House Democrats. The attacks on Wright's ethics, which first surfaced in the spring of 1987, steadily grew and widened until by May of 1989 House Democrats abandoned almost all pretense that he could survive as Speaker.

As they prepared for the disgrace of Speaker stepping down, House Democrats were dealt another blow: the announcement by Majority Whip Coelho that he, too, would resign from the House rather than face a lengthy ethics investigation into his financial affairs. (He had failed to disclose a $50,000 loan and profits from an investment in junk bonds.) Uneasy about the prospects of a prolonged inquiry and unsure that in a future secret ballot his colleagues would be willing to advance him to the number two position of majority leader, Coelho decided to leave the House and seek his fortune in investment banking in New York (Jackson 1990). Democratic lawmakers were deeply chagrined by the prospect of having to replace two of their top three elders, both of whom had been tarnished by ethics scandals. Congress—House and Senate—had been through months of brutish partisan combat; the task facing the House Democrats was to reconstruct their leadership and to do so quickly and in a way that blurred memory of reasons for the openings in the lineup in the first place. A major concern was whether the leadership troubles would affect Democratic prospects in a series of upcoming special elections as well as the 1990 races.[3]

Contests for leadership posts are among the most fiercely fought conflicts in Congress in spite of their low visibility (Brown and Peabody 1987). The outcomes often turn on personal rather than policy concerns. All four congressional parties tend to select ideological middlemen (Peabody 1976); still, the calculations involved in supporting a candidate can be highly complicated, touching on regional and generational factors, committee loyalties, assessments of future benefits, and leadership styles. Sometimes personal rivalries may reach back for decades.[4] The fact that leadership races are decided by secret ballot makes it difficult for the contestants themselves to be sure of who voted for whom and why. (Candidates usually build into their vote a certain amount of slippage due to misinterpretation of support or outright lying.)

The unprecedented circumstances that produced the midsession openings in the House Democratic leadership, complicated by the pressures of severe time restraints, made those races even more Byzantine than usual. For the past decade, most leadership contests in both bodies have been waged before the start of a congressional session, when members are not yet heavily involved with legislative duties and a sense of new beginnings is in the air. Normally also a long lead time permits campaigning for leadership positions; recent leadership races have extended over years, not months.[5] But here were prospective leaders forced to put together campaigns in the middle of a session in a matter of days.

Far from eager anticipation, the atmosphere surrounding the races in 1989 was one of broad-ranging uneasiness, intense fatigue, and not a little fear. As one House leader characterized the mood of the House: "Everyone was concerned about the future, *their* future. They were asking: How far is this going to go? Is this going to bring us all down?" All these factors—the first forced resignation of a Speaker in the history of the House, the resignation of the party whip, the taint of scandal surrounding the Democrats, the condensed time frame within which to select new leaders, the disheartened and anxious mood that pervaded Democratic councils—placed the leadership contests of 1989 in a special category. If there were ever a time when established patterns of succession might be challenged, June 1989 would have seemed to be that time.

THE RESIGNATION OF SPEAKER WRIGHT

On that last day of May in 1989 just before Speaker Wright asked to be heard on a question of personal privilege, the members had voted unanimously to approve two resolutions honoring the late Claude Pepper (D., Fla.), who had died the day before at the age of eighty-nine. The first resolution paid tribute to this cherished member of the House; the second permitted his remains to lie in state in the Rotunda of the Capitol—a rare honor. Pepper, chairman of the House Rules Committee, had become a legendary figure over his four decades in Congress. He had first won election to the Senate from Florida in 1936 but was defeated in the 1950 primary by George Smathers in a vitriolic and controversial campaign tinged with the tactics of McCarthyism. Pepper ran for the House successfully in 1962 and had retained his seat since then. A fervent champion of the elderly, he was one of the few members of Congress who could lay claim to a national constituency. Even as House members concluded their testimonial to this deceased colleague, rumors circulated that they were about to witness the final scene in the political death of their Speaker.

By turns theatrical, combative, and confessional, Jim Wright spoke for an hour almost to the minute to his colleagues in Congress, the Democrats boisterous at times, interrupting with applause, the Republicans more cynical and reserved. The Speaker defended himself against charges that he had used his high office for personal gain or deliberately circumvented House rules. He reflected on his leadership style and commented on the changes that had taken place in the institution he had made his home for thirty-four years. He climaxed his oration with an emotional plea for an end to the partisan hostilities—what he termed "the mindless cannibalism"—that had racked the House.

What led to the political demise of Jim Wright?[6] A number of factors seem to have played a role. In a world where personal relationships can advance or impede agendas and careers, Wright's personality was a volatile mix of partisan pride, steely determination, and a tendency to go it alone. Looking back, a cluster of events figured strongly in Wright's loss of support among his colleagues on both sides of the aisle.

On one level, Jim Wright could point to one of the most impressive records of a modern-day Speaker. On the domestic front, he had led the members of his party to craft an ambitious legislative agenda and then pass it. That agenda included antidrug legislation, welfare reform, aid for the homeless, a clean water act, and transportation and trade measures. In foreign affairs, Wright took the most activist stance of any twentieth-century Speaker, inserting himself directly in the negotiations surrounding the end of hostilities in Nicaragua. But his involvement in what the executive branch thought of as its exclusive preserve also earned Wright the enmity of the White House and other high government officials. One Democratic leadership aide pointed to Wright's direction of U.S. policy toward Central America as an example of where the Speaker "broke down the rules of the game. He crossed boundaries," observed the aide, "by getting into foreign policy. And Republicans cared a lot about that issue."[7]

Jim Wright was willing to pull every lever of power available to work his will in the House, but he was less willing or able to build the infrastructure of personal relationships that can sustain a leader through difficult times. As the attacks against him grew more public and intense, he did not have at his disposal a large reservoir of good will and personal loyalty. In the end, he could rely only on the Texas delegation and his top leadership lieutenants to stand by him. One senior Democratic House member and committee chairman observed of Wright's isolation: "We were friends, but he was a loner. He never came to me. He never called—'Give me five minutes.' A lot of people would have rallied around him, but we never got that phone call." The same refrain appears in the remarks of another powerful member and committee chairman: "He was so much of a loner. A decent guy, a friend of mine, but he became suspicious about a lot of people. With all due respect, Jim Wright, I think, lacked confidence in himself." Wright himself acknowledged the shortcomings of his leadership style in his resignation speech. Looking back on his career as Speaker, he asked himself, "Have I been too partisan, too insistent, too abrasive, too determined to have my way? Perhaps. Maybe so."

A series of questionable legislative maneuvers by Wright also worked to erode his political base with Republicans, and, eventually, with his own Democrats. In the fall of 1987, Wright indulged in a heavy-handed display of the Speaker's powers when, as presiding officer, he used House rules to invoke a long count on a critical vote on a budget reconciliation bill. By extending the voting time beyond the customary fifteen minutes, Wright allowed one of his aides to round up a junior Texan and persuade him, at considerable reluctance, to change his nay to aye. What first looked to be a stunning Democratic loss was converted into a dramatic 206–205 victory. House Republicans were furious and Newt Gingrich, the Georgia Republican who had earlier instigated ethics charges against Wright, gained further adherents to his cause, most notably Minority Leader Michel and Whip Dick Cheney (R., Wyo.) (Barry 1989).

A midwestern Republican who had good working relationships with many Democrats observed flatly: "Jim Wright would still be Speaker if he hadn't twisted Jim Chapman's arm, publicly, on that reconciliation vote. . . . Every member had to have some emotion—a gut feeling. It just plain wasn't right. It was a comprehensive demonstration of arrogance that went beyond what the rank-and-file member should have to stomach." A senior Democratic committee staff member sympathetic to Wright noted that after the reconciliation vote, "Republicans developed a bias against anything Wright was doing for fear that it would further advance his power as Speaker. I don't think any minority generated such a fear against any leader in such a short time going back for decades."

In February 1989, Wright was forced into a decision to allow a vote on a controversial pay raise bill (thereby dooming it to defeat), which angered members who felt that the Speaker had exposed them unnecessarily to a torrent of public criticism.[8] He lost the support of a number of his own party members. A ten-term Democrat on the Appropriations Committee flatly declared that the pay raise issue "cost him his job." He went on to say: "We could understand the pressure, but that was his job. Trying to protect his job, it cost him his position. If he had hung tough I think he'd still be here. They could have forgiven him a lot of things." Another Democrat, a liberal from the Northeast, observed of the pay raise: "The strategy was not thought out—the raise was too large, the procedure too cute. But Wright was unfairly blamed."

Then on 11 May 1989, in the midst of the final stages of the Ethics Committee investigation (formally launched a year earlier), Wright suffered a further setback when his chief legislative floor aide, John Mack, was forced to resign because of a crime of sixteen years earlier (a violent assault on a young woman) that was brought to light the week before in a story in the *Washington Post* (*CQ Almanac* 1989:39).

Beyond personal failings and legislative missteps, larger, broader forces were at work in the downfall of Jim Wright. Many members, mostly Democratic, blamed the media and the "feeding frenzy" that accompanied a controversial story.[9] A member of the leadership loyal to the Speaker spoke of lingering "anger" in the caucus over the media's treatment of Wright. "The press had gone overboard. They had gone after the Speaker. It was overkill." Another member, a senior southerner, referred to the "crucifixion" of the Speaker. Yet a third member, a southerner with leadership experience, agreed: "Jim Wright was, in my opinion, driven out by the media. They were hell-bent on driving him out. In the final days, it was the media that eroded his base of support in the House. The media never allowed this system to operate." In his book on the fall of the Speaker, *The Ambition and the Power,* John Barry makes a strong case for interpreting the ouster of Wright as a partisan coup, the result of both an overaggressive independent prosecutor, Chicago attorney Richard J. Phelan, and House Republicans led by Gingrich and his Conservative Opportunity Society, who saw a chance to exert some real power in the institution where they had been in the minority for thirty-five years.

Certainly, the fate of Jim Wright cannot be seen apart from the partisan power struggle that gripped Capitol Hill throughout the 1980s.[10] By the time the Ethics Committee took up the Wright case, the landscape was already littered with the political corpse of Robert Bork, and John Tower was soon to follow.[11] The bitter presidential campaign of 1988 had injected a new level of rancor and distrust in relations between the parties. A fitting denouement to the drama of Jim Wright's loss of the speakership was the victory in March 1989 of Newt Gingrich as the House Republicans' choice as whip to replace Dick Cheney (who had been appointed Secretary of Defense after the failed Tower nomination). Gingrich prevailed by two votes (87–85) despite Minority Leader Michel's support of Edward R. Madigan of Illinois. In the competing styles of these two candidates for the position of number two in their party leadership and likely heir apparent to Michel, House Republicans faced a clear choice: Gingrich, the partisan provocateur and public firebrand, versus Madigan, inside workhorse and legislative craftsman.[12]

An even broader interpretation of the events on Capitol Hill in 1988 and 1989 may be found in Benjamin Ginsberg and Martin Shefter's new book, *Politics by Other Means* (1990), in which they argue that our national government is locked in a cycle of divided rule that carries on most of its partisan and institutional wars by means other than electoral, such as media revelations, personal scandals, special prosecutors, and congressional investigations.

"THE HOUSE OF REPRESENTATIVES SHALL CHUSE THEIR SPEAKER"

Throughout 1988 and 1989, the relatively calm center in the swirling storm surrounding the Speaker and his troubles was Majority Leader Thomas S. Foley. He was untouched by scandal (although later he would be subjected to a Republican partisan smear). Cautious and prudent by nature, loyal to the speakership, respectful of the institution of the House and respected by the vast majority of its members, known as a bridge-builder and conciliator, Tom Foley was the heir apparent to Jim Wright for weeks before Wright announced he would resign rather than keep battling ethics accusations.

The formal transfer of power from Wright to Foley began on the morning of 6 June when the Democratic Caucus chose Foley as its nominee with no opposition. Wright offered his lieutenant's name in nomination. Tony Coelho, who was serving his last week in the House before resigning, gave one of the seconding speeches. In a parallel procedure, the Republican Conference chose Robert Michel, their minority leader, as their candidate for Speaker. When the full House met later that day to choose its Speaker, Foley was elected on a straight party-line vote of 251–164 to be the forty-ninth Speaker of the House. In ceremonial fashion, former Speaker Wright handed the gavel he had wielded for the past two and a half years to Speaker Foley.[13]

In one sense Foley's legislative career appears to be based on fortune; he always seems to be at the right place at the right time. But the perception that he has been lucky at each of the critical junctures of his career is a strong testament to his sagacity, measured style, and willingness to master both the substance of legislation and the process by which it is enacted.

Born in Spokane, Washington, on 6 March 1929, Foley attended Gonzaga High School, a Jesuit school, and after transferring to the University of Washington from Gonzaga University, received his B.A. degree in 1951 (table 14-2). He began law school then interrupted it to do graduate work in international affairs, but returned to earn his law degree in 1957. He began practicing law in Spokane, intending to follow in the footsteps of his father, Superior Court Judge Ralph Foley, a legendary figure in Spokane and the longest-serving judge in the state's history. The younger Foley served as a deputy prosecutor and then assistant

Table 14-2. Profile of Thomas S. Foley

District:	Washington (5)
Elected to Congress:	1964
Date of birth:	6 March 1929
Previous leadership positions:	Majority leader (1987–89)
	Majority whip (1981–86)
	Chairman of the caucus (1977–80)
	Chairman of the Democratic Study Group
	(1974–76)
Committee(s) and rank[a]	Agriculture Committee (2), previously (1)
(1 = chair):	House Administration (7)
Winning percentages in	1988 — 76%
last five elections:	1986 — 75%
	1984 — 70%
	1982 — 64%
	1980 — 52%
Voting ratings:[b]	ADA, 85
	AFL-CIO, 86
	ACU, 4

Source: This and subsequent profiles are from *Politics in America 1990,* edited by, Phil Duncan. Washington, D.C.: CQ Press. Voting ratings are from 1988.

[a] In the Ninety-ninth Congress.

[b] ADA, Americans for Democratic Action; ACU.

attorney general before coming to Washington, D.C., in 1961 to work as a clerk and special counsel of the Senate Committee on Interior and Insular Affairs under the chairmanship of Senator Henry M. (Scoop) Jackson (D., Wash.).

First elected to the House in 1964 as part of the Johnson landslide (although he was far from an eager candidate, filing for the race within minutes of the deadline and only after the importuning of his political mentors), Foley replaced Walter Horan, an eleven-term GOP conservative. This junior congressman developed an early reputation as a knowledgeable and issue-oriented legislator. Representing the wheat and apple growers of the Inland Empire of eastern Washington, Foley sought and obtained seats on the House Agriculture and Interior Committees, from which he could look after the interests of his constituents. Through the luck of the draw, he was the second of eleven Democratic freshmen who went on Agriculture and the third on Interior. A self-styled "middle-of-the-road" Democrat, Foley earned high marks from his colleagues for his mastery of the often arcane subject matter and complex politics of the issues under his committees' jurisdiction, particularly farm legislation. Over the years, he helped steer through Congress several major agricultural bills. And working with Senator Jackson, from his Interior Committee base, Foley was able to obtain a third powerhouse for Grand Coulee Dam—no mean feat for a freshman.

In 1974, in a pattern that was to be repeated fifteen years later, Foley rose to the chairmanship of the Agriculture Committee because a leader was deposed. One of the casualties of the reform sentiment brought to the House in the wake of Watergate was the elderly and conservative head of the Agriculture Committee, Bob Poage of Texas. With chairmanships now open to the approval of the caucus, House Democrats voted Poage out. Due to a number of retirements, Foley, with only ten years of seniority, was next in line. Foley was again the reluctant candidate; he had spoken in support of retaining Poage. But once the caucus acted, he accepted the chairmanship.

From there, Foley continued an incremental rise within the House hierarchy from chairman of the Democratic Study Group (1974–76), to chairman of the caucus (1977–80), to appointive whip in 1981.[14] The fact that he ascended uncontested in 1987 from whip to majority leader (as Jim Wright moved from majority leader to Speaker) was a testament to Foley's strength as a respected party leader and his skill at making his advancement look almost inevitable (Brown and Peabody 1987). For during the leadership contests of 1986, Tom Foley, though respected and well-liked, had no guarantee he could become floor leader, especially without opposition. Historical precedents offered few assurances. Of the past five whips, only three (Carl Albert, Hale Boggs, and Tip O'Neill) became floor leaders. Moreover, intensive multicandidate struggles for majority leader had occurred in 1970–71 and 1976 with, first, Hale Boggs of Louisiana (who had served as whip) and, later, Jim Wright (only a deputy whip) emerging as victors (Peabody 1976; Oppenheimer and Peabody 1977). Presumably, one or more senior members or committee chairmen such as Dan Rostenkowski or John Dingell could have challenged Foley for the majority leadership, but they did not (for reasons elaborated upon in Brown and Peabody 1987).

The principal factors behind Foley's success in moving up to the majority leadership included an organized, aggressive, yet low-key campaign conducted largely out of public view; the perception that Foley as majority leader would serve as a "balance wheel" to Jim Wright in terms of style, temperament, and approach to leadership; and the failure of any committed challengers to emerge to test Foley's support. Of course, one reason for a lack of competitors was the perception of Foley's imposing strength. As one high-ranked Democratic leader observed, "You don't have opponents for a reason. It's because opponents don't think they can win."

These same factors, with only modified nuances, were at work two years later in June 1989 as Foley emerged as the overwhelming consensus choice for Speaker. He had served as a capable floor leader and taken on some unusually tough assignments, including Democratic point man on budget negotiations. He had complemented, some said humanized, the House leadership team; Wright and Coelho both had a strong edge in their dealings with their colleagues and tended to be highly partisan. Tom Foley represented a kinder, gentler face to the members of his own party and to the Republicans. Although his soothingly nonpartisan style and cautious approach had come under criticism in the past, it seemed the perfect balm for a House riven by distrust and rancor.[15] His years in leadership had earned Foley an enormous amount of affection, trust, and respect. His colleagues had twice floated his name for national office, both in 1984 and 1988. In a 1988 survey of senior Hill staffers, Foley was named the most effective House member by a substantial margin.[16] And Foley had an added skill: he was good on television. Over the previous eight years, he had served as a major media spokesman for the House Democrats, and his relaxed style and low-key delivery was much better suited to the cameras than the intense demeanor, preachy tones, and rhetorical flourishes of Jim Wright. Nor had Wright's predecessor, Tip O'Neill, been particularly comfortable or adept with the media.

In a sign of how scurrilous the partisan climate had grown, Foley's ascension was to be marred by a controversy surrounding a memo prepared and distributed by the Republican National Committee (RNC) that attacked Foley and linked him to Rep. Barney Frank (D., Mass.), who had revealed his homosexuality in 1987. The memo was denounced by Republican leaders, including President Bush and, later, by RNC head Lee Atwater, and the staff member responsible for writing the document was fired. But bitterness and distrust continued to mark the dealings between the parties and provided an anxious backdrop for the remaining Democratic leadership races.

SORTING OUT THE OPTIONS: DEMOCRATIC HOUSE LEADERSHIP IN FLUX

Back in January 1989, when the 101st Congress began, hardly anyone believed Wright's hold on the speakership was at risk. But by the time the Ethics Committee reported its charges in mid-April, it was no longer a question of if, but when, Wright would step down. Democrats hoping to move up the leadership ladder began maneuvering for position in the post-Wright regime. It was a precedent-breaking time in the House. There were no blueprints to follow. No Speaker had ever been forced to resign. But the very fact that Democrats felt that the political ground was moving beneath their feet led them to take comfort in the known and tried and not risk more surprises. This yearning for a peaceful and predictable transition, along with Foley's popularity, explained the early emergence of the majority leader as Wright's uncontested successor. But what of the subsequent openings in the leadership lineup once Foley moved? As Jim Wright's troubles crystallized, but before Tony Coelho's grew more damaging, most Democratic members were probably in favor of a leadership transition that simply advanced incumbents up one notch. That would have elevated Foley to Speaker and Whip Tony Coelho to majority leader.

The Competition for Majority Leader

For many reasons, Tony Coelho, as whip, did not have the same "lock" on the position above him on the ladder as did Foley. As mentioned earlier, the House had seen two strongly fought battles for majority leadership. The progression from floor leader to Speaker has traditionally been so pronounced in the House that in choosing a majority leader, members know they are designating the heir presumptive to the Speaker. (That they knew this in 1986 when they chose Foley as leader helped to ease his ascension in 1989.) Moreover, while Foley had served in the formal leadership since 1977, Coelho had been whip for only two and a half years. These factors did not preclude elevating Coelho from whip to leader, but they made his rise much less assured.

Complicating the usual labyrinthine politics of leadership races was the uncertainty in the spring of 1989 about what positions would be open, and when, and the reluctance of most House Democrats (especially those contemplating a race themselves), while Speaker Wright still held office and was under attack, to speculate publicly about the prospects for leadership change in the future.

Coelho's hopes to rise unchallenged to the majority leadership were greatly diminished with the appearance of news stories in mid-April 1989 about profits he reaped as a result of a junk bond investment and the circumstances surrounding his obtaining a loan to finance the deal. It was just the sort of allegation to play into many members' misgivings about Coelho's dealings with wealthy donors to the Democratic party.[17] The stories, coming as they did in the midst of Wright's troubles over financial improprieties, sent a shiver down the collective spine of the members of the Democratic Caucus. Could the Democrats afford, possibly on the heels of their Speaker's resignation, to elevate to majority leader someone who might soon be facing similar charges? Coelho could not count on an uncontested step up to majority leader, and he might have to fend off a challenge to stay whip.

Coelho's problems further confused an already hazy leadership picture. Names surfaced as possible candidates for majority leader. Chief among them was Richard A. Gephardt of Missouri, chairman of the Democratic Caucus from 1985 to 1988, who had remained in the House after a losing bid for the Democratic presidential nomination in 1988. Widely perceived as "squeaky clean" and someone who had survived the intense personal and financial scrutiny of a presidential campaign, Gephardt combined political stature with ethical protection. But Gephardt, long a close associate, even a friend, of Tony Coelho, had signalled a reluctance to challenge him in a head-to-head race (Jackson 1990). (Weeks earlier, when it had looked more probable that Coelho could mount a successful bid for majority leader, Gephardt had considered running for whip as a way to get back in leadership.)

Losing Jim Wright of Texas, southern Democrats, the largest regional grouping in the party, wanted to continue to be represented in top leadership. Hence the entry of Ed Jenkins, a moderate conservative from Georgia first elected to the House in 1976 along with Gephardt and similarly a member of the powerful Ways and Means Committee. Jenkins had intermittently been mentioned for leadership over the last half-dozen years. After conferring with his southern colleagues, he was prepared to present himself as the South's candidate for leadership.

Other members were eyeing the possible openings on the leadership ladder and trying to assess their chances. When it appeared, for a time, that the whip position might not be open (i.e., Coelho would stay in the number three spot rather than risk a tight contest for the number two spot) and that the majority leadership might be the only opening, Dan Rostenkowski (D., Ill.) and John Dingell (D., Mich.) may have flirted with the prospects, as they had in 1986. Lee Hamilton of Indiana, a respected figure in the House and a lawmaker of unquestioned integrity, was also mentioned as a possible candidate. Hamilton had co-chaired the special joint committee that investigated the Iran-Contra affair in 1987 and was considered an expert on foreign policy and economics. But he quickly indicated he was not interested in a formal leadership post. Some members who were already on the ladder but aspired to higher posts also considered the majority leadership, even if briefly. Caucus Chair William Gray (D., Pa.) was one.

As Wright's situation grew more grave and Coelho came under intensified media attack, the prospect of leadership contests down the entire ladder became more probable. Furthermore, these would be "open" races that would entail a distinct calculus. As one leadership aide put it, "Once [a race is] open, a feeling sets in among members: Why not me?" The normal prelude to such contests—testing the waters, deciding on what position to run for, organizing support—was, of necessity—truncated, provisional, and conducted mostly out of view. No prospective leader felt comfortable mounting a full-blown, highly visible campaign that took as its premise the forced resignation of the Speaker of the House. As one leadership aide characterized this period, "Clearly there was going to be change. But it was a funny period. No one was really talking to one another. Everyone was eyeing everyone else. But no one was sure who was going for what."

The Competition for Majority Whip

Unlike the top two leadership posts, no clear line of succession for the whip had fully emerged by 1989. Until 1987, the whip was not even an elective position but one appointed by the Speaker in consultation with the majority leader. Appointed whips, of which Foley was the last, included John Brademas of Indiana (who had been chief deputy whip, another appointive post) and John McFall of California (who had pre-dated Bradermas as chief deputy whip). Tony Coelho, as already noted, had advanced to the post by election of the Caucus after serving as head of the Democratic Congressional Campaign Committee (1981–86). Perhaps if the majority whip had still been an appointive position, the chief deputy whip slot would have been viewed as the logical training ground for it. But once the whip was made elective, a different dynamic was at work. Certainly, the chairman of the caucus, elected by his party peers, could increasingly lay claim to consideration as holding the number four position in the hierarchy and, therefore, as in line for the whip.

This emerging precedent put the caucus chair, Bill Gray, in a beneficial position. Gray had been elected to the chairmanship only six months before, after an almost two-year campaign for the job against determined competitors.[18] Gray, a black minister from Philadelphia, began a sure-footed climb up the leadership ladder upon his arrival in the House in 1978 and was known to be ambitious for higher posts. The current chief deputy whip was seven-termer David E. Bonior of Michigan, who had been appointed to the position in a surprise move by Wright in 1987. Wright was looking for a liberal midwesterner to round out his leadership team, and Bonior fit the bill. Elected to the House in 1976, tapped for the Rules Committee in 1981, and chosen as one of seven whips in 1985, Bonior, too, was on a leadership track, albeit with a lower profile than Gray.

Even if an "everybody-move-one-rung-up" approach to the leadership changes in 1989 had been accepted as a way to achieve peace within the Democratic ranks, it would have pitted Bonior and Gray against each other in a contest for majority whip. But there were other forces at work in the House that made such a neat succession unlikely. For any member for whom the results of the 1986 leadership races had been a disappointment or represented thwarted ambition, here was a chance to try again, a chance that in a normal course of events would not have arisen for another decade but was now available within a sparse two and a half years. Though launched more or less discreetly, at least half a dozen campaigns were well underway the week before Jim Wright delivered his farewell address to the House. As one high-ranking Democratic leader observed: "This place is like stretched skin. If you step on it in one place, it sends vibrations to other places. You can't run a race for leadership in secret. The House is a ganglia of political nerves."

THE RACES TAKE SHAPE: THE RESIGNATION OF TONY COELHO

On 26 May, the Friday before the Memorial Day weekend, Tony Coelho released an exclusive to the *New York Times*:[19] effective 15 June, his forty-seventh birthday, he would resign from the House of Representatives. The publicly announced reason for his decision was that he did not want to put his colleagues or his family through a drawn-out investigation into his finances.

Coelho had long maintained that he did not feel wedded to the House, that he could envision a life after Congress. His powerful ambition was on display for all to see. Even before his first election to the House in 1978, he expressed reluctance at being just another member of Congress. From the moment he won the whip office in 1986, there was speculation about whether he would be content to follow the route of his predecessors and wait patiently in line for his chance at advancement. His hard-charging style quickly created some tensions within the newly installed leadership team in 1987 (Barry 1989). And there were reports even before the Wright investigation that Coelho would not wait the possible ten to twenty years it might take to reach the speakership, but instead would consider challenging Foley directly for the job if and when Wright left office. A prime motive behind Coelho's decision to resign, therefore, was his assessment that questions about his junk bond deal were going to keep him from moving up the leadership ladder. And if he couldn't move up, he'd rather exit.

Several of Coelho's colleagues saw this reasoning at work. Said one: "If Coelho had stayed, he might have been kept majority whip. His ego couldn't stand it. So he got out." Another member, a liberal from the East, had the same analysis: "[The junk bond disclosure] was enough to interfere with his advancement to majority leader—that was the crucial thing, I think. Otherwise, he'd have been a whip forever. He would have had the problem of persuading others to vote for him for majority leader, on a secret ballot. Coelho couldn't have been jumped over without suffering greatly in terms of effectiveness. You have to emphasize the importance of the secret ballot. Democratic members would be thinking, 'Why take a chance?'" The money he might make for himself and his family as a New York investment banker was probably a strong secondary consideration in Coelho's decision to resign (Jackson 1990).

Coelho had told a number of his colleagues of his plans the day before the story ran in the *Times*. He let Gephardt know so that his friend could be released from his personal pledge not to run against him for majority leader. Absent Coelho, the way was now clear for Gephardt to escalate his own campaign. Word also got to several of the leading candidates for the position Coelho currently held. The whip spot would be vacant as of 15 June. That message, in a moment, starkly clarified what had been murky and inchoate campaigns (almost pseudocampaigns) for an office that, up to then, no one knew for certain was going to be vacant. Now, regardless of what happened to Wright and the shuffling at the higher rungs of the ladder, this much was clear: there was going to be a multiple-candidacy race for whip.

The news had an immediate and galvanizing impact on the two members who had given the most thought to a contest for whip: Caucus Chair Gray and Chief Deputy Whip Bonior. Within hours of hearing the news from Coelho, their offices were transformed into operational headquarters, with staff manning the phones to seek the support of as many members as possible. It was no easy task; this was the holiday weekend, and members were flung across the country in their respective districts and some across the globe as part of traveling delegations. In a sign that the two candidates anticipated imminent movement within the leadership (even if they were not sure when and how), they had each taken the precaution of contacting all members before the start of the holiday recess to find out where they could be reached outside Washington.

At the time Coelho made his decision, it was also widely assumed that Jim Wright would soon be stepping down. On 31 May, five days after the Coelho announcement, he did. The shaken Democrats were now faced with the prospect of rebuilding their leadership. After the Democratic Caucus met to select a nominee for Speaker on Tuesday, 6 June (the date set by Wright when he would relinquish his speakership), they would reconvene the next Wednesday, 14 June (the day before Coelho was to resign), to choose a new majority leader and majority whip as well. Depending on the outcome of those races, other contests might also be in the offing.

A CONSENSUS CHOICE FOR MAJORITY LEADER

With the departure of Jim Wright, it would be only the third time in this century that a state of the old Confederacy would not be represented in the leadership. Ed Jenkins of Georgia (table 14-3) described as "the perennial Dixie bridesmaid but never a bride,"[20] considered himself the southern candidate for leadership, representing a regional constituency in apparent danger of losing its historic place at the top echelons of the congressional party. Elected to Congress in 1976 from a northern Georgia district of farms and factory towns, Jenkins was known for behind-the-scenes negotiating skills. Conservative in political temperament but personally friendly with many liberals, he had been tapped by leadership on several occasions, most recently to serve on the Iran-Contra investigating committee (1987). He was eighth-ranking member of the Ways and Means Committee and had played a strong role in many of the issues under its jurisdiction, particularly trade and taxes. He considered Dan Rostenkowski, his chairman, a likely supporter.

The member to emerge as the overwhelming favorite for majority leader, however, was Richard Gephardt (table 14-4). By the first week in June, he was clearly the man to beat. Gephardt was one of those congressmen marked as a rising star almost from the moment he entered the House in 1976. He had been chosen as protégé by fellow Missourian Richard Bolling, an influential force in House politics and later chairman of the Rules Committee. Bolling had helped Gephardt secure a seat on the Ways and Means Committee in his first term. By the time he ran for majority leader, he ranked ninth on that committee, one slot below Jenkins. He also served on the Budget Committee for five years before being elected chairman of the Democratic Caucus in 1984.

In a career move unusual for House members, Gephardt threw his hat in the presidential ring in 1987, winning the Iowa caucuses but losing steam by the crucial string of "super-Tuesday" primaries in the spring of 1988. In his bid for the presidency, he received the endorsement of scores of his fellow House members, many of whom traveled throughout the country to appear with him at rallies and fundraisers. As a result of his campaign, he became one of the few members of the House to build a national reputation. By the time the Democrats met on 14 June to choose the majority leader, the result was all but a foregone conclusion. Gephardt received more than twice as many votes as Jenkins, 181 to 76.

Table 14-3. Profile of Ed Jenkins

District:	Georgia (9)
Elected to Congress:	1976
Date of birth:	4 January 1933
Previous leadership positions:	None
Committee(s) and rank (1 = chair):	Budget (4) Ways and Means (8)
Winning percentages in last five elections:	1988—63% 1986—100% 1984—67% 1982—77% 1980—68%
Voting ratings:	ADA, 45 AFL-CIO, 64 ACU, 54

What was behind Gephardt's success? First he already had a formidable base of support among his colleagues, a large number of whom had backed his bid for president. As one supporter put it: "Ed Jenkins had no chance. Gephardt was just too strong. Members thought: 'I endorsed him to be my candidate for the presidency; how could I not support him for leader?'" That Gephardt had endured the pressures and scrutiny of a presidential campaign, and maintained a clean bill of health, was an important factor for Democrats worried about the political fallout of the ethics scandals surrounding their leaders. His high national profile (for a House member) also added luster to his selection. To allay the fears of his colleagues about his immediate future ambitions, Gephardt pledged he would not be a candidate for president in 1992.

If Gephardt had a solid growing reputation external to the House, his credentials and personal ties to members were also of a high order. As former Caucus chair, he had experience in leadership politics; he had already shown a style—low key, earnest, willing to listen—well suited to advancement in the House. He was personally well liked and, with more of a partisan edge than Foley, seen as good counterpoint to the new Speaker. Moreover, the Missourian was known as a thoughtful and hard-working legislator. He had played an early, formative role in the tax reform effort and had taken the lead on competitive trade issues. Richard Gephardt epitomized the driving, pragmatic, issue-oriented, media-conscious, new breed of political leader. As one Democratic leadership aide put it, "Gephardt gave us an outsider's purity and an insider's stability."

Fresh from the campaign trail for the highest office in the land, Gephardt also was able to put together in short order a well-organized, highly

Table 14-4. Profile of Richard A. Gephardt

District:	Missouri (3)
Elected to Congress:	1976
Date of birth:	31 January 1941
Previous leadership positions:	Chairman of the caucus (1985–88)
	Deputy Whip (head of task forces) (1983–84)
Committee(s) and rank (1 = chair):	Ways and Means (9)[a]
Winning percentages in last five elections:	1988—63%
	1986—69%
	1984—100%
	1982—78%
	1980—78%
Voting ratings:	ADA, 75
	AFL-CIO, 92
	ACU, 10

[a] In the 100th Congress and 101st Congress, 1st session.

disciplined campaign for majority leader. He had recently hired Thomas J. O'Donnell, a top operative from the Democratic Congressional Campaign Committee (DCCC), to begin planning for the next possible presidential bid in 1992. Instead, this staff member, the weekend before he he was officially on board, found himself intensely involved in the logistics of an internal leadership context. Gephardt, working with O'Donnell and two other staffers, made round-the-clock telephone calls contacting 190 members in three days. While the two endeavors—running for president of the United States and running for majority leader of the House— clearly have their separate strategies and demands, the fact that Gephardt could command an experienced and savvy staff helped him mount, in a very short time frame, an effective vote-getting operation. (In House leadership races, top staff persons are more likely to play an important support role than their Senate counterparts. This is largely a function of the need to keep track of a greater number of members.)

By contrast, Jenkins ran a low-key, lackluster campaign. On 1 June, he sent out a letter to all Democrats announcing he was running for leader and asking for their support. He offered himself as someone who could "bridge the gap across ideological and geographical distinctions" and warned that members "need look no further than recent national elections to witness the results when citizens with moderate or conservative views perceive that our party has excluded them." But Jenkins did not solicit votes in a visible or aggressive manner. As one observer reflected," Jenkins announced, but didn't do much. There was not much going on from his end." One aide for an incumbent member of the Democratic leadership announced that Jenkins was more attuned to the process of passing legislation than running for a leadership post. "You know how legislation is done. You don't require people to say anything. They just have to vote. It's not the same for leadership races." Whatever the reasons, Jenkins's campaign was not up to the demands of an extensive caucuswide contest for a major leadership post. Also working against Jenkins was his conservatism. A liberal member tersely said: "Members recognized that in electing a majority leader, they were electing a future Speaker. Jenkins was just too conservative."

The existence of Jenkins's candidacy served to highlight the fact that the South was losing its place in the leadership ranks and could be calculated to keep pressure on the new Speaker to add a southern leader. Many members felt that this was the primary reason for Jenkins's bid; even if he had no hopes of winning, a strong showing would force party leaders to take notice and attempt to maintain active southern involvement in ongoing and future party councils.

As was the case two years before, when the Democrats were choosing their leadership team at the start of the One-Hundredth Congress, the selection of Speaker and majority leader were comparatively tame side shows to what became a hotly contested race for whip.

OPEN COMPETITION FOR WHIP

In one sense, the race for whip got underway when potential aspirants first sensed privately that Wright would be forced to step down, but when such private assessments could be publicly acted upon was another matter. Representatives Gray and Bonior, the two members most clear in their objectives, felt free to launch their campaigns officially when Coelho announced his resignation. Candidates who had not previously considered a bid (or at least not in any sustained way) reconsidered as the leadership landscape started shifting in response to the political shocks of Wright's and Coelho's leave-taking. Two members who fell in this category were eight-term member Henry A. Waxman of California, and six-term member Beryl Anthony, Jr., of Arkansas.

Waxman didn't begin testing the waters publicly for a leadership run until after Coelho's announcement, although he had made tentative inquiries among his California Democratic colleagues. An inducement was the fact that Coelho was resigning and leaving the fractious yet large (twenty-seven members) California Democratic delegation without a principal spokesman at the highest reaches of the House. But his campaign was somewhat ambiguous from the start. Waxman, first elected in 1974, was a proven legislator and coalition builder who headed the Health and Environment Subcommittee of the Energy and Commerce Committee. Ahead of his time in using financial resources to fuel an internal ascent in the House, Waxman's ability to raise money (much of it from the entertainment world centered in his Los Angeles district, which includes Hollywood) and willingness to share it generously with his colleagues had helped secure a contested chairmanship for him in 1979. From this powerful legislative vantage point, Waxman was a key actor in major health and environmental legislation often pitted against John Dingell (D., Mich.), his strong-willed chairman, who represented the auto makers and workers of Detroit and Michigan.

In a contest for whip, Waxman could theoretically anticipate majorities of two big blocs to support him: the Democratic members of the Energy and Commerce Committee, and the members of the California delegation. Moreover, Waxman was still a prodigious fundraiser who had continued to contribute to the campaigns of his fellow House members. Waxman spent a week exploring a whip bid and lining up supporters, but in the end he decided he did not have a broad enough base of support and removed himself from the race. A week before the election, on 6 June, he announced he would not be running. Optimistic estimates put the number of Waxman supporters at thirty to forty members, but at least one northeastern liberal advanced the view that Waxman could count on less than ten members. In abandoning his race, Waxman came out in support of Gray, but Bonior was to claim that he had gained a majority of Waxman's supporters.

Another member who got a late start in the leadership race but who stayed in the contest until the voting was DCCC Chairman Beryl Anthony (table 14-5). Elected in 1978 from the southern part of Arkansas (his district has the largest percentage of blacks in the state), Anthony is a southerner of moderate political instincts with closer ties to the leadership than many of his region, including Jenkins. A former prosecutor and a protégé of Jim Wright, Anthony had early on displayed fund-raising skills, particularly among business interests, and in 1987 the Speaker supported his candidacy to head the DCCC after Coelho became whip.[21] Anthony also held a seat on the Ways and Means Committee (he was ranked fifteenth), to which he had been appointed in his second term, and counted Chairman Rostenkowski among his supporters.

Following the maestro of fund-raisers, Tony Coelho, as head of the DCCC was not easy, but Anthony more than held his own, increasing the amounts the party raised in 1987 and 1988 and helping the House Democrats make a net gain of three seats in the 1988 elections. Anthony,

Table 14-5. Profile of Beryl Anthony, Jr.

District:	Arkansas (4)
Elected to Congress:	1978
Date of birth:	21 February 1938
Previous leadership positions:	Chairman of the Democratic Congressional Campaign Committee (1987–)
Committee(s) and rank (1 = chair):	Ways and Means (15) Select—Children, Youth and Families (7)
Winning percentages in last five elections:	1988—69% 1986—78% 1984—98% 1982—66% 1980—100%
Voting ratings:	ADA, 80 AFL-CIO, 92 ACU, 16

like Coelho, was able to extract support from business as well as from traditional contributors to Democratic coffers, especially labor groups (Jackson 1990).

Beyond Ways and Means as a base of support, therefore, Anthony could look to his position as chairman of the DCCC as an asset. The history of leadership races had showed that these fund-raising positions could be stepping stones to higher posts: Tony Coelho had used his tenure to launch a successful campaign for whip, echoing a move a decade and a half earlier by Tip O'Neill. In the Senate, George Mitchell had been elected to lead the Democrats after heading up their campaign committee and helping win back the Senate for his party in 1986. As Coelho had most recently shown, aggressive and enterpreneurial leadership of the fund-raising arm of the congressional party brought with it the gratitude of candidates, particularly incoming freshman.

Anthony was also in a good position to take advantage of the concerns of southerners, an important segment of the Democratic party, but these two assets turned out to be more theoretical than practical. Anthony's position at the DCCC worked against him in one respect: members were reluctant to force a midterm change in control of the DCCC, especially with a half dozen special elections looming, including the seats held by Wright and Coelho.

The southern strategy failed because Gray, in a repeat of a remarkable alliance of northern and southern support that had helped him win the caucus chair six months earlier, had already locked up a good number of southern votes before Anthony got into the race seriously. As Anthony started making contact with members, especially his southern colleagues, he faced a disquieting realization: Gray had already been there and in many cases had come away with a firm commitment. Anthony discovered that Gray's reach was extensive; many supporters of the caucus chairman were calling others on his behalf. Anthony felt dispirited that he could not by himself hope to cover as broad a terrain as Gray had apparently already traversed. Anthony stayed in the race but never garnered enough support to be considered a likely winner. He ended up with thirty votes.

A Two-Week, Two-Way Contest

The contest rather quickly reduced itself to a two-way race between David Bonior and Bill Gray.

David Bonior. Bonior (table 14-6), forty-four years old, a low-key and serious-minded liberal legislator, had been first elected to the House in 1976 and had, by 1989, established himself well within the first orbit of leadership. With more than eight years' experience as a leadership spokesman on the Rules Committee, he had gained generalized exposure to almost all members and had emerged as a critical expediter of legislation important to the Speaker and majority leader. Appointed one of seven deputy whips in 1985, he seriously considered a run for chairman of the caucus in 1986 (if Gephardt had decided to limit his tenure to one term), and then was appointed chief deputy whip at the beginning of the One-Hundredth Congress (1987–88). His appointment surprised many members who had expected Speaker Wright to choose either a southerner or one of the rising young stars, Steny Hoyer (D., Md.) or Vic Fazio (D., Calif.).[22] Moreover, as chief deputy whip, Bonior spearheaded several task forces on issues important to the Democratic majority, most recently one on trade. His highest profile role was in leading the fight to cut off U.S. aid to the contras in Nicaragua and, more generally, in helping organize his party's approach to U.S. policy in Central America.

Born and raised in Detroit, Bonior earned a B.A. from the University of Iowa in 1967 and returned to academics several years later to earn a master's degree in history from Chapman College in California in 1972. Before coming to Congress, Bonior had served two terms in the Michigan House of Representatives, but his career had been eclectic; he spent time as a probation officer and adoption caseworker as well as serving in the U.S. Air Force during the Vietnam War (1968–72). Bonior remained stateside during that conflict but felt strongly that the veterans of his generation's war had not received respect or fair treatment from their government. Once in Congress, he pushed strongly on behalf of these veterans, helping form the Vietnam-Era Veterans Congressional Caucus

Table 14-6. Profile of David E. Bonior

District:	Michigan (12)
Elected to Congress:	1976
Date of birth:	6 June 1945
Previous leadership positions:	Chief deputy whip (1987–)
	Deputy whip (1985–86)
Committee(s) and rank (1 = chair):	Rules (5)
Winning percentages in last five elections:	1988–54%
	1986–66%
	1984–58%
	1982–66%
	1980–55%
Voting ratings:	ADA, 95
	AFL-CIO, 100
	ACU, 4

in 1977 and co-authoring a book on the subject, entitled *The Vietnam Veteran: A History of Neglect* (1984).

A college athlete, and still avid runner and basketball player, Bonior combined strong competitive instincts with a laid-back demeanor, an almost scholarly detachment, and an unrivaled talent for teamwork. He was the only one of the leadership contestants, and one of the few members of Congress, to sport a beard.

Bonior represents the Twelfth District of Michigan, one of those pivotal political constituencies that are looked to as barometers of national trends. The district includes modestly affluent, blue-collar suburbs that were spawned after World War II as successive waves of Polish-, Italian-, and Belgian-Americans left Detroit. Originally rooted in the Democratic party, these voters, heavily Catholic, became increasingly disaffected with the liberalism of the 1970s and were edging Republican. Ronald Reagan carried the district in 1980 and 1984. George Bush got 61 percent of the district vote in 1988. In that same year, Bonior won reelection to his seventh term but was held to 54 percent of the vote, even though he outspent his opponent three to one (*Almanac of American Politics 1990*: 614–17).

After a history of relatively easy victories, Bonior's performance in 1988 signaled that he was not part of the trend toward safe incumbencies. But this fact seemed only marginally to affect his chances of becoming whip. Bonior was pleasantly surprised to discover that his entry into the race had excited widespread interest and overwhelmingly favorable reaction in the Detroit papers and other local press. Far from hurting, his leadership prospects appeared to be greatly helping, his future electoral prospects.

Going into the whip contest, Bonior had a number of internal advantages. After four years in the higher levels of the whip organization, with the hours upon hours of interaction with the rank and file such duties entailed, he could stress his experience in the trenches and his importance as a conduit to the leadership. His colleagues viewed him as fair and effective, someone who did his homework and, in his operating style, epitomized the politics of inclusion. For example, he had worked tirelessly on the Contra aid issue, helping to craft and recraft leadership positions in order to counter the Republican administration and yet gain the support of the majority of Democratic members. If a key to legislative leadership is listening, Bonior had mastered the skill (Barry 1989). Trusted by leaders and respected and admired by his colleagues on both sides of the aisle (with the possible exception of those who opposed his anti-Contra efforts), Bonior had few enemies in the House of Representatives.

The Michigander also had the active support of a number of exceedingly powerful members: John Dingell, the dean of his state's delegation and chairman of the Energy and Commerce Committee; Joe Moakley of Massachusetts, the new chairman of the Rules Committee (who ascended to that post on the death of Claude Pepper); William D. Ford, the chairman of the Civil Service and Post Office Committee who was also from Michigan. Bonior eventually laid firm claim to the support of at least a dozen committee chairmen. He also gained the backing of all but two of his state's eleven-member Democratic delegation.

As the prospects for openings in the leadership became more and more apparent, Bonior and his staff began to intensify their strategic thinking and sort through their options. Bonior viewed the whip position as the main, indeed the sole, focus of his efforts. Not to run for the post if it became open, he felt, would relegate him to the backwaters of leadership, or bump him from the leadership circle entirely.

But Bonior also enjoyed a close relationship with Wright, Foley, and Coelho. These men were clearly the four horsemen of the 100th Congress and the early 101st Congress. (Gephardt, who served as caucus chair from 1985 to 1988 would probably have been included but was only marginally involved because of the demands of his presidential campaign, which kept him away from the House for most of 1987 and 1988.) As he contemplated running for higher office, Bonior was especially sensitive to setting in motion any strategy that might mistakenly signal his lack of confidence in the Speaker's ability to survive. This was the ambivalence for aspiring leaders in 1989: on the one hand, to heed the lessons of the past, which taught that successful leadership races depended on early starts and well-organized efforts and attempts to collect commitments; and, on the other, to accommodate to the special conditions of the present races, which ruled out any overt move to fill a leadership position that was not yet vacant.

Still Bonior had begun testing the waters discreetly. When he got the news on the night of 26 May that Tony Coelho was going to resign, he put his efforts into high gear. He and the three staff persons from his chief deputy whip office were back in their Capitol office early Saturday morning to begin what was to be a marathon session of phone calls to members, most of whom by this time had left the capital to go back to their districts, seek vacation time, or travel abroad as part of various official congressional delegations. Working out of the chief deputy whip's small suite of rooms on the first floor of the Capitol, Bonior kept up a steady barrage of phone calls throughout the long holiday weekend. Using the phone numbers gathered earlier by his staff, he tracked down scores of his colleagues those first few days, letting them know he was running for whip and seeking their support. As he made his calls Bonior discovered, as would Anthony later on, that Gray had already reached many members. One of the most dramatic examples for Bonior involved attempts to contact a large congressional delegation traveling in the Near East. When Bonior finally got through to them in Turkey, he learned that Gray had found them first. In one call, Gray had been able to talk to eight of the delegation, undoubtedly locking in the support of several of them.[23] Over the next several days, Bonior could also detect that Gray was gaining support among southerners.

Bonior also formally wrote to all 259 members of the Democratic Caucus. Giving his view of the main role of the whip as "someone who listens" and keeps "an open door to all Members," he emphasized his leadership experience and skills; his involvement in issues of concern to the caucus, including Central American policy and trade and environmental issues; his championship of the rights of Vietnam veterans and of the disabled.

A group of Bonior supporters stepped forward to act informally as a steering committee for his race. This cadre came together more on their own impetus than at the invitation of the candidate, but he welcomed their efforts.

As the members began returning from the Memorial Day weekend—with Jim Wright's resignation expected daily, and with but two weeks until Coelho's resignation was to go into effect—Bonior threw himself into the race full-time. He kept up his contact with colleagues, refining his counts, checking them against the soundings of the members of his

Table 14-7. Profile of William H. Gray III

District:	Pennsylvania (2)
Elected to Congress:	1978
Date of birth:	20 August 1941
Previous leadership positions:	Chairman of the caucus (1989)
Committee(s) and rank (1 = chair):	Appropriations (25) District of Columbia (4)
Winning percentages in last five elections:	1988—94% 1986—98% 1984—91% 1982—76% 1980—96%
Voting ratings:	ADA, 95 AFL-CIO, 100 ACU, 0

steering committee, and seeking second-ballot commitments if a first was not forthcoming. And in what has become a standard practice in House races, he fed all this information into office computers, where it could be tabulated and examined.

Bonior entered the race feeling that his chances were decent to good. He naturally considered Gray his strongest competitor but was forced to upgrade that assessment to front-runner as his calls continued to reveal a broad base of support for the caucus chairman. As front-runner, Gray's approach to the race was that of Coelho in the 1986 whip race: an all-out effort for a victory on the first ballot. For the Bonior camp, considering that the race always appeared to be a multicandidate race, the strategy was to attract enough support to force a second ballot. (Under caucus procedures, if no candidate receives a majority of votes on the first ballot, the candidate with the fewest votes is automatically forced out and the balloting immediately continues.) Bonior reasoned that if Gray were kept from a first-ballot victory, he, Bonior, would do well in picking up the supporters of Anthony, Waxman, or any other fallen candidates. In a head-to-head battle with Gray, and with second-ballot commitments lined up, Bonior thought he might prevail. Since Anthony stayed in the race until the balloting, Bonior's strategy had a chance of succeeding.

Bill Gray. Born in 1941 in Baton Rouge, Louisiana, William H. Gray III (table 14-7) moved with his family at age eight to Philadelphia when his father, William H. Gray II, took over as pastor of the Bright Hope Baptist Church, following *his* father, William H. Gray I. After graduating from Franklin and Marshall College in 1963, he earned a master's degree in divinity from Drew Theological School in 1966 and one in theology from Princeton Theological School in 1970. He also did graduate work at the University of Pennsylvania and Temple University. In 1964 he became an assistant pastor at Union Baptist Church in Montclair, Pennsylvania, and then moved back home to Philadelphia when his father died in 1972, to follow in his father's and grandfather's footsteps as pastor of the Bright Hope Baptist Church.

Given the importance of religion to politics in black communities all over America, it was not surprising to find the six-foot, two-inch articulate young minister challenging Robert N. C. Nix, an aging incumbent who had represented the Second District with only marginal distinction since 1958. After narrowly losing a bid against Nix in 1976, Gray beat him rather easily in 1978.

If safe seats remain necessary if not sufficient conditions for House party leadership contenders, the Rev. Bill Gray's Second District of Pennsylvania is in stark contrast to Bonior's increasingly marginal Twelfth District of Michigan, or even Speaker Foley's conservative base in eastern Washington state. Gray's district includes most of Philadelphia's Center City high-rise and office centers, much of North and West Philadelphia (where the MOVE row house firebombing took place in 1985), and the centuries-old stone and row houses of Germantown. Once predominantly middle-class, blue-collar, and white, these neighborhoods are mostly black now. More than 80 percent of the Second District's residents are black. Holding one of the least competitive seats in the post–World War II House, Gray won by 98 percent in 1986 and "slipped" to 94 percent in 1988 (*Almanac of American Politics* 1990:1033–35).

Comfortable in the pulpit (he still preaches almost every Sunday) or in small-group confrontation, able to combine cerebral persuasion with inspirational rhetoric, Gray's rise to the top leadership ranks in the House has been meteoric, rivaling, sometimes surpassing, the advancement of his Democratic generational peers, Coelho and Gephardt. Since his first term, he has sought and successfully won a series of positions that required class- or caucuswide support. He was chosen freshman representative on the Steering and Policy Committee (which hands out committee assignments for the Democrats). Two years later, he gained a seat on Appropriations and in his third term was selected chairman of the Budget Committee. In December 1988, in a strong showing against two other candidates, he succeeded Richard Gephardt as chairman of the Democratic Caucus.

Gray was not shy about his further ambitions; in any case, the caucus chair, because it is limited to two two-year terms, is a "sunset" leadership post. Gray had just won his chairmanship barely six months ago, after a long and hard-fought campaign. But in the face of the unexpected opening of whip, with its promise of a more secure perch on the leadership ladder, Gray did not hesitate. (In fact, he had earlier contemplated running for majority leader, even if it meant going up against Coelho.) The fact that Gray had just completed a prolonged run for caucus chair was perhaps his strongest asset in his race for whip. The organization that had helped him win in December 1988, complete with thirty or forty key supporters (or whips) from all sectors of the party, was still largely intact. Gray had only to activate it for a new campaign for whip. As one observer said of the Gray operation, "They had been saying 'thank you' for a long time."

Gray could also rely on other key areas of support: the twenty-three member Black Caucus; the twelve-member Pennsylvania delegation (including John Murtha, an influential House "mover and shaker");[24] and Democratic members of the Budget and Appropriations Committees. (After nine years' service, Gray had risen to twenty-fifth rank among thirty-five Democrats on Appropriations.) Moreover, Gray's past leadership campaigns had been marked by a coalitional richness that had its roots in the racial politics of the North and South. A prominent black politician (who also happened to be born and spend part of his childhood in Louisiana), Gray was in frequent demand to speak on behalf of his southern colleagues in their districts, many with substantial and increasingly active black minorities.[25] A Democratic aide explained: "An important factor here is the changing demographics of the South. The members in districts with large black populations feel vulnerable, precarious. . . . This is where Bill Gray can give them what they need." As the whip campaign progressed, Gray claimed almost a solid phalanx of support from Democratic members in Georgia, North Carolina, and South Carolina. He also was considered to have substantial support in Florida and in Texas (conservative leader Charles Stenholm was to second his nomination).

Not only had Gray stumped extensively for his southern colleagues in prior elections, he had contributed financially to the campaigns of scores of Democratic members.[26] Gray could also expect to generate support for his whip candidacy from other would-be leaders whose own career aspirations depended on Gray's victory, that is, those interested in the chairmanship and vice chairmanship of the caucus. Steny Hoyer of Maryland, for example, the current vice chair, wanted to run for the chairmanship. Other Democratic members were waiting in the wings for what eventually would be a two-way race. And the potential field for vice chair included Vic Fazio of California and Martin Frost of Texas, who felt that the size and importance of their delegations earned them a sinecure in Democratic leadership. The field for vice chair would eventually grow to four members. Thus, without an opening in the caucus chairmanship, the career ambitions of a number of leadership-oriented members and their close supporters would have been thwarted. Committee aspirants as well stood to benefit from turnover in leadership.[27]

Another Surprise

As the whip race got underway and the candidates began stepping up their whirlwind campaigns, condensing the planning and contacts and activities of months into days, yet another bombshell dropped: a leak first broadcast by *CBS Evening News,* that the Republican-controlled Justice Department was investigating Bill Gray. Later reports said that the FBI was looking into an alleged payroll-padding scheme in Gray's office. With a cloud of scandal already enveloping the Democratic leadership, and with less than two weeks before the election, the news could have permanently derailed the Gray campaign. Relying on his own political instincts and judgments, Gray opted not for a passive defense but a strong offense. He immediately called a press conference, vehemently denied any wrongdoing and castigated the Justice Department under Attorney General Thornburgh for allowing, or perhaps even planting, the leaks in the first place.

Gray then directed a saturation campaign of rebuttal toward his Democratic colleagues: he formally demanded an inquiry into the leaks; he sent all his colleagues a videotape of an *NBC News* report that Gray was not the subject of any investigation; he obtained and distributed signed affidavits from his staff both in Washington and Philadelphia disputing the allegations of any no-show employees; he called in the members of his steering committee for the whip race and briefed them on how to respond to the concerns of their colleagues. His chief competitor in the race, David Bonior, also immediately issued a statement of support for Gray: "I know Bill Gray to be a man of honor and integrity. . . . It is inconceivable to me that there could be any truth to last night's news reports concerning Congressman Gray."

Although he countered strongly, the reports of the Justice Department investigation nevertheless diverted Gray's attention and energy from the whip race. Some observers thought that Gray had been on his way to amassing a clear and formidable lead until the ethics probe and that he lost considerable momentum after that. Gray's vote counters estimated that the FBI leak cost their candidate twenty-five to thirty votes. But a minority dissented from that view. One member voiced this opinion: "It made people hesitate at first. But then there was a backlash. It appeared it was a setup by Thornburgh. That nullified any negative effect. It may have helped him. It was probably a wash." In any event, Gray's swift, robust rebuttal confined the damage to a minimum. He was helped because he could question the political motivation and timing behind the Justice Department's actions. In the highly polarized House, this would engender sympathy. The Democrats did not want to elect another leader who carried ethical baggage. But neither did they want to be seen as succumbing to cheap partisan tricks. And Gray had demonstrated his mettle, that he could withstand controversy and give back as good as he got.

The probable result of the incident was that a larger number of members than usual remained undecided until just before the balloting (or committed themselves but privately reserved the option to change their vote) to see if the charges against Gray would be substantiated or unmasked as partisan maneuvering. Responding to Gray's insistent demands for clarification, the Justice Department, forty-eight hours before the caucus vote, issued a statement declaring that Congressman Gray was *not* a target of any investigation and that he had fully cooperated with their preliminary inquiry.

By the morning of the vote, the whip contest had come down to Gray versus Bonior. Anthony had stayed in the race and had earned the commitments of at least two dozen or more members, but his campaign had never caught on in a way that made him a serious contender. His candidacy was too little, too late. From the outset, Gray had been thought to have the lead, but it was unclear how his support might have eroded as a result of the Justice Department leaks. A close vote was expected. Bonior felt he at least had the votes to deny Gray a first-round victory.

The caucus convened at 9:00 A.M. on Tuesday, 14 June. It was closed to the press and the public. At about 11:00 A.M., the results of the majority leader race were announced. Richard Gephardt decisively defeated Ed Jenkins on the first ballot, 181 to 76. Jenkins came out to talk to the press and explained: "I was trying to get the one-third of the party that feels somewhat isolated up to the table."

By 11:30 A.M., attention within the caucus had turned to the most competitive of the races, the selection of a new majority whip. Nominating speeches[28] were made on behalf of each of the three candidates, and then the balloting began. The final tally showed: Gray, 134; Bonior, 97; and Anthony, 30. It was a surprisingly strong first-ballot win for Gray, with three votes to spare.

Just before 1:00 P.M. the new leaders held their first press conference in the Rayburn Room adjacent to the House floor. Standing under a large portrait of George Washington, Speaker Foley introduced the new majority leader and the majority whip. He then announced that, after consulting with Mr. Gephardt and Mr. Gray, he was reappointing David

Bonior as chief deputy whip. Beryl Anthony was also asked to continue as head of the DCCC. Both men acquiesced. The new post-Wright leadership team was in place.

Coda

Gray's promotion set the stage for another leadership election for caucus chairman, held 21 June. This race attracted as candidates Steny Hoyer of Maryland, the current vice chair of the caucus; Barbara Kennelly of Connecticut; and, for a while, Mike Synar of Oklahoma, who had tried for the post in 1988 and lost to Gray. Hoyer easily prevailed over Kennelly, 165 to 82 (Synar dropped out before the balloting). Hoyer's victory led, in turn, to a final vacancy in the Democratic leadership lineup: the caucus vice chair.

In a sign of the spirited competition that surrounds even midlevel and lower leadership posts, no fewer than four candidates actively campaigned for vicechair: Vic Fazio of California, Martin Frost of Texas, Marcy Kaptur of Ohio, and Richard J. Durbin of Illinois. Many members saw the race primarily as a two-man contest between Fazio and Frost, both from large state delegations that found themselves without representation after the Coelho and Wright resignations. On the first ballot, the vote was Fazio, 113; Frost, 69; Kaptur, 37; Durbin, 34. Because no one had a majority, a second ballot was taken among the top three vote getters. Fazio won a majority on that round with 147 votes to Frost's 74 and Kaptur's 32. The lineup left the Democratic leadership without any woman or any representative of the party's southern and conservative wing. In Steny Hoyer and Vic Fazio, the Democrats had chosen attractive lawmakers (the one elected in 1981, the other in 1978) who though young, were seasoned operatives in House politics.

DYNAMICS OF THE WHIP RACE

The whip race of 1989, like its counterpart in 1986, emerged as one of the most competitive of the multitiered Democratic leadership contests, and the front-running candidates for whip, like their predecessors two years earlier—Tony Coelho, Charles Rangel, and others—ran aggressive, highly organized campaigns that relied on intensive member-to-member contact, constant assessment and refining, and carefully crafted appeals for support. The outcome of the 1989 leadership races turned on a host of factors. Some of them, like the quest for personal commitments, regional identity, committee associations, and a myriad of calculations as to which candidate can best advance a member's career aspirations and agendas, are perennial. But some are more specific. Certainly the 1989 confrontation was sharply affected by media reports of an investigation by the Justice Department involving Rep. Gray. At another time in the history of the House, such an unconfirmed rumor might have caused less consternation. But after the Wright and Coelho ordeals, House Democrats were extraordinarily wary of empowering any candidate whose background or future behavior might lend itself to ethical scrutiny.

The 1989 contest highlighted another controversy in leadership races—that between elective and appointed backgrounds. That Gray only six months before had put together a successful coalition to win the caucus chair helped him greatly when the whip position opened up. Moreover, he had previously had to seek Democratic Caucus approval for his appointment to the Appropriations Committee and the chairmanship of the House Budget Committee.[29] In putting together the coalition of support for these positions, Gray early on aligned himself with those outside his natural base of big-city liberals and the Black Caucus. Gray, taking nothing for granted, set about again from scratch to gain support among his colleagues for this new race. But logistically, he benefitted from the fact that his whipping operation for the caucus chair was easily resuscitated, and substantively, he benefitted from the fact that a majority of the caucus had only months before given their support to him as he entered the formal ranks of party leadership.

David Bonior was a strong opponent; he had gained the respect and trust of his colleagues in the performance of his job as chief deputy whip. He could point to a direct and substantive record, serving as he had for the past two and a half years within the leadership structure. But Bonior had been appointed to his post by Speaker Wright. He had not won his job by vote of the caucus. This highlighted an important difference between the House careers of the two men.

Race was also a factor in the whip contest. It was not so much the fact of Bill Gray's skin color that figured in his victory—in the 1986 whip race, Charlie Rangel, a black representative from Harlem had been soundly defeated by Tony Coelho—but how Gray used his race to assist southern colleagues in the most important area of *their* political lives: reelection. The fact that Beryl Anthony, a southerner himself with an assertive leadership style, could not contest Gray's hold on the majority of members of his region was a further testament to the Pennsylvanian's success at forging a southern strategy.

Money, the "mother's milk of politics," also figured in the outcome of the whip contest, although probably not to the degree some political journalists contended it did. Over the last decade, donations to colleagues have become commonplace, if still controversial. Both Gray and Bonior distributed campaign funds through personal PACs. And Beryl Anthony, as chair of the fund-raising arm of the congressional Democrats, signed all the checks that Democratic candidates received. Gray easily outpaced his two competitors in the financial realm. During the 1987–88 election cycle, he had transferred from his own personal campaign fund nearly $45,000 to sixty Democratic House candidates, plus another $128,000 from his leadership PAC, the Committee for Democratic Opportunity, to ninety-two Democrats. Over a parallel period, Bonior's campaign fund gave $14,000 to twenty-three Democrats, and the PAC he co-chaired gave $49,600 to thirty-six Democrats. Donations like these draw attention and support for an aspiring leader but are rarely a deciding factor in and of themselves.

One middle-ranking member of the party hierarchy commented that leadership "decisions are based on how they [the members] feel for you personally and what you can do for them." Gray's financial generosity contributed to a general perception that he was someone who could do a great deal for members. Two years earlier, a senior member of leadership told a story that helps explain Gray's appeal: "A senior member was invited by Bill Gray to a [Jack] Valenti [head of the Motion Picture Association of America] event—to a screening of the movie *Manchurian Candidate*. His response was 'I guess Bill is in a position to provide those things.' Now this member could get anything he wanted from Jack Valenti. But it's a signal."

Every leadership race is conducted according to its own internal rhythms. Outside groups generally hold little sway, and their interference, if too aggressive, if often resented. The choice of House and Senate party leaders usually turns on personal relationships and felt institutional needs, not policy matters. The constituency is clearly the members themselves. Moreover, the vote is always conducted by secret ballot. The 1989 whip race was something of an exception, to the extent that David Bonior was hurt by his positions on two highly charged issues: abortion and Israel.

A Roman Catholic representing a largely Catholic district, Bonior hewed to a strong antiabortion stand. He did not take a visible role in the ongoing debate over the issue nor attempt to persuade his colleagues, but his voting record spoke for itself. It may have cost him the support of a few Democratic members, particularly among women in the House.

His voting record on issues affecting Israel probably hurt more. Bonior had cast several "anti-Israel" votes over the years on such matters as arms sales to Saudi Arabia, trade and weapons initiatives that would have benefited Israel, and support of PLO efforts to join the United Nations' World Health Organization. The week before the election, several Jewish publications ran similar stories assessing the contenders for the House races in terms of their records on Israel. Reporting that Jewish groups were favoring the election of Gephardt as majority leader and Gray as whip, one article went on to say: "If Bonior is elected, Yasir Arafat and the PLO will have a good friend in the Democratic leadership. . . . Moreover, elevation to the Whip's job would give him an inside track to the top leadership jobs, and that could bring an unhappy change in Israel's fortunes on Capitol Hill." By contrast, Gray was cast as "a friend of Israel who has played a positive role in the Black Caucus and as a member of the very important and powerful Appropriations Subcommittee on Foreign Operations, which has jurisdiction over the annual $3 billion foreign aid package for Israel" (*WJW*, 5 June 1989). Bonior undoubtedly lost votes among several northeastern and California liberals who would have been supporters if not for his record on Israel. It is always problematic to isolate the reason for a lost vote, or to assess how many votes turn on a single factor. In this case, the number was no doubt small, certainly under ten. But Bonior only needed four votes to force Gray into a second ballot run-off, where the outcome might have been different.

Aspiring leaders who continue to address major issues face a balancing act on the leadership ladder. Bonior was reminiscent of Jim Wright in this regard. Tip O'Neill followed a safer, more process-oriented approach. Foley, though deeply involved in legislation throughout his career, has managed in large part to mute his issue basis (on such matters as gun control and trade policy). The more salient and polarizing the issue, however, the more difficult it is to downplay one's stance. Bonior's position on abortion and support for Israel place him outside the national mainstream of his party (if not outside the sentiments of his district). Richard Gephardt, representing a similar blue-collar suburban district in Missouri, initially took centrist positions on abortion and busing, but his presidential aspirations forced him to move to the left. Bonior faces a similar dilemma if he hopes to advance further along the leadership path. Bill Gray—with a strong organization still largely intact from his caucus race; with impressive support across the ideological, regional, and racial spectra of the party; with a demonstrated ability as a gutsy partisan fighter and effective political strategist; and with proven talent at raising funds and articulating ideas, and sharing both with his colleagues—garnered the votes of a majority of the caucus in a first ballot triumph to join Foley and Gephardt in the newly reconstituted House Democratic leadership team.

LESSONS OF THE LEADERSHIP ELECTIONS OF 1989

What are the lessons of the House Democratic leadership elections of 1989? What are the intermediate and long-range implications for party leadership in Congress? Occurring as they did in the middle of a session and in an atmosphere of intense partisan rivalry, these contests present a unique opportunity for students of party leadership and Congress to further comprehend the complexity of the process because the ways in which these contests either followed or deviated from past practices and norms help us to gauge the strength of those practices and norms and to assess their future applicability.

Incumbency

First, the outcomes of the races confirm several established trends. The power of incumbency, always a critical variable in leadership contests, was somewhat muted in the 1989 races when two of the top three House leaders were forced to resign. Nevertheless, the 1989 contests show that in competing for top party posts, *those already in leadership positions are favored to advance.* No challengers emerged to contest Majority Leader Foley's ascent to the speakership. Former Democratic Caucus Chairman Richard Gephardt had ridden the crest of a national bid for office in seeking his party's presidential nomination, but had also forged an impressive career within the House. Gephardt, therefore, was an unusual commodity; he was an insider who had gained a measure of renown on the outside. Once Tony Coelho dropped out of consideration, this combination made Gephardt an overwhelming choice among his Democratic colleagues for majority leader, and he subsequently won easily.

All three final contestants for the whip position already held leadership posts and were seeking advancement. Moreover, Gray, Bonior, and Anthony could point to predecessors, each of whom had used his position as a springboard to the office of the majority whip. Of the three posts held, however, only the caucus chair is strictly elective. (The chair of the DCCC requires confirmation by the caucus, but the Speaker's nominee always prevails.) This gave Gray the advantage of having previously run a successful caucuswide campaign. The fact that he had conducted the campaign less than a year before his whip race added to his competitive edge.

Whether elected or appointed, lower-ranking leaders feel pressure to advance to fill openings above them on the ladder. As one leadership aspirant noted, "This place is weird. It tends to reward people who indicate they are interested." An aide to a Democratic leader characterized the mind-set of prospective leaders this way: "You don't want to look noncompetitive. . . . You don't know how many chances there will be. You can't afford to pass them up. You don't want to look like you're not a player." The weak campaign of Ed Jenkins of Georgia and the almost noncandidacy of Henry Waxman of California underscore the fact that lawmakers who concentrate on narrow areas of legislation, even if they acquire expertise that makes them highly influential in the policy arena, may be at a disadvantage in building the broad base of support needed to emerge victorious in a leadership contest. A middle-level leader clearly interested in advancement spoke of this dilemma: "The more you are involved in specific cases, the less time you can devote to leadership. Take [Congressman X]. He is a leader, a political force in [a major American city]. But because of his involvement in ——— issues, he's not in formal leadership."

The races for majority leader and whip also showed once again that candidates who are slow to organize or seem hesitant in lining up commitments from their colleagues lose valuable momentum and support. Jenkins's effort lacked focus and assertiveness. The campaign of Beryl Anthony suffered from a slow start. In today's leadership races, a contender cannot afford to ponder his or her options with the troubled air of a Hamlet, waiting for an auspicious sign for action. Those who prevail in leadership contests more likely follow the example of Henry V, wresting from the environment, the circumstances, and their colleagues every point of advantage.

Region

Regional considerations continue to affect leadership race outcomes, but they are significantly less decisive than in prior decades. Said one leader from the West: "I never felt it [region] was much of an issue. The House has gone beyond that. In the old days it was a more important factor. It's more important when it's not person to person. Once it's retail [i.e., running a leadership race], it's not that important. I never believed it was a determining factor for members." Another high-ranking leader observed: "It's not a big issue except for people who want to make it an issue—to give them a reason for rationalizing a candidacy."

Despite the appeal of the campaigns of Jenkins and Anthony to keep a southerner in leadership, both men were rather decisively rejected by the caucus. Even though they represent one of the largest regional blocs in the House, southerners must make a bridge to other regions, traditionally the Northeast, in order to be a moving force in leadership contests. One moderately liberal southern member observed: "You can't win without Boll Weevil support on the floor, but they don't have enough votes to get a position on the leadership directly."

To address the concerns of southerners, Speaker Foley, the first Speaker from the Far West, very soon after the leadership elections alluded to the possible creation of a new leadersip slot to which he would appoint a representative from the South. Negotiations surrounding such a position came to naught.[30] On 25 October 1989, however, Foley appointed three new deputy whips to fill spots left open by advancing leaders; the new whips were Butler Derrick of South Carolina, Charles W. Stenholm of Texas, and Esteban Edward Torres of California.

In the future, it will not be just the South looking for representation in leadership. The 1990 census combined with congressional redistricting will bring about important shifts in political power in the 1990s, from the North and East to the South and West, from Michigan, Ohio, Pennsylvania, and New York to Florida, Arizona, Texas, and California. Already the largest delegation in the House, California is predicted to pick up six or seven seats by 1992; Texas, three or four; and Florida, three or four. The most favorable current Democratic scenario gives that party complete control of these state legislatures and at least two of the three governorships, making it likely that the House Democratic delegations from these states after 1992 will be substantially enhanced.

As indicated earlier, the California delegation felt keenly the loss of Tony Coelho as whip, helping to launch Henry Waxman's stillborn campaign to succeed Coelho and maintain the influence of the largest state delegation. Waxman abandoned his attempt, but a fellow Californian, Vic Fazio, won the vice chairmanship of the caucus. Except for Fazio, no Democratic member from a Sun Belt state currently holds a leadership position. The delegations from these states are chomping at the bit and will surely make a push for greater representation in top leadership whenever vacancies occur in the Congresses to come. The question remains, however, whether the House has once again stabilized its leadership hierarchy for at least a decade. In the meantime, aspiring leaders from the Sun Belt regions may have to console themselves with aggressive attempts at intermediate positions such as caucus chair and vice chair, chairmanship of the Budget Committee, and head of the DCCC. In the inevitable purposive calculus that every member undertakes every two years, some of the most ambitious members will opt to run for the Senate or other statewide office.

Money

The 1989 leadership contests confirm a finding of the 1986–87 races: The use of PACs by leaders or leadership aspirants to raise funds to distribute to House Democratic candidates continues to play a significant, but not determinative, role in the selection of party leaders (Brown and

Peabody 1987). In the whip contest, the candidate who raised and distributed to his colleagues the most money—Gray—prevailed. But if money were the most significant factor, then Waxman, a prodigious fundraiser, would have made much stronger showing.

In the majority leader race, money was less of an issue. Richard Gephardt, concentrating on paying off the debt of his presidential campaign, was in no position to funnel great sums to his colleagues. Ed Jenkins, in the words of one fellow southerner, "never even bothered to set up a PAC."

Helping members with financial contributions for their election campaign is not a new practice for aspiring House leaders. Over the last decade, however, the process has become more sophisticated and widespread. How powerful an influence is money in leadership races? When asked about the charges that Gray had "bought" his whip job, one member heatedly disputed the connection: "That's b---s---, a nonsense argument, just not applicable. Look at [Congressman X]; he's raised a lot of money for members. He only had a handful of votes, he had nothing, [Congressman Y] and a few others. He couldn't even carry [a metropolitan area]. So that money argument is a nonstarter. . . . You can't do that much with $5,000 or $10,000, and after all, it's a secret ballot. It makes a good impression, but just because you receive a contribution, that's a long way from saying you should support someone for leadership. It doesn't mean s--t."

One leadership aide who has been intimately involved in running a leadership race assessed the impact of money this way: "Sure it helps. I consider it "table stakes"—it's the ante to be able to play the game. It's so helpful that almost everybody does it. But that means it's not that much of a help. It doesn't give you a great advantage because everybody does it." One House leader, a skilled fund-raiser, opined: "I don't think it gets you votes. But it can hurt if you don't have it. Not having it is a problem. . . . It's not necessarily the amounts. Rather it's a signal that I can help you. Your ability to help is important."

The point is that members want many things from their leaders (and their aspiring leaders), and campaign contributions are only one aspect of their expectations. True, members have come to expect their leaders to assist them in their campaigns, through appearances in the district as well as financial assistance. In campaigns that can now cost hundreds of thousands of dollars, the several thousands provided by their leaders (the limit is $5,000 for the primary and $5,000 for the general election) may not provide the margin of victory, but the contribution communicates to a member an important fact about a candidate for leadership, and that is his or her willingness to respond to a member's needs.

But established leaders seeking a higher office are well positioned to perform a myriad of services helpful to members, not only raising money, but giving speeches, helping with committee assignments, easing the passage of legislation. In the campaign arena, leaders not only have better access to funds but can introduce a member to a wide range of extra-congressional contacts: national party figures and wealthy individual contributors, interest groups, PACs, civic associations, and even media exposure. To the extent that a leader is able and willing to activate these contacts and resources to help his colleagues, and thereby ascend higher on the leadership ladder, the escalator trend for House Democrats is reinforced.

Modified Insider-Outsider Strategies

In his classic study of the majority leadership race between Carl Albert and Richard Bolling following Speaker Rayburn's death in 1962, Nelson W. Polsby identified two distinct strategies of influence as embodied by each man's campaign: Albert's careful working of the members with low-key appeals to friendship and loyalty versus Bolling's reliance on extra-congressional sources such as special interest groups and the media to bring pressure to bear on members. Polsby concludes that Albert prevailed in that race because his "insider" strategy was better suited to the operation and norms of the House than Bolling's "outsider" approach (see chap. 12). Of course, no candidate can run a significant challenge without substantive insider strength.

The 1989 House Democratic races (as well as the House Republican race for whip in 1989 and the 1988 race for Senate majority leader) reinforce a trend seen in the 1986 House Democratic races (Brown and Peabody 1987), on the basis of which we set forth a modification of Polsby's analysis. Success in late twentieth-century contests, we argue, calls for an "insider" strategy that makes increasing use of "outsider" skills, most particularly, raising money and generating a favorable national profile for House Democrats. All the leading contenders for majority leader and whip based their approach and appeals to colleagues along traditional "insider" lines. They contacted as many colleagues as possible, stressed their qualifications in terms of experience, willingness to serve members, and loyalty to the institution. But in the two areas where members themselves increasingly stress leadership abilities—fund-raising and media performance—the candidates, especially the winners, willingly displayed their strengths.

Gephardt's national reputation, far from an impediment, seemed to give him an edge in the contest for leader. As one leadership aide analyzed Gephardt's appeal: "The colleagues you can only do on the inside—one-on-one meetings and lunches, helping them with legislation, contributing money, going to the districts. The outside role is where he is interested in pursuing an agenda for the party. Where he thinks the party should be going. This is where the presidential expertise comes in."

Gray, too, was known beyond the Beltway far more than most of his colleagues. In a *Wall Street Journal* profile, Gray, then caucus chair, was described as "clearly a high-flying national figure." The article describes his schedule for a single day: "He got off a plane from London [where he had spoken to financiers], delivered a speech at a Baptist church here [in Washington] and then ate dinner at his favorite French restaurant before boarding a corporate jet bound for rural Georgia to speak on behalf of a colleague" (6 Dec. 1988, A26). Gray could be a thrilling speaker, rousing church and college audiences with his oratory. But he also performed well on the news programs and talk shows, holding forth on more arcane matters like the budget and defense spending. His speaking and media skills were well recognized, so much so that his campaign avoided emphasizing the topic for fear of inciting jealousies among other powerful House figures. Thus Gray, unlike Bolling in 1962, was able to get around the possible resentment of other members at his "outsider" skills.

In Foley, Gephardt, and Gray, the House Democrats chose a leadership team with a high national profile. As comfortable before the television cameras as working the aisles in the House chamber, they were the most telegenic team ever to serve as party leaders. They all possessed a demonstrated ability to play the outside game as well as traditional congressional cloakroom politics.

BROAD IMPLICATIONS FOR AMERICAN POLITICS AND LEADERSHIP

A New Generation of Democratic Leaders

With the election of Foley, Gephardt, and Gray, control of House leadership shifted to a new generation. While Foley, at age sixty and with twenty-five years in the House before he became Speaker, is no "young Turk," he is on the other side of the generational divide from Jim Wright and Tip O'Neill, his immediate predecessors. Born in 1929, the new Speaker was the first to have come of age politically after World War II, and his outlook is more that of a post–depression era Democrat than one steeped in the crisis itself. Elected to Congress in 1964, a decade before the Watergate class, Foley nonetheless was a key architect of the reforms that reshaped the House in the 1970s, and as mentioned earlier, he was a direct beneficiary of the revolt against seniority on several occasions. Foley is also the first Speaker to hail from the frontier of the United States—the Far West. His ascendancy signaled the end of the "Boston-Austin" axis by which Massachusetts and Texas (or Oklahoma) alternated for more than five decades as the home states of the top leaders in the Democratic hegemony.

Gephardt and Gray were both born in 1941, the year the United States entered World War II, and came to Congress in the wake of Watergate. As befits politicians of the eighties, the new leader and whip practiced an individualistic brand of campaigning and conformed to the discipline of television and its demand for concise and biting messages. Gephardt, with a dozen years in the House at the time of the election, and Gray, with ten, had far less seniority than all previous majority leaders and most whips (less than all whips since 1962). In fact, not one of the candidates for majority leader or whip was elected before 1976. Though shorter than those of leaders in the past, the apprenticeships served by these members were varied and intense. All of them grew up in and helped give form to a House leadership environment characterized by the politics of inclusion (Sinclair 1983; Loomis 1988).[31]

Richard Gephardt, working years earlier in the caucus under the tutelage of Chairman Gillis Long (D., Md.), had sat through endless meetings and discussions to craft Democratic party policy agendas that could claim the allegiance of a majority of the congressional party and attract the attention of the larger public. William Gray had honed his consensus-building skills as chairman of the Budget Committee during a period of great inter- and intraparty divisions. David Bonior, as deputy and then chief deputy whip, was adept at leading the task forces that leadership increasingly used as extensions of the whip operation. One of Beryl Anthony's first moves as head of the DCCC was to spread power by naming six regional co-chairs of the fund-raising committee. Pragmatic, nonideological, skilled at coalition building, comfortable with sharing power—these men, altogether with Caucus Chair Steny Hoyer and Caucus Vice Chair Vic Fazio, are the new face of leadership in the House of Representatives. For out of this group will likely emerge the first Speaker of the twenty-first century.

The Leadership Ladder

The strong post–World War II pattern of House Democratic succession— from whip to majority leader to Speaker—has, up to now, depended on infrequent changes in leadership and the willingness of would-be leaders to wait in line for their turn. Do the events of 1989 augur any changes in this tradition? Has the leadership ladder been weakened?

In filling the open spots in their leadership after the political demise of Wright and Coelho, House Democrats showed a respect for tradition that might be viewed as all the more remarkable for the unusual circumstances surrounding the races. In choosing Foley, the Democratic Caucus continued the party's practice of half a century of elevating the majority leader to the speakership. Gray was also moved one rung up the ladder from caucus chair to whip. (Without a firm line of ascent to whip, even if the caucus had chosen Bonior or Anthony, the selection could not be interpreted as precedent shattering because both men were already part of the inner leadership circle.)

The race for majority leader could not help but break past practice since the next in line, Tony Coelho, was resigning from the House. (If Coelho had stayed and been passed over for majority leader, there might have been early evidence of a breakdown in the leadership ladder.) The choice of Gephardt for majority leader, a known quantity and former caucus chair, someone with an impressive set of skills and background that made him attractive to a party struggling with scandal and a deteriorating image, cannot be seen as a challenge to established patterns, but rather as a consensus choice to revitalize a weakened leadership.

One development that may serve to weaken the leadership ladder in the future is the *frequency* of leadership turnover. The new majority leader and whip, for example, may not make the House their final career. Gephardt promised his colleagues he would not run for president in 1992, but he will only be fifty-six in 1996. Gray, as one of the most prominent black politicians in the nation, has been mentioned as a possible cabinet appointee or vice presidential choice on a national ticket. He may even consider, at some point, a run for the Senate. (A career option now seen as viable with Governor Wilder's victory in Virginia.) The implications of frequent leadership openings are difficult to predict. One result—and there is some evidence that this is already occurring—is the enthusiastic encouragement by younger members of their more senior colleagues in leadership to move on to other careers and thereby free up valuable rungs on the ladder. Thus, would-be leaders can be expected to lend generous support to incumbent leaders who are considering a run for office outside the House.

With less longevity built into leadership careers, incumbent leaders may also find themselves more vulnerable if they are perceived as ineffectual, prone to scandal, or an embarrassment to the party. Moreover, given the increasing amounts of time, resources, and energy that have flowed into leadership races in recent years, more frequent contests would absorb a great deal of the attention of the House, not without costs.

Patterns of Recruitment and Advancement

Congress is like other organizations: if the methods of recruitment and advancement change, the people at the helm are likely to be different. Until 1987, the whip—widely considered the first rung on the leadership ladder—was appointed by the Speaker in consultation with the majority leader. They tended to select as their lieutenants like-minded people of similar political and ideological backgrounds and with demonstrated loyalty to the House and to the leader(s) sponsoring them. Above all, there had to be a measure of deference to the established leaders and House norms. And so Sam Rayburn acted as mentor for Carl Albert, John McCormack sponsored Tip O'Neill, Foley learned from O'Neill, and so on (Brown and Peabody 1984). Top leaders also used appointive positions under their control to shape a team with regional or ideological balance or both. The criteria in such appointments was often suitability and adaptability, not necessarily force of personality or intellect.

In an effort to broaden the base of political power in the House, younger Democrats pushed to make the whip elective, and in 1987 Tony Coelho became the first elected whip. Coelho himself presaged a new approach to leadership races. His campaign for whip was a late twentieth-century model of high-tech, entrepreneurial politics and a prototype of future multicandidate contests in the House, both Democratic and Republican (Brown and Peabody 1987). The very qualities that made Coelho a successful candidate for whip—he was highly organized, aggressive, able to build an independent base of support (including a strong financial base)—might have worked against him if he had had to be appointed to the job. Established leaders do not like to have to keep looking over their shoulders at potential competitors.

It is interesting to speculate about who would be whip in 1990, after Wright, if the position had remained appointive. As a loyal lieutenant who had won the confidence of leadership and forged close bonds with Foley, David Bonior might have been the Speaker's first choice. In temperament and style, and in the personal relationship he had established with other leaders, Bonior more nearly fit the mold of past appointees to the position.[32]

All of these trends—younger members moving into the leadership circle, more frequent and possibly more competitive races for party posts, a circumscribed role for established leaders in tapping future leaders—may signal an era of renewed vigor and vision for the House. Still, a few questions linger. First, can highly charged and highly ambitious leaders develop the skills of collegiality to work together effectively as a team? There were obvious tensions in the Wright-Foley-Coelho triad, mainly triggered by uncertainty over Coelho's career ambitions. A similar dynamic possibly, but not likely, will develop in the new leadership team. A second concern is whether leaders who seek a career beyond the House will be properly protective of the institution and its prerogatives. If their plans include a bid for national office, how will that affect the shaping of the congressional party agenda? Finally, will the declining role of party leaders in choosing their successors remove a valuable filter for deciding who can best advance the interest of the party and the institutions? This parallels a concern often voiced on the national level that Democratic party regulars and office holders are not accorded a large enough role in choosing nominees for president.

It is useful to note that the two House leaders who were forced to relinquish their posts in 1989 both got onto the leadership ladder by election, not by appointment: Coelho, the Democrat's first elected whip, and Wright, who made a successful lateral grab onto the leadership ladder in 1976 in the hard-fought contest for majority leader against John McFall (D., Calif.), Richard Bolling (D., Mo.), and Phillip Buron (D., Calif.) (Oppenheimer and Peabody 1977; Barry 1989).

Speakership Change in the Context of a Divided Government

At 1989's American Political Science Association meeting in Atlanta, David Mayhew posed the important question: Does it make a difference whether party control of the American national government is unified or divided? Among his major findings, Mayhew concluded that: "A Congressional mind-set of problem-solving and a logic of needing to build broad coalitions in order to win at all seems to work toward evening out lawmaking across conditions of unified and divided control" (1989, 125).

The transition in the House from a polarized, strife-ridden, partisan atmosphere under Speaker Wright to a more moderate, conciliatory, bipartisan mood under Speaker Foley has already had a number of important consequences, not the least of which is enactment of the Ethics Reform Act of 1989. The successful passage of this legislation to ban honoraria for House members and raise congressional pay by a third over two years was in stark contrast to the failure of a larger pay raise that was derailed by public outrage at the beginning of the year.

Respect, trust, and comity among party leaders are important variables in determining whether or not legislation dealing with difficult issues such as deficit reduction, savings and loan association's bailouts, distribution of the (vanishing) peace dividend, or meaningful campaign finance reform will succeed or be doomed to defeat. To repeat what Peabody argued more than two decades ago: "A congressional party's philosophical approach, the kinds of legislation it promotes, its strategies of imple-

mentation—all hinge to a considerable degree on the individual personalities, political backgrounds, and state and regional outlooks of its principal leaders" (1967, 675).

Despite the fact that Speaker Jim Wright and President George Bush
grew up with overlapping careers in Texas and national politics, there
seems little question but what Tom Foley and George Bush have a deeper,
more sympathetic relationship with the attendant, likely positive consequences for legislative compromise and implementation of policy upon
which both can agree. The comprehensive clean air legislation, currently
in conference, is one of the more dramatic examples of how a smooth
working relationship between the White House and Capitol Hill, including prominently in this case Senate Majority Leader George Mitchell,
can yield progress.

Foley possesses a set of balancing skills that may be more suited to an
era of divided government than the confrontational approach of his predecessor. In the words of one prominent Washington lobbyist with extensive Hill experience: "Foley understands the members; he massages
their egos. He listens to others more than Wright. Sure, he has an agenda,
but it's much more low key. Foley is like Rayburn, in that he tends to
bring out the best in people." This temperance style, combining elements
of cooperation and competition, comes across in the new Speaker's own
words. When asked by *National Journal* reporters last month, "Do you
suffer from an excess of decency?" Foley replied: "Guilty. . . . I'm willing,
I guess, to take the criticism that there's too much, I'm not going to say
decency, that's your word, that there's too much conciliation or cooperation. But, on the other hand, I think you're going to also see, from
time to time, that I'm not unwilling to take the argument, where I think
the case is strong, against the President" (*National Journal,* 18 Aug. 1990,
2019). In these sentiments, Foley may be in tune with the feelings of his
colleagues. As one of them said, "Most of what we do here is nonideological and nonpartisan. Invariably, enmities *are* contained."

Throughout this paper, as well as in our earlier research, we have
suggested that the choice of one contender over another *does* make a
difference, and therefore is likely to have both short-range and immediate
career benefits as well as larger institutional and public policy considerations. Explicitly we are making a case for the existence of what Fred I.
Greenstein once referred to as "action dispensability . . . the circumstances
under which the actions of single individuals are likely to have a greater
or lesser effect on the course of events" (Greenstein, 1967, 633). As
Greenstein was quick to point out, the answers are always a matter of
degree and require added research to confirm or deny. With Greenstein,
then, we would agree that the question of how important personality is

in any given context is, "in the final analysis . . . not susceptible to a general or definitive answer" (641). It all depends on the environment of unfolding events.

Thus, when asked how much difference it makes whether Foley or Wright is Speaker, we must refer the readers to the broader context within which the question arises. But we *can* conclude that the difference between the short-lived, if assertive, leadership of the Democratic team of Wright, Foley, and Coelho, and the new, post-1989 team of Foley, Gephardt, and Gray has already had major consequences, developments that are likely to shape House and national politics well into the 1990s if not the twenty-first century.

POSTSCRIPT

On 20 June 1991 Majority Whip William H. Gray III (D., Pa.), shocked his colleagues by announcing he would resign from the House and his leadership position to accept the presidency of the United Negro College Fund. His resignation set off the third reshuffling of the House Democratic leadership hierarchy in less than five years. Two members of the existing party leadership—Chief Deputy Whip David E. Bonior of Michigan and Democratic Caucus Chairman Steny H. Hoyer of Maryland became the prime contenders to succeed Gray as whip. In a secret ballot vote in the Democratic Caucus on 11 July 1991, Bonior won going away. The vote was 160 to 109. Despite his loss, Hoyer remained chairman of his party's caucus, eligible for another term as chair in the 103d Congress (1993–94).

NOTES

1. Recent revisionist views, including those of former member of Congress Richard Bolling (D., Mo.) and political scientist Ronald M. Peters, Jr., assign a more powerful reign than is commonly assumed to Speaker Carl Albert (1971–76). Writing in the June 1990 *American Political Science Review*, Bolling describes Albert as a "highly intelligent and skilled legislator who . . . was quietly responsible for much of the success of the efforts to modernize and even reform the House and its committee system" (84:646–47). In *The American Speakership: The Office in Historical Perspective* (Baltimore: Johns Hopkins Press, 1990), Peters claims that Albert "accomplished historic change in the House of Representatives and in the office of the speaker. Under Carl Albert the speakership accumulated more institutional power than at any time since 1910. The Congress asserted its role in government in a way that had not been witnessed in decades" (205).

2. In a 10 April 1989 profile of Thomas Foley for the *New Yorker*, John Newhouse quotes Rep. Pat Williams (D., Mont.) on the leadership team of Wright, Coelho, and Foley: "Jim is the captain, Tony the oar drummer, and Tom the navigator" (48–84).

Our study relied upon more than thirty interviews with key participants and staff, most of which are unattributed because of their sensitivity.

3. As of June 1989, in addition to the vacancies soon to result from the resignations of Wright and Coelho, there were four other vacancies in the 101st House caused by recent deaths or resignations.

4. The playing out of personal ambitions and rivalries surrounds each House race with a rich history. One irony of the 1989 reordering of leadership was that Jim Wright's political demise brought about the ascension of two members, Thomas Foley and Richard Gephardt, each of whom was an ally of one of the more formidable representatives in the House's recent history—Philip Burton (D., Calif.) and Richard Bolling (D., Mo.), respectively. The intense Burton-Bolling rivalry came to a head in the 1976 race for majority leader, which Jim Wright won on the third ballot by one vote, largely because Burton and Bolling were intent on eliminating each other (Oppenheimer and Peabody 1977).

5. Recent examples of lengthy leadership contests include the 1986 races, which got under way a full two years before the vote, when Speaker O'Neill in 1984 announced his pending retirement and the 1988 caucus chair race, which was conducted over two years. (In the latter case, the early start was premised on the expectation that the incumbent caucus chair, Gephardt, would step down before the end of his second term in order to devote his energies to his presidential bid. But, at the prompting of Speaker Wright, Gephardt retained his post until the end of the One-Hundredth Congress.)

6. Certainly anyone interested in this question should read John M. Barry's *The Ambition and the Power* (1989). One weakness of Barry's book is endemic to "inside-story" treatments, and that is the researcher's tendency to rely on the world view of sources who have given him access. (Barry himself offers a fascinating account of how he researched his book in "Playing the Inside Game" in *Extensions,* a publication of the Carl Albert Center, Summer 1990:3–6.) A second weakness—one that is hard on political scientists but devastating to the political actors portrayed in Barry's account—was the lack of an index! Fortunately, this was corrected in the paperback version.

7. Wright himself tracks the attack on his ethics to his involvement in U.S. policy in Central America. "From that moment there was nothing but hostility from the Administration," Wright told reporters at a luncheon held the day after his resignation. "There was a determination on the part of certain people in the other party to see to it that I was removed." (*CQ Almanac* 1989:40).

8. The proposal was to give members a 51 percent pay raise. A vote was not required by the procedures operating at that time; without a vote the raise would have gone into effect automatically. By switching strategies, circulating a poll among Democratic members, and then promising opponents a floor vote on the proposal, Wright was thought to have badly mishandled an issue of great sensitivity to his colleagues and made himself vulnerable to their questioning of his political judgment and eventually to their withdrawal of support.

9. For diverse views from journalists and political scientists related to this issue, refer to "Congressional Ethics and the Role of the Media," in *Congressional Ethics Reform Hearings before the Bipartisan Task Force on Ethics,* U.S. House of Representatives, 101st Cong., 1st sess., 20 Sept. 1989. For a general examination of interaction between the media and Congress, see Michael J. Robinson, "Three Faces of Congressional Media," in Thomas E. Mann and Norman J. Ornstein, eds., *The New Congress* (Washington, D.C.: AEI, 1981).

10. The souring of partisan relations could perhaps be traced at least to early 1985 and the acrimony surrounding the contested seating of Frank McCloskey as representative from the Eighth District of Indiana after a disputed election. "Republicans— even those usually not given to partisan warfare—saw in the attempt to seat McCloskey a blatant and arrogant abuse of power by the House Democratic majority." Alan Ehrenhalt, ed., *Politics in America, 1986* (Washington, D.C.: Congressional Quarterly Press, 1985), 520.

11. Interestingly, Wright had issued a statement of support for his fellow Texan, John Tower before the Senate vote.

12. See John J. Pitney, Jr., "Republican Party Leadership in the U.S. House." (Paper delivered at the Annual Meeting of the American Political Science Association, 30 August–2 September 1990, San Francisco.)

13. In his inaugural speech Foley characteristically reached for conciliatory rhetoric and pledged to Republicans "a spirit of cooperation and increased consultation." Bob Michel, in his remarks, signaled that the rancor over Wright's treatment of the minority had not subsided. Taking issue with the former Speaker's portrayal of the mood of the House as one of "mindless cannibalism," Michel retorted: "Now it's a catchy phrase, but the distinguished members of the ethics committee, equally divided from both parties, are neither mindless nor cannibals" (*CQ Almanac* 1989: 40).

14. Foley was the last of the appointed whips; he never had to test and win the support of the caucus for the number three position. He assumed the duties of whip in 1981, taking the place of John Brademas of Indiana, who was defeated for reelection. So Foley was the junior member of the leadership team of Tip O'Neill and Jim Wright, who had assumed their positions in 1977. Furthermore, Foley was selected only after Dan Rostenkowski of Illinois, who as chief deputy whip was next in line, turned down the job to take up instead the chairmanship of the Ways and Means Committee.

15. Speaker O'Neill was fond of saying that Tom Foley could "see three sides to every issue." Liberal Barney Frank (D., Mass.) was quoted a month before the embattled Wright resigned as saying of Foley, "His only fault is about a half an inch too much caution. But in this case [the selection of the Speaker], that served him very well." (*National Journal*, 29 Sept. 1989, 1034).

16. *Roll Call*, 7 Feb. 1988, 1.

17. Two years before in running for whip, Coelho faced questions about his fundraising tactics. A key supporter at the time, who helped run Coelho's campaign, spoke of "reach[ing] out . . . to those 'doubting Thomases' about his [Coelho's] ethics or the overly political aspects of his career." The appearance in 1988 of a book by *Wall Street Journal* reporter Brooks Jackson, *Honest Graft*, highlighting the role of money in politics and featuring Tony Coelho and his operation at the Democratic Congressional Campaign Committee, did little to alleviate their concerns.

18. In that contest for caucus chairman the results were Gray, 146 votes; Mary Rose Oakar of Ohio, 80 votes; and Mike Synar of Oklahoma, 33 votes.

19. The choice of the *New York Times* was not accidental. Coelho felt that only that paper had given balanced coverage to his story; he was furious at the *Washington Post* and the *Los Angeles Times* for their reporting of his financial dealings (Barry 1989, 752).

20. The phrase is from *Evans-Novak Political Report*, 23 May 1989.

21. Anthony had to work for the DCCC post in 1987. His possible competition included two aggressive, accomplished young members: Vic Fazio of California and Steny Hoyer of Maryland. Anthony, known to be good at raising money from business,

also made a concerted effort to enlist the support of labor leaders to his cause in order to signal to the caucus and its leaders his good ties with this still-important constituency of the Democratic party.

22. Both Hoyer and Fazio were probably hurt in this selection process by their close assocation with newly elected whip Tony Coelho. Fazio had been Coelho's campaign manager for whip. Hoyer had allegedly told the *Baltimore Sun* that a victorious Coelho would appoint him chief deputy whip. The presumption apparently offended Wright, who jealously guarded his appointment power. It was also probable that the incoming Speaker wanted *his* close allies, and not those of his whip, to be brought into the leadership circle.

23. Gray raised some eyebrows by enlisting the aid of the Capitol operators to place his telephone calls to canvass Democratic members for his whip race. In a tight race with limited time and resources available, such logistical support can be a distinct advantage. Of course, getting to members is one thing; convincing them to vote for you is another.

24. John Murtha himself was a symbol of Gray's broad reach in the House. This consummate inside player represents a small-town, white ethnic constituency centered in the infamous Johnstown, Pennsylvania. In a recent profile in the *National Journal*, Christopher Madison writes that Murtha "came to Washington less than a year before the now-famous Watergate class elected in November 1974, but he clearly belongs to the 'old politics' that the Watergate class quickly challenged. He is the antithesis of the new breed Members, the ones Rostenkowski, a Murtha crony, derisively calls, the 'blow-drys' " (11 Aug. 1990, 1947–51).

25. Thirty years ago, before the Voting Rights Acts of 1965, the picture was less clear. Still, Adam Clayton Powell, representative from Harlem, told Rep. Gillis Long of Louisiana during the latter's reelection campaign in the mid-1960s: "I can come down and run against you or run for you, whichever will do the most good."

26. The issue of contributions figured in the caucus chair race, which Gray easily won against his opponents, Mary Rose Oakar (D., Ohio) and Mike Synar (D., Okla.). Gray had made extensive use of his leadership political action committee (PAC), distributing more than $115,000 to colleagues in the year leading up to the race. In contrast, Oakar had raised and distributed $8,000. Synar did not even take PAC money in his own reelection campaign. (*Wall Street Journal*, 6 Dec. 1988).

27. The reason Bob Carr didn't back his fellow Michigan liberal David Bonior for whip, according to some reports, was that Carr stood to advance faster within the Appropriations Committee (where Gray is ahead of Carr on the Transportation Subcommittee) if he backed Gray. Gray may have told Carr he could become subcommittee chair if the current chair, Bill Lehman (D., Fla.), gave the position up in the near future (*CQ Insight*, 23 June 1989). The only Democrats in the Michigan state delegation who did not sign a letter supporting Bonior were Carr and John Conyers, a member of the Black Caucus.

28. Candidates usually attempt to obtain nominators and seconders who reflect the widespread nature of their support. Gray's nominators, for example, were: Gaydos (Pa.), Dellums (Calif.), Torres (Calif.), Byron (Md.), and Stenholm (Tex.)—a dean of his delegation, a black, a Hispanic, a woman, and a respected conservative southerner.

29. To win the Budget spot in 1984, Gray had had to campaign against a rule change that would have allowed the two main contenders for the post, James R. Jones of Oklahoma and Leon E. Panetta of California, to remain on the committee. Gray sidestepped the Jones-Panetta contest and concentrated on defeating the rule change

and then offering himself as a candidate. Winning the chairmanship of the Budget Committee, therefore, was like running for a leadership job. It was a way for Gray to get organized for other, bigger races and to test his strength against rivals.

30. The problem arose of what position to create for a southerner and where to locate it on the ladder, which masked a deeper concern: would this newly created post interposed within the hierarchy be construed as a threat by the whip or deputy whips? If the post were viewed as an intermediate step between the leader and whip or the whip and deputy whips, it would create dissatisfaction among the incumbents in those positions. On the other hand, if the post were not of sufficient stature, a senior southerner would not be willing to accept it. How could a prospective appointee justify the expenditure of time and effort, let alone the potential political risk in his district, unless the position was of high rank?

Another factor might have spelled the end of the southern leadership spot. One Democratic leadership aide reported: "After the capital gains fight—the southerners challenged Foley on the first big issue of his speakership—the leadership said, 'That's it.' Even Foley couldn't countenance that."

31. The leaders themselves were highly self-conscious about the generational transition. In his 1 June 1989 letter seeking support from his colleagues, Gephardt included this passage: "John Kennedy said in 1961 that it was time for a new generation of Americans to lead our country. Now I believe it is time for a new generation of Members to lead the Congress."

32. Foley had, in fact, told Bonior before the whip race was over that if he failed, he would reappoint him chief deputy whip.

REFERENCES

Almanac of American Politics 1990. Michael Barone and Grant Ujifusa, eds. Washington, D.C.: National Journal.

Barry, John M. 1989. *The Ambition and the Power, the Fall of Jim Wright: A True Story of Washington*. New York: Viking.

Brown, Lynne P., and Robert L. Peabody. 1984. "Dilemmas of Party Leadership: Majority Whips in the U.S. House of Representatives, 1963–1982." *Congress and the Presidency* 11:179 96.

———. 1987. "Patterns of Succession in House Democratic Leadership: The Choices of Wright, Foley, Coelho, 1986." Paper delivered at the Annual Meeting of the American Political Science Association, 3–6 September 1987, Chicago.

Canon, David. 1989. "Institutionalization of Leadership in the U.S. Congress." *Legislative Studies Quarterly* 14:415–43.

Ginsberg, Benjamin, and Martin Shefter. 1990. *Politics by Other Means: The Declining Importance of Elections in America*. New York: Basic Books.

Greenstein, Fred I. 1967. "The Impact of Personality on Politics: An Attempt to Clear away the Underbrush." *American Political Science Review* 61:629–41.

Jackson, Brooks. 1990. *Honest Graft: Big Money and the American Political Process*, rev. ed. New York: Alfred A. Knopf.

Jones, Charles O. 1970. *The Minority Party in Congress*. Boston: Little, Brown.

Loomis, Burdett. 1988. *The New American Politician: Ambition, Entrepreneurship, and the Changing Face of Political Life*. New York: Basic Books.

Mayhew, David R. 1989. "Does It Make a Difference Whether Party Control of the

American National Government Is Unified or Divided?" Paper delivered at the Annual Meeting of the American Political Science Association, 31 August–3 September 1989, Atlanta.

Nelson, Garrison. 1977. "Partisan Patterns of House Leadership Change, 1789–1977," *American Political Science Review* 71:918–39.

Oppenheimer, Bruce, and Robert L. Peabody. 1977. "How the Race for House Majority Leader Was Won—By One Vote." *Washington Monthly,* Sept. 1977:46–56.

Peabody, Robert L. 1967. "Party Leadership Changes in the United States House of Representatives." *American Political Science Review* 61:675–93.

———. 1976. *Leadership in Congress: Stability, Succession, and Change.* Boston: Little, Brown.

Politics in America 1990, edited by Phil Duncan. Washington, D.C., CQ Press.

Ripley, Randall B. 1967. *Party Leaders in the House of Representatives.* Washington, D.C.: Brookings Institution.

———. 1969. *Majority Party Leadership in Congress.* Boston: Little, Brown.

Sinclair, Barbara. 1983. *Majority Leadership in the U.S. House.* Baltimore: Johns Hopkins University Press.

———. 1989. "House Majority Party Leadership in the Late 1980s." In *Congress Reconsidered,* 4th ed., edited by Lawrence C. Dodd and Bruce I. Oppenheimer. Washington, D.C.: CQ Press.

———. 1990. "Strong Party Leadership in a Weak Party Era—The Evolution of Party Leadership in the Modern House." Paper delivered at the Conference, "Back to the Future: The United States Congress in the Twenty-first Century," Carl Albert Center, University of Oklahoma, 11–13 April 1990.

Wright, James Claude, Jr. 1984. *Reflections of a Public Man.* Fort Worth: Madison.

Index

Abortion, 354, 355

Adams, Sherman, 25

Agriculture Committee, 329, 330; and amendments, 198; assignment requests to, 84, 85, 87; leadership style and performance of, 157, 158, 160, 161

Albert, Carl, 287nn. 35 and 40; and campaign for majority leadership, 264–65, 266–70, 275–76, 277, 278, 279–80, 281, 360; district constituency of, 288n.45; as majority leader, 231, 264, 280, 360; leadership progression of, 268, 313, 321, 330, 364; as majority whip, 268, 269, 273, 274, 293; popularity of, in the House, 268, 273, 280; relationship of, with Rayburn, 285n.22; seniority of, in the House, 285n.20; as Speaker, 321, 367n.1.

Albosta, Donald, 128

Alexander, Bill, 297, 298

Allen, Leo, 247

Ambition and the Power, The (Barry), 327, 368n.6

Amendments, 206n.2; committee position and sponsorship of, 191–96, 197, 200–201, 202, 207n.10; and committee proposals, 165, 172, 173, 175, 178, 196–201, 204–5; contestedness of, 179, 183, 197; and multiple referral, 178, 182–83, 202; number of sponsors of, 186–89, 196; outcomes of, 179,

183–85, 197, 202; recorded voting and volume of, 169, 172, 176, 177, 179, 180–81, 183–84, 185, 186–87, 202, 204; rules governing, 175–76, 178, 180, 183, 199; seniority and sponsorship of, 189–91, 196, 202; types of, 206n.1; volume of, 169, 171–72, 173, 174, 179–83, 185, 197, 202

American Bar Association, 26

American Business and Public Policy (Bauer and de Sola Pool), 1

American Federation of Labor-Congress of Industrial Organizations (AFL-CIO), 277

American Political Science Association, 365

Americans for Constitutional Action, 150

Americans for Democratic Action (ADA), 113, 115

Anderson, Glenn, 124

Anthony, Beryl F., Jr.: and campaign for majority whip, 340, 341, 342–43, 346, 347, 351, 356, 357, 363; as DCCC chairman, 293, 341–42, 352, 353–54, 362, 369–70n.21

Appleby, Paul, 5

Appropriations Committee, 39; and amendments, 197–99, 200–201, 202; assignment to, 101, 103–4n.19, 110; chairs and subcommittee chairs of, 121, 122, 125–26; Defense Subcommittee,